FIVE CENTURIES OF JEWELRY IN THE WEST

FIVE CENTURIES OF JEWELRY IN THE WEST

by Jean Lanllier
and Marie-Anne Pini
Preface
by G. Boucheron

Arch Cape Press
New York

This 1989 edition published by Arch Cape Press,
a division of dilithium Press, Ltd.,
distributed by Crown Publishers, Inc.
225 Park Avenue South, New York, New York 10003

Printed and bound in Hong Kong

ISBN: 0-517-67240-5

h g f e d c b a

TABLE OF CONTENTS

PREFACE

Sir,

You honor me greatly by your request for a preface to your book. I am deeply moved by it for several reasons: First, because of my professional connections with jewelry. I am a craftsman and the designing and making of jewels plays a major part in my life. Secondly, for reasons of sentiment, because this craft which I practice and love is a tradition of my family. I am the third generation of Boucherons with an establishment in the Place Vendôme. In addition I am always glad to take advantage of any chance to restate my love for jewels. This brings me to another source of gratification—that in this case I shall not be alone in praising the beauty of jewelry. Throughout this book your authors unfold a fascinating story. Your book fills a void which I have long felt and of which I have become increasingly aware through the many letters I receive from all over the world asking for information and material on jewelry. I am delighted to see the publication of a book to meet this need, wholly devoted to the most beautiful of all jewels—those set with precious stones.

I have no doubt that your book will have a very favorable reception, for interest in jewelry is spreading and expanding as never before. It is true that this interest has an economic aspect inasmuch as the intrinsic value of precious metals and stones, unlike that of our fluctuating money, never changes. It is a better investment than ever to buy a high-quality jewel. The investment improves in proportion to the quality of the jewel and as a result, even the investor who begins by seeing it only as good business will come to appreciate the artistic quality of the object he buys. This is increasingly true of members of the jewelry business, who often come to see it as an important art form.

I personally believe that there is something unreal about jewels. No description, however accurate, can ever fully convey their magical character. This is why, if we want to understand them, we must try to understand their history and find out why and how they came to be designed in their present form.

Like all works of art, a jewel is made for a specific person or occasion. It exists by virtue of an underlying purpose which we must discover. Like all the arts, jewelry responds to the need for beauty in life—in this particular case, the adornment of human beings—the eternal craving for ornament which was born with the human race and is its exclusive privilege. Like all the arts, jewelry demands detailed knowledge of the craft and technique with its possibilities and limitations; and I should like to stress this point. It is not enough to have a new idea, a good design, perfect execution and top-quality materials in order to make a jewel. Many people have tried and have produced marvelous objects and fascinating trinkets whose only fault is that they are unwearable—they are anything but jewelry. Just as a great artist would be more likely to draw costumes than dresses if he were asked to produce a couture collection, the sculptor, painter or architect makes works of art rather than real jewels. You illustrate some examples in this volume. Their aesthetic value is often indisputable, but are they ornaments meant to be worn or symbols, lines and volumes translated into gold and diamonds?

Our craft, you see, has its laws and demands. They sometimes limit our imagination and fancy a little, but the discipline they impose is remarkably productive. I could discuss it at length, but I prefer to leave that to your authors, whose researches I have followed with interest, knowing how carefully and lovingly they have set about retracing the history of jewelry.

They could tell you, if it still needs reiterating, how delighted I was to see the conception and progress of a book which means so much to me. It is even dearer now that you have asked me for a preface, and I hope that it will contribute by its success to a wider public interest in the art which is so dear to me.

G. Boucheron

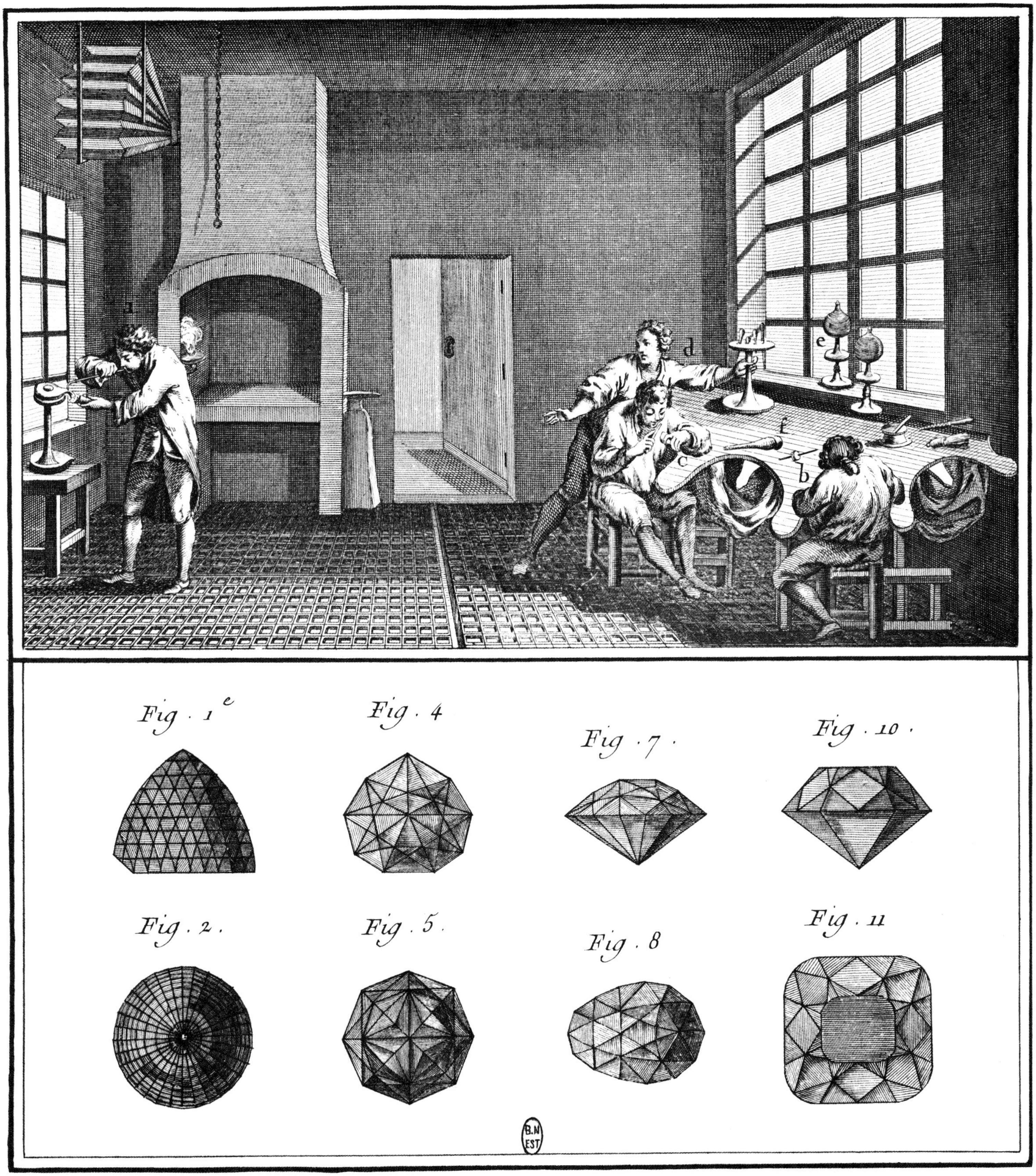

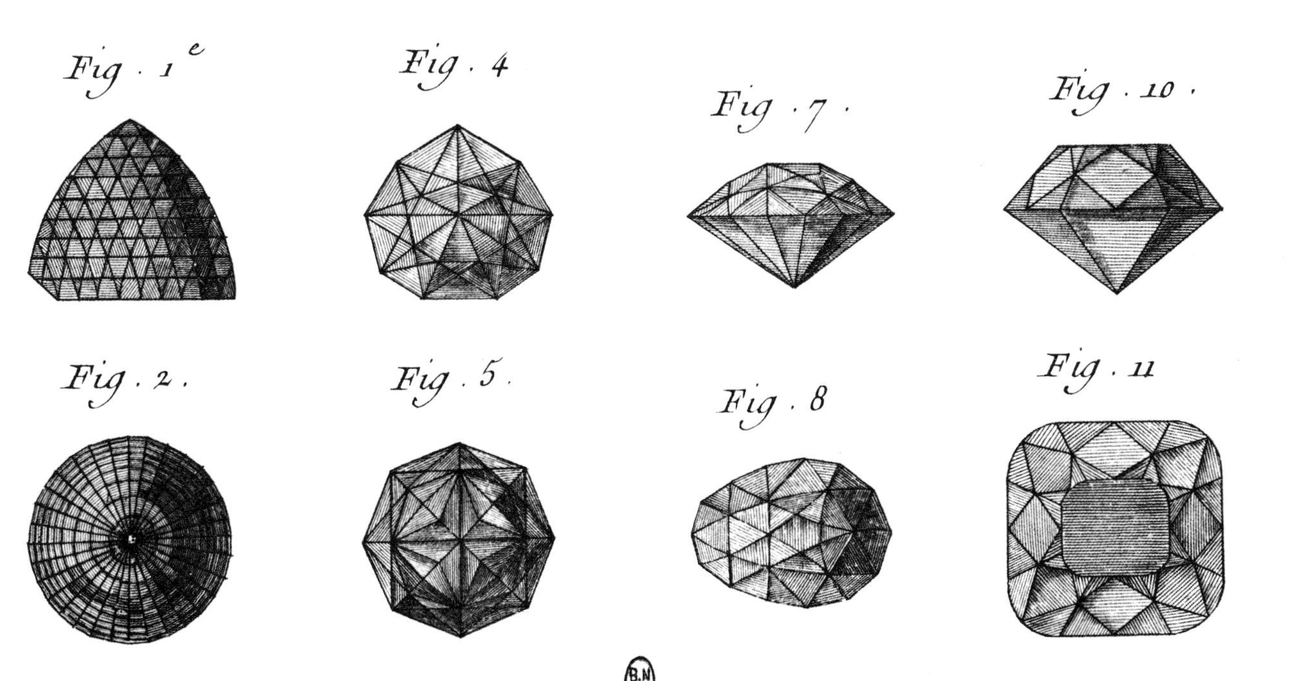
Fig . 1e
Fig . 4
Fig . 7 .
Fig . 10 .
Fig . 2 .
Fig . 5 .
Fig . 8
Fig . 11

Acknowledgments

This book on jewelry could never have been completed without the kind assistance of the European and American jewelers who have consented to be a part of it. They placed ample records at our disposal and incessantly encouraged us in the undertaking.

The photographs of ancient jewels reproduced here were mainly supplied by museums where we have always been welcomed most kindly. We would particularly like to thank Mrs. Bury, Assistant Keeper of the Jewelry department, Miss Cordrey and Mr. Maxwell of the Victoria and Albert Museum; Mr. Seyd of the British Museum; Sgr. Guido Gregorietti, chief curator of the Poldi-Pezzoli Museum in Milan, who is also the author of a book on the history of jewelry; Dr. Gudmund Boesen, director of Rosenborg Castle Museum in Copenhagen, and Miss Adams, of the Cooper Union Museum in New York.

Many antiquarians, managers of shops and collectors have freely cooperated with us. We would like to mention Mr. Kenneth Snowman, author of a book on Fabergé and director of the house of Wartski in London; Mme. Heger de Löwenfeld and Mme. Edith de Bonnafos of the Galerie Stadler, who supplied us with material on Braque's jewelry, The Masenza and Fumanti Galleries in Rome, Sra. Panicali of the Marlborough Gallery and Sra. Pomodoro of Milan.

We would also like to express our gratitude to the Diamond Information Center in London and Paris, to the house of Christie in London, and to M. Voeltzel, director of the Atelier Vendôme.

We extend our warmest thanks to all of them.

Chapter 1

THE SCIENCE OF JEWELRY

THE SCIENCE OF JEWELRY

Anyone who was privileged to work with precious metals was once known as a goldsmith. The name goldsmith, which corresponds to the Latin *aurifex,* was the only term in use up to the end of the Middle Ages, and those to whom it referred might be engaged either in making large civic and religious items or the small personal ornaments later known as jewelry, or in setting precious stones. Nowadays we can differentiate between the goldsmith who makes gold, silver, copper or tin into functional or decorative ecclesiastical or civic objects for the altar or table; and the jeweler who makes objects meant as personal ornaments, chiefly in gold or platinum, the metal (precious or otherwise) serving as the sole medium for the artist's design (*bijouterie*). This term also applies when the decorative effect of the piece is achieved by grouping a certain number of stones as a painter uses the colors on his palette, the precious metal being used as unobtrusively as possible only when it is essential for the setting (*joaillerie*).

The jeweler shapes the metal with an eye to the stones to be set, and in the final analysis these reveal the merits or defects of his work. He forms the shape and movement he has designed from the lump of gold or platinum and the setting demonstrates the art and skill of his hand even before it is finished and enhanced with the sparkle of gems. But the hitherto blank and soulless jewel is destined to be clothed in all the seductions of stones which give it life and impact. The successful choice of these stones is another aspect of the jeweler's art.

Jewelry is a complete branch of art in and of itself. Various assistants may be co-opted but no specialists, because in jewelry there is only one technique—that of the jeweler.

The first and most valuable of the jeweler's assistants is the setter, whose extremely delicate task consists of mounting the stones in the metal prepared by the jeweler. It is he who puts the finishing touches to the jewel, and "there is no piece so badly prepared that a skillful setter cannot improve it, on the other hand there is none, however perfect, which a clumsy setter cannot spoil."

Apart from the setter the modern jeweler needs the collaboration of a number of auxiliaries: the perforator who cuts out parts of a piece manually, or by machine following a prepared line, and the polisher who removes tool marks from the metal and gives the shine needed for the presentation of the jewel. The crafts of perforation and polishing employ exclusively female workers.

In addition to setters, draughtsmen, chasers, engravers, and enamelers, stonecutters should also be counted among the jeweler's assistants. Stonecutters work gems to achieve the maximum of sparkle and beauty. The modern jeweler has to draw heavily on the stonecutter's art, and the latter has now succeeded in adapting to the jeweler's design the rigid and inflexible principles that ruled his art until recent years.

In Paris the jeweler has all these collaborators at hand and this opens up boundless possibilities for the most daring creations. In spite of this, French taste loses none of its flexibility and discrimination, and the restrained, harmonious national genius continues to pervade the successive productions of this art form.

As to the jeweler's raw materials, there are, of course, the precious metals—gold, platinum and silver. However, the most important part is obviously played by diamonds, precious and semi-precious stones, pearls and enamels. A summary of useful information about them follows.

Rough diamonds. De Beers.

Rough diamonds. De Beers.

The Diamond

The diamond consists of pure crystallized carbon. Its density is 3.5. It is the hardest material, but also very transparent and the most refractive. However, despite its hardness it is also very brittle. In the world of minerals the diamond is king. Its points can cut all the other crystals while its facets cannot be penetrated by their attacks.

To find the reason for its invincible strength, we must penetrate the crystalline structure and study it patiently. The structure of all atoms follows the same plan, with a central nucleus around which satellites revolve at considerable distances, like planets in a solar system. The nucleus with its complex and still mysterious composition is positively charged. The satellites are all identical and are simply points of negative electricity. These are the electrons. The whole forms a neutral electrical system.

Ninety-two specific atoms numbered from one to 92 correspond to the 92 natural elements. The atomic number indicates the number of satellite electrons of each atom. The carbon atom has the number six. Six electrons, then, surround its nucleus, which includes six positive electrical charges.

In all atoms the satellite electrons are spread over several "shells." Two gravitate in the first shell counting from the nucleus, and the second and third shells have room for eight electrons each. Then come the shells which can contain up to 18 or even 32 electrons.

When a complete shell encloses an atom the distribution of its electrons forms a spherical symmetry. As a result, it is so stable that it breaks off all contact with the outside world. This is true of the atoms of the series of gases known as "inert" gases, i.e., helium, neon, argon, krypton, and xenon, which combined neither with each other nor with other atoms and have no effect on any atom of any substance, whatever its state. Apart from these few special atoms all the others form combinations and associations.

Two of the six electrons of the carbon atom gravitate in the first shell and the other four in a second orbit approximately five times as large. The carbon atom, having four electrons in the second shell, has four electrons too many to be "noble" in the manner of helium (no. 2) and four too few to be "noble" in that of neon (no. 10). It is therefore possible for it to lose or gain four electrons.

Distributed symmetrically over the eight points of a cube, the four outer electrons of the carbon atom can obviously only cover one corner out of every two. They therefore no longer form the shape of a cube but that of a tetrahedron or a pyramid made up of four equal triangles.

This tetrahedral shape is all very well, but such a situation is nonetheless intolerable for the carbon atom which has to have eight electrons for its second shell. The ideal, not without grandeur in the case of the carbon atom, is to achieve this without involving any foreign atoms. Therefore, four atoms gather around it; each of them contributes one of its four electrons and places this in one of its four spaces. In exchange they each take one of its four electrons and put these in one of their four spaces. Then each of them calls on three more atoms to fill their three remaining spaces, and so on. Thus, starting from a central atom, an infinite molecule develops, and this gigantic molecule is a diamond in which each atom, functioning as a "central" atom, exerts its force of attraction on the four "adjacent" atoms surrounding it, while each atom, functioning as an "adjacent" atom, responds to the force of attraction of the four "central" atoms surrounding it.

In every diamond formed like this, the compensating forces emanating from each nucleus and exerting a counterbalancing attraction on the electrons in their common shells are so powerful that nothing but another diamond can break off a single one of the millions of trillions of atoms joined in this way.

The source of what we call the hardness of the diamond is the extraordinary cohesive power of this wonderful atomic structure. For graphite is also crystallized carbon, but in the structure of graphite one of the four outer electrons of the atom is left free.

For carbon atoms to be linked as they are, in a diamond

by the four electrons attracted in opposite directions in their common shells, such exceptional and consequentially rare conditions must be united so that graphite is sold by the ton and diamond by the carat.

This miracle of crystallization, the unique and huge diamond molecule, arises from the fact that the carbon atom has four electrons in its second electronic shell. There is only one atom in the world, atom no. 6, carbon, which has or could have four electrons in its second electronic shell.

The diamond, then, will never lose its crown. Its throne is beyond the reach of every other crystalline substance. The powers of this edifice of light can never be equaled or surpassed.

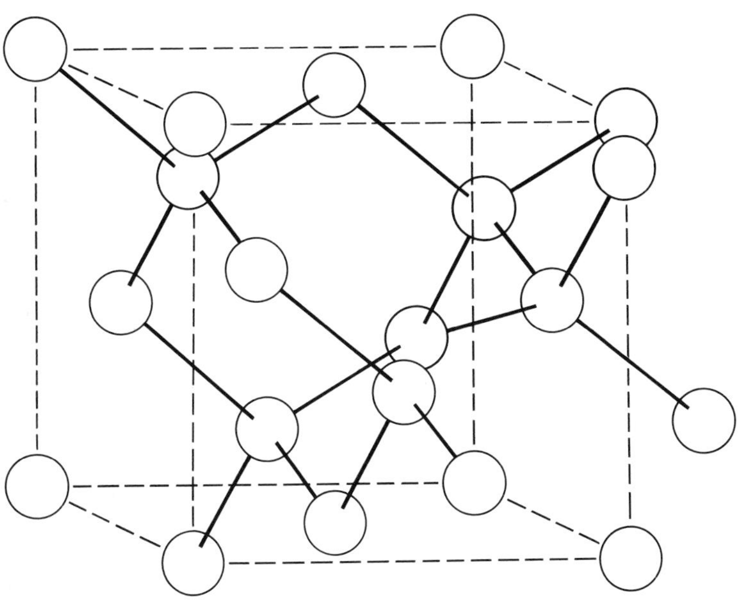

Atomic structure of the diamond. Drawn by Michel Labarthe.

The diamond crystallizes in the cubic system. This is the most symmetrical of all crystalline systems. When a diamond is growing in magma, the one original crystalline network multiplies indefinitely in three dimensions by the addition of strongly linked atoms even before a volcanic eruption throws it up to the earth's crust. Starting from its basic element, invisible even to the most powerful microscope, differences in the growth rate of the faces can produce shapes which occur when the edges of the cube are truncated. Thus the commonest form of the diamond is the octahedron, which is a polyhedron with eight triangular faces. Other derivatives are the rhombic dodecahedron with twelve faces and the hexoctahedron with 48 faces. Crystals with cubic faces are rare.

The great symmetry of the cubic crystalline system is determined by its exceptional number of elements of symmetry, i.e. the center of symmetry, the planes of symmetry and the axes of symmetry.

Some special properties result from this, and these are put to use in cutting down diamonds. It is certainly the hardest known mineral, but its hardness is by no means equal in every direction since the cohesion of some of the planes of atoms is slightly weaker than the electronic forces linking them to adjacent atoms.

This is true of the planes of atoms lying parallel to the faces of the octahedron. The operation of cleavage consists of taking advantage of these directional properties rapidly and forcibly to split the diamond into two by means of a steel blade applied in the appropriate direction and struck with a maul.

This can be compared to the action of a woodcutter's axe splitting a tree-trunk. The axe blade penetrates between the veins and makes the trunk split along the plane with the weakest cohesion between its fibers.

There are four possible cleavage directions lying parallel to the faces of the octahedron, each pair of which are alike. A diamond can therefore be split into a large number of thin parallel leaves.

Diamond experts have experimented with the strength and resistance of these fragments. A wheel charged with

Rough diamonds passing over "greaser" (moving table coated with grease). De Beers.

diamond dust will not bite into the faces of the octahedron. However, it has recently been discovered that diamonds can be sawed in directions where the atoms are slightly less densely packed in the crystal network. These directions are roughly comparable to pathways through a thick forest which cut across the main avenues.

The possibilities for sawing include: three directions lying parallel to the possible faces of the cube, each pair of which are alike, and six directions lying parallel to the possible faces of the rhombic doedecahedron, each pair of which are alike. Compared with the theoretical sawing planes, the angle of the saw allows for a slight variation in the cutting planes lying parallel to the faces of the cube, but the angle must be exactly parallel to the faces of the rhombic dodecahedron because if it deviates it collides with the cleavage planes and they stop it.

Sources of diamonds

Diamonds are found in two types of ground. The first type includes deposits in their original position, consisting of funnels or "pipes" which occur most commonly in South Africa and Brazil. The deposits at Kimberley in Cape Province, Jagersfontein and Bostop in the Orange Free State and the Premier Mine in the Transvaal are examples of this type.

The other category is the residual or alluvial deposit, a detrital formation which seems to result when primary deposits disintegrate after the diamonds have successfully withstood mechanical and chemical erosion. The chief examples of this type are found on either side of the mouth of the Orange River, in Lichtenburg and Namaqualand (discovered in 1924-5 and 1927-8), the Belgian Congo (discovered in 1907 and mined in 1913), Portuguese Angola (1916), the Gold Coast (1919), Tanganyika (1939), Sierra Leone (1920), Equatorial Africa (1931), West Africa (1935) and Southwest Africa (1907). Secondary deposits have also been discovered in Brazil.

World production of diamonds

The world's most important producer is South Africa. In 1928 production reached a total of 4,370,000 carats, which was 80 percent of world production. At this time some amazingly rich deposits had just been discovered in Namaqualand (1,000,000 carats in 1929). As a result, production was voluntarily restricted to avoid upsetting the world market. In 1945 production from the Union of South Africa rose to 1,141,000 carats, or 8 percent of the world production of 13,781,591 carats.

World production nowadays is about 35,200,000 carats, of which 97 percent come from Africa. However, only 20 percent of this enormous quantity of diamonds are suitable for jewelry. In 1965, for example, only 7,152,000 carats had the requisite quality for jewelry making. In fact, 95 percent of the diamonds from the Belgian Congo and

Different shapes and colors of rough diamonds. De Beers.

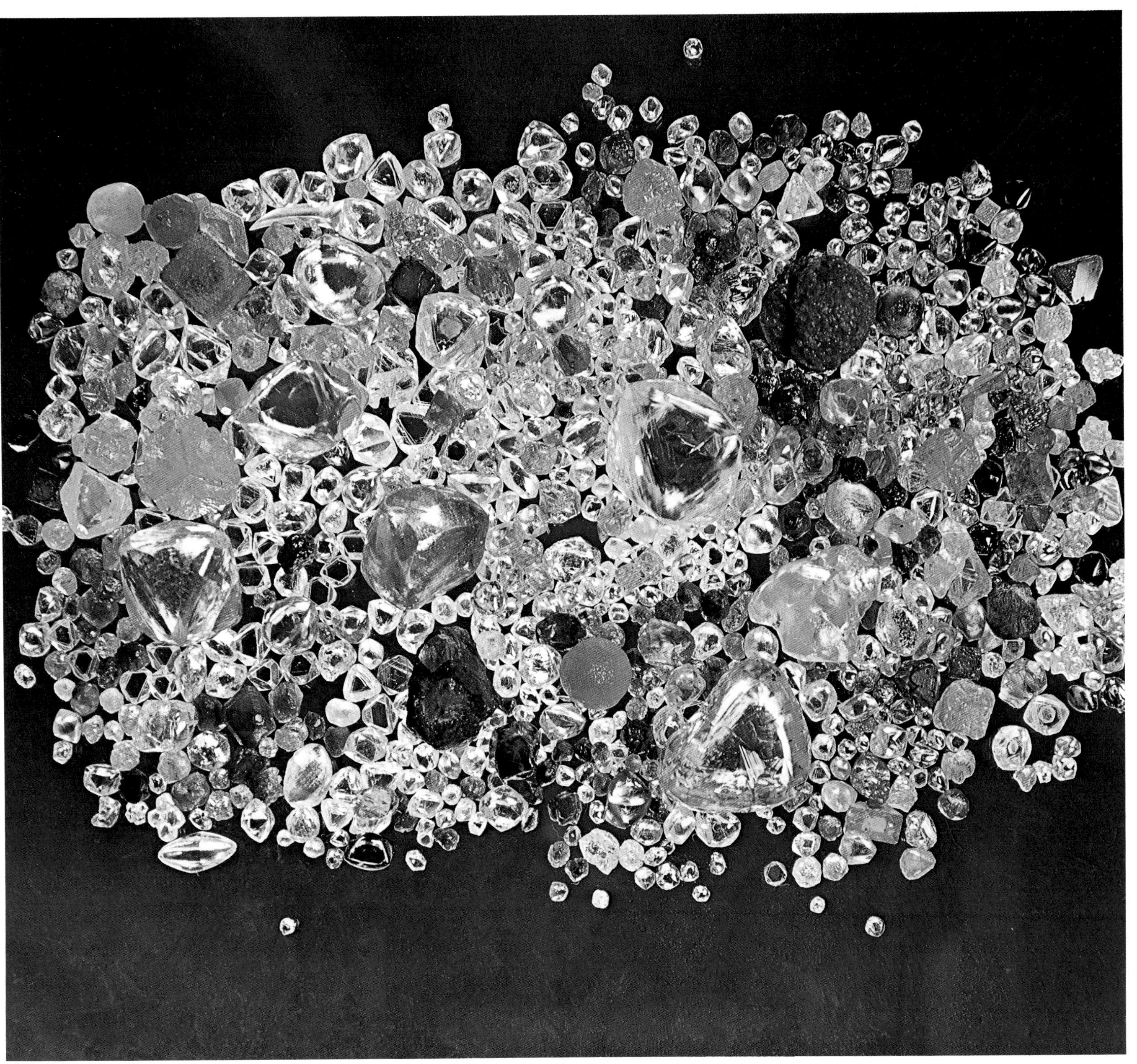

from 50 percent to 70 percent of those from Ghana, Angola, Sierra Leone, Guinea, the Central African Republic and Tanzania are "boart," or diamonds suitable for industrial use only. Southwest Africa and Namaqualand provide a very high proportion of gem diamonds (about 80 percent).

The Diamond Syndicate

In the years following 1867, when the first diamond was found in Kimberley, the small operators banded together to form anonymous societies. These split into two groups, Cecil Rhodes' "de Beers" group and the Barnato brothers' "Jagersfontein" group.

In 1900, the de Beers group and the Barnato brothers formed "The Diamond Syndicate" for the purpose of regulating production according to demand so as to keep prices high.

In 1928, the Syndicate became "The Diamond Corporation" and in 1933, the South African government, which had hitherto remained independent, joined the association. All the members agreed, should the need arise, to accept prearranged reduced percentages and only to sell through the association.

Leading producers in other countries who have no direct part in "The Association of Diamond Producers" are linked to it by exclusive sales contracts of set duration. In 1939, the rough diamond trust controlled between 95 and 97 percent of world production.

In 1940, the Syndicate had to do battle with a Canadian named Williamson who had stumbled on deposits in Tanganyika estimated to be as rich as those of Kimberley, and who wanted to retain his independence. Eventually, however, he too joined "The Diamond Trading" group.

The "Cullinan diamond" at the time of its discovery. De Beers.

The "Cullinan diamond" after cleavage by Asscher. De Beers.

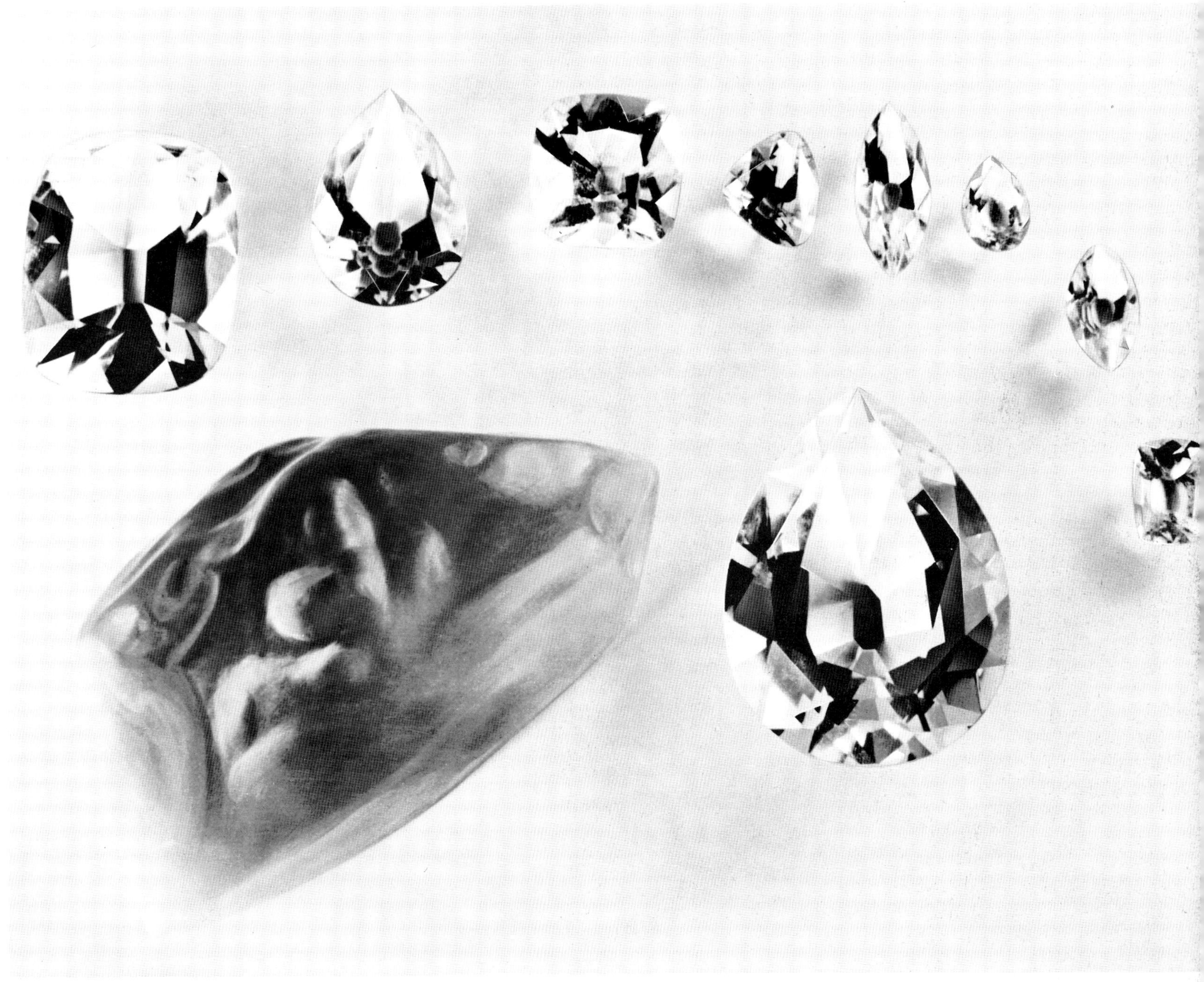

The "Cullinan diamond" and the nine brilliants cut from it. De Beers.

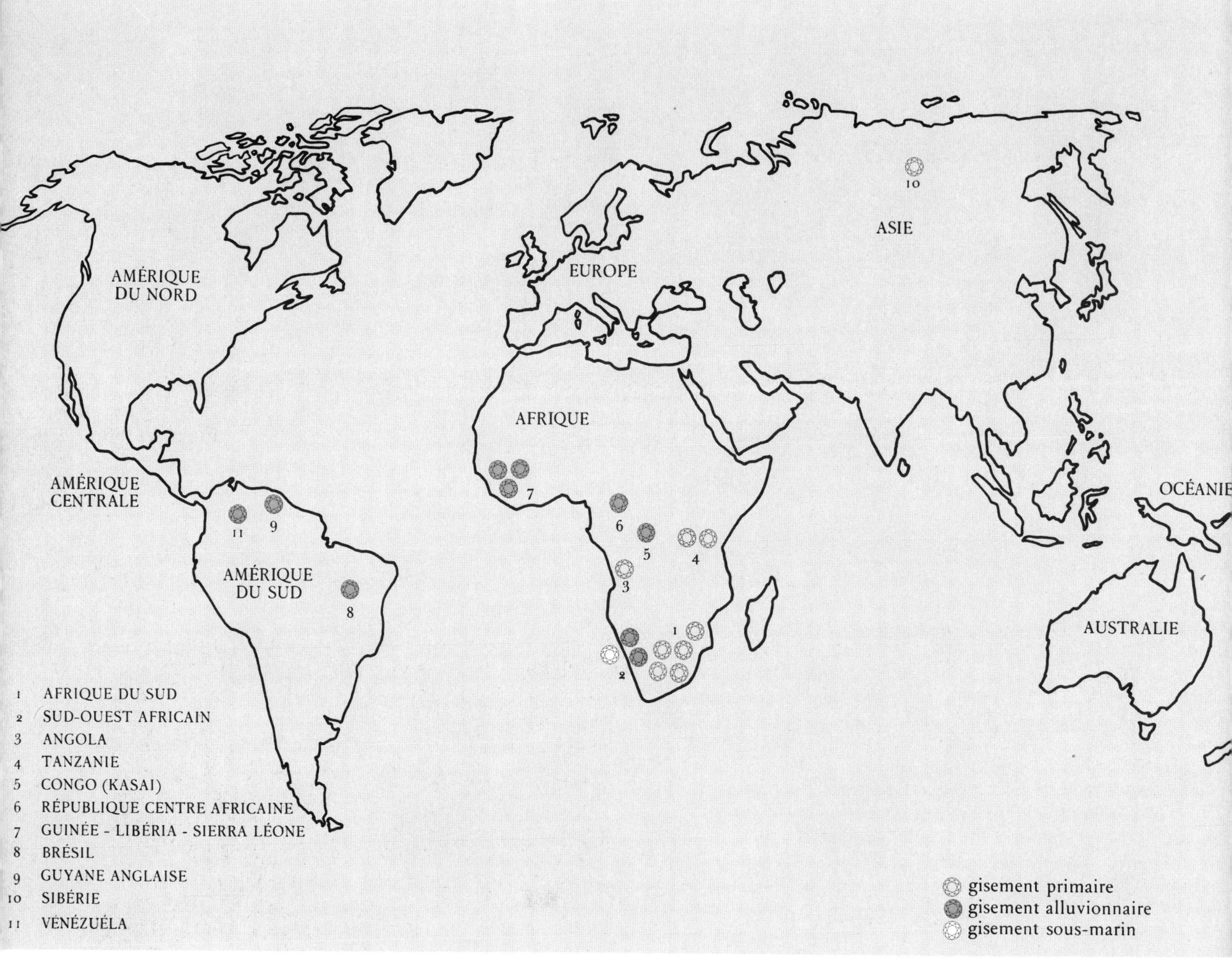

Map of diamond sources throughout the world. De Beers.

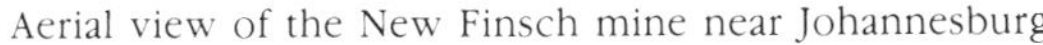

Aerial view of the New Finsch mine near Johannesburg.

Workings of the Consolidated Diamond Mines, South Africa.

The organization of the London market

The diamond market in London is based on the following organizations:

—"The Diamond Corporation," which controls nine-tenths of world production. It administers stocks and apportions them according to demand. It controls and regulates the fluctuations of the market and works directly with its members.

— "The Diamond Development," which is a branch of "The Diamond Corporation." It works more specifically with companies not affiliated with the de Beers group.

— "The Diamond Trading," which is the sales unit specializing in distribution of stock-in-trade and supplying the clients' needs.

Aerial view of the Kimberley pit during the first rush, c. 1884. De Beers.

— "The Diamond Boart Development," which was founded specifically for handling the enormous quantities of "boart" (black stones unsuitable for cutting and used as industrial abrasives) from the Belgian Congo.

The Syndicate's general policy is to maintain the greatest possible stability in the high price of the merchandise.

The sale is made only on the seller's terms. Once a month the Syndicate gives what are known as "sights" in London to a certain number of accredited clients, who must buy the lots assigned to them. These lots contain stones of all sorts from different sources, and they cannot be broken up. They are extremely valuable, and payments are made in cash. The smallest lots are of the order of 5,000 carats.

After sorting them into matching groups, these direct buyers in turn sell their purchases to a variety of customers for both gem cutting and industrial use.

The London classification of rough diamonds
The main London categories for the classification of rough diamonds are as follows:

Crystals: clear stones, usually octahedral in shape.

Irregular cleavages: stones before cleaving.

Spotted stones: (first and second quality) stones containing some kind of impurity.

Macles (naats): stones that are hard to cut because they consist of two or more crystals that interpenetrated at the time the diamond formed. In certain cases the stone crossed, or rather furrowed, by a sort of grain known as the "naat." In these cases the grain runs in two different directions which meet in such a way that a feasible intermediate direction has to be found in order to cut into the face; this always proves to be very hard.

Coated stones: stones with an opaque milky grey or black coating which that it impossible to judge their purity in the rough state.

Boart: black, shapeless stones full of impurities that cannot be cut. They are suitable for use in industry as an abrasive.

Cutting the gem diamond
Diamond cutting consists of four different operations.

Cleaving: this operation is carried out whenever it is advisable to divide a rough stone into two or more parts if the grain of the stone allows the desired division to be made.

Sawing: this is done before or after cleaving as necessary, with the aid of a special machine, the basic part of which is a saw consisting of a phosphor-bronze disc from ten to twelve centimeters in diameter with its rim impregnated with diamond dust mixed with oil. Sawing is only practiced when cleaving is impossible.

Bruting or *rounding:* this is the first of the actual cutting operations. Stones which have been given a suitable shape for cutting either by nature or by cleaving or sawing are first roughed out by bruting. This operation is carried out on a bruting machine.

Cutting and *faceting:* this is the final operation, and gives the stone its definitive form.

In 1476, Louis Van Berken, a native of Bruges, discovered how to polish diamonds with an iron mill he had invented. Charles the Bold, Duke of Burgundy, heard of this and sent Van Berken three large stones to polish to the best of his ability. The work was executed to the entire satisfaction of the duke, who was delighted and rewarded Van Berken with 3,000 ducats.

Van Berken settled in Antwerp, a city renowned for the skill of its stone cutters, and with the help of his companion cut many stones, including the famous "Sancy" diamond which had been imported from India as a rough stone and belonged to Charles the Bold.

Under Spanish domination the cutting industry moved to Amsterdam. However, the fame of the stone cutters of Antwerp persisted, for in 1787-8 when some diamonds belonging to the Crown of France needed recutting, they were sent to Antwerp. The job was done so well that M. Chantreine, who was chief curator of the diamonds and in charge of the operation, bestowed magnificent gifts worthy of a king of France on everyone who had a share in the enterprise. (*Antwerp Gazette,* 26 February 1788)

Cutting is always carried out by means of a machine, the basic parts of which are an iron plate impregnated with diamond dust and a tool known as a "dop" which is simply a holder for the diamond.

Each of the operations of cleaving, cutting, bruting and faceting is a professional specialty executed by a skilled craftsman.

A cutter is reckoned to be capable of working 23 saws. Four cutters can supply 60 faceters. One bruter is needed for every five faceters.

The rough diamond loses about 60 percent of its weight before it becomes a "perfect" brilliant. Every brilliant, whether it weighs half a carat or twenty carats, is cut in the same way, the large stones with exactly the same number of facets as the small ones.

The "brilliant" has 58 facets including the table and the culet. The table side, which is known as the crown, includes about a third of the stone and the pavilion side about two-thirds. The thickness of an average stone is about two-thirds of the diameter of the girdle. The diameter of the table is about one-third of the diameter of the stone, the other third on each side being occupied by facets sloping towards the crown; these are known as quoins, bezels or templets, stars and cross facets (also known as skill or girdle facets). The table should be in

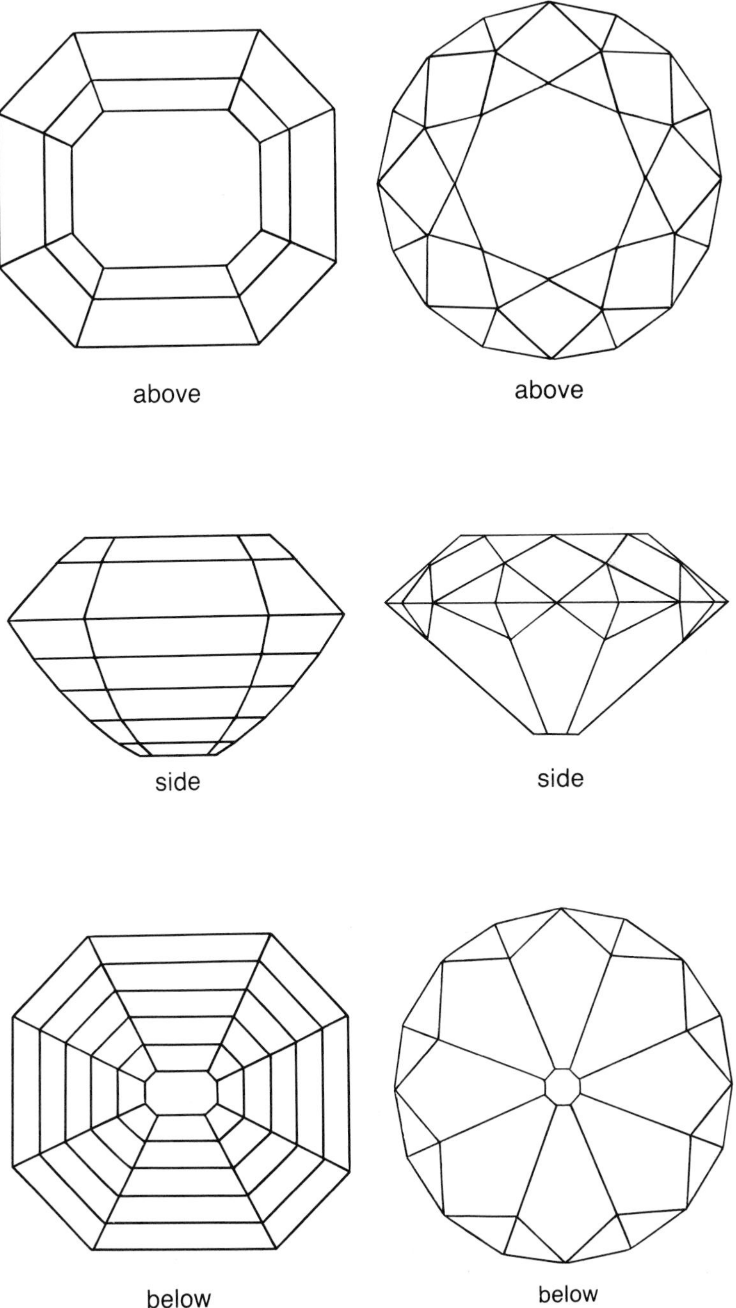

The rose and brilliant cuts. Drawn by Michel Labarthe.

the exact center of the stone and should be horizontal in relation to the girdle. This is also true of the culet, which is simply a miniature facet, but which must nevertheless be accurately placed exactly in the middle of the stone and must form a tiny regular octagen which can be seen in the middle by looking through the stone perpendicularly from the crown.

The smallest stones, i.e., those weighing less than four to six stones to the carat, are usually cut 32/24, 16/16 or 16/8, the first number referring to the number of facets of the crown and the second to those of the pavilion. Stones weighing less than fifteen to the carat are cut 8/8, eight facets each to the crown and pavilion.

Pure stones with shapes which do not entail too much loss are occasionally cut into fancy shapes such as the "marquise," "briolette," "pendeloque," "baguette," and "emerald" cuts (the latter is a square or rectangular shape with the corners cut off).

The "rose" cut is used for all kinds of stones, but it is particularly suitable for those which are too flat to make brilliants without excessive loss. This cut consists of a sort of dome resting on a flat base. The dome has twenty-four facets.

The cutting industry throughout the world

A large number of Jewish craftsmen were employed in the industry of gem diamond cutting which was chiefly centered in Antwerp and Amsterdam until 1939. It was completely disrupted by the German invasion, and the skilled labor force scattered and took refuge almost all over the world—in New York, South Africa, Cuba, Israel, Canada and even Puerto Rico and Santo Domingo.

Nowadays, the greatest diamond cutting center is Antwerp, where there are more than ten thousand workers. The second greatest is Israel, with nearly three thousand. In other countries such as the Netherlands, France, Germany, South Africa, Cuba and the USA, the figure rarely exceeds one thousand.

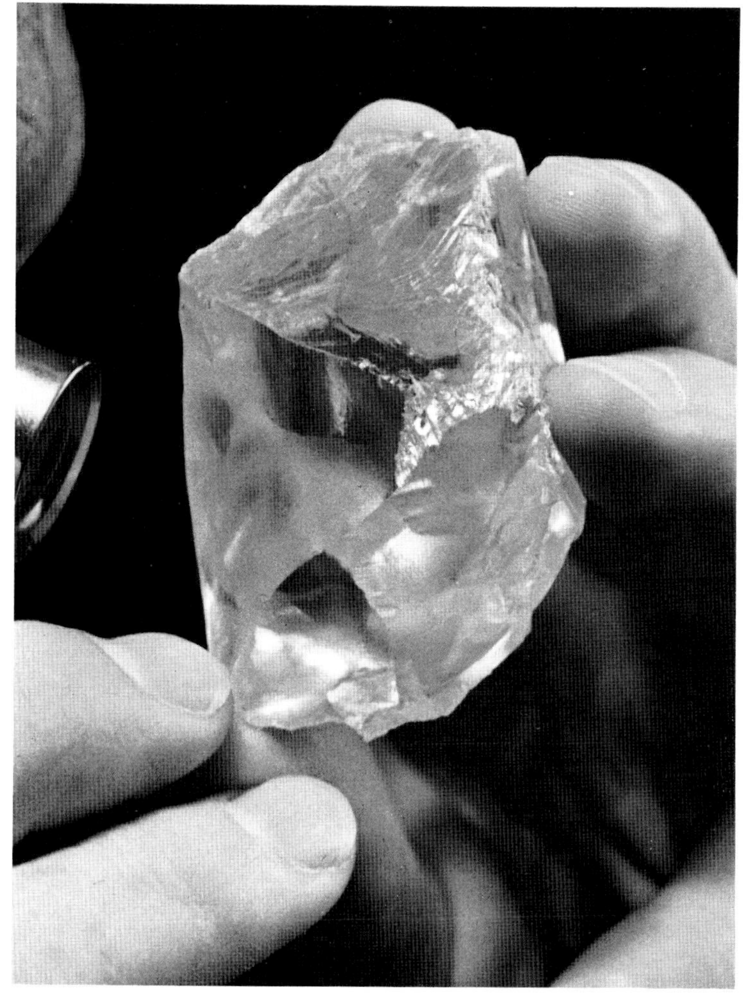

Examining a diamond under a magnifying glass. Harry Winston, New York.

Some diamond cuts. De Beers.

Different cuts and colors of diamonds. De Beers

The industry in France

The French diamond cutting industry is located in the Saint-Claude region of the Jura, the Paris district and Trévoux in Ain, where there are fifteen diamond houses. The Jura region specializes in small stones weighing up to four to the carat (8/8, 16/16, 32/24) and baguettes.

The Paris district, on the contrary, specializes in stones weighing from one to four carats and stones weighing over four carats. The Swiss gem cutters of Geneva and Bienne should also be mentioned.

Some famous diamonds

A few diamonds, sometimes named after an owner, have become historic because of their outstanding size and beauty, and these stones are often surrounded by legends. Among them are the "Sancy" (54 carats), the "Regent" (140.5 carats), the "Guise" (33 carats), and the "Florentine," a greenish-yellow diamond of 137.27 carats which once belonged to the Medici family and is now lost. The "Blue Tavernier" diamond weighed 112 carats before cutting. One part of it is now the "Hope" diamond (44.5

carats) in the Smithsonian Institution, Washington, and another is the "Blue Brunswick" (13.75 carats). The "Koh-i-noor," which was presented to Queen Victoria in 1850, weighed 186 carats before recutting, and now weighs 108. Among older stones the "Orloff" diamond (199 carats) which adorns the Romanoff sceptre (Diamond Treasury, Moscow) should also be mentioned.

From the end of the 19th century onwards, the South African mines were noted for the number of outstandingly large stones they produced. The "Cullinan" diamond was found there in 1905. It was the biggest diamond in the world (3,106 carats), and yielded nine big stones and 96 smaller ones. The finest pieces of this diamond, "Cullinan I," (530.2 carats), "Cullinan II," (317 carats), "Cullinan III," (94.5 carats) and "Cullinan IV" (63.6 carats) belong to the Crown of England and are kept in the Jewel House of the Tower of London. The "Excelsior" diamond (995 carats) was discovered at about the same time.

More recently there are the "Jonker" (726 carats), the "Star of South Africa" which went from 83.5 to 47.5 carats after cutting, the "Jubilee" (245.35 carats), the "Victoria" (184 carats), the "Stewart" (123 carats), and the "Tiffany" (128 carats). These are the weights after cutting.

The "President Vargas" (726.6 carats), which made 29 stones, and the "Star of the South", which weighed 261.9 carats before and 128.8 carats after cutting, were both found in Brazil.

Finally, a diamond weighing 601.25 carats was found in the South African province of Lesoto after which it was named.

Precious stones, semi-precious stones and enamels
Precious stones are subdivided into precious stones proper, i.e. diamonds, rubies, emeralds and sapphires, which are used for fine jewelry, and semi-precious stones, which are used for everyday jewelry and the decorative arts. Corundum, which is usually transparent or translucent and is the next hardest substance to diamond, should also be counted among the numerous species of minerals to which precious and some semi-precious stones belong.

De Lapidibus Preciosis: woodcut. Bibliothèque Nationale, Paris, Cabinet des Estampes.

DE LAPIDIBVS
PRECIOSIS.

Parure: gold, rubies and brilliants. Van Cleef & Arpels, Paris.

Parure: gold, platinum, sapphires and brilliants. Van Cleef & Arpels, Paris.

The Ruby

The ruby is a corundum. There are several qualities of ruby known by different names. In decreasing order of value they are as follows:

— The Burma ruby, known as the "ruby of rubies." Its color ranges from scarlet-red, so-called "pigeon's blood," to crimson or even purple-violet. Its density is four.
— The Siam ruby, which is the color of lees of wine, and darker than the Burma ruby.

All corundums (ruby and sapphire) have a rhombohedral crystal (six faces composed of equal lozenge [rhomboid] shapes). Rubies have a considerable sparkle, their refractive index being 1.76. They have the property of shining brightly.

Some beautiful rubies come from Ceylon. They are cut on the spot in the so-called "Indian cut" and then recut in Europe. The Indian cut is completely different from the European. The Indian stone cutter aims to bring out the maximum color with the minimum of weight loss without troubling about a symmetrical cut. Recutting, in which Parisian jewelers specialize, removes from 20 to 40 percent of the stone's weight. The cutting is carried out in steps, like that of an emerald. The cabochon shape is still used for less transparent stones and especially for star rubies.

The famous "Côte de Bretagne" ruby remained uncut for many years. It had several flaws, and it was believed that these could not be removed without substantially diminishing the value of the stone. However, a cutter was found who was skillful enough to take advantage of the flaws in carving the ruby into the shape of a dragon with outspread wings. It can now be admired in this form in the Louvre Museum in Paris.

The Sapphire

The color of the sapphire varies according to its source.

— The Kashmir sapphire is the most sought-after—indeed, it is virtually unobtainable because the original mine is no longer worked. Its color is kingfisher blue with a slight velvety opacity.
— The Ceylon sapphire is a slightly lighter blue and more transparent. The finest Ceylon sapphires are almost kingfisher blue.
— The Burma sapphire is darker than the Ceylon and more transparent than the Kashmir. The characteristic color of the Burma sapphire is royal blue.
— The Australian sapphire is darker than the Burma and regarded as the poorest and cheapest type.

A great deal of research has been conducted into the origins of the sapphire's blue color. Early in this century a group of chemists demonstrated that it was the result of a combination of iron oxide and titanium oxide.

In chemical analysis the sapphire, like the ruby, consists of almost pure aluminum. Sapphires occur along with rubies in the rivers and streams of Ceylon, Thailand and Mogok in Burma. Experience thus confirms the chemists' conclusion as to their common origin. Its crystal is the same shape and its physical and chemical properties are identical.

Sapphires are cut in very much the same way as rubies. In Ceylon the "Indian cut" is used. In Europe, sapphires and rubies are generally cut as oval brilliants from the "Indian cut." Sapphire crystals are larger than those of the ruby. Deposits of sapphires are fairly numerous. The rough stones are often covered with a dull crust although they are often clear inside it. They are found in Ceylon, India, Thailand, Australia, Cambodia, Burma, Tanzania, the USA and even in France, near Rougeac in Haute-Loire.

The substance of the sapphire is the hardest after the diamond. This is one of the reasons for the rarity of engraved sapphires throughout the ages. The best-known is the seal of King Alaric of the Visigoths who died in 410. It shows a royal bust in full face wearing garments like those on the coins of Theodosius' successors, with the inscription "Maricus Rex Gothorum." This curious intaglio is in the Imperial Treasury in Vienna.

One of the most beautiful known examples is the stone which Charles Barbet quotes as a sapphire belonging to the kings of France. It is actually mentioned in the 1791 catalogue of the jewels of the Crown of France. This sapphire was found in Burma. It has neither flaw nor fault, and weighs 132 carats. It is lozenge-shaped with six bezels and all its faces polished flat. It is in the Mineralogical Museum in Paris.

The Emerald

The name emerald is applied to the green variety of beryl which gets its color from chromium. It is a natural silicate of aluminum and beryllium.

Emeralds occur in several shades of green. The dark or bright green color of meadow grass is the rarest and most sought-after. These stones are the most valuable and indeed, one of the jeweler's favorite gems.

The best-known and most productive mines are those of Muso in Colombia. However, there are others in Rhodesia and Australia. The East African mines in the neighborhood of the Red Sea known as "Cleopatra's Mines" were very well known in the ancient world, but they are almost exhausted today. Several emeralds from these mines were famous in the Middle Ages. Among them was the emerald which adorns the top of the papal tiara, a gift from Napoleon I to the reigning pontiff. Pliny states that Nero used a fine, specially cut emerald to watch the games at the circus.

In 1830 some emerald mines were discovered in Siberia. They have yielded some high-quality stones, but these can easily be distinguished from other emeralds by their color, a green slightly tinged with yellow.

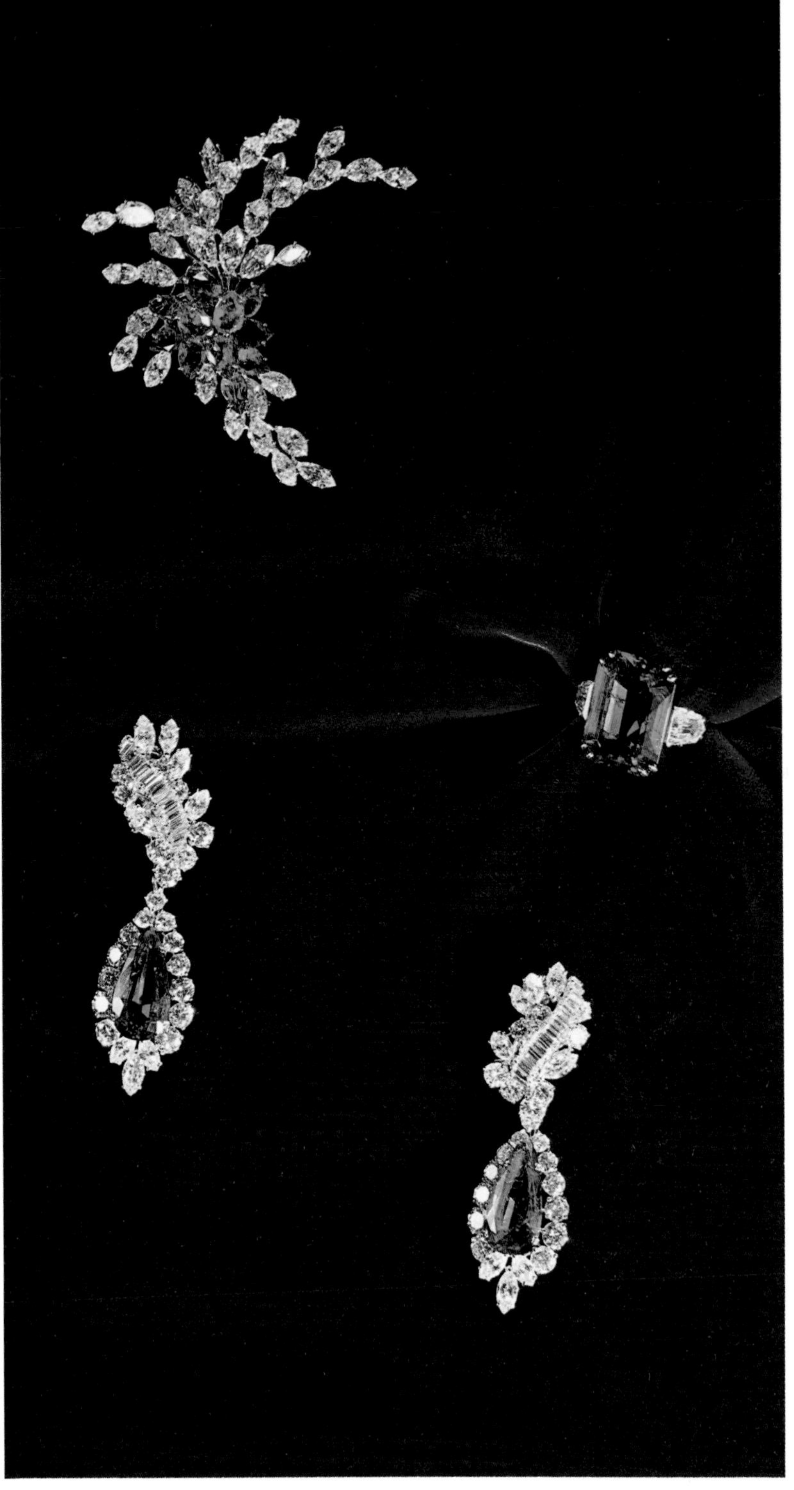

Brooch, eardrops and ring: emeralds and brilliants. Boucheron, Paris.

The Pearl

The pearl is not a precious stone, but its beauty and its importance in jewelry-making justify its inclusion in the same class as its companions the ruby, the emerald and the sapphire.

A large number of shellfish, usually bivalves, contain more or less spherical calcareous concretions known as pearls. Those which come from the pearl oyster or meleagrina are called native pearls. The best specimens come from the Indian Ocean, the Persian Gulf (Bahrein) and Ceylon (Manaar). They are also fished off Madagascar, Tahiti and New Caledonia. The value of a pearl depends on its shape and weight, which is expressed in grains (a grain is 0.05 grams), its color, which may be white, pink, yellow, grey or even black according to the species of oyster it comes from, and its shine, which is known as the orient.

The only specimens that can legally be called pearls or native pearls are those produced naturally by the pearl oyster without human intervention. Pearls produced by the same species of oyster as a result of the introduction of a foreign body around which the pearl secretion is gradually deposited should only be called "cultured pearls," never native pearls.

Artificial pearls are made of small globes of blown glass lined with a liquid known as *essence d'orient* made from fish scales, and then filled with wax. These beads can only be displayed under the name imitation pearls.

There is another way of making artificial pearls which consists of filling blown glass globes with wax and covering them with a coat of *essence d'orient.* Pearls produced by this process look more natural and less glassy. They reproduce the sheen of native pearls much more closely.

Earrings: platinum, brilliants and pearls. Chaumet, Paris.

Enamels

Enamel is a paste of colored and vitrified glass attached to metal by fusion. Metal oxides incorporated into the material in proportions of one to six percent impart the color. The melting point of enamel is inversely proportional to its color and hardness. Enamel has long been used to decorate metal and at some periods of history its popularity even rivaled that of precious stones. It has infinite possibilities in goldworking but its use in jewelry is much more restricted and varies according to the age and fashion. Time has no effect on it, and humidity and air do not alter it. Its colors do not fade when exposed to daylight and sun.

Various ways of applying enamel to metal have been developed. Every period had its own processes. Until the mid-14th century, the inlaying process was customary. Until this time, it functioned as a colored coating. From the 15th century onwards, it was used as an element in painting.

The inlaying process is twofold. Therefore it has two names: inlaid or true *champlevé* enamel, and *closionné* enamel. Hollows are cut in a metal plate with a burin, graver or chaser leaving in untouched relief the strips forming the details, outlines of figures, ornaments and folds of the design. The enamel is placed in the hollows in powdered form. The plate prepared in this way is heated in a small furnace called a "muffle." When the metal becomes red-hot, the enamel melts and adheres to the plate, which, after firing and cooling, is polished with pumice and a rotary burnisher to remove the ridges and irregularities caused by the firing.

Cloisonné enamel is simply a variant of inlaid enamel. Instead of being reserved on the plate, metal strips are soldered to it.

In the 14th century, translucent enamel was run over chased metal worked in relief. The intensity of the color increased with the thickness of the vitreous paste so that even monochrome enamel could produce the effect of painting. One of these plaques can be seen in the Louvre Museum. Even though the design and ornament seem rudimentary and primitive, the glow of the color is charmingly attractive.

After the close of the 15th century, painted enamels succeeded colored enamels. The metal of each plate was covered with a fairly thick coat of white enamel on which, after firing, the painter drew figures in vitreous colors that had been ground to the finest powder and lightly mixed with gum. Painted enamels have to be fired as many times as there are different colors, each firing being short—one or two minutes. Blacks, blues and greens are applied first, then the lighter colors and finally white and pink. Since each color requires a new firing in this order, the same object may pass into the furnace more than twenty times, as necessary.

The enameller uses a foil to give greater brilliancy to some parts of his work. This is a thin leaf of silver or gold applied on a layer of enamel and covered with another layer of translucent enamel which causes the precious metal to shimmer and glow more intensely as the light shines through.

In the 17th century, the process changed from painting with enamel to painting on enamel.

Whatever the process, *cloisonné, champlevé* or painted, enamelling is always a time-consuming job requiring highly skilled craftsmen with a thorough knowledge of their art who are prepared to expend great care and extreme accuracy on their work. The slightest carelessness in the last firing can ruin all the previous work.

Chapter 2 THE RENAISSANCE

THE RENAISSANCE

Pendant: Cupid. Enamelled gold, rubies and pearls. South German, late sixteenth century. Victoria & Albert Museum, London.

A consistent factor in the history of man is that he does not take care of essentials first and then deal with trivialities, but tackles necessities and apparent inessentials simultaneously. A taste for ornaments did not appear when man had conquered the more pressing dangers and was free from the most urgent cares, but at the very time when he was struggling inch by inch for survival. It is certainly true that human nature includes a certain tendency to frivolity. This is clearly apparent among primitive peoples but only survives in the modern western world among women.

A jewel, however, is not just a thing of beauty; it has a profound magical, religious and social significance, has become an essential part of dress and plays an important part in public life. This is true of all ornaments, even the most primitive such as a bone amulet or even a simple sign painted on the body, but it is even more true of jewelry which consists by definition of the most valuable materials at man's disposal. For the act of wearing gems and pearls indicates a great deal more than wealth or frivolity. It is a sign of the privilege and merit which were once reserved for the cream of society, the princes and noblemen of this world. The history of jewelry covers more than the evolution and development of techniques, shapes and fashions throughout the ages. It is also a reflection of society and government. It is loosely connected with history and personal records, and fluctuates with political, economic and social conditions. The history of jewelry is not only part of the history of art, but also of signs and symbols.

Jewelry has always fulfilled the same function, but from the Renaissance on its role became more clearly defined. At this time plentiful supplies of gold and gems and technical improvements set the scene for the birth of a true art form, that of the jeweler. Portraits of rulers, nobles and heroes show them literally covered with precious metals and gems, stiff and rigid in an absolute carapace of stones and metal, their fingers paralyzed by several dozen rings, their necks weighted by thick chains, their bodies hidden under thick stuffs further loaded with scattered gems and pearls. It was not until later that insignia were distinguished from ornaments. From the fifteenth to the eighteenth centuries the Orders of the Golden Fleece, Malta and the Holy Ghost were real masterpieces of jewelry. The double significance of jewelry is still reflected in the hierarchy of metals, bronze honoring the glorious start of a career to be crowned first with silver and ultimately with gold. Even if merit is only shown by an unobtrusive ribbon* nowadays we still speak of a "decoration."

The idea of beauty and splendor has always been associated with bright light. The display of jewels and stones which sovereigns have always loved, especially since the Renaissance, bears witness to more than their extravagance and vanity. It could be said without exaggeration that it was part of their duty to the state. The famous journeys of the fifteenth and sixteenth century kings and queens to all their chief cities with their sumptuous and interminable trains strengthened the rulers, authority and furnished them with evidence of their people's love and loyalty. However, these occasions were also severe physical trials. Imagine the royal visitors, in the August heat or November fog, stiff and uncomfortable in robes which sometimes weighed more than 44 pounds, with sceptre, orb and crown, traversing all the main streets and stopping at churches and crossroads to show themselves because it was their duty, and because it was also the wish of their people, who were often miserable and sometimes crushed by taxation, but who rarely murmured against court extravagance.

* i.e., The Légion d'Honneur

A number of prerogatives existed in the strongly hierarchical society of this period and new ones were continually being created. Certainly everyone was acutely aware of all the shades of meaning of the art of dress, which was regarded as symbolic. It was a matter of some importance whether the cloak was worn on the left shoulder or the right. Social class or an affiliation could be recognized by such details, and there were very specific rulings on these points. Similarly, certain expensive materials, fabrics and metals were forbidden to people of low degree and after the Reformation, to heretics on one side or the other—Calvinists in Catholic places, Catholics in Protestant countries. Not all women had the right to wear silk and pearls. Not all men might sport a gold chain. These were not just signs of wealth, but also of class privilege. When the middle classes were consolidating their wealth and power, edicts and laws were passed in every kingdom in Europe to control these *nouveaux riches* who wanted to set themselves up as equals of kings, and, in various independent cities, sometimes succeeded. The middle classes could not claim any mark of honor by birth. Professional qualities only brought advancement if successfully placed at the service of the sovereign. The bourgeois explorer, businessman or artist might then be ennobled, and the first sign of royal favor would be a rich gift, usually a gold chain with a medallion adorned with precious stones framing the royal portrait. This should prove again, if more proof is needed, that jewelry has more than a monetary value. Apart from being an object of great price it is a symbol and a sign.

It was even more than that at the beginning of the Renaissance when it had been endowed with a quasi-magical power. For a long time, people believed in the virtue of certain stones. "Every bishop wears a sapphire in his pastoral ring," says the *Mercure Galant* of 1678, "to remind him of his duty to help victims of the plague and cure them by means of the virtue which nature has vested in this precious stone." Because of a similar belief fragments of emeralds, pearls and gold were added to potions for plague victims who could afford it. In the sixteenth century, a single jewel could also recall the glory of a king or any episodes of his reign worthy of immortalization in gold and gems.

Jewels were sometimes presented by a king or a noble to commemorate a specific event, and the jewel took on new meaning and additional value not only from its material but from its shape, design and date. The pendants of the Elizabethan epoch provide many examples. The most famous of these commemorate the defeat of the Invincible Armada and the profitable expeditions of Francis Drake. Many jewels bear inscriptions, devices or little poems to explain their meaning. Unfortunately, some of these texts are obscure and we cannot always tell to what they refer. Their language is secret and this is often true of the whole symbolism of shapes and colors. There is a whole little-known side of Renaissance jewelry, which often has a double or triple meaning. This brief review of the apparent and cryptic characteristics of the jewels of this period may be useful in helping us to a better understanding of the evolution of jewelry if we bear it in mind throughout the history of technique and form. The material, shape, value and history of the jewel made it significant long before it became a work of art.

Insignia, emblems and ensigns (pilgrim badges) all belong to the same category. An ensign was a jewel that men and women wore in their hats, headdresses or hair. It was originally just a mark of identity, sometimes of a valuable object that showed that the owner had taken part in an important pilgrimage. This type of ensign, inherited from the Middle Ages, persisted until the mid-eighteenth century, but the significance of the ornament changed. After the end of the fifteenth century the badge gradually lost its religious meaning and modest simplicity. It became the most important jewel and was often very rich and finely executed. It also gave free reign to the craftsman's ingenuity and the owner's fancy and grew richer in

Holbein: design for a pendant with the monogram HI (Henry VIII and Jane Seymour?). An emerald in the center and three pearls. Pen and watercolor. British Museum, London.

Hat badge: low relief in enamel, gold, diamonds and rubies. The conversion of St. Paul. Italian, sixteenth century. Waddesdon Bequest, British Museum, London.

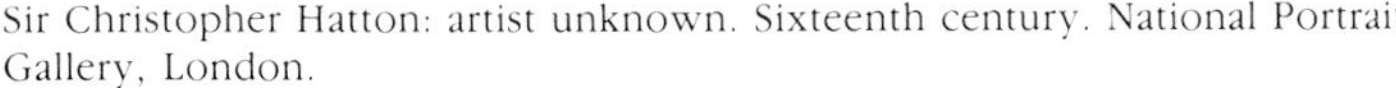
Sir Christopher Hatton: artist unknown. Sixteenth century. National Portrait Gallery, London.

The Infanta Isabella Clara Eugenia: engraving after a portrait by Pourbus. Bibliothèque Nationale, Paris, Cabinet des Estampes.

material and design, changing from a talisman to a precious object that illustrated the wearer's character. During the Renaissance, it was a mark of identity and no longer indicated membership of a group but rather the individuality of the owner. Emblems, devices and symbols, very often enigmatical, abounded on them. Contemporary portraits and drawings show that every distinguished person had many hat-badges. Unfortunately, very few of them have survived. When enameled gold went out of fashion, these hat-badges met with the same fate as many other jewels;

Queen Elizabeth I:
painting commemorating her visit to
Sir Henry Lee on September 20, 1592.
National Portrait Gallery, London.

Collar of the Order of the Garter presented to Frederick II of Denmark by Elizabeth I in 1582. Rosenborg Castle, Chronological Collection of the Danish Kings, Copenhagen.

they were dismantled for the sake of the precious stones and the ancient setting was abandoned without regret.

However, some amazingly rich and varied examples can still be seen in the museums of London, Vienna, Paris and New York. The shapes and subjects are so diverse that it is very difficult to attempt a classification. They include biblical and mythological scenes and a number of cameos and intaglios, either antique or copied from the antique, which were very fashionable from the end of the fifteenth century on, especially in Italy. This article readily lent itself to all sorts of fancies since it could take any shape whatsoever and there were no limits to its weight and size. As to the material, it was the same as that of all the other jewels of the period—gold enameled with bright color or white and precious stones with the colors set off by white enamel or diamonds.

The same taste for glitter and clear colors, blends of red and green or blue and red, and the same use of several techniques and materials on a single piece occur everywhere in this period. The exquisite workmanship which is one of the chief characteristics of this era should be stressed. In the course of the subsequent centuries, gold was rarely to be enameled with such skill and even details handled with such talent. The invisible side of a hat badge or brooch, only one face of which was ever visible, was generally enameled with a finely executed design. Jewelers' designs, which often showed both sides of a piece, indicated that this pursuit of perfection was universal among artists until the seventeenth century.

Before we leave the subject of head and hat ornaments, we should also mention the brooches that were worn in the headdress, especially in England, and the hat-bands that were sometimes worth a veritable fortune by themselves. Diamonds, rubies, emeralds, sapphires and pearls mounted in gold or silver were attached to them like ordinary buttons. The most typical fifteenth and sixteenth century ornaments could often be worn in many different ways. Along with jewels that had a fixed purpose and permanent form, rulers and men of quality owned an impressive number of single pearls and gems with which they

Sir Henry Sidney: artist unknown. Sixteenth century. He is wearing a pendant showing St. George and the dragon. National Portrait Gallery, London.

scattered their clothes. The ideas of jewelry, ornament and dress revealed by this custom are widely different from our own, but not without charm, apart from a few excesses. The gown, cloak and hat, and sometimes the ladies' hairstyles were designed to include and set off precious ornaments. Pearls and gems were not added as an afterthought, but were a basic part of the garment or headdress. Movable decorations could therefore be used and reused according to every new idea. This was also the reason for the variety and number of jewels, since each ceremonial outfit and every state robe could require its own set of jewels. Europe of the fifteenth century was suddenly inundated with gold and gems and made the most immediate, abundant and striking use of them. Fashion profited handsomely by this new wealth, which transformed not only styles of dress, but even habits of thought. Little by little, man gained confidence in himself and in the world.

The great works of art are not alone in reflecting this transformation. The man of the Renaissance consolidated his position in contrast with the medieval lord by his manner of dressing and the very luxury with which he adorned himself. He regarded himself as increasingly worthy to wear things which had formerly been the prerogative of the king or of God. Fashions also reflected this new era, as did the current economic theories. Large sums were invested in gold and precious stones; collections were formed, trade increased and goldsmiths' and jewelers' work was more abundant than ever before.

A history of jewelry beginning in the Renaissance opens in a climate of pride and passion. It would be out of place here to analyze the changes in thinking that henceforth liberated the idea of profit from guilt feelings and allowed wealth to be displayed without shame, but it is important to show their consequences in the realm of jewelry. People no longer saw only frivolity, selfishness and vanity in jewelry, but also a new joy in living and a steadily increasing wish to make the most of the beauty in the world.

Men and women of rank covered themselves with jewels and displayed them as advantageously as possible

Hans Collaert: design for a pendant (Miscellaneous collection of sixteenth and seventeenth century jewelry designs). B.N., Paris, Cabinet des Estampes.

within the rules of dress. The clothes and jewels set each other off. After the headdress ornament came the pendant, the form and position of which gave it a privileged role in Renaissance jewelry. It put the essential finishing touch to all gold chains and was the ornament which was best adapted to the current style of bodice. Low necklines or yokes showed it off and all eyes were drawn to it.

The pendant as a form was not a Renaissance creation. It had existed in previous times and one of its direct ancestors was the reliquary pendant decorated with cabochons. The craftsmen of the Renaissance, however, produced a great variety of styles and designs and made it the most characteristic jewel of the period. Infinite ingenuity and skill were lavished on pendants, and though it is true that many elements were borrowed, they were perfectly adapted to their new function. They sometimes seemed to be the ideal medium for realizing all the artist's dreams. Some Spanish pieces are like candelabra; others from Italy are reminiscent of niches for statues and architectural ornaments, park palings or even tombs. The craftsman seems to have been able to give freer rein to his imagination in this miniature candelabrum or *tempietto* than in models where a degree of seriousness was always obligatory. The laws of equilibrium and gravity were less imperious and the improbable became possible. The comparatively modest size of the pendant allowed the use of only the most precious materials, and special mention must be made of the ingenuity shown in the use of the baroque pearl. It was transformed into a triton's torso or a dragon's body, jewelers took advantage of all its irregularities and flaws, head and limbs of enameled gold set with precious stones were added and the ugliest were integrated into the most exquisite shapes. The "Canning Jewel" in the Victoria and Albert Museum, an Italian pendant of the late sixteenth century, is an outstanding example, displaying astonishing daring and freedom. It is highly typical of its epoch and unites the taste for fantastic characters and masks which was common in all the arts, the profusion of colors and materials described in the section on hat-badges, and great technical skill. Incidentally,

The "Canning jewel:" pendant. Gold, enamel, diamonds, rubies, pearls and a baroque pearl. Italian, perhaps Tuscan, late sixteenth century. Presented by Mrs. Edward Harkness. Victoria & Albert Museum, London.

it should be noted that there are three pearls at the base of the pendant, a sort of inevitable threefold rhythm which recurs in nearly every piece of this kind. The function of these pearls is not purely decorative; they either balance and stabilize an assymetric composition or stress the main lines of the object in its role as central ornament of the wearer; they underline the basic function of the pendant with its real or simulated weight, while accentuating the vertical movement pointing downwards. In the case of the "Canning Jewel," the movement of which is oblique, they are the only regular foundation element.

There are many pendants in the form of a niche, often flanked by pilasters, containing one or more figures. They occur in all countries, but especially Italy and Germany. The type probably originated in the peninsula, and was often derived from real or imaginary architecture and sculpture. However, Germany soon adopted this motif and carried it to excess. The architectural setting then gradually became very important. Golden columns were enriched with table-cut stones and the piece was loaded with a profusion of ornaments, figures and details far removed from the Italian taste. The Florentine, Venetian and Milanese masters described these pendants somewhat disparagingly as *alla fiamminga* or *alla tedesca*.

The motifs and shapes of pendants are very varied. There are religious subjects (the Virgin and Child, the Crucifixion, saints), mythological subjects, allegories and fantastic creatures. The Venetians were fond of the ship motif which lent itself perfectly to this type of jewel, but there are also many pendants of this shape from England and Spain. The pendant could just as easily be a simple medallion richly decorated with gems and enamel framing a portrait. It frequently opens to show yet another treasure. Such, for example, is the heart-shaped "Darnley Jewel", that Lady Margaret Douglas had made in memory of her husband, who was killed in 1571. The center is ornamented with a cabochon sapphire surrounded by red, green and blue enamel motifs and emblems of Faith, Hope, Victory and Truth. The whole is surmounted by a crown set with precious stones concealing two hearts joined by

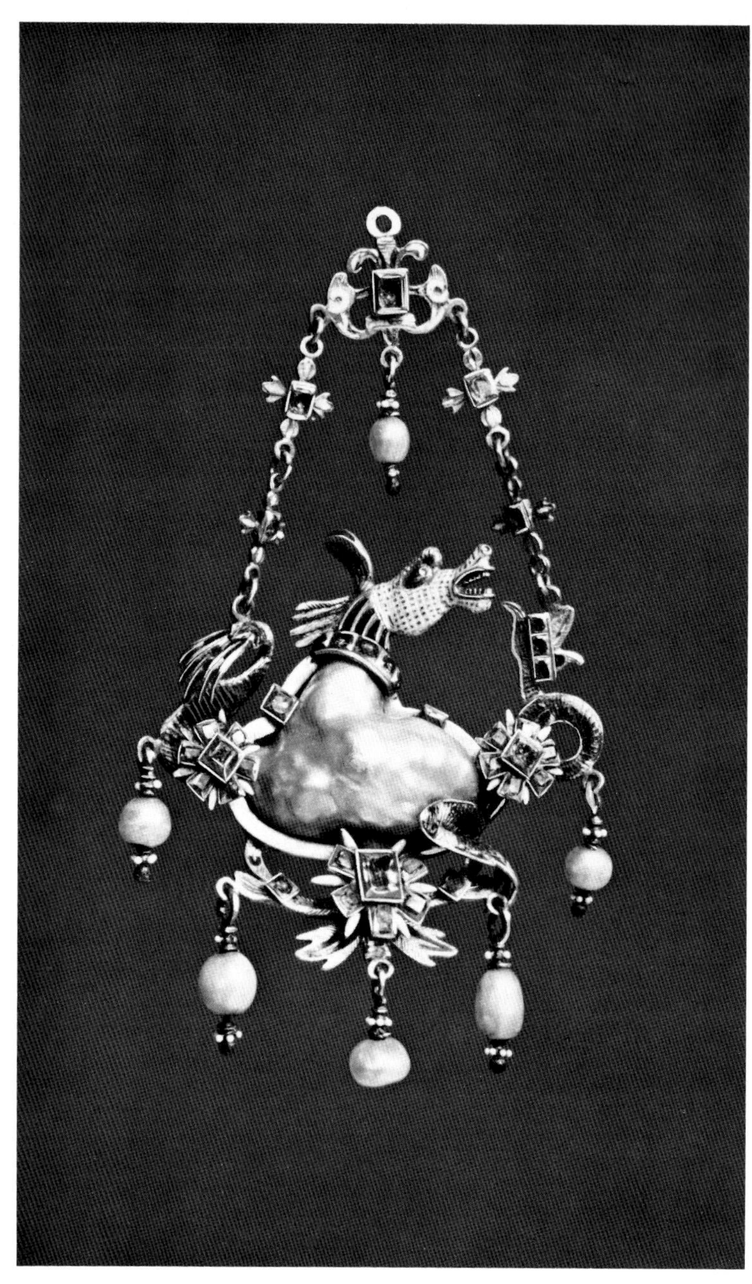

Pendant: gold, enamel, rubies, emeralds, a baroque pearl and green enamel on the body of the hippocamp. Its collar is decorated with rubies and the chain with emeralds. Waddesdon Bequest, British Museum, London.

Pendant: Diana, a stag and a dog. Gold, enamel, a diamond, emeralds, rubies and pearls. Italian, sixteenth century. Salting Bequest, Victoria & Albert Museum, London.

a golden knot. The reverse of the jewel is richly enamelled and decorated with symbolic and allegorical figures of rather obscure meaning. It bears an inscription and can be opened. It must once have contained a miniature. The front of the jewel can also be opened. Its construction and the abundance of allusions and symbols are complex. Others are simpler, but in the same spirit. A fair number have survived, especially in England, where Elizabeth I was loaded with gifts on the least occasion. The finest and most valuable pendant, a flower all in gold, diamonds, rubies and opals bearing a cameo and pearls was given to her as a Christmas gift in 1581. There are also pendants in the shape of letters which might be the owner's initials or religious symbols like the IHS jewels which are so common in Denmark.

Pendant: gold and diamonds. On the reverse, the instruments of the Passion in gold and enamel. Formerly the property of William Howard. English, c. 1600. Victoria & Albert Museum, London.

Arnold Lulls: design for a pendant with the letters IHS. Early seventeenth century. Victoria & Albert Museum, London.

Pendants were also worn on the girdle and in some countries in the ears. Earrings occur most frequently in Spain, and far from being a feminine prerogative, they were the current fashion for men. They could be fairly large and were usually decorated with faceted stones, usually emeralds, or gems engraved with a design. The Sicilians and Italians sometimes wore earrings but they preferred a smaller size. The fashion spread over the rest of Europe towards the end of the sixteenth century—many kings wore a pearl in their ears—but it did not last for long. The majority of women, who still wore coifs and wimples, rarely wore earrings. As for girdle pendants, they too are numerous and varied. To begin with, the belt itself was often leather, covered with velvet, embroidered with gold and silver and decorated with stones and pearls. The buckle and the terminal offered many possibilities to artists. In addition, many useful small articles were carried among the folds of the ample garments of the time, attached to a chain hanging from the belt. These included keys, prayerbooks, pomanders and watches that were themselves beautifully worked and decorated with stones and enamel.

Hat-badges, brooches and pendants were the most typical Renaissance jewels, the latter always being accompanied by richly enameled chains, some links of which contained a ruby, emerald, sapphire or diamond. But there are many other types of jewels, among which rings with or without stones figure prominently. Kings, queens and nobles often wore them on all their fingers and even their thumbs. These, too, were enameled and ornamented with engraved or plain gems. They often had a symbolic meaning such as interlaced hearts and joined hands, and inscriptions were common on betrothal and marriage rings. But like hat-badges and pendants, rings could also enclose a mythological or biblical scene, or again an intaglio. Few ancient rings survive, since they were usually reset at a later period after jewelers had discovered the best way to bring out the sparkle of the stone. In the sixteenth century, the metal claws, or *collet*, which held the stone still largely encroached upon it and hid it, and it was often necessary to put a colored foil between the setting and stone to reinforce its brilliance and intensify its color. However, there are many portraits where every jewel is shown in such detail that we can see quite clearly which types of rings were most fashionable in the Renaissance era.

All the fingers were adorned but bracelets were only rarely worn. For a long time, fashion decreed very long sleeves covering the whole wrist, sometimes ending in a lace ruffle. A bracelet would have been invisible and this ornament was rare until the seventeenth century. However, it is interesting to note that some painters show bracelets either on the wrists or above the elbow when they paint a nude figure. They are often circlets which look like enameled gold, with one or more stones in the central portion. The subject of a "Woman at her Toilet," so dear to the Mannerist painters, furnishes many examples. However, some women, especially in England, could not resist the lure of bracelets. They used to have their sleeves slashed so that the jewels on their arms could be seen. The same process was used for gloves in order not to conceal rings.

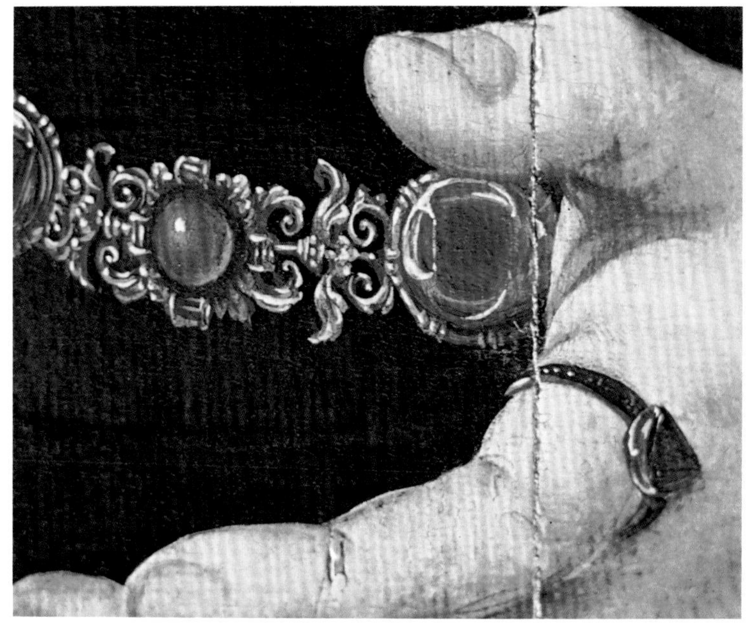

Portrait of Anna van Bergen, Marquise de Vere: Mabuse. Isabella Stewart Gardner Museum, Boston.

Detail of portrait

Possibly, this brief examination of the most common forms of Renaissance Europe does not follow the evolution of tastes, styles and fashions in every country, as such a study would be very difficult. Craftsmen, models, jewels and rich men traveled, and there were few countries in which a national style developed. Princesses' dowries brought new pieces into the treasures of foreign kings, and these would quickly be copied, interpreted and adapted. Jewels were sold and exchanged. Everyone of high rank was expected to dazzle his hosts by the profusion of his jewels whenever he went on a diplomatic mission or a courtesy visit. Here and there the spirit of emulation arose, impelling everyone to exhibit greater wealth and novelty. As to the craftsmen, they settled wherever the greatest patrons summoned them or took them into their service. Besides, there were many who had engravings made of their jewelry designs and published them in volumes which might circulate all over Europe. It has always been very difficult to locate a jewel accurately because the interplay of influences and the movements of craftsmen so obscure the trail.

Attributions raise the same problems. In the last century, the hand of the celebrated Cellini was often discerned in pieces with which he had nothing to do, and German influence was subsequently somewhat mistakenly recognized in pendants from a variety of provenances. But Bavaria is very close to Italy, Spain dominated the Netherlands, Mary Stuart was queen of France for a few years, and Italian influence, which might seem to be pre-eminent, sometimes arrived in a distant land only by way of German or Flemish adaptations. Dürer assimilated the Italian style perfectly, but for all that he never lost his personal touch. Holbein worked for Henry VIII and carried out the orders he was given, but did his designs belong purely to the English school? It is impossible to answer this question by postulating an international style, but it is equally impossible to try to isolate the characteristics of each country.

The craftsmen of the main production centers were not necessarily natives of the country where they were working or even permanent residents. We should always remember the frequent movements of objects, their owners and makers, the tangled networks of influences and the diversity of contributed and borrowed elements. It is true that the whole of Europe adopted Italian fashion—which was itself inherited from the ancient world although only a few aspects were known—but it is also accepted that this style was enriched by borrowing from Gothic, Turkish and Arab elements. Itinerant craftsmen who joined the suites of diplomats, courts of sovereigns and powerful merchant families in their clients' own countries had to satisfy both traditional and contemporary taste. Their rivalry was conducted on two apparently contradictory fronts. This was the source of their originality, and also of our difficulties in assigning them to clearly defined categories.

Finally, an examination of the most active production centers of the Renaissance must take chronology into account, since all the centers did not arise at the same time, but succeeded each other after competition. These vicissitudes nearly always follow historical, social and economic events, which also explain the presence of a great master in one place or another. Such a man would bring with him a whole train of pupils and assistants who

Holbein: design for a lozenge-shaped pendant with diamonds and pearls. Pen and wash drawing touched up with yellow. British Museum, London.

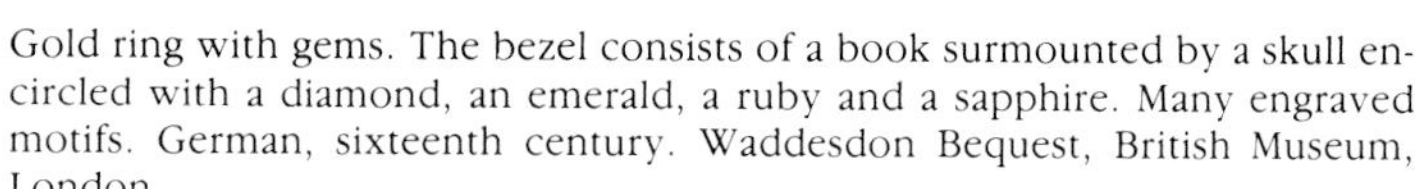

Gold ring with gems. The bezel consists of a book surmounted by a skull encircled with a diamond, an emerald, a ruby and a sapphire. Many engraved motifs. German, sixteenth century. Waddesdon Bequest, British Museum, London.

Holbein: design for a necklace with floral motifs decorated with gems and pearls. Pen and wash drawing. British Museum, London.

would leave in their turn to try their luck all over Europe.

Italy was obviously the leading spirit, and the richest and most active cities there were Florence and Venice. After them came Naples and Milan, the latter producing a lot of jewels, but also a fair number of fakes of all sorts, such as "antique" cameos and intaglios of recent date that were all the rage in Europe, and pearls made of glass filled with wax that were in great demand for decorating clothes. The Florentines and Venetians certainly had artificial jewels, too, but the real pieces which survive put them at the head of high-quality producers from the fifteenth century on.

There is no need for detailed description of the prodigious activity of Florence in all the arts. Cosimo dei Medici, an enlightened patron, protected such masters as Brunelleschi, Ghiberti and Donatello. Then came Lorenzo the Magnificent, who surrounded himself with scholars and artists and patronized all the creative arts. On the other hand, it is a fact that many Florentine painters, sculptors and architects served their apprenticeships with a goldsmith. This was true of Cosimo dei Medici's three great protégés and of Botticelli, Pollaiuolo, Verrochio and Ghirlandaio, to quote only the best-known. Andrea del Sarto furnishes another example in the sixteenth century. The majority of these great masters, then, passed some years of their youth in a goldsmith's workshop, and the training they received there was very important. For example, it reveals the power of the Florentine goldsmiths' guild and the respect in which their art was held. The craft was not insecure in the fifteenth century; on the contrary, it was highly profitable, and provident fathers delighted to dedicate their sons to it. There was an abundance of choice for apprenticeship. In the years after 1400, there were 44 shops on the Ponte Vecchio alone, and the jewelry trade flourished in the Calimuzza and Canto di Vacchereccia. A hundred years later, business was even more prosperous. Florence had opened up Eastern trading houses

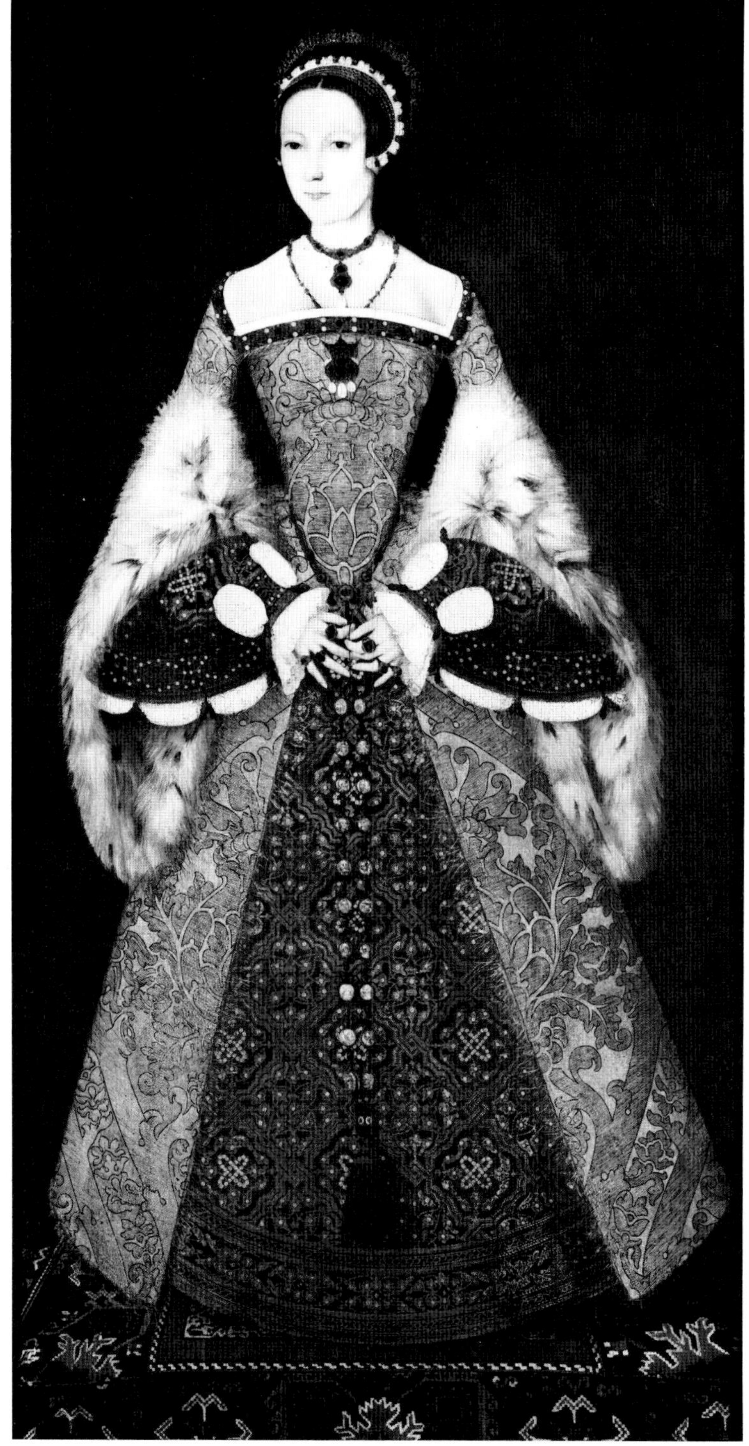

Portrait of Lady Jane Grey: artist unknown. Sixteenth century. National Portrait Gallery, London.

and all the merchandise of the orient flooded into the city. It came first to the apothecaries and druggists who belonged to the fine arts, i.e., an important guild. They actually did business in all Levantine goods, drugs and spices, but also in precious stones.

There was no shortage of customers, for Florence had been one of the richest cities in Europe for more than a hundred years. Devoted to luxury and beauty, wealthy Florentines ordered sumptuous ornaments and craftsmen had their hands full to execute all their orders. They lavished infinite care on their work. The Florentine tradition of technical perfection was very active among her craftsmen. It certainly affected the young artists they trained. We can recognize it in their later works, especially when they painted jewels. They expended all their genius on these paintings, but they did it as connoisseurs and initiates, and thus they provide extremely valuable evidence. The jewels with which they decked their models were always practicable even when they are perhaps not real, and whenever they imagined an ornament, it is more than probable that the painted jewel would be copied by craftsmen who expanded their repertoire with elements drawn from paintings. It must also be remembered that in an era when artists and craftsmen were still indistinguishable, great masters were often asked to provide designs for all sorts of ornaments. In fifteenth century Florence, painting, sculpture and goldworking were closely linked, progress in one advancing the other, and all the arts benefited from these continual exchanges.

Florentine craftsmen and artists not only had good customers, they had patrons—rich and cultured men who accepted new forms readily. Several generations of the Medici family encouraged the contemporary arts and surrounded themselves with collections of treasures. Those of Lorenzo were famous, and included some very fine intaglios. From his youth, the Magnificent showed a pro-

Pendant: hunter with dogs. Gold, enamel, gems and pearls. German, last quarter of the sixteenth century. The Michael Friedsam Collection, Metropolitan Museum of Art, New York.

Pendant: Charity with three children. Gold, enamel, rubies, diamonds and emeralds. Style of Erasmus Hornick, Augsburg (?). German, late sixteenth century. Waddesdon Bequest, British Museum, London.

Pendant: Cleopatra. Gold, enamel, hyacinths, diamonds, rubies and emeralds. Italian stones c. 1550, German setting c. 1590. Nymphenburg Castle, Munich. 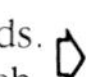

Pendant: a three-masted ship. Gold enamel and pearls. Venetian, late sixteenth century. Spitzen Collection, Victoria & Albert Museum, London.

nounced taste for sumptuous ornaments. For his marriage, he wore a scarf embroidered with roses entirely carried out in pearls. The same motif decorated his black cap, which was set off by a feather made of gold threads with a pearl, diamond or ruby on the tip of each. The famous Benvenuto Cellini worked with Michelagnolo di Viviano, one of the Medici family's master jewelers. This colorful character is very often named in the context of jewelry, but in fact it is practically impossible to attribute a single surviving Italian piece to him. We only know his creations from his own descriptions, and he seems to have been more interested in sculpture and large pieces of goldwork than in personal jewelry. During the 1530s, he worked for the papacy, and he says that he made a pin with a big diamond in the center for Clement VII's cape and a papal ring adorned with a colored diamond for Paul III. In 1545, Duchess Eleonora of Toledo ordered a golden girdle set with stones from him. We do not know what became of

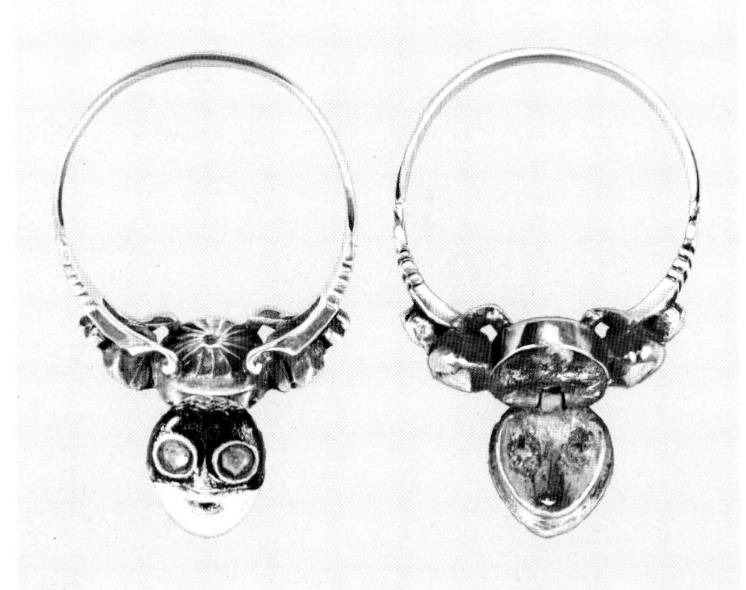

Gold ring: the bezel consists of a head in black and white enamelled gold with brilliants for eyes. Italian, sixteenth century. Poldi-Pezzoli Museum, Milan.

these pieces, and if Cellini made any other jewels, the same thing applies to them as all the other Italian Renaissance jewels—we do not know which artists were responsible for them.

Florence shared with Venice the privilege of being "the great depot for the supply of jewels, pearls and objects of finery." (J. Lucas-Debreton, *Everyday Life in Florence in the Time of the Medici,* London 1960). Venice was a rich city and the greatest port in fifteenth century Europe. In spite of the Turkish threat and the dangerous rivalry of other cities, commerce and industry flourished in this town full of merchants and seamen. Trade with the East furnished sugar, spices and precious stones, and also opened the way to all sorts of influences which are not so clearly apparent anywhere else in Europe. At the same time, Venice was in touch with Germany, England, France and Flanders. All this called for very strict organization. Certain buildings were "fortified at public expense at a specified time of year. To these buildings," writes Sabellico, "four long ships from Syria and four more from Egypt brought perfumes, silk, precious stones and pearls. Three more brought gold, gems and slaves from Libya. . . . four brought salt, carpets and emeralds from beyond the Bosphorus," and the town grew richer. Austere to begin with, the patricians gradually learned the ways of luxury. Their palaces became more sumptuous and their wives sought rare stuffs and precious materials for their clothes.

From the end of the fifteenth century on, travelers remarked on this opulence. In 1490, Philippe Devoisin marveled to see robes "bejeweled each one to the value of more than thirty or forty thousand ducats." The Doge and his wife had to outdo everyone else in splendor. They were even obliged to do so by a law which commanded the Doge to wear an ermine collar fastened to his robe by gold buttons twelve times a year. Albrecht Dürer's letters to his friend Pirkheimer in 1506 hint at the city's activity in the precious stones and jewelry trade. For the painter profited by his stay to make several purchases. "I am sending a sapphire ring by this courier, as you urgently requested me. I could not conclude the deal any sooner, since I spent two whole days visiting all the goldsmiths from Germany and Italy and making comparisons and haven't found a single ring as good as this for the same price. I bought it by dint of prayers for 12 ducats four marcelli from a man who was wearing it on his own finger. And no sooner had I bought it than a German goldsmith who saw me wearing it offered to buy it for three ducats more." (March 8, 1506) (Albrecht Dürer, *Lettres et Ecrits théoretiques,* text and translation by Pierre Vaisse, ed. Hermann, Paris 1964). Dürer bought emeralds and the ring with the sapphire which he mentions in his letter, and asks his friend if he wants a diamond bracelet. He always hoped to make a good bargain by sending stones to Nuremberg to be sold there for a higher price.

Nuremberg, too, was a rich and flourishing city which was visibly expanding. Inhabited by daring merchants who would unhestitatingly embark on even the longest voyages, it was remarkably prosperous from the fourteenth century on. It was situated at an important crossroads, in contact with the east via Italy and with northern Europe, and was therefore open to a variety of influences. It was the home of Wolgemuth and Dürer, and also the scene of many inventions such as the watch. Its prosperous merchants formed a powerful aristocracy who were quickly captivated by the new art of luxurious living. Many goldsmiths settled there, among whom was Dürer's father, "a gallant man and skilled in his art," according to his son, who served several years apprenticeship in the paternal workshop. Nuremberg attracted a large number of distinguished artists who either settled there for periods of varying length (e.g. Erasmus Hornick, who lived there from 1559 to 1566) or worked there all their lives (e.g. Peter Flötner, Matthias Zundt and Virgil Solis). It is sometimes difficult to accurately attribute pieces in museums to one of these goldsmiths and jewelers, but, nevertheless, an idea of their style can be formed because nearly all were engraved or had engravings made of the jewelry designs that inspired Europe for many years.

There were other flourishing German cities where very fine jewels were made. In Munich, the Dukes of Bavaria

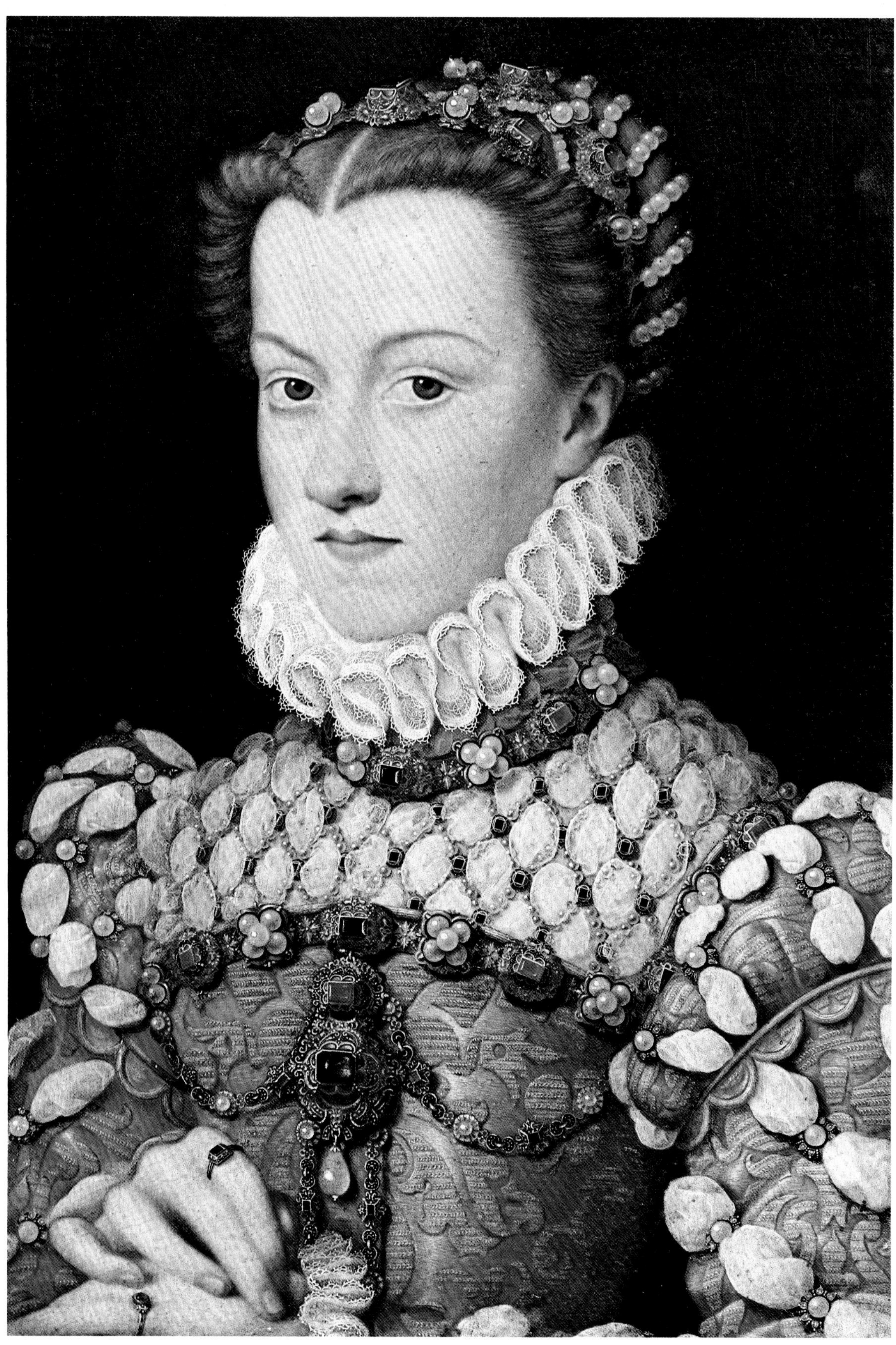

Clouet: portrait of Elizabeth of Austria.
Musée du Louvre, Paris.

encouraged the luxury arts, and Duke Albert V took the famous Hans Mielich into his service. Theodore de Bry settled in Frankfort in 1560 with his sons, and the new style he introduced, with its rich decoration, delicate figures and varied motifs, where animals mingled with fruits, flowers and grotesques, influenced contemporary work quite profoundly.

However, the greatest of them all was the powerful city of Augsburg, with its merchants and bankers, like the Fuger and Welser families, who often proved to be discriminating patrons. Geographically, the town occupied the privileged position of intermediary between north and south and, by virtue of its contacts with Venice, between east and west. It had the political status of Imperial City, i.e., it enjoyed an exceptional degree of independence. Commerce, and industry benefited from these advantages. Pius II said that Augsburg was the richest city in the world. A statement like this is disputable, but it is certainly true that Jacob Fugger, one of its illustrious citizens, was reputedly the richest man in the world. This prosperity attracted all sorts of craftsmen in the late sixteenth century, including a large number of goldsmiths and jewelers whose names are recorded. Among them were Daniel Mignot and Erasmus Hornick, whom we have already encountered at Nuremberg and who became a citizen and independent artist in Augsburg. He did not spend the rest of his life in Germany, however. In 1582, he moved to Prague, another important center of the late sixteenth century, largely owing to Rudolph II. Hornick is an example of the great itinerant craftsmen, who, even in their old age, did not hesitate to quit an apparently prosperous situation to try their luck in an unknown country. Born in Antwerp, which he had to leave for religious reasons, he died in Prague in 1583. Others, such as the Milanese jeweler Donato della Porta, traveled even further. He worked in Hungary, where King Matthias Corvinus and King Ladislas II were renowned in the fifteenth and sixteenth centuries for the splendor of the courts and their jewelry collections. The latter king had only one rival in his kingdom who was richer than himself. This was Archbishop Tamas Bakocz, who even succeeded in dazzling the citizens of Rome. In Budapest museums, there are several precious relics of this era, when lords wore ceremonial robes of gold thread adorned with hundreds of diamonds, and pendants with nearly as many precious jewels.

In the history of France, the profound transformation of ideas, arts and customs under Italian influence, which is known as the Renaissance, took place in the sixteenth century.

Chronological divisions of history may be necessary, but they are always conventional and categorical. They do not match the natural course of events, which is more subtle and unrolls without interruption, bringing about successive changes slowly and gradually. At the height of its development, a transformation like the Renaissance, that affected all branches of thought and ways of life, also encompassed the conservative elements, which, refusing to be submerged, kept persistent offshoots alive far beyond their accepted termination date.

In France, four centuries of struggle between the monarchy and the feudal lords ended in victory for the lilies. French unity became a fact when the throne rose on the ruins of the feudal system.

Once they had united all the interior provinces under their rule, the monarchs, new to power and greedy for conquest, sought for lands further afield. They crossed the Alps from 1497 to 1515 in pursuit of the succession to the kingdom of Naples and attempted to conquer Milan between 1515 and 1544. Charles VIII, Louis XII and Francis I went in search of a crown but brought back arts, customs and doctrines. The struggle was vain but the confrontation had dazzling effects. From the second half of the fifteenth century on, contacts with Italy increased, and exchanges, not only of embassies, but of members of the clergy, scholars, and above all, artists, were many. Faced with the more sophisticated intellectual life in Italy, the French were soon decisively drawn towards the ancient civilization of the south.

Nevertheless, Benvenuto Cellini, the sculptor, goldsmith, engraver and author of several jewelry designs,

Chain of office: gold, enamel, artificial emeralds, spinel ruby, diamonds and pearls. Munich, c. 1565, perhaps after a sketch by Hans Mielich. Nymphenburg Castle, Munich.

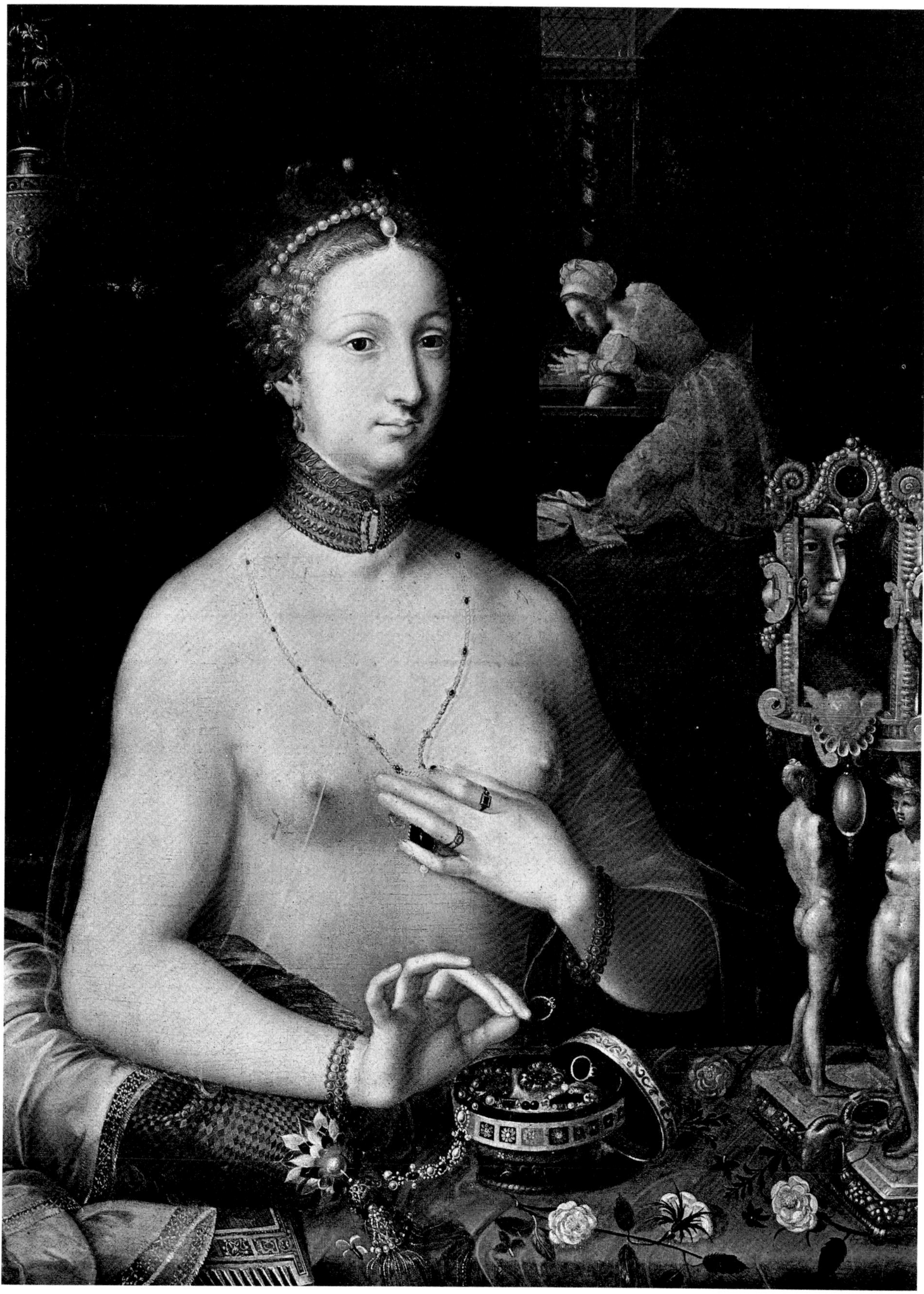

School of Fontainebleau: *Woman at her Toilet.* Musée des Beaux Arts, Dijon.

Detail of preceding page.

Virgil Solis: design for two pendants. Victoria & Albert Museum, London.

summoned to France in 1540 and endowed by Francis I with a pension of 700 gold *écus* a year, naturalization papers and the title of Lord of Petit-Nesle with a life interest in the castle, did not influence jewelry as profoundly as his compatriots, Primaticio, Leonardo da Vinci and Il Rosso affected French painting. At the time the illustrious Italian goldsmith settled in the mansion at Petit-Nesle, some outstanding French jewels and goldsmith's work bearing the marks of the purest Renaissance style were already in existence.

It was not until fifty years later, i.e., the mid-sixteenth century, that the French Renaissance freed itself from Italian influence to follow an authentically national path.

Daniel Mignot: design for a pendant. Bibliothèque Nationale, Paris, Cabinet des Estampes.

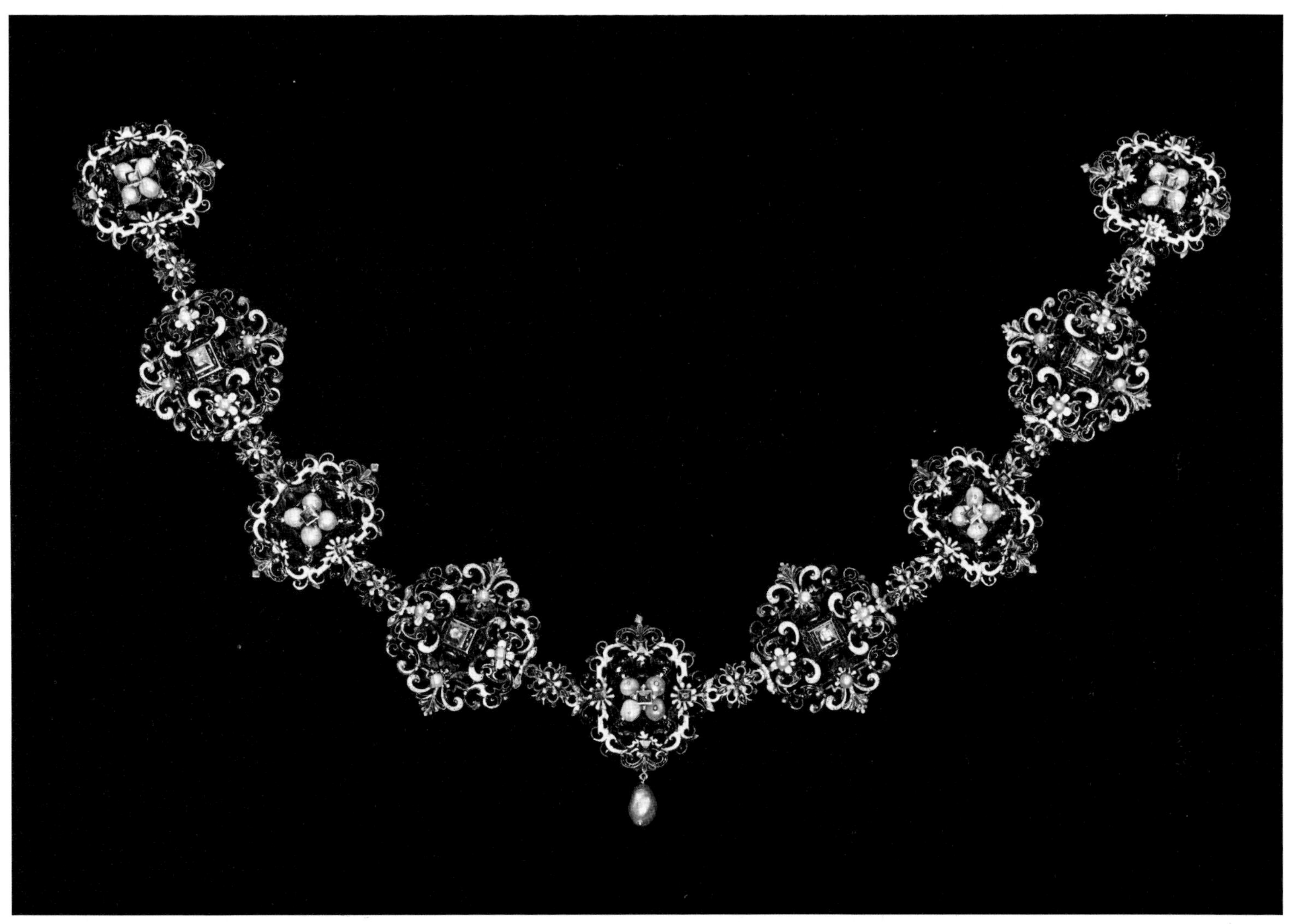

Gold chain: enamel, pearls and diamonds. German or Austrian, 1540-80. Kunstindustrimuseet, Copenhagen.

However, Renaissance preoccupation with the ancient world had a decisive and lasting effect on France, where its traces could be discerned for more than three hundred years to come, and are still apparent in our own times.

At this point, a development took place which affected the art of jeweler and goldsmith alike. They were the direct interpreters of the tastes and tendencies of aristocratic clients who had a smattering of Latin learning and were proud of their superficial ideas about the ancient world. Consequently, goldsmiths and jewelers, who had hitherto been complete artists, gradually ceased to supply the inspiration for their own works and became no more than executants. From this time on, they usually confined themselves to reproducing faithfully, in workmanship of

Boyvin: design for pendants (Miscellaneous collection of sixteenth and seventeenth century jewelry designs). B.N., Paris, Cabinet des Estampes.

such excessive finesse and delicacy that it looks as if the chiselling was carried out through a magnifying glass, ornaments designed to their specifications by productive engravers, the best-known of whom were Boyvin (1530-98) and Etienne Delaulne (1519-83).

All those compositions show great respect for form. However great the richness of the ornament, it never spoils the purity nor obscures the original idea. There could be no better evidence to show how far French goldsmiths and jewelers escaped Benevenuto Cellini's influence than a comparison of Boyvin's or Delaulne's work with that of the Italian master. The latter demonstrates the artist's ardor and the exuberant wealth of his imagination. Excess of these qualities produced a profound change for the worse, and gave an impression of decadent taste.

However, it was not just aesthetic values that had changed. Techniques, particularly those of jewelry, had also been altered with the discovery about 1476 of a method of cutting diamonds and precious stones in facets, endowing jewelry with a hitherto unknown lightness and flexibility in the following century.

While jewelry was going through this formative period in the sixteenth century, the most fashionable ornaments were a sort of cap consisting of a gold net studded with diamonds and rubies; "chaplets," which belong equally to the goldsmith's and jeweler's art; pendant medallions of various sizes showing human figures decorated in low relief enamel; gilded or golden belts for the richest women, like the one which Valentina Visconti of Milan gave to one of her court ladies "decorated with 120 pearls and 13 balas rubies" (spinels), according to the *Accounts of the Hôtel of the duc d'Orleans* (the popularity of gold belts and châtelaines in all ranks of society became so great that royal edicts had to be passed to restrict them); *ferronnières* (chains fastened in the middle with a jewel worn around the forehead, as shown in the portrait of *La Belle Ferronnière* by Leonardo da Vinci); and the medallions, which were not worn around the neck like pendants and were known as "portraits" or "*enseignes.*" Women wore them in their headdresses and men in their hats. They were made of gold, enamel and gems, though the badge with the image of the Virgin of Embrun that Louis XI wore in his felt hat, was made of lead.

Courtly love of ostentation, strengthened by the taste for luxury, pretty things and easy living developed by the nobility of Medicean Italy; the enrichment of the middle classes by business prosperity; and royal patronage—many reasons combined to encourage all the luxury arts, among them that of the jeweler, which was the best medium for displaying the wealth of a house or family to all the world. The extravagant tastes of the people of the sixteenth century show clearly in the inventories and portraits of the period and the output of the jewelers' workshops can be estimated from them.

The inventory which Catherine de Medici's creditors drew up on her death in 1589 does not include a single jewel, but this was probably because the Queen-Mother forgot to take them with her when she hurried away from the Hôtel de Soissons after the day of the Barricades.

An event which took place in the reign of Francis I should be mentioned at this point. It is important because it marks the starting point from which jewelry developed under Louis XIV, Louis XV and Louis XVI.

The accession of Francis I brought to the throne of France not only the sovereign who was the greatest patron of the arts, but also the king who displayed the most extravagant gallantry.

The affectionate son of Louise of Savoy and beloved

School of Leonardo da Vinci: *La Belle Ferronnière*. Musée du Louvre, Paris.

Portrait of Francis I, formerly attributed to Clouet. Musée du Louvre, Paris.

brother of that most romantic lady, Marguerite d'Angoulême was described after his ceremonial entry into Paris "on his armored horse all accoutred in white and cloth-of-silver, doing wonders to show before the ladies."

The king and his reign are represented in popular imagination by this picture of a curveting monarch with nobles and ladies pressing around him. He was a brilliant talker and a charming letter-writer, a poet and even a musician, and women played so large a part in both his private and public life that he had to bestow a splendid official position on his mistresses. It is no exaggeration to say that his gallantry is the chief reason for his later renown.

He was a kingly figure who seemed to understand everything and "conversed to a marvel;" he could write the charming song:

My pretty darlings,
Whither way?
Will you be changing
Your place every day? . . .

and could also frame his fine soldierly pen to the famous phrase about the "life which is saved" along with honor. This king, whose portrait we see in the Louvre in his white satin doublet banded with black velvet and black cap with a white feather, was an unbelievably prodigal patron, who was born to love jewelry and allowed himself the pleasure of giving it.

By the Treaty of Cambrai in 1529, known as the "Ladies' Peace," which reconciled the king of France with Charles V, Burgundy and its dependencies were preserved for the French crown, the sons of the French king were released from prison in Madrid, and Francis I received the hand of Eleanor of Austria, dowager queen of Portugal and sister of his rival.

A few months after the treaty was signed, Eleanor, accompanied by the Dauphin and the Duc of Orleans, left Madrid for Paris. Francis I had gone ahead of the princess, whom he met on July 7, 1530, near Mont-de-Marsan,

Boyvin: design for a pendant. B.N., Paris, Cabinet des Estampes.

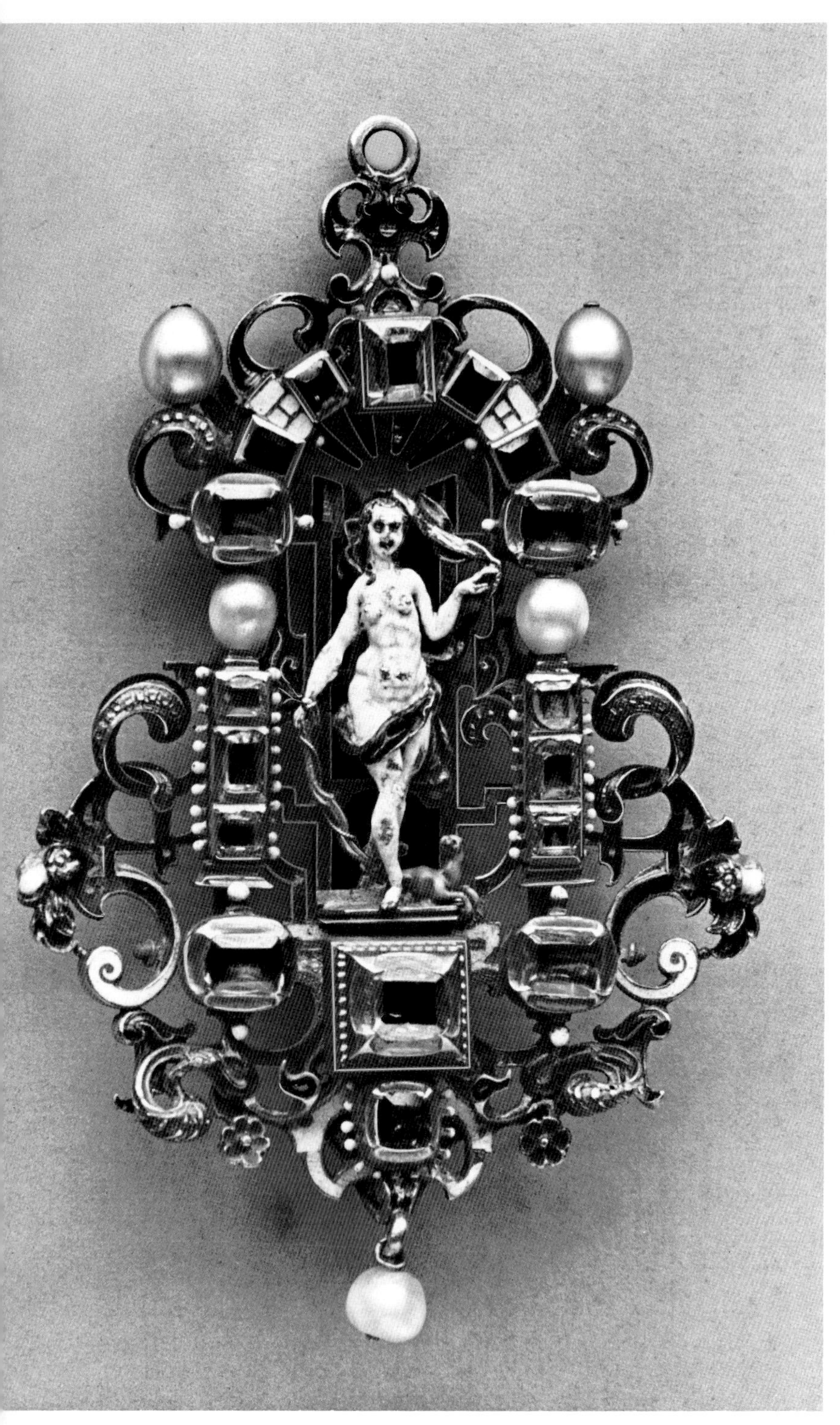

where the marriage was solemnized and consummated. Twenty days later, the queen, with the princess, made her state entry into Bordeaux and received from the king the collection of "Crown Jewels" which he had just made Crown property a month earlier by letters-patent dated June 15, 1530.

Francis I announced that he had collected this treasure to belong to his successors in turn, i.e., to the state, ordaining that "any alteration of the said jewels, their evaluation, weight, delineation and lead models shall be verified in their presence before they issue their obligatory letter-patent reserving them for their successors to the Crown."

This document illustrates the legal nature of the donation. When he made the jewels, which had been his own up to June 15, 1530, into state property, Francis I attached a specific condition to his gift. This was that the articles which composed the donation should be inalienable as long as the state of France should last.

Francis I only presented part of his jewels to the Crown. He kept many more for his personal use than he handed over. It is important, therefore, to distinguish between the Crown Jewels that were inalienable state property, and the king's personal jewelry that he could dispose of as he pleased. In order to make the distinction between the two types of jewels clearer, the Treasury was held accountable and responsible for the Crown Jewels, while the others concerned no one but the king, who much later unhesitatingly and quite legitimately forbade the Treasury councilors to interfere with them.

"The Crown Jewels of which Eleanor had the use were under the care of Jeanne des Tombes, Lady of Arpajon, one of her ladies-in-waiting.

The personal jewels of Francis I were under the care of the keeper of his privy purse, Jean de la Barre, knight, Governor and Provost of the city of Paris." (G. Babst)

Pendant: Diana. Gold, enamel and gems. German, c. 1600. Michael Friedsam Collection, 1931, Metropolitan Museum of Art, New York.

Anne de Caumont, wife of François d'Orléans. Collection Gaignières. B.N., Paris, Cabinet des Estampes.

The queen also had her personal jewels that she had brought with her from Madrid in addition to those presented to her by the king. Eleanor could adorn herself not only with her own jewels but with those belonging to the crown, of which she had the use for her husband's lifetime.

In his letter-patent, Francis I decreed that the "lead" of the stones must be kept every time they were remodeled. This phrase needs a few words of explanation. The density of lead (11.34) is nearly three times that of diamond (3.5). On the basis of this relative density, whenever there was a rough diamond, it was reproduced in lead and this lead was then cut to exactly the same shape that was planned for the diamond. Once this had been done,the stone was handed over to the diamond cutter, who cut it to the same shape as the lead. By means of this process, it was known before cutting that the finished stone should be one-third the weight of the carved lead. The "leads" of each stone were kept and served to establish the stone's identity.

The royal jewel collection as it was founded by Francis I contained eight pieces of a total value of 272,242 *écus soleil.** There were seven "bagues" and a big necklace of eleven diamonds cut indiscriminately in tables and points which had belonged to Queen Claude, Francis I's first wife.

The word "bague" (ring) did not then have its current meaning. In ancient law, the expression "*bagues* and jewels" indicated all the jewels and ornaments given by the husband to the wife before marriage as a wedding present. In the sixteenth century, while *anel* or *anneau* meant the ordinary finger ring, the word "bague," which had been used in the fifteenth century to refer to one's jewels, clothes and baggage, only applied to jewelry in general and especially to pendants. In his French dictionary, the

* An *écu soleil* was worth approximately $2.00.

Pendant: gold, enamel, diamonds, rubies and pearls. The Adoration of the Magi. The reverse is enamelled. Style of Daniel Mignot. Munich, early seventeenth century. Waddesdon Bequest, British Museum, London.

Attributed to Hans Collaert: design for a pendant. Victoria & Albert Museum, London.

Marquis de Laborde quoted this phrase from Antoine du Bourg, the king's Privy Councilor: "to give it (the stone) to make an ornament for the neck as desired." (G. Babst)

The seven "bagues" of the Royal Jewels were two triangular jewels, a brooch with the diamond known as the "Pointe de Bretagne" (the Breton Point) and another brooch with a large square table-cut diamond with high bevels (both these brooches had a pendant black pearl), a ruby known as the "Côte de Bretagne" (the Breton Coast) in its setting, another ruby known as the "Fève de Naples" (the Neapolitan Bean) and a big square-cut emerald mounted in gold.

On October 28, 1533, after long negotiations, the marriage of Henri Duc of Orleans, Francis I's second son, with Catherine de Medici, Pope Clement VII's niece, was celebrated at Marseilles. Clement VII had been obliged to pawn one of the finest diamonds of the papal tiara at the Strozzi bank to pay his niece's dowry. It appears that this was not enough, for the Treasurer of France expressed his astonishment when he did not receive the stipulated quantity of gold and silver. According to Brantôme, the representative of St. Peter replied that "beside all these things, to make a dowry worthy of such a marriage, he had promised by his authentic instrument three pearls of inestimable value, the splendor of which three great kings coveted with the utmost solicitude—the towns of Naples, Milan and Genoa." Naturally, the promise was never kept, but it was humorously commemorated by naming the three finest Royal jewels "The Neapolitan Bean," "The Milanese Point," and "The Genoese Table."

On the death of Francis I on March 31, 1547, Queen Eleanor, keeping only the ornaments "which the late king had given and bestowed upon her," returned the Crown Jewels to Lord Charles de Cossé-Brissac, Grand Pantler of France and representative of the new king of France, Henri II, "entailed and attached to the House and Crown of France." (G. Babst)

The royal jewelry collection subsequently expanded considerably, notably by the addition of several diamonds from a bequest by Mazarin bearing his name and some purchases made by Louis XIV from Tavernier, the Indian explorer, which included the "Blue" diamond. In the reign of Louis XV, it was enriched by the "Regent" diamond, a stone weighing 136 carats.

Babst's history of the Crown Jewels of France is full of intriguing surprises. It is not, as one might be tempted to think, merely the story of the official Crown Jewels. They served as pledges for loans. They assured Henri IV of the resources to which he largely owed the success of his work. They were of nationwide importance under every government, even the revolutionary ones; among other services they rendered were the brilliant charge of Lasalle's hussars at Rivoli and of Kellermann's cavalry that decided the battle of Marengo, and which was only possible because the Crown Jewels of France financed the purchase of horses for the French cavalry.

A law dated December 10, 1886, repudiating the inalienability of the foundation, decreed the sale of the Crown Jewels of France except for a few which were placed in the Louvre. The sale realized 7,095,665 francs net.

This review of the great European centers has shown that each king and each powerful city attracted to his kingdom or within its walls the goldsmiths and jewelers whose work contributed to their patron's prestige. Many of these artists, however, only settled temporarily. We have briefly followed the wanderings of Hornick of Liège. Theodor de Bry, who worked in Frankfort, also came from Liège, as did Hans Collaert, who emigrated to Germany with his two sons and was one of the most celebrated goldsmiths of his time. All these Flemings made their jewels "in the German style." Corvinianus Saur from Bavaria was summoned to the court of Christian IV of Denmark, and under Henry VIII and Elizabeth, artists from all parts assembled in England, including John of Utrecht, Alexander of Brussels and John Baptista de Consolavera, not forgetting Holbein, whose jewelry designs were often executed by Hans from Antwerp, known as John Anwarpe.

From England to Hungary and Flanders to Spain we encounter the same difficulties when we try to isolate the characteristics of any style. We must, therefore, confine ourselves to mentioning the great number of jewelers of Flemish origin at all the courts and great cities of Europe, competing with the Italians and soon with the French, adapting themselves to the tastes and positions of their patrons and the raw materials available in the country where they worked. They supplied the queen of England with many ornaments in colors cleverly chosen to express what she wanted to symbolize and the Spanish kings with religious jewels, including many emeralds. But the same taste for valuable and colorful ornaments predominated everywhere, and the fashion for jewels "in the Flemish style" succeeded the Italian style. Gradually, at the end of the sixteenth century, nearly all jewelry became heavier and more ponderous, and moved towards a realism which seems to belie the material of which it is made, to return at the end to simplicity, or, it might almost be said, to abstraction. But this last stage of development already takes us into the early years of the seventeenth century.

Chapter 3 THE CLASSICAL PERIOD

THE CLASSICAL PERIOD

Daniel Mignot: design for a pendant and other ornaments. B.N., Paris, Cabinet des Estampes.

It may seem paradoxical that fewer jewels have survived from the seventeenth century than the sixteenth. We might expect that with the passage of time, more pieces would be preserved. However, jewelry does not obey this rule, and its history follows an entirely different pattern. Paintings or buildings gradually acquired value as historical documents. Some seventeenth century restorations already showed respect for even the strangest and more unintelligible styles. The reverse is true of jewelry. It was dismantled and reset more frequently than ever before, without the least concern for the original design, which soon came to be regarded as little more than a background to be altered at will, or as an indispensable setting for the stones, the most important feature.

In fact, the seventeenth century was an important turning point in the history of ornaments as it was in this period that real jewelry originated. By the end of the Middle Ages, it had already lost its religious and magical talismanic significance. The classical period took little interest in the symbolic or narrative meaning of the design, and jewels became essentially decorative. There was, however, no decline in aesthetic or technical standards; on the contrary, the actual material of the jewel became more important than the form in this brand new avatar. From this point of view it could be said that jewelry became

Necklace: gold, enamel, brilliants, rubies and two pearls. Italian or South German, early seventeenth century. Poldi-Pezzoli Museum, Milan.

Onyx cameo with the kerchief of St. Veronica. Silver-gilt, enamelled silver, gems. Probably from Augsburg, second half of the seventeenth century. Nymphenburg Castle, Munich.

more abstract, not because it entirely abandoned naturalism, but because it drew an infinite variety of stylized decorative motifs from nature. Flowers, feathers and bows were to be the favorite themes which were to banish the Dianas, Neptunes, fabulous animals, Saint Georges and ships for many years.

The chief reasons for this development were certainly of a technical nature. Jewelers now knew how to cut stones and impart a hitherto unattainable sparkle and beauty. They also knew how to make the setting so light as to be almost invisible, so that the sapphire, emerald and ruby were no longer spots of color enhancing a design, and the diamond was no longer a blank surface to set off the glowing colors of the enamel. Jewels no longer needed either a frame or story to bring out their full effect. All their richness was now revealed and the setting was now

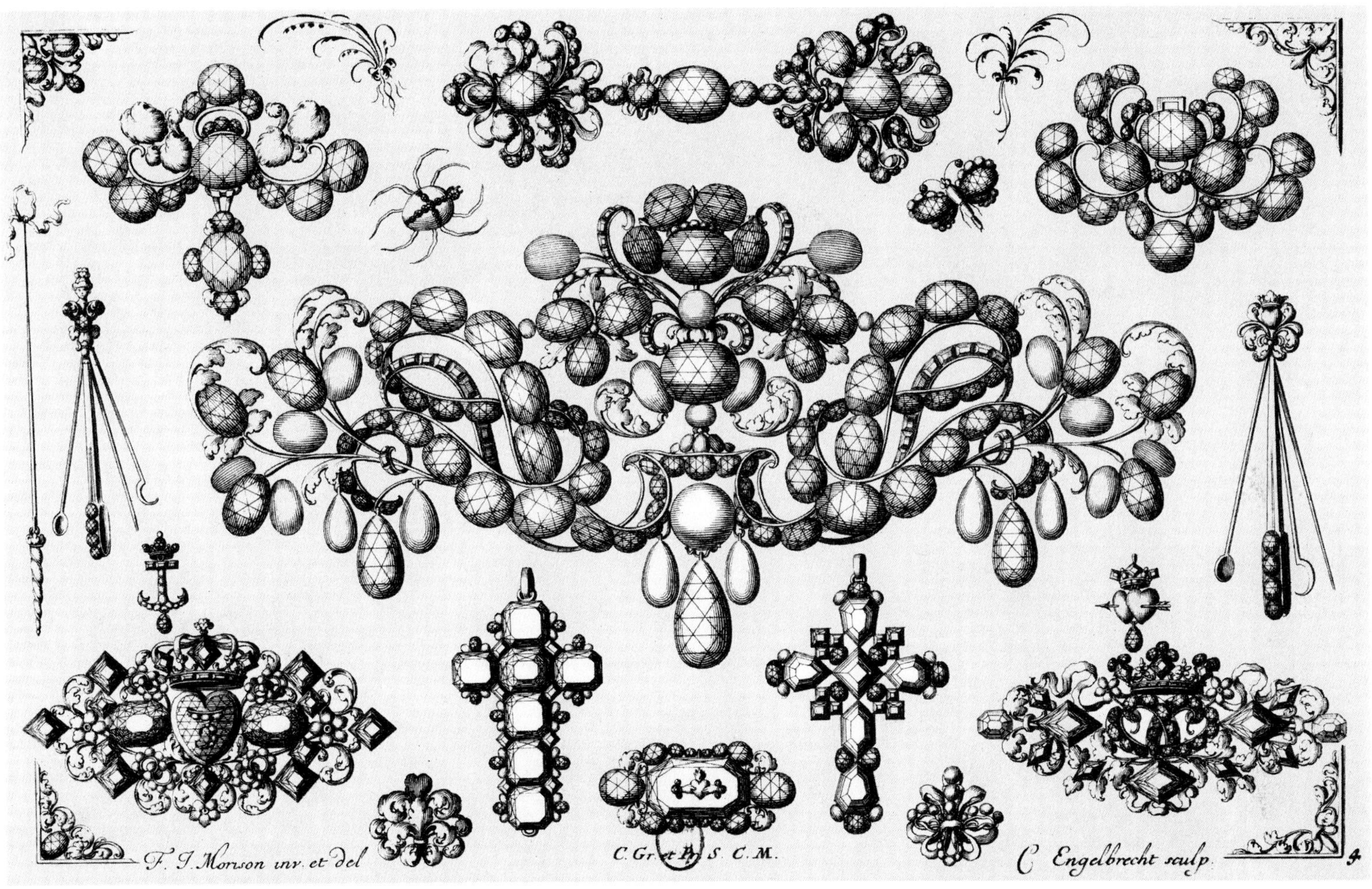

Friedrich Jacob Morison: designs for jewelry (Miscellaneous collection of sixteenth and seventeenth century jewelry designs). B.N., Paris, Cabinet des Estampes.

relegated to a secondary role of diminishing importance. Changing fashion also played a part. The thick velvets of the preceding century were succeeded by lighter fabrics. This was the great age of Lyonnaise silks and filmy laces. An architectonic or sculptural jewel such as a pendant in the form of a triptyche or niche would contrast too strongly with such fragile materials. An ornament with emphatic lines was out of place on such irridescent, unsubstantial garments. There were practical as well as aesthetic reasons for the change—a heavy jewel cannot be attached to a light fabric. It would spoil the whole line of a dress or cloak and would look none the better for it.

Technical progress and changing fashion, however, do not fully explain the transformation of jewelry. Another contributing factor was the emerging distinction between artist and craftsman, or between the major and the minor

Friedrich Jacob Morison: designs for jewelry (Miscellaneous collection of sixteenth and seventeenth century jewelry designs). B.N., Paris, Cabinet des Estampes.

arts. Artists appropriated the almost exclusive right to make use of symbolism and to commemorate notable events, allegories, battles, mythological scenes and edify martyrs. The arts became specialized and so did the artists. Connections between painters and goldsmiths became distant and jewelry moved away from painting and sculpture.

Further divisions arose within each group. Portrait and still-life painters belonged to a distinct circle, or lower standing than historical painters. Jewelry was also made by different specialists, and the goldsmith was not always jeweler, enameler and gem-cutter. He yielded precedence to the jeweler, but often employed the others to work for him. The jeweler designed the piece and carried out the most difficult and choice parts. The role of the goldsmith and enameler gradually became more insignificant.

Anonymous: design for an aigrette and two pendants. Italian, seventeenth century. Victoria and Albert Museum, London.

This explicit division between art and craft perhaps limited the scope of each but compelled each artificer to explore all the avenues left open to him in his own field and to make the fullest possible use of them. Jewelers no longer sought to follow painting and sculpture, and abandoned historical and religious motifs, complex compositions and symbolism.

But jewelry was no less important for being preeminently decorative. The factors which restrained it in one direction set it free in another. What it lost in realism it gained in imagination, and this is posibly where its originality lies. When the Renaissance jeweler selected a floral motif he had observed, real shapes and colors and fidelity to the model dictated his execution. His colleague of the classical period did not worry about local color or differences of texture. He made a whole flower out of dia-

Pendant: pelican. Gold, enamel, amethysts, emeralds and pearls. Hungarian, seventeenth century. Victoria & Albert Museum, London.

monds, or, to put it more accurately, a jewel based on the shape of a flower. The genesis of what we regard as pure jewelry was not a purely technical process; it was also an aesthetic phenomenon. It also answered a new conception of the function of the ornament; its decorative role became more obvious; it freed itself from any literary, religious and historical references, and its symbolic function was expressed in the material, precious stones and especially diamonds. It could therefore be adapted to any type of setting, so long as it gave precedence to the precious stone. Jewels were very often removed from their settings and this is why there are so few seventeenth century jewels but so many volumes of designs, innumerable variations on a rather limited number of motifs—those which yield the place of honor to the gem. There was one more change in the function of jewelry, which became ornamental rather than representational, and gradually a feminine prerogative. This should not be regarded as a mere caprice of fashion since it had a profound effect on the history of jewelry. This change in customs was closely related to the transformations of technique and forms in that women, except for queens, filled a social role which gave them less reason than men to display complex symbolic jewels. Female ornaments indicated birth and wealth rather than merit. It adorned rather than illustrated. It is difficult to distinguish cause from effect, and opinions on this subject are certainly divided. But there is a close relationship between the new characteristics of seventeenth century jewelry and the fact that it was increasingly designed for women.

Jewelry did not change overnight. In some countries, traces of the transformation could already be discerned by the end of the sixteenth century, while in others, they did not appear until much later. It was more apparent in some regions, more unobtrusive in others. It was also accelerated or slowed down by historical events. Everyone knows how many wars and revolutions took place in the early seventeenth century. They impoverished Spain; Germany and Bohemia were soon devastated; England was no longer a refuge from violent upheavals after the death

Clasp in the form of a trophy. Gold, enamel and diamonds. Augsburg, 1603, by H. Beuerl. Nymphenburg Castle, Munich.

of Elizabeth, and the Netherlands still had many long years to wait for real stability. The chief centers of the late sixteenth century remained important for some little time, but the richest cities and the most brilliant courts were soon to vanish from the political and artistic scene after the passage of the armies and the inevitable accompanying looting. The Thirty Years War was fatal to many of the great German cities that had flourished for so long, and it ruined Prague, which had played a prominent part until 1612.

At the height of their wealth, Bohemia and Hungary preserved their traditional splendor and luxury. Men and women wore garments embroidered with gold and pearls, and lavished countless fortunes on their own persons. Men attached highly ornate daggers and swords to belts enriched with diamonds and precious stones. They sported medallions and brooches, also richly adorned with gems in their hats that sometimes bore an aigrette which was either a real feather or a jeweled ornament. This headdress decoration was very popular in the late sixteenth century and often contained square table-cut diamonds set in gold or silver. Women wore them in their hair which they covered with pearls, or they chose a smaller brooch also in the shape of a feather. Their clothes were even richer than those of the men, and they added large corsage ornaments that covered their bodices with pearls and gems, pendants set in a brooch often shaped like some form of plant life, several rows of pearls around the neck, pairs of bracelets and rings on nearly every finger. This fashion was not confined to Bohemia and Hungary, but these countries were outstanding in early seventeenth century Europe for the fabulous wealth and abundance of jewels to be seen there.

The seventeenth century in France was the *Grand Siècle,* the glory of which is often attributed exclusively to Louis XIV, although his predecessor Louis XIII also had some claim to it. Louis XIV was born in 1638 and did not take power into his own hands until the death of Mazarin in 1661. By that time the French Academy had already been in existence for twenty-six years the *Discours de la*

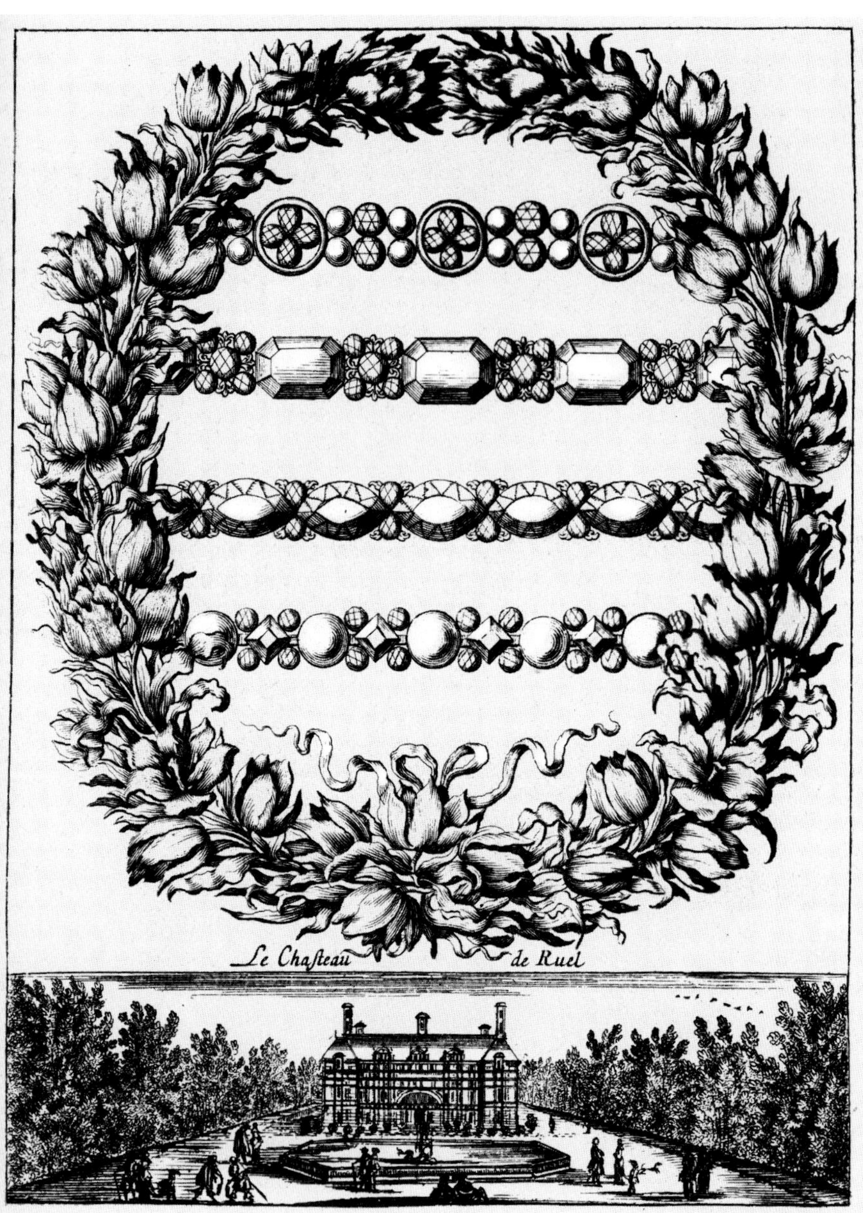

Balthasar Moncornet (1600-68): designs for jewelry, c. 1665. Victoria & Albert Museum, London.

Méthode and the first production of *Le Cid* had appeared in 1637 and *Les Provinciales* in 1656-7.

When Mazarin died on March 9, 1661, Louis XIV was twenty-three and a half years old. Everyone thought him handsome. He had a fine presence and an air of grandeur which gave his gait a natural majesty although he was not tall. He was polite, and no king ever gave his commands so graciously or saw that they were obeyed so strictly. His intelligence was average ("less than mediocre," wrote Saint-Simon), but he was able to grasp difficult problems once they had been explained to him and he liked to have them explained. He was a hard worker, and neither illness nor the appalling doctoring of the period was allowed to interfere with the undeviating regularity with which he sat down to work. He enjoyed being king, of which he said, "The rank is great, noble and delightful." (*Mémoires* Vol. II, p. 518, ed. Dreyss).

Louis and Colbert wished to encourage production and discourage imports as far as possible, and they believed that if factories were set up, this would be the best way to increase the number of workers, and to deploy the investors' capital to the best advantage.

The royal factories were the finest in the land and best of these was the Gobelin works, which was responsible for supplying the king's majesty with high-quality luxury goods, including the rarest gems and the most splendid ornaments. Administered by Colbert, and directed by Le Brun, it was both a workshop and a training school for industry, arts and crafts.

From the time of Philip the Fair to that of Louis XIV, a series of decrees known as Sumptuary Laws severely restricted goldsmiths' and jewelers' freedom to work. These laws, issued from time to time under the *Ancien Régime,* were meant to restrain the unbridled extravagance which overran all classes of society and were believed to be at the root of the rising cost of living. One historian, Jean de Saint-Gelais, believed that, under Charles VIII and his successors, "you could scarcely enter any workman's house nor any other in the wide land but you

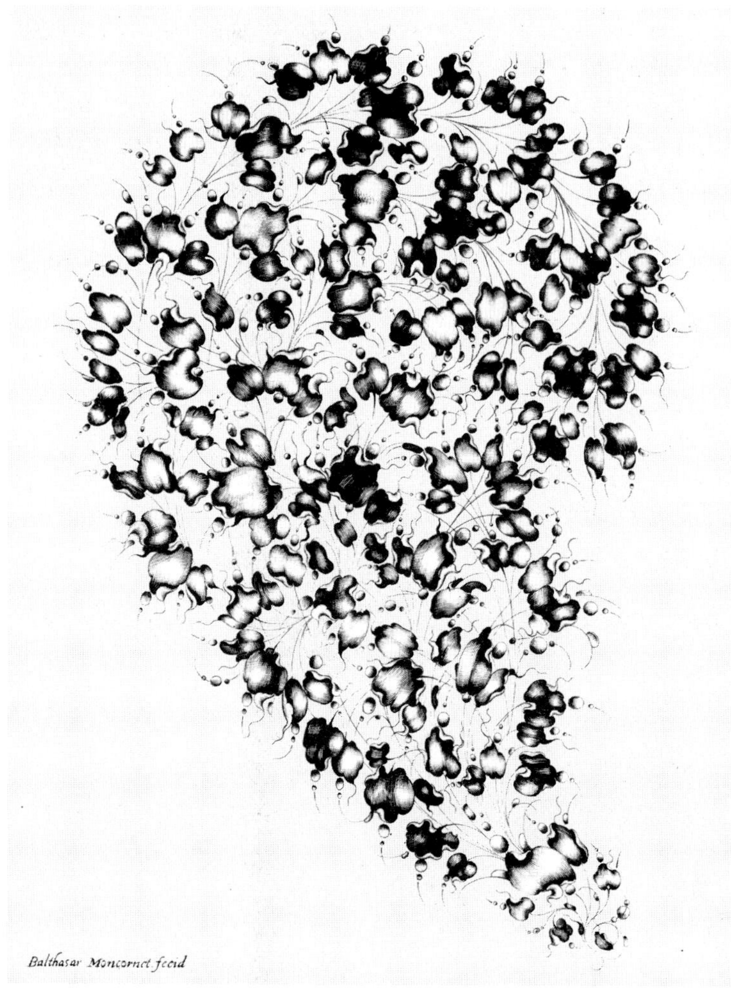

Balthasar Moncornet: jeweled spray. *Le livre de toutes sortes de feuilles pour servir à l'art d'orfèvrerie,* Paris, 1634. Victoria & Albert Museum, London.

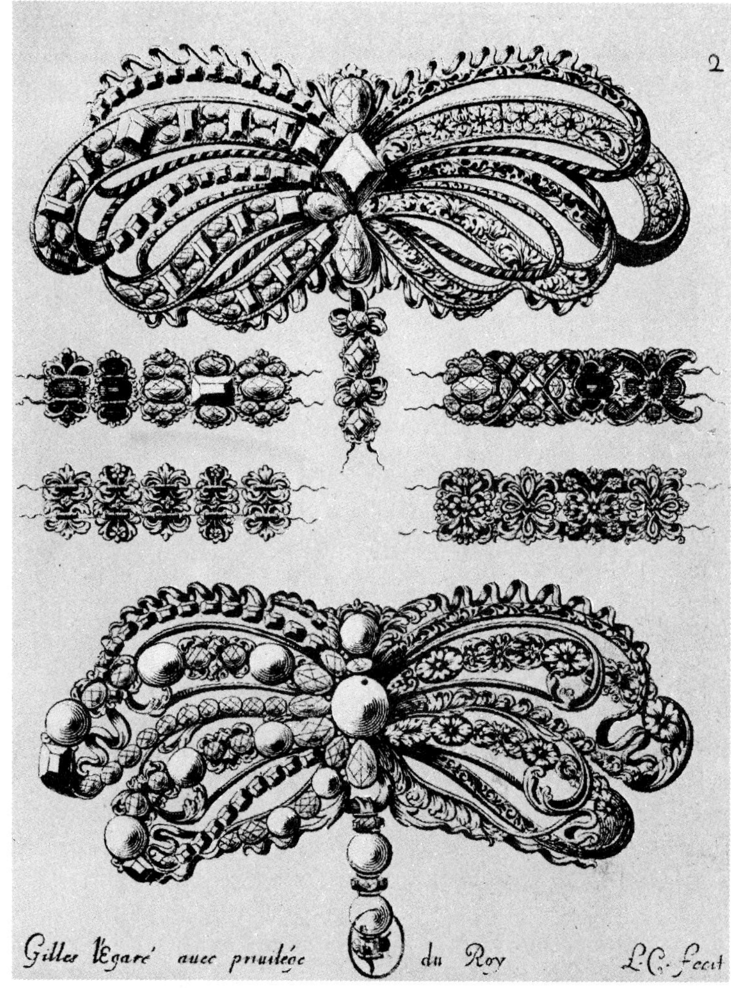

Gilles Legaré: two knots of brilliants and pearls. *Le livre des ouvrages d'orfèvrerie fait par Gilles Legaré* (Miscellaneous collection of sixteenth and seventeenth century jewelry designs). B.N., Paris, Cabinet des Estampes.

might find silver vessels." (Jean de Saint-Gelais, *Histoire de Louis XII*)

In fact, the kings tried to combat extravagance, mainly by restricting the industrial use of precious metals in order to improve the quality of the coinage, and thus restore their people to wealth and well-being. There were two mistakes in this policy: first, they did not understand the real reasons for the rising cost of living and for the crisis they provoked; and secondly, they were mistaken as to the efficacy of sumptuary laws for controlling luxury.

These sumptuary laws do not seem to have troubled jewelers very much, since they used very little metal in comparison with the quantities needed by a goldsmith making furnishings and tableware. The kings hoped to bring this quantity of gold and silver flowing back into the mint. In the reign of Louis XIV, when luxury was at

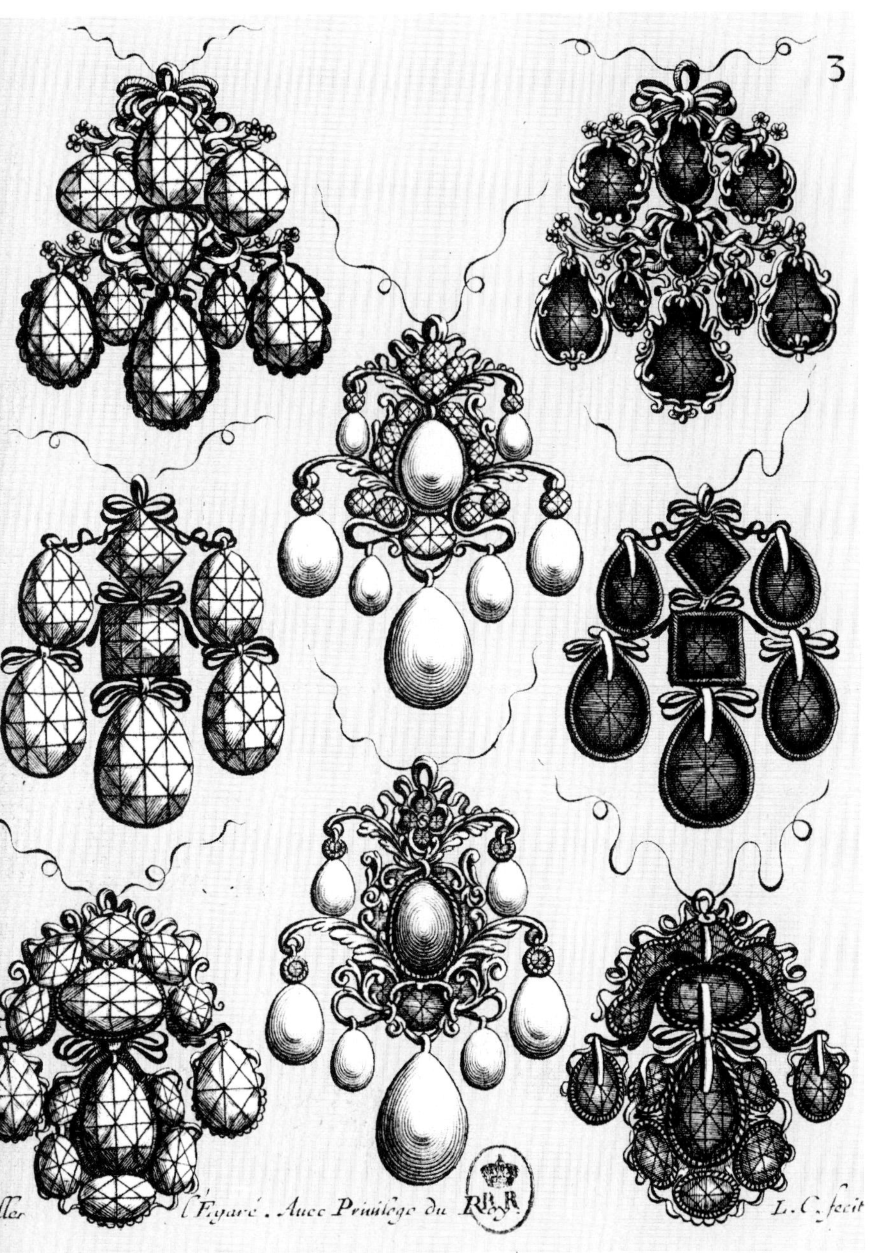

Gilles Legaré: design for eardrops. *Le livre des ouvrages d'orfèvrerie fait par Gilles Legaré* (Miscellaneous collection of sixteenth and seventeenth century jewelry designs). B.N., Paris, Cabinet des Estampes.

its height, the greatest number of edicts to restrain it were issued.

The art of jewelry originated a few years after the discovery in 1476 of diamond and gem cutting, when gems brought back from India began to spread through Europe by explorers and traders such as Chardin and Tavernier, who explored the site of Golconda, 11 kilometers from Hyderabad. Golconda was the legendary treasure house destroyed by Aurengzeb in 1687, a source of diamonds, rubies and sapphires, and a gem cutting and polishing center. Mazarin, like a true Italian, loved jewels. He encouraged the gem cutting industry and developed French taste for jewels by acquiring the twenty-six finest diamonds of his time from Tavernier and Chardin and bequeathing them on his death to the Crown of France.

With the collaboration of Pierre de Montarsy, his personal jeweler, Louis XIV raised the art of jewelry to great heights. The importance of Pierre de Montarsy must be stressed in this context. Now that the gem cutting process had been perfected, the king's jeweler proved to have true genius in the art of gem setting which is the foundation of the jeweler's art. With his simplicity and clarity of expression, he succeeded in freeing the jewel of all the excesses of the early Renaissance to such an extent that he might be called the Malherbe of jewelry.*

During this period, jewelry was divided into two branches; in the first, the ornament was carried out by executing the selected motif entirely in precious metal, pearls and gems not being employed except in exceptional cases as accessories (*bijoulerie*). In the second, the jewel was designed to bring out the best in the gems, the setting being only the most unobtrusive vehicle possible (*joaillerie*).

As the period progressed, goldworking became industrialized, and smiths specialized in different types of pieces to achieve mass production. However, there is still only one technique in jewelry—that of the jeweler—and only

* Malherbe: a classical reformer of French poetry roughly contemporary with Shakespeare (trans.)

one design—that of the individual jewel—and this excludes mass production.

If one traces the history of the seventeenth and eighteenth centuries in the portraits of Versailles, ornaments are fairly clear indications of fortunes and customs. It is interesting to see the role and the importance, the design, the style and the value of jewelry from the Valois to the Revolution. It can then be readily understood how a duke could wear on his person and give to his wife and mistresses the price of his castles and lands. It also illuminates the tactics of Louis XIV who, by encouraging his courtiers' leanings towards extravagance, made the unparalleled splendor of his reign into one of the instruments of his policy, impoverishing the nobility, the better to curb and reduce them.

The king himself set the fashion for extravagance with his court attire spangled with gems. Mme. de Montespan, the most splendid of his mistresses, had a set of jewels to match the color of every one of her dresses.

The nobility's passion for jewelry was extraordinary. Never before had so many gifts of jewels been made. Leafing through the pages of the *Mercure Galant,* there is all too much choice.

In November, 1678: "Shortly before the departure of Mme. la Comtesse de Soissons, Mme. Royale sent her a rich diamond bracelet valued at 3,000 *pistoles.* It was taken to her by the Comtesse de Saint-Maurice to whom the princess gave a very fine diamond as a token of her affection and esteem."

In May, 1680: "I told you in our last issue that the king of Spain was always very gallant. This monarch, having been out hunting, sent his quarry to the queen on his return and had her informed that if this dish should please her taste, he would take care to have her served with a salad which she should find well-seasoned.

"The next day a salad was brought to her from the king. It was a gold plate of wonderful workmanship full of emeralds and rubies sprinkled with pearls and topazes. The green stuffs were represented by the emeralds, the vinegar by rubies, the oil by the topazes and the salt by

Gilles Legaré: design for rings. *Le livre des ouvrages d'orfèvrerie fait par Gilles Legaré* (Miscellaneous collection of sixteenth and seventeenth century jewelry designs). B.N., Paris, Cabinet des Estampes.

Pendant: gold, enamel, sapphires, rubies, emeralds and diamonds. Dutch, second half of the seventeenth century. Presented by Dr. Joan Evans. Victoria & Albert Museum, London.

the sprinkling of pearls, and as greenery should predominate in a salad, there were many more emeralds than all the others."

This custom of presenting jewelry was so widespread that a princess who wanted to mark her esteem and affection for her confessor naturally chose to give him a jewel. In that terrible night of disaster which Bossuet describes, among the dying Madame's last words were to tell her chief lady-in-waiting, in English which Bossuet, who was present, did not understand, "When I am dead, give M. de Condom the emerald I had made for him."

Improved methods of cutting and setting stones and plentiful supplies of diamonds brought about major changes in jewelry. The diamond assumed the pre-eminence it has kept up to the present day. In the ballet of Apollo, in which Louis XIV appeared at Versailles in all his glory, he wore more than ten thousand *livres* worth of diamonds set in buttons in his costume. He had a predilection for this type of button. In 1685, he ordered 118 buttons, each set with a diamond to the value of 1,033,463 *livres* from Pierre de Montarsy. The same year he bought a set of waistcoat buttons for 1,191,468 *livres* and also "was at charges" for garter-buckles, for a pair of which he paid 351,258 *livres* in 1685.

The courtiers vied with each other in senseless extravagance. Lauzun boasted one day that he was wearing 300,000 *livres* worth of jewelry on his clothes and the Comte de Saint-Germain's shoe-buckles were reckoned to be worth 200,000 *livres*.

The women's up-swept hair encouraged the creation of "girandoles," diamonds, pearls and precious stones clustered in mobile drops and serving as earrings. Rings, necklaces, bracelets and all the classic ornaments were worn and around their necks women wore "waterfalls" (*flots*) of brilliants, the ancestors of the modern diamond *rivières*. The fashion for cameos persisted, but the early Renaissance enamel mounts were often replaced by brilliants.

By the end of the reign, France was in severe financial difficulties because no one had any idea how to confine

Necklace: gold, enamel, diamonds, a pearl and rock crystal pendant. French, second half of the seventeenth century. Bequest of Lady Alma-Tadema. Victoria & Albert Museum, London.

expenditures within the limits of income. As the king grew old, he secretly married Mme. de Maintenon about 1697, after the death of Maria Theresa, and submitted to her influence in religious matters. Bereavement followed bereavement at court. There were no more fêtes and ceremonies. "Everything is dead here," wrote Mme. de Maintenon, "Life has been swept away from us." "We hear nothing at all from the court," says Madame (the Princess Palatine) in 1712.

Pierre Gaxotte, writing about the age of Louis XIV in his history of the French, very rightly stresses its contradictions. "It was a century of magnificence and straitened means; of political expansion and economic deflation; of great enterprises and small resources." Other factors could be added, such as excessive legislation by Colbert, the minister who was keenest on free trade, and the fact that the trade guilds grew richer while their standing grew lower.

After France comes Germany with its still-powerful cities like Augsburg, Nuremberg and Munich. Several jewelers' designs from these centers have survived, and some of them show traces of the beginning of a change in style. At the end of the sixteenth century, heavily decorated architectural pendants spread from Germany all over Europe and even influenced Spanish jewelry. Little by little, reaction set in, even in Germany, against these excesses. They began to strive for greater simplicity, purity and regularity, and pendants became lighter and tended to be symmetrical with fewer figures on them. However, the two styles coexisted for several years. Theodor de Bry died in 1598, but Hans Collaert lived until 1622, and his jewels lost none of their exuberance. For a long time he remained the inspiration for jewelers all over Europe. Daniel Mignot of Augsburg, who represented the opposite trend, published engravings from 1590 on. The models for jewels he offered are outstandingly light; the setting is much less visible and is merely a framework of simple shape and symmetrical design to hold the gems. Birckenhultz belonged to the same school. He produced lighter jewels with more openwork and often without figures. He gradually abandoned sixteenth century forms to concentrate on jeweled brooches and aigrettes, sprays of flowers and feathers. The same divergence of styles took place at Amsterdam, where P.R.K. remained faithful to the earlier style for a long time, while Jacques Honervogt very soon adopted plant motifs treated as true jewelry.

On the subject of Holland, we must mention the extraordinary craze which seized all the inhabitants from the richest to the poorest and the most ignorant to the most

Pendant: gold and diamonds. North Portuguese, late seventeenth century. Victoria & Albert Museum, London.

learned. This collective madness had appalling economic consequences and led to the ruin of many families, but it also brought about a change in the repertoire of forms, especially in jewelry. The rose had long been regarded as the queen of flowers and symbol of purity. However, just before 1620, it was abandoned in favor of the tulip, the emblem of elegance and delicacy, which came to be loved with a positively insane passion. This new fashion came from France and infected all Europe, but chiefly the Dutch, who were the main producers. Tulip bulbs were beyond price, everyone grew them, bought them and resold them, and this was not the end of it. The decorative arts were substantially affected by this epidemic and the tulip became the favorite flower motif. It was soon superseded by the pea pod, especially aigrettes.

The excesses of tulip mania were only one very pronounced aspect of the taste for more or less stylized plant motifs, which became general in the seventeenth century. They were adapted to all purposes. Even watches were shaped like leaves, flowers or fruit, as we see from designs by Jacques le Blon and Jacques Hurtu. This new repertoire of motifs spread through Europe very swiftly, and we cannot tell the provenance of many pieces with any more certainty than in the preceding century. Craftsmen traveled as much as ever and except for the Spanish, who remained shut off from new influences, all countries produced similar jewels inspired by the most prized designs. To which school can the works of Arnold Lulls be ascribed? He was born in the Netherlands, and became jeweler to Anne of Denmark, whom he followed to England early in the century to work there. Or those of Michel le Blon, who probably came from a French Huguenot family, was born in Frankfort, employed by Queen Christina of Sweden and died in Amsterdam in 1656? There are few countries with an individual style. Nearly everyone adopted the style which developed in seventeenth century France. It was exported all the more easily because many Protestant jewelers settled in neighboring countries, particularly in the second third of the century. The French also originated the decorative motif of the ribbon bow,

Aigrette: topazes, amethysts and diamonds. Spanish (?), late seventeenth century. Poldi-Pezzoli Museum, Milan.

love-knot and fan, especially for brooches entirely covered with diamonds known as *Sévignés*.

Countries with a national style were rare, and each chose from the common repertoire whatever seemed most suitable to their own tastes and needs. For example, many aigrettes were worn in England in the time of James I. It was for this type of ornament that Arnold Lulls provided so many of his designs that are absolutely typical of seventeenth century fashion. The lines are clean and the golden scrolls of the setting are almost invisible. The gems—rubies, sapphires, emeralds and diamonds—are given pride of place. The aigrette was attached to the end of a pin which was pushed into the headdress. The early seventeenth century was the peak period of English jewelry. James I and Anne of Denmark devoted large sums to the purchase of jewels, and their jewelers were held in high repute in court and society in general. They enjoyed the same respect as the best artists, and were generally fairly well off since they also exercised the profession of money-lending. George Heriot of Edinburgh followed the king to London and entered his service with William Herrick and John Spilman. Many foreigners also came to spend a few years in England, and English jewels betray German, French and Flemish influences.

Posy-rings are probably the only specifically English jewelry of this period. These are rings bearing inscriptions, usually a short couplet like "In thee my choice I do rejoice," in memory of a happy or sorrowful event. Other ornaments were the same as elsewhere, i.e. *Sévignés* and necklaces of bows and sprays. However, very few of them survive because, although Charles I sought to prove himself worthy of his predecessors by employing James Heriot (George's half-brother), Philip Jacobson, Thomas Simpson, John Acton and William Terry as court jewelers, he was very soon forced to sell his jewels or pledge them as security for the loans he had to raise.

During the civil war, veritable fortunes were put up for sale and bought by the merchants of Amsterdam who immediately took them to pieces to recover the gold and gems. The king was not the only one to sacrifice his jewels.

Pendant: gold and pearls. Spanish, late seventeenth century. Poldi-Pezzoli Museum, Milan.

Corsage ornament: silver-gilt, emeralds and pearls. German, early eighteenth century. Victoria & Albert Museum, London.

His faithful supporters as well as his most implacable enemies sold everything they had and devoted the money they raised to their cause. The Cheapside Hoard probably contains the largest number of pieces from this period, but it is only the ordinary stock of a good-class London jeweler; none of the pieces are exceptionally well-designed or costly. It was found by accident when a house in the city was being demolished in 1912, and it is more interesting as an indication of general fashion trends than as a collection of choice specimens. It includes necklaces, bracelets and earrings of light and graceful design and demonstrates the importance of gems—emeralds and amethysts in this case—as well as the popularity of floral motifs.

Enameling was rare but stones were often highly finished and cut with facets or in the rose cut. Cabochons were no longer made. There is hardly a single example to be found in Europe after 1640. England produced a very famous piece dating from the reign of James I. This is the Lyte Jewel, now in the British Museum, a medallion enclosing a miniature of the king. One side is decorated with the letter "R" in diamonds and the other is enameled. It contains 25 table-cut and four rose-cut diamonds.

The second third of the century after the victory of the Puritans was not very propitious for English jewelry, which was chiefly devoted to mourning jewels, *memento mori* and medallions commemorating the death of Charles I that were worn as unobtrusively as possible. A miniature of the king was often concealed inside a diamond watch case. It was customary to give a present to everyone who attended a burial. The family of the deceased offered rings with the painted or carved portrait of the departed with the eyes represented by two small diamonds. These rings sometimes accompanied a gift of gloves or hat-ribbons decorated with stones that played the same part as the medieval ensigns. All the mourners wore the same sign of remembrance to demonstrate the fidelity of their affection.

Austerity, however, was confined to the Commonwealth period, for in the reigns of Charles II and William

Studio of Allan Ramsay: portrait of Charlotte of Mecklenberg-Strelitz (1744-1818), wife of George III. National Portrait Gallery, London.

III jewelry returned to favor. From this time the most celebrated jewelers received a knighthood, which shows how important they were at court. The first was Sir John Vyner who made the king's crown; then came Sir John Chardin, the famous French-born merchant and traveler who was one of the first to establish commercial links with Persia and India. The revocation of the Edict of Nantes compelled him to emigrate, but his journey was made under the most favorable conditions since he was able to take a huge quantity of precious stones with him.

Finally, Sir Francis Child was appointed court jeweler towards the end of the century in 1689. He concentrated on making jewels for the king to present to ambassadors. Native and foreigner worked side by side in London, which became a very important meeting place and trade center. Jewelry could not but profit from the contributions of these varied influences and in spite of their political and economic problems, the king of seventeenth century England encouraged it. Largely because of their patronage, it acquired a quality and fame it never subsequently lost.

If England was open to foreigners, Spain closed in on itself and was not affected by changes of fashion and technical improvements until long after the rest of Europe. The traditional austerity of fashion persisted through almost all the seventeenth century, and portraits of the time of Philip IV show that the farthingale was still worn in his reign. Kings wished to impose the same severe restraint on the wearing of jewels, but the number and frequency of the sumptuary laws indicates that the Spanish were hard to convince. Nevertheless, although nearly as much jewelry was worn, the style changed because the sumptuary laws passed by PhillipIII in 1600 forbad the making of jewels with relief figures except for church use. Jewelers therefore curtailed their repertoire of decorations but extended that of shapes, at least in the early part of the century. Partisans of austerity indignantly and publicly denounced people who even had gold and silver nails in their shoes. In 1630, Alonso Carranza addressed to Philip IV his "Discourse against Wicked Dress and Lewd Orna-

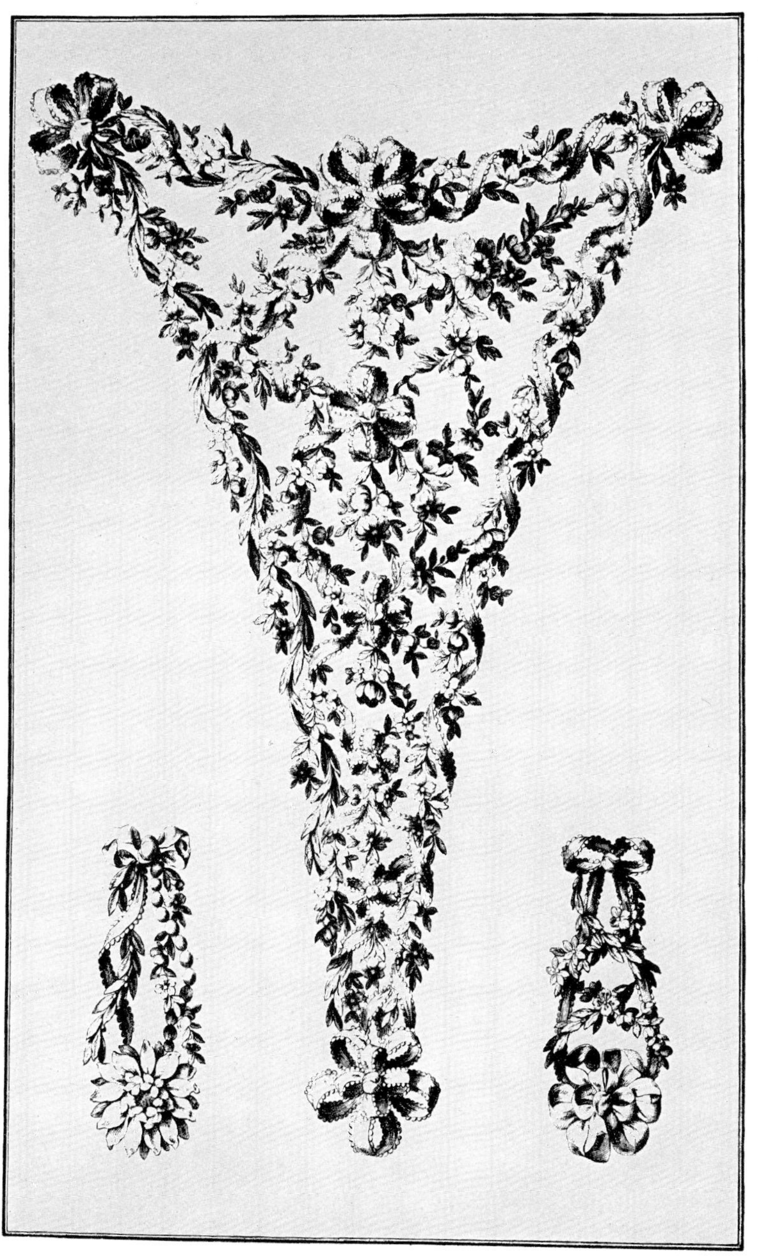

L. van der Cruycen: design for a corsage ornament. *Nouveau livre de desseins concernant la joaillerie,* Paris, 1770. B.N., Paris, Cabinet des Estampes.

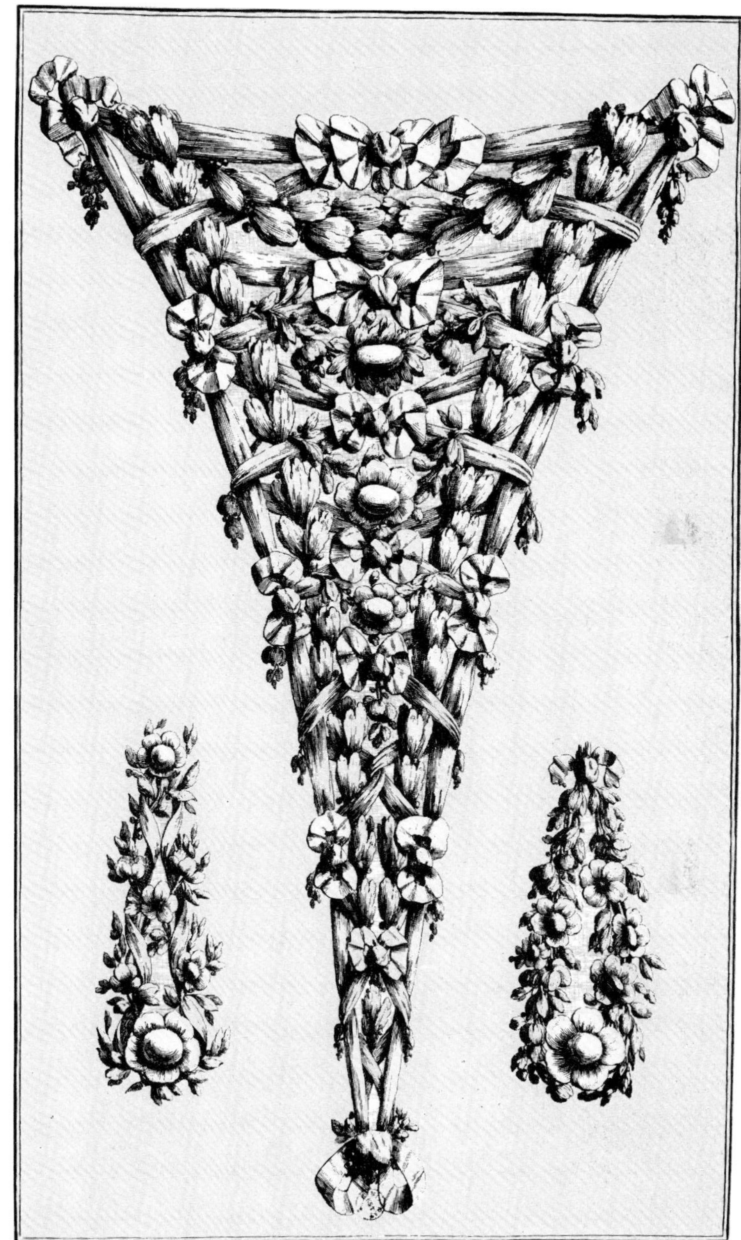

Maria: corsage ornament. *Premier livre de desseins de joaillerie et bijouterie inventés par Maria et gravés par Babel,* Paris, c. 1765. B.N., Paris, Cabinet des Estampes.

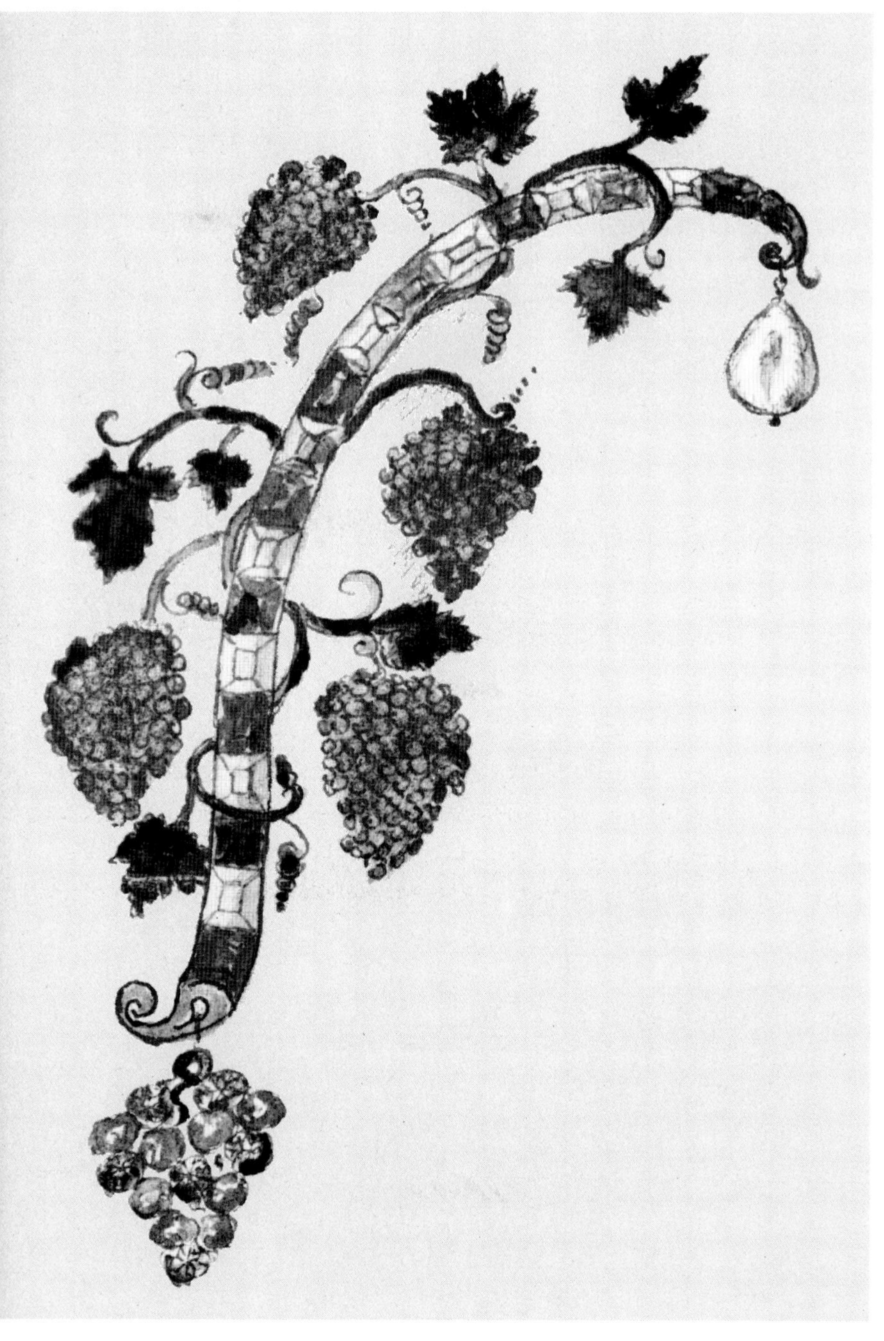

Arnold Lulls: design for a jeweled ornament. Victoria & Albert Museum, London.

Arnold Lulls: design for an enamelled and jeweled pendant with three pendant pearls. Victoria & Albert Museum, London.

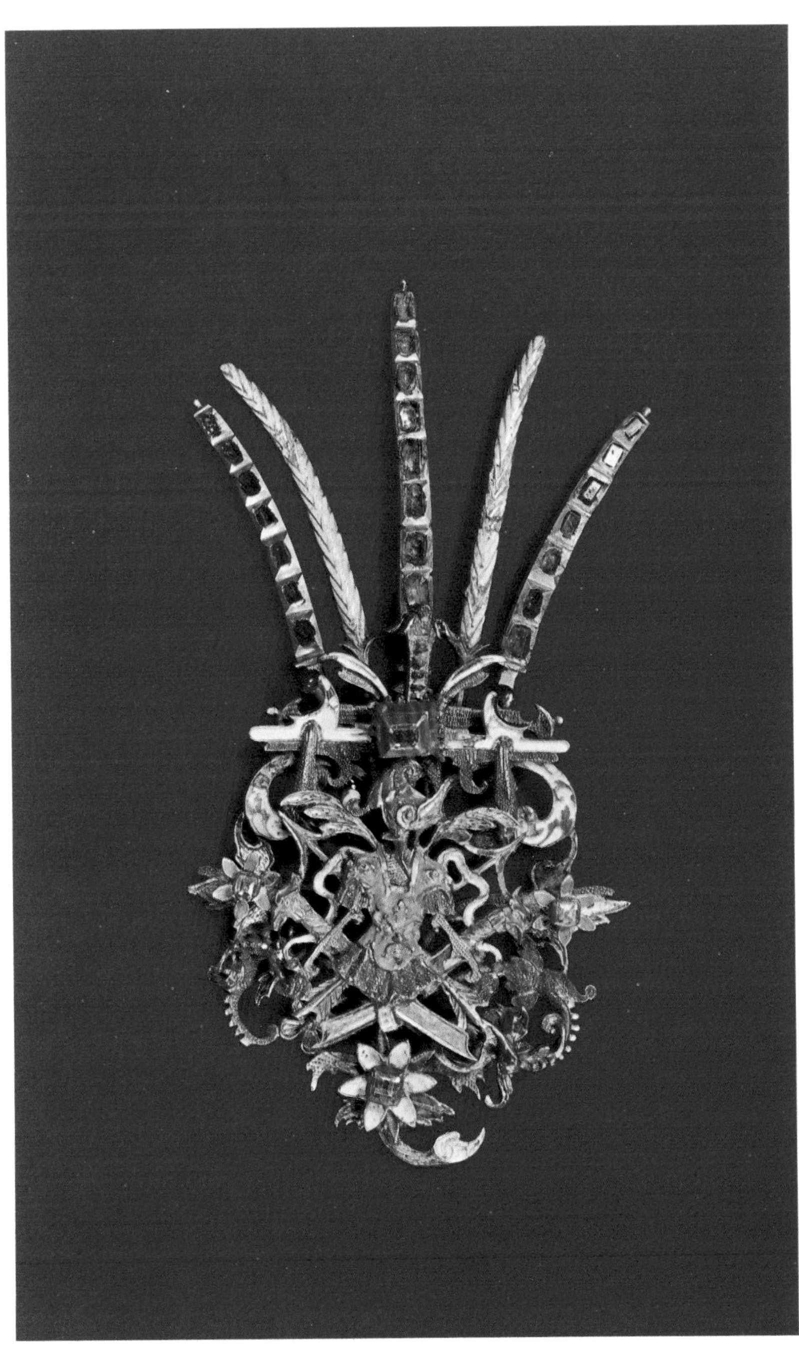

Aigrette: gold and gems. A trophy with four diamonds surmounted by five plumes, three with rubies and diamonds. Style of Daniel Mignot. German, seventeenth century. Waddesdon Bequest, British Museum, London.

ment." New restrictions were imposed but not always observed, particularly those limiting the number of stones which might be used in any one jewel. Spanish women preferred to wear a single huge piece of jewelry, usually decorated with emeralds or diamonds, and sometimes matching earrings. These corsage ornaments were sometimes *lazos* (like the French bows), the designs of which closely resemble Gilles Legaré's work.

This was probably the only common ground between Spanish practice and the fashion and technique adopted in Paris. In her account of her travels in Spain, Mme. d'Aulnoy distinguishes clearly between them: "The Spanish," she writes, "wear girdles made entirely of medals and reliquaries. They have many gems, the finest that could be seen. These are not used for a single set of ornaments, as most of our French ladies wear. They have as many as eight or ten, of diamonds, rubies, emeralds, pearls and turquoises in all manner of shapes. They are very badly set. The diamonds are almost completely hidden and only a small part can be seen. I asked them why, and they told me that they consider gold as beautiful as gems. But for my part I think their lapidaries do not know any better. I make an exception of Verbec, who could do it perfectly well if he would only take the trouble.

"The ladies wear big jeweled ensigns high on their dresses with ropes of pearls or ten or twelve knots of diamonds hanging from them and attached at one side of the body. They never wear necklaces but they have bracelets, rings and earrings that are much more than a hand's breadth long and so heavy that I cannot imagine how they can wear them without tearing their earlobes. They put on everything they think pretty."

This description, which dates from the end of the century, clearly shows how far Spain lagged behind current fashion. Gems were still set so as to be almost hidden, earrings were disproportionately large and necklaces were not worn. In the rest of Europe in this period, women wore a black velvet ribbon with a medallion decorated with diamonds containing a miniature around their necks. Hairstyles now left the ears uncovered so that earrings

Pendant: gold, enamel, emeralds, garnets and pearls. Hungarian, c. 1700. Victoria & Albert Museum, London.

could be worn, but these were a fairly reasonable size. Everyone tried to make the setting as light as possible and to keep everything but the gem out of sight. This was the chief preoccupation of late seventeenth century jewelers, among whom was Johan Melchior Dinglinger. He was in the service of Frederick Augustus I, Electoral Prince of Saxony, who became King of Poland in 1697. Born in 1664 in Biberach-am-Riss, Dinglinger was one of those goldsmiths and jewelers who deserve to be called the Cellini of his age—the supreme accolade, earned only once in a lifetime or perhaps even less. From his youth, he showed unparalleled talent and inventiveness, and he was still only a journeyman when he started to work for the Saxon court where his exceptional talents had been recognized. All the Dresden jewelers were busy copying their Augsburg colleagues, but Dinglinger's boldness and originality soon attracted attention. He was one of the first to introduce an exotic note into his work in the Turkish or Chinese style, which was beginning to be fashionable. He also borrowed several forms from the ancient world, but he never tempered his own exuberance. In the treasuries of the Grünes Gewölbe of Dresden there are some splendid jewels either from his hand or his workshop. A whole series of ornaments in coral, sapphire, brilliants and pearls consisting of aigrettes, pins, necklaces, hair ornaments, shoe buckles and Orders of the golden Fleece can be seen here, the richness and fine workmanship of which bear witness to both the luxury of the court and the skill of the master. He also made statuettes, vases, tableware, cups and goldsmith's work, and his jewelry proves him to be one of the most brilliant and typical artists of the late seventeenth and early eighteenth centuries.

His work ushers in one of the most brilliant periods of European jewelry, when every court strove to surpass its rivals and to set an example of luxury and taste. A man like Dinglinger served both these aims admirably. He has been compared to Cellini, but this is both flattering and inaccurate. Perhaps he could also be regarded as a forerunner of Fabergé. He was a goldsmith, a jeweler and an enameler, which was unusual in this period. He worked with his brother and his son and taught them all the secrets of his own exceptional skill. The quality of workmanship in some of his pieces is very close to sixteenth century work. The Dinglinger family contributed to the fame of the Dresden court and then to that of Poland, the luxury and wealth of which was envied throughout Europe. Frederick Augustus had a palace with some rooms paved with

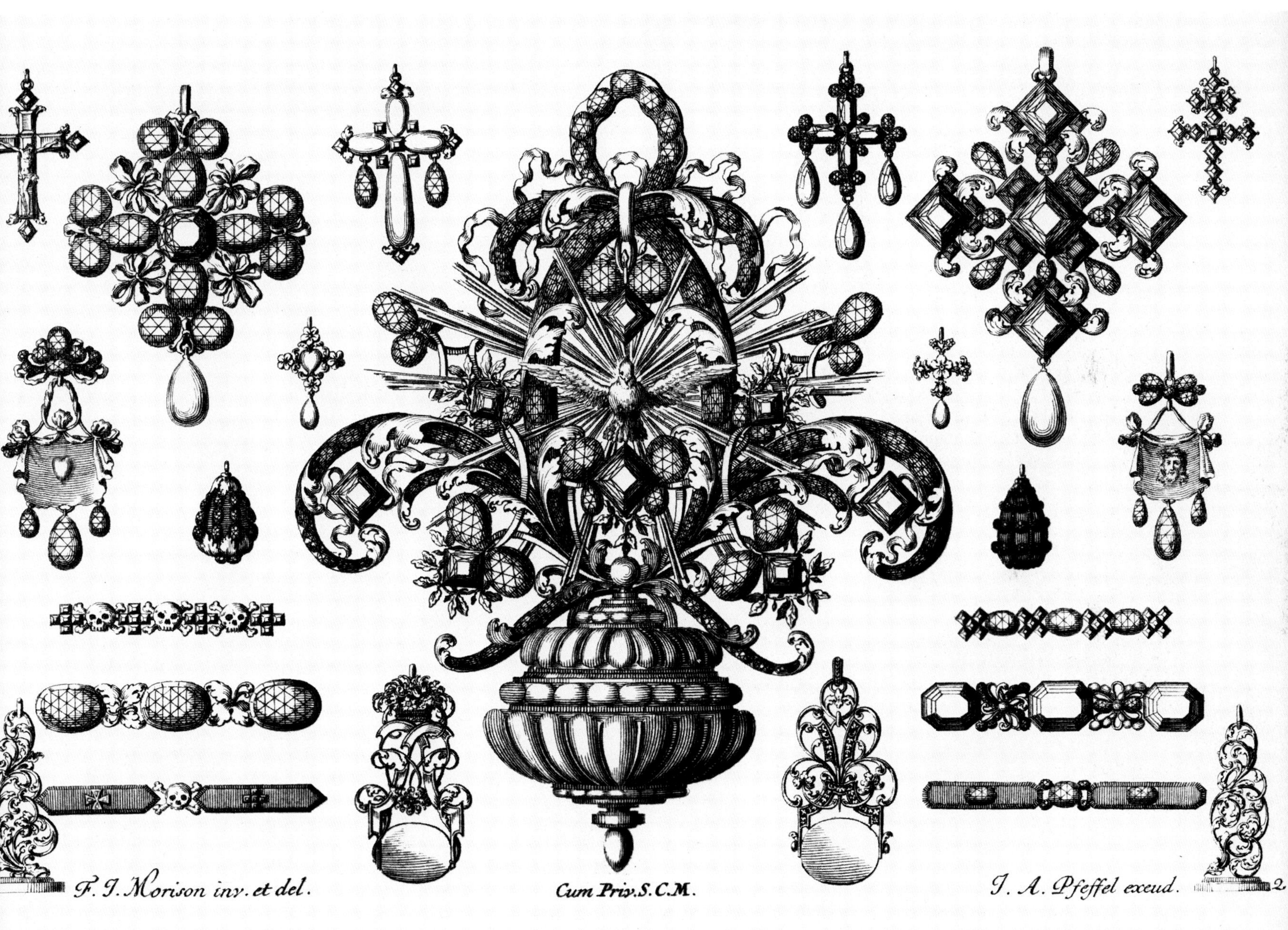

Friedrich Jacob Morison: pendant, cross and other ornaments. *Designs for Jewelry and Gold and Silversmiths. Work* engraved by J-A. Pfeffel and C. Engelbrecht. c. 1690, Victoria and Albert Museum, London.

Necklace with motifs of knots and roses: gold, silver and brilliants. Second half of the seventeenth century. Poldi-Pezzoli Museum, Milan.

gilded marble in which was a very fine collection of paintings and tapestries. His elegance and prodigality were proverbial. When he fell in love with Fraulein von Kessel he gave her diamonds worth sixty thousand ducats; then came the turn of Aurora von Konigsmark. A diamond *parure* was the first gift she received when she finally consented to yield. The prince's suite followed his example. We need only mention Graf von Bruhl, whose wardrobe contained no less than 500 outfits and 47 furs and who, to set them off, could choose from the 102 watches and 87 rings of which he was the happy owner. He owed his ministerial post partly to the reputation of his fortune.

The court of Dresden was perhaps the most brilliant in Germany, but it was by no means unique, and it should be remembered that these numerous little sovereign courts (there were more than three hundred of them) were very advanced cultural centers in this divided country. The Electoral princes did not rule very wide realms but they were powerful and immensely rich and never missed a chance to demonstrate the fact. They had nearly all been dazzled by Versailles and for the next half century they were to apply their minds to imitating the French model. They expended enormous sums on this ambition, which led Montesquieu to say, "Versailles has ruined all the German princes." But their impoverishment took some time to show, and meanwhile the German courts of the first half of the seventeenth century were distinguished by all the outward signs of wealth. French merchants were always welcome there; they were entrusted with the creation of court dress decorated with gems and pearls, and the models they offered were enthusiastically accepted. There, too, wealth and power were expressed primarily through dress; rules of etiquette with a curious mixture of excessive rigidity and insatiable love of causing a sensation were complied with. Soon the wearing of a sort of uniform became obligatory in many courts.

In Dresden, men wore red and gold, women blue and gold. The Elector required his guests at Nymphenburg to wear a green coat and a waistcoat with blue facings. It goes without saying that these outfits were adorned with

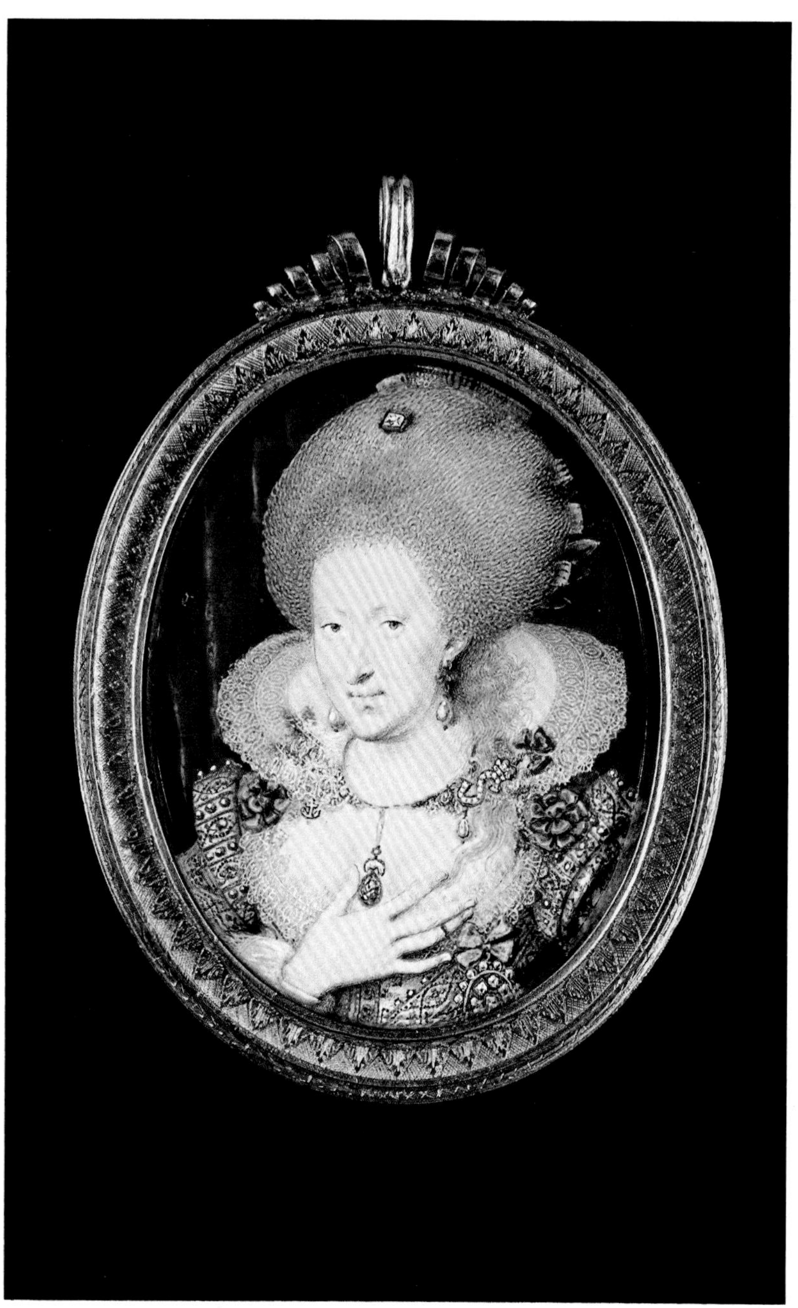

Isaac Olivier: portrait of Anne of Denmark. Medallion. The Queen is wearing a rich necklace with pendants, earrings and an ornament in her hair. National Portrait Gallery, London.

Brooch in the form of a dove: silver, diamonds, rubies and emeralds. French, late eighteenth century. Presented by Dr. Joan Evans. Victoria & Albert Museum, London.

necklaces, aigrettes, bracelets and earrings for the ladies, while men often had diamond buttons and priceless shoe-buckles (a pair of buckles might be set with more than a hundred diamonds). Palaces, art collections and staggering fêtes were not enough for these princes; they also had to have a treasury containing some exceptional piece, preferably a precious stone of outstanding size and cut which might have a famous legend attached to it. Frederick Augustus had an extraordinary green diamond, Francis I, a yellow diamond weighing 133 carats known as the "Florentine," and the royal house of Bavaria, the blue Wittelsbach diamond.

Beside such a display of wealth, the everyday life of the Austrian court might have seemed austere. But when a ceremony interrupted its regular progress, the Empress Maria Theresa would appear covered with gems among a gathering as brilliantly adorned as any of the German courts. The remains of these treasures can still be seen in a few museums. Dresden, Vienna and Munich are famous for their collections, but many jewels were taken to pieces and reset in the new fashion during the nineteenth century so that once again we must look to portraits to supplement our information.

There are a great many of these because portraits were very fashionable in the eighteenth century since few people of rank did not have their features recorded for posterity. German and Austrian paintings show how faithfully women followed the French fashion for a wide, low neckline, tight bodice and very full skirt. Neck ornaments were simple, often just a medallion threaded onto a velvet ribbon. The hair was much more bejeweled; pearls and aigrettes of all sorts were worn in it, and ears of corn, flowers, feathers and birds were mounted on metal springs to bring out the sparkle. The favorite earring was the pendant with three drops. Both wrists were often encircled by several rows of pearls. Here and there on the sleeves and skirt a few brilliants enhanced the sheen of the fabric. An ornament sometimes occurs which might be taken for embroidery at first sight, but which is actually a group of gold plates covered with gems and pearls forming a long

Pouget: designs for aigrettes, pompons and hair ornaments. *Pierres précieuses*, 1762. B.N., Paris, Cabinet des Estampes.

Johann Heels: design for jeweled ornaments with enamelled backs. Late seventeenth century. Victoria & Albert Museum, London.

triangle over most of the bodice from the neckline to the waist. Every volume of designs seems to devote the last five or six pages, reserved for its masterpieces, to this ornament. The stomacher was chiefly restricted to queens and princesses by its size, design and price, but it was also the most admired and envied piece, and the court jeweler lavished all his skill and imagination on it. It shows the survival of the traditional links between dress and orna-

Pendant: the "Lyte Jewel." An oval pendant, gold, enamel, 21 table diamonds and four rose diamonds. English, early seventeenth century. Waddesdon Bequest, British Museum, London.

ment. Women also wore several rings, often fairly large, which were sometimes marquise-shaped. The diamond was the favorite jewel, but it is not unusual to find rings with a large colored stone surrounded by brilliants.

There is a comparatively large number of volumes of jewelry designs from this period, but they do not achieve the quality of the works published in the previous centuries. The best come from Paris, but they were also published by Germans, British and Italians. Why were there fewer models when precious stones, particularly diamonds, were so frequently used for ornaments, when (thanks to the mines of Golconda and Brazil that were now being worked), finer and bigger diamonds could now be had for a relatively reasonable price, and when the brilliant cut made the most of their effect? Precisely because the stone itself was now the dominating element. This is the reason given by Bourget at the beginning of the collection of ornaments he published in 1712. He advises his reader that he is not offering many designs for jewels: "It seems thoroughly pointless to me," he writes, "since fashions change and moreover, designs are worked out to accord with the number and size of diamonds available for the work." These few words define the line of conduct adopted by nearly all the jewelers in Europe, although with the passing of time we can pick out appreciable variations in style.

The jewels of the early eighteenth century show traces of the rococo feeling which was overrunning the decorative arts. They are often asymmetrical and combine natural motifs and abstract ornamental elements. Many of them have the appearance of tiny three-dimensional sculptures and some artists drew a sharp dividing line between flat and relief ornaments. After the close of the seventeenth century, the designs of Friedrich Jacob Morison, the famous Viennese jeweler, ushered in this new tendency, which was followed by Bemmel of Nuremberg, D. Baumann, Johann Heel and J. Leopold, all of Augsburg.

It also occurred in Italy. The Santini family of Florence produced many variations on the bow motif carefully emphasizing the gems. Grondini of Genoa who worked in

Duflos: designs for necklace, aigrette and eardrops. *Receuil de dessins de joaillerie, dessinés par Augustin Duflos, joaillier du Roy d'Espagne,* Paris, 1767. B.N., Paris, Cabinet des Estampes.

Brussels about 1715, Carlo Ciampolini and D.M. Albini, author of *Disegni moderni di gioglieri,* were also attached to the rococo style. It was not until about 1760 that a new style appeared; it owed much to the discovery of Pompeii and the passionate interest aroused by this event in everything which was—or looked—ancient, although some countries were only affected by the virtues of simplicity after a long resistance. The neo-classical style of dress and ornament also originated in Paris and, without wishing to denigrate the rest of Europe, it must be admitted that with a few exceptions, nearly everyone turned to Paris for inspiration and sometimes for craftsmen.

The beginning of the French Regency* was distinguished by the purchase of the most famous of the Crown diamonds. On the suggestion of the banker John Law, this magnificent cut stone weighing 136 carats was bought from Thomas Pitt by the Regent Philippe d'Orléans for the sum of 2,500,000 livres, whence the name "The Regent." This stone is now in the Louvre in Paris.

In 1722, when Louis XV was twelve years old, he went to Notre Dame to attend a Te Deum celebrating the alliance with Spain. His majesty wore the "Regent" on his epaulette, and in his hat was the "Sancy" diamond, another magnificent stone once worn by Charles the Bold of Burgundy and one of the eighteen diamonds bequeathed to the Crown by Mazarin.

Between 1715 and 1792, France was never invaded and grew richer as a result of agricultural improvements, the enclosure of common land and expansion of trade. Interest in science and the arts increased, and the art of jewelry seemed pleasant and attractive to an intelligent and cultured society in reaction against the bigoted austerity of the end of Louis XIV's reign.

Unfortunately, an unforeseen catastrophe brought these prosperous years to an end. The financial enterprise known as "Law's System" ended in 1721 in utter disaster and bankruptcy. Its liquidation brought ruin not only to the Treasury but to Parisian trade and the ordinary people who had plunged into the wildest speculation and were the first victims. The peace which reigned at the time and had been unbroken for twenty years apart from the war of the Polish succession (1733-4), a war that was neither long nor costly, enabled the French to repair their financial situation by economy and hard work.

* The minority of Louis XV, 1715-23. (trans.)

Maria: design for eardrops. *Premier livre de dessins de joaillerie et bijouterie inventés par Maria et gravés par Babel,* Paris, c. 1765. B.N., Paris, Cabinet des Estampes.

L. Van der Cruycen: design for a necklace. *Nouveau livre de desseins concernant la joaillerie,* Paris, 1770, B.N., Paris, Cabinet des Estampes.

Mondon: large knot for court dress. *Premier livre des pierreries pour la parure des dames.* B.N., Paris, Cabinet des Estampes.

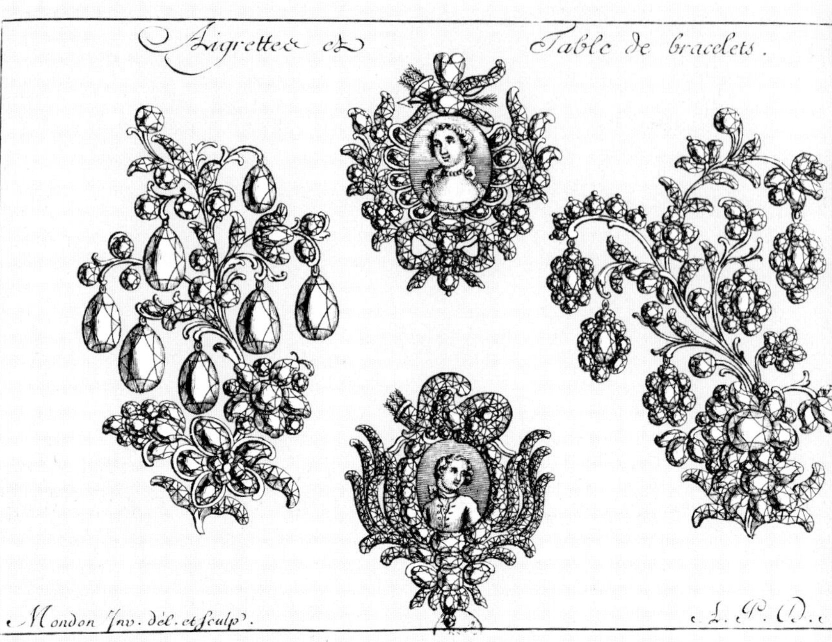

Mondon: aigrettes and bracelet clasps. Ibid.

However disastrous the ultimate results of Law's System, commerce, industry and even agriculture reaped some benefits from it, particularly as regards the easy turnover of goods at ever-rising prices.

Luxury, too, reached new heights during the successful years of Law's System. The court had been deprived of fêtes and pleasures during the later years of Louis XIV's reign and now meant to make up for lost time. Speculators suddenly found themselves rich and hastened to display their wealth in exhibitions of splendid goldwork and costly jewels. Despite the sumptuary laws of February 4, 1721 which forbad "the wearing of diamonds, pearls and precious stones," people of all ranks strove to secure as many as possible to buttress the enormous fortunes represented under the System by a piece of paper, which the more provident people were already beginning to distrust. However, in the year 1721, Louis XV softened the rigors of the preceding year by explaining to his subjects that his intention, like that of his predecessor, had "never been to forbid the reasonable use of jewels or silver plate . . . . but only to prevent gold and silver from being exhausted in useless and superfluous goods." This tolerance, combined with the severe fiscal measures that the financial condition of the country required, brought luxury within reach of the masses. From then on it was accessible to a greater number of rich men. The period produced a great many of frequently charming articles which, in contrast to really high-quality jewelry, could be classed as trinkets, e.g. snuff-boxes, perfume boxes, pomanders, châtelaines, cruets, and cane-knobs, among others.

High-class jewelry, on the other hand, was increasingly restricted to the court and the princely households. The jewelers of this period were Rondé, Jacquemin, Lemper-eur, Leblanc, G.M. Bapst and even Strasse, who gave his name to a glass process he invented that was supposed to simulate diamonds, but would never have deceived anyone.

The series of royal mistresses began discreetly enough in 1733 with Mme. de Mailly, followed by Mesdames de Vintimille, de Flavacour, de Lauraguais and the Duchess of Chateauroux. Then came Antoinette Poisson, later Lenormand d'Etoiles, who became la Marquise de Pompadour in 1745 and duchess in 1752 by the favor of the king, who presented her at court in September 1745. The court and the royal family were furious. The courtiers could not bear to see the office of royal favorite, which had formerly been the prerogative of the nobility, fall into the hands of a common financier's family.

The young marquise's reign lasted twenty years, during which she appointed herself overseer of the pleasures of that perpetually bored monarch Louis XV. She was witty, intelligent and artistic, and patronized arts and letters, although she did not have the influence over the arts with which she is sometimes credited.

When engraved stones and cameos came back into fashion, Mme. de Pompadour had two bracelet clasps made for herself with portraits of Henri IV and Louis XV surrounded by diamonds and emeralds. Jacques Guay, her favorite engraver, set up his equipment (a small lathe for engraving hard stones) in her rooms at Versailles and initiated his patroness into the secrets of his craft. Some of the stones she engraved were nearly as good as her teacher's work.

Mme. de Pompadour was made Lady-of-Honor to the queen in 1756 and continued to exert her influence until she died in Versailles in 1764.

The comtesse du Barry was presented to the king in 1768 and succeeded Mme. de Pompadour as official favorite. She had a following at court and lived in a very luxurious style, receiving 300,000 *livres* a month from the court banker Beaujon. Her jewel casket was famous, but her outlay on jewelry was really quite modest compared

Gold ring with a sapphire surrounded by 22 brilliants. French, eighteenth century. Poldi-Pezzoli Museum, Milan.

with the enormous sums paid by Louis XIV to Pierre de Montarsy. She paid 91,000 *livres* to her jeweler Aubert for furnishings, and in one year, "various goods such as rings, swags, tassels, necklaces, bangles, bracelets, shoe buckles, seals, pencil-cases and watch-cases."

Unlike Mme. de Pompadour, Mme. du Barry had no political ambitions, although in the later years of the reign she was compelled to exert her influence against her declared enemies.

Early in the century, ladies wore upswept hair styles that favored the type of earrings known as "girandoles." Since the old king admired the low hair styles of two English ladies who visited the court, where they caused a furor, French women subsequently dressed their hair *à l'anglaise* in the days that followed. This hair style, with short locks cut off at three fingers' length, passed from Versailles to Paris, whence it spread all over France. Women frizzed their hair in big curls and wore a jewel or a feather in it, or a little plumed cap—*coiffure à la culbute,* in the contemporary phrase.

"Augustin Duflos, who made Louis XV's coronation crown in 1722, left a volume of his designs in which there are aigrettes made to look like feathers, bunches of wild flowers and ears of corn." (Jean Babelon)

Male dress became simpler. Full garments disappeared along with lace, ribbons and huge perukes. Coats were closer fitting and more sober, and the wig was made close to the head with a low crown or, as the saying was, "four hairs in front."

"When the Turkish ambassador Mehemet Effendi came to Paris, he was shown three of Louis XV's costumes. One was adorned with pearls and rubies, one with pearls and diamonds and the third with some very fine diamonds. When he received the ambassador, Louis XV wore flame-colored velvet adorned with gems valued at more than 25 million and weighing 34 or 40 pounds. He wore a clasp with big diamonds in his hat. The same day, the Regent wore a waistcoat of blue velvet all embroidered with gold with a big clasp of diamonds in his hat, and the Order of the Holy Ghost and the Golden Fleece set with diamonds. All the gentlemen were very splendidly dressed." (H. Carré)

Part of a diamond necklace belonging to Marie Antoinette.

The king died on May 10, 1774. The succession to the throne was ensured by one of his grandsons, the Dauphin Louis, who had married the Archduchess Marie Antoinette of Austria in 1771.

When Louis XV died Louis XVI, who was born on August 24, 1754, was only twenty years old. The Comtesse de la Marche described him to Gustavus III of Sweden as "spiritless, unintelligent and illiterate." However, he had plenty of sense. "This man is rather weak," his brother-in-law Joseph II said of him, "but he's no fool."

He slowly learned by experience to assess men and events, but he lacked initiative and his qualities of generosity and conscientiousness aggravated this failing by increasing his indecision. His brother, the Comte de Provence said of the king's mental processes, "It's like trying to hold greased ivory balls together."

Marie Antoinette was more intelligent than the king, and

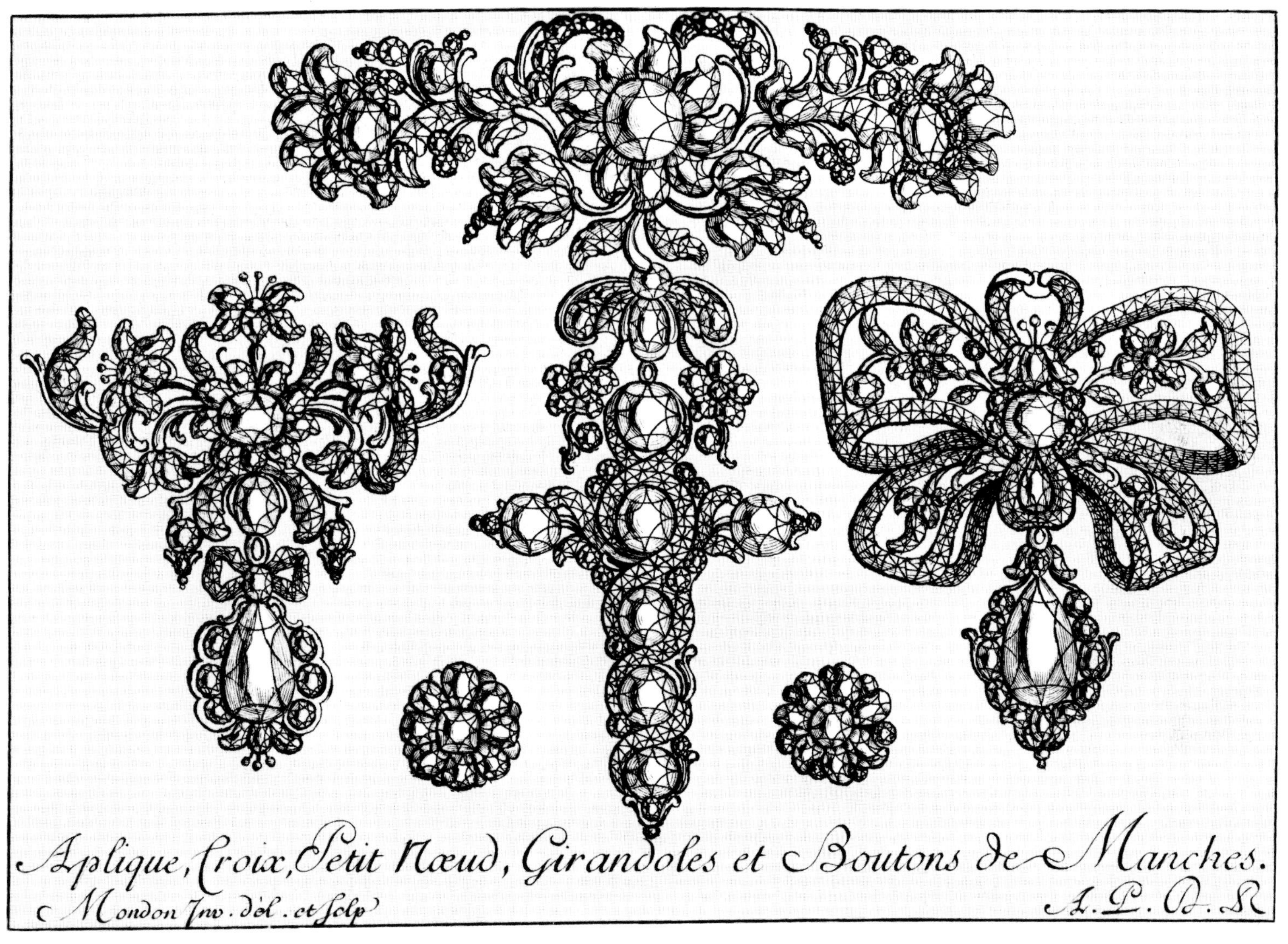

Mondon: ornament, cross, small knot, eardrops and sleeve buttons. *Premier livre des pierreries pour la parure des dames,* Paris, after 1750. B.N., Paris, Cabinet des Estampes.

capable of resolute action, but very ignorant and equally indifferent to the arts and all branches of culture. She had no liking for extravagance, spectacles and pleasure. Her somewhat indiscreet attachment to the princesse de Lamballe and the comtesse Jules de Polignac, who commandeered all the state posts for their own families, turned most of the court against her. At the same time the people, who disapproved of her policy of protecting Choiseul and dismissing Turgot, made no attempt to hide their dislike and called her "the Austrian woman."

Her unpopularity was redoubled by a lamentable swindle known as the "necklace affair," of which the queen was perfectly innocent, and which she did not even hear about until it was all over.

The jewelers Boehmer and Bassange were selling a magnificent necklace, which they offered to the queen for 1,600,000 *livres,* to which she returned the too-often-forgotten answer, "France needs ships more than diamond necklaces."

Cardinal Louis de Rohan, Bishop of Strasbourg and Grand Almoner of France, wanted to be reconciled with the queen, whom he had offended, and let himself be taken in by a confidence trickster, the Comtesse de la Motte (1784). She persuaded him that the queen was longing for the necklace. He bought it on credit from the jewelers and in Mme. de la Motte's rooms, handed it over to a certain Rétaux de Villette, who had been introduced to him as the queen's representative but who was really only the comtesse's lover. Rohan could not pay the first installment. Louis XVI was told about it and began by imprisoning the Cardinal in the Bastille; as a crowning blunder he laid the matter before the Paris *Parlement.* The affair then became almost exclusively political, the magistrates being divided into two camps: one devoted to the ruling party and the other systematically hostile to the queen. The general public sided with the accused. The acquittal of Rohan on May 31, 1786, was both a protest against arbitrary imprisonment and a means of humiliating the queen. Rohan was exiled to his abbey of la Chaise-Dieu. Mme. de la Motte was condemned to be beaten with rods, branded on the shoulders and incarcerated in la Salpetrière. The jewelers recovered 680,000 *livres* from the Cardinal's revenues. There was a tremendous scandal, of which Goethe said, "The necklace trial was the overture to the Revolution."

The Revolution was indeed near, and during its course, in deference to the austere principles of the Incorruptible, any sign of luxury, even modest shoe-buckles, could be dangerous. The delightful art of ornament and jewelry slept until better days would dawn.

Brooch: silver-gilt with rose diamonds. Eighteenth century. Kunstindustrimuseet, Copenhagen.

French jewelry enjoyed one of the most brilliant ages of its history in the period before the Revolution, and its influence was felt nearly everywhere. Perhaps only England and Spain preserved any individual characteristics and created a national style. Elsewhere, everyone followed the French lead, and what they could not equal in inventiveness they tried to surpass in richness. We have already seen this happening in Germany and we shall meet with the same thing in Russia.

Pouget: jeweled spray. *Pierres précieuses,* Paris, 1762. B.N., Paris, Cabinet des Estampes.

79
B.R

In Italy, too, jewelry was often quite good but rarely showed much originality. The Italian nobility did not live so brilliantly as they once had, it is true. They were often poor, and cared more for keeping their treasures than adding to them, and seldom displayed them. The letters of Président de Brosses give his impressions of his travels in Italy, and we learn from them that Italian women sometimes did not wear their jewels, like the fair Venetian who lived in the Palazzo Labia: "She showed us all her gems, perhaps as fine as any in Europe. She had four complete sets in emeralds, sapphires, pearls and diamonds. They were all carefully shut in caskets, since she was not allowed to wear them, women of noble birth only being permitted to wear colored stones and garments during the first year of their marriage."

What de Brosses says is true; the purchase of gems and ornaments was no more than an investment, and it is not surprising if designs lacked inventiveness. An ornament condemned to stay shut in a casket except for one year per generation did not call for much originality or imagination. High society in Florence was more brilliant, since ladies attended assemblies "covered in diamonds," but these gatherings were not very frequent. As for Naples, the president regarded it as "the only town in Italy which really feels like a capital," but Naples was still strongly influenced by Spain and was a very exceptional case. Indeed, Italy had to wait until the next century to produce any jewels or craftsmen of outstanding quality.

The Spanish, on the contrary, suddenly broke away from their past and their traditions of baroque luxury in the second half of the eighteenth century, and their jewelry can be classed as among the most interesting of the period. French influence was undoubtedly present, and one of the great craftsmen who worked in Spain was the Frenchman Augustin Duflos. Although it was inspired by the new trends and techniques, Spanish jewelry managed to preserve an individual flavor. While the diamond reigned supreme in Paris and nearly all the other stones had been abandoned in its favor, colored stones were still worn in the court of Madrid. The emerald was still the most popular, and combinations of reds, yellows and mauves using diamonds with rubies, topazes and amethysts were sought. These blends of tone and color variations were one of the characteristics of eighteenth century Spanish jewelry, and it can be distinguished from products of other countries by them. Although Augustin

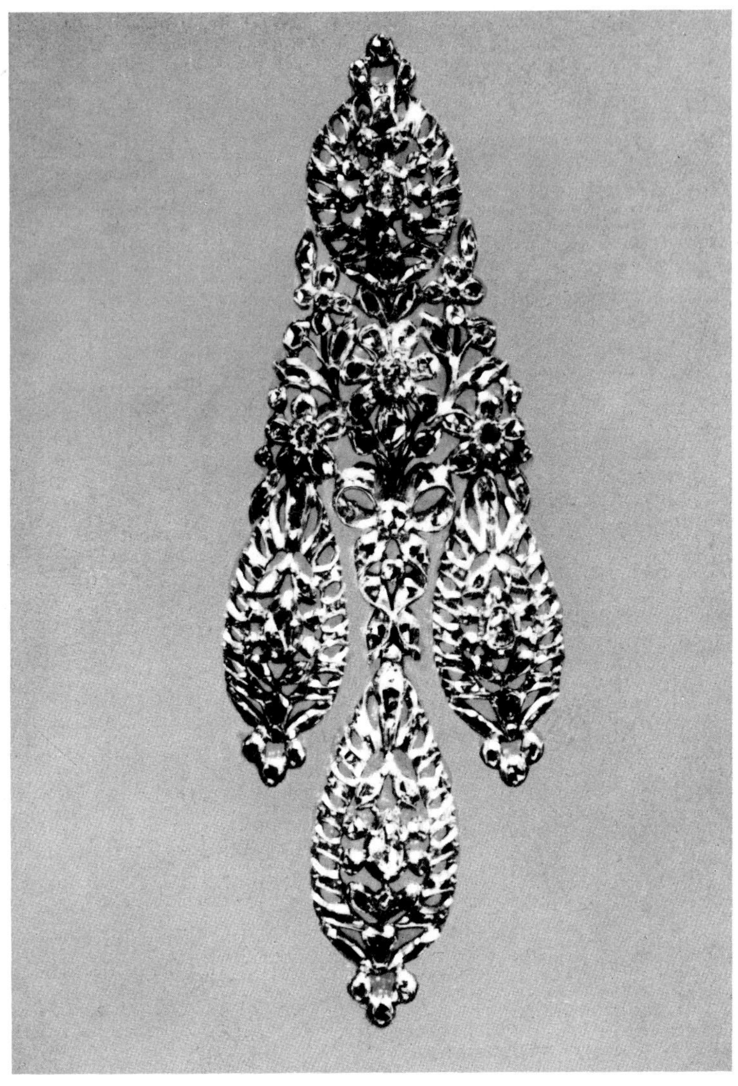

Eardrops: silver and diamonds. Spanish, eighteenth century. Treasure of the Virgin of the Pillar, Victoria & Albert Museum, London.

Necklace: gold, enamel, rubies and emeralds. Italian, eighteenth century. Victoria & Albert Museum, London.

Sebastiano Meyandi: design for a necklace and eardrops. Italian, c. 1755. The Cooper Union Museum for the Arts of Decoration, New York.

Duflos was a Frenchman, he expresses in the preface to his book his regret that the ladies of Paris had abandoned colored stones, and states that some ornaments are improved by the addition of stones other than diamonds. The brief text which precedes the designs has several claims to interest. Duflos clearly distinguishes between pieces without relief such as necklaces, earrings and ribbon knots, for which, he says, very elegant outlines are necessary, and relief pieces such as stomachers, aigrettes, side knots and royal Orders, which are almost worked in the round. The jeweler's chief concern was with lightness and flexibility. Duflos proclaimed himself the apostle of the new style when he published his designs in which he said that he "hoped to lead (the ladies) back to noble and simple taste, which is more suitable for adornment and sets off their natural graces better than the twinkling

Corsage Ornament: Gold, enamel, emeralds and diamonds. Flower motif. Spain. Beginning of the eighteenth century. Treasure of the Virgin of the Pillar. Victoria & Albert Museum, London.

display that they have long favored." He hoped to see them preferring "fine brilliants, however small, to vast flowered or pendant earrings that weigh down their ears." Duflos set himself apart from Parisian modes by his attachment to colored stones, and he was also a prophet in that he foretold the dominant trend in jewelry many years before it actually happened. He also wrote an invaluable record of the different styles in vogue in his time, and of Spanish taste in this period. Colored stones not being out of fashion there, the art of enameling that had been neglected for some years in the rest of Europe and would only return to favor with copies from the antique, was still practiced very skillfully.

Portugal is very close to Spain in geographical terms but it seems to have been much more affected by French influence so much so that it is very difficult to tell imported French pieces from jewels made locally by Portuguese craftsmen. Parisian style and fashion triumphed there as they did in Italy and Germany. One of the few countries to remain aloof from French influence, like Spain, was England. The English always had reservations about the rococo style. Even at the beginning of the century, English jewelry shows an austerity which was never completely eliminated by continental influence. There is another interesting aspect of English work of this period. Artists from all over Germany, France and Holland often came to London, where they settled and worked for long periods, if not for their whole lives. However, British jewelry kept its individual characteristics without rejecting foreign contributions. England paradoxically achieved a leading position in relation to other continental courts which were often far richer. London was not so brilliant as Versailles but its prestige was almost as high, and it is an equally curious fact that we know for certain that most of the aristocracy owned hardly any jewels. They usually hired jewelry for great occasions. However, vast quantities of

Flowers: gold, enamel and diamonds. Spanish, late eighteenth century. Victoria & Albert Museum, London.

jewels were rented and court dress was covered with ornaments. Queen Charlotte was one of the few people in the kingdom who owned her jewelry in this period. The carcan necklaces, ropes of pearls, bracelets and stomachers with which she adorned herself were mostly gifts from the Nawab of Arcot. British originality did not extend to the creation of new forms of jewelry. Like everyone else they wore aigrettes, birds, flowers, butterflies mounted on movable stems, girandoles and bracelets decorated

Buckles: silver, rose diamonds and steel. Eighteenth century. Kunstindustrimuseet, Copenhagen.

Set of brooches: silver and diamonds. English, second half of eighteenth century. Victoria & Albert Museum, London.

Parure: silver and chrysoberyls. Portuguese, late eighteenth century. Presented by the Rt. Hon. Sir C.W. Dilke, Bart, Victoria & Albert Museum, London.

Necklace: silver, topazes, brilliants and rose diamonds. French or Italian, eighteenth century. Poldi-Pezzoli Museum, Milan.

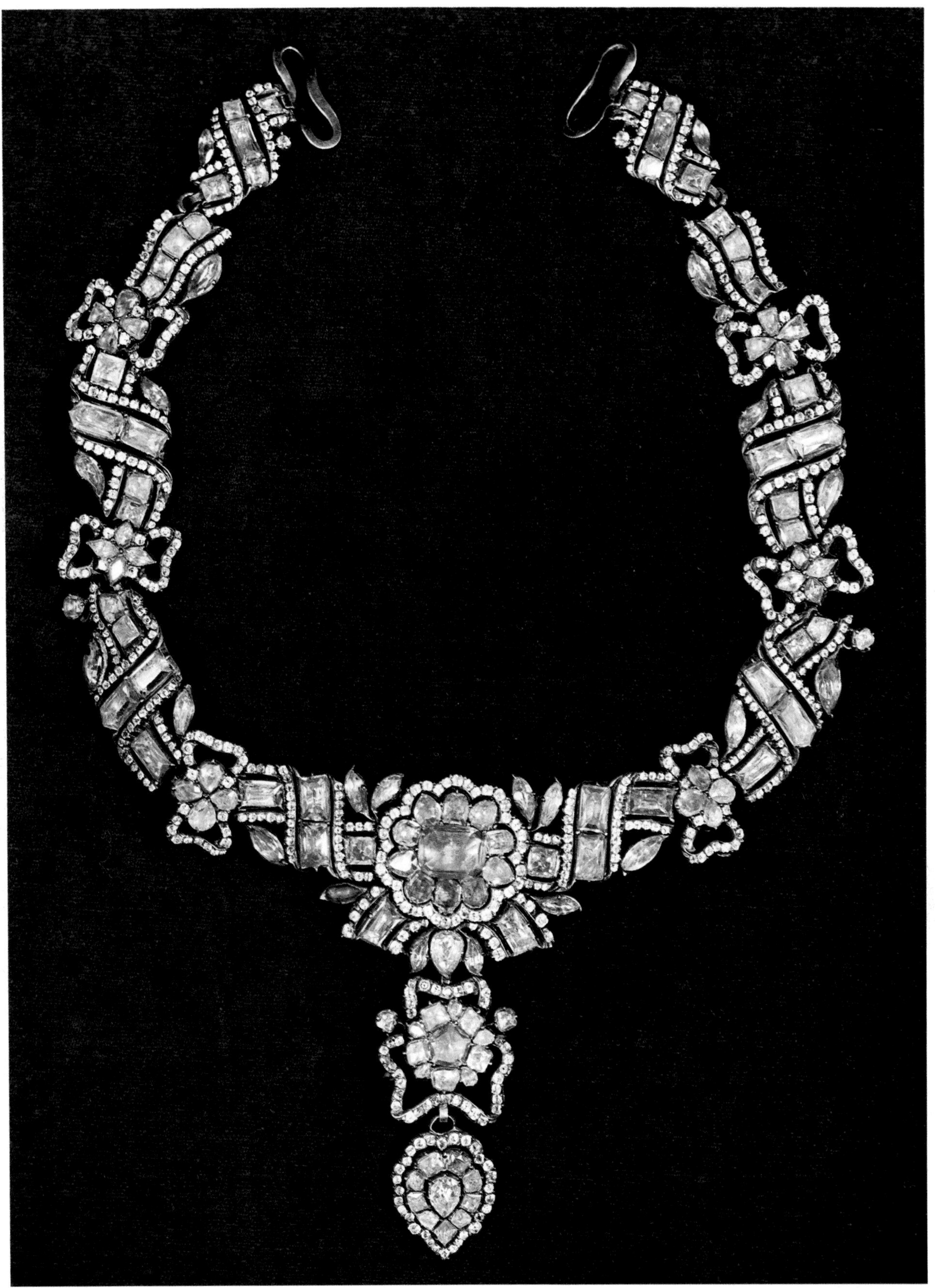

with cameos and marquise stones. Some forms, however, were more popular than others. The fashion for mourning jewelry reached its peak during the eighteenth century, especially when enamel returned to favor.

We must also mention the extraordinary number of châtelaines and watches, the latter designed and worn as ornaments rather than functional instruments. They were often decorated with brilliants, enamel and precious stones, and accompanied by all sorts of trinkets. The decorative nature of this ensemble is confirmed by an amusing detail. Men and women habitually wore two watches: one told the time but the other usually did not work and was exclusively decorative. However, this by no means prevented British clock and watch makers from enjoying a high reputation throughout Europe. A great variety of shoe buckles were made in England, and although the output was so large, every pair had some little detail which set it apart fom all the others. For nearly a hundred years, men had yielded the privilege of covering themselves with jewelry to the ladies; their own aspirations to elegance and the taste for costly things which they still preserved were expressed discreetly through the medium of these various buckles. However, this also made them an easy prey to the robbers who infested all the roads in Europe. Therefore, when they wanted to travel, they had to replace the ornaments on their shoes with something less valuable but no less showy.

This may not be the origin of the large output of imitation jewels which is also characteristic of eighteenth century England, but it is certainly a contributing factor. Crystal, steel and some substitute for gold such as pinchbeck—an alloy of copper and zinc named after the watchmaker who invented it—silver-plated copper and marcassite were used. This industry is far removed from high quality jewelry, but it deserves mention because its clients came from all ranks of society and its makers were something more than vulgar imitators. Among them were the famous Wickers and Netherton, who advertised, as well as some fine jewels, "A Variety of False-stone work in Aigrettes, Earrings, Buckles, etc . . . ." These valuable ornaments are interesting, because in some periods when family treasures had to be sacrificed to national defense, they were the only jewelry a good citizen dared wear. It then became a point of honor to wear nothing but crystal and steel, which were not always devoid of beauty. More than a hundred years later, decorative arts learned some valuable lessons from the restraint necessitated by this period of poverty. It was perhaps no accident that the first signs of the new movement appeared in England.

However, before describing the upheavals which radically changed the face of Europe at the end of the eighteenth century, there is yet another country to be discussed. It did not come into the picture before this time, but it suddenly eclipsed London, Madrid, Dresden and perhaps even Paris by its splendors. This was the vast and mysterious land of Russia, which many people regarded as barbarous. Under Catherine II it became a major power in Europe, and supplemented its national traditions with contributions from the west. Talk of its fabulous treasure had already been heard in the seventeenth century, and travelers who ventured into this distant land came back spellbound. "The Raschodnoy Casna . . . is full of innumerable jewels of all sorts, chiefly pearls, more of which are worn in Russia than all the rest of Europe. I have seen in the treasury at least fifty changes of dress for the Emperor, with jewels around them instead of braid, and robes entirely embroidered with pearls and others embroidered with a band of pearls a foot, six inches or four fingers wide. I have seen half a dozen bed covers all embroidered with pearls and sundry other things. There are also rich jewels, since some are bought every year and are kept in the treasury in addition to those which are presented by ambassadors." (Capitaine Margeret, *Estate de l'Empire de Russie et Grande Duché de Moscovie,* 1669)

Before the reign of Peter the Great, however, Russia had looked to the east rather than to Europe and the style and

Necklace, earrings, and diamond brooches. Russian, c. 1750. Christiés Auction. London, 1963.

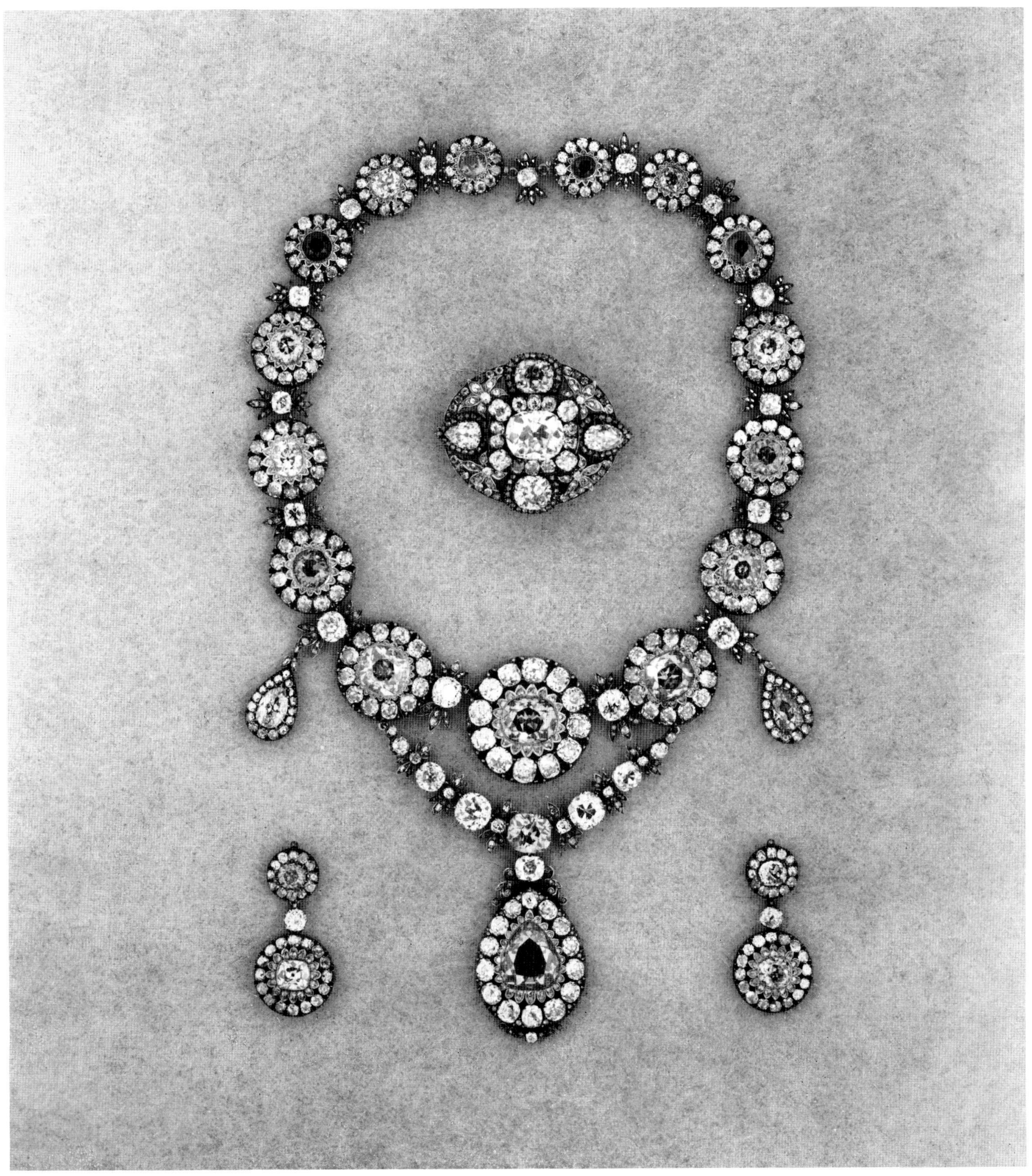

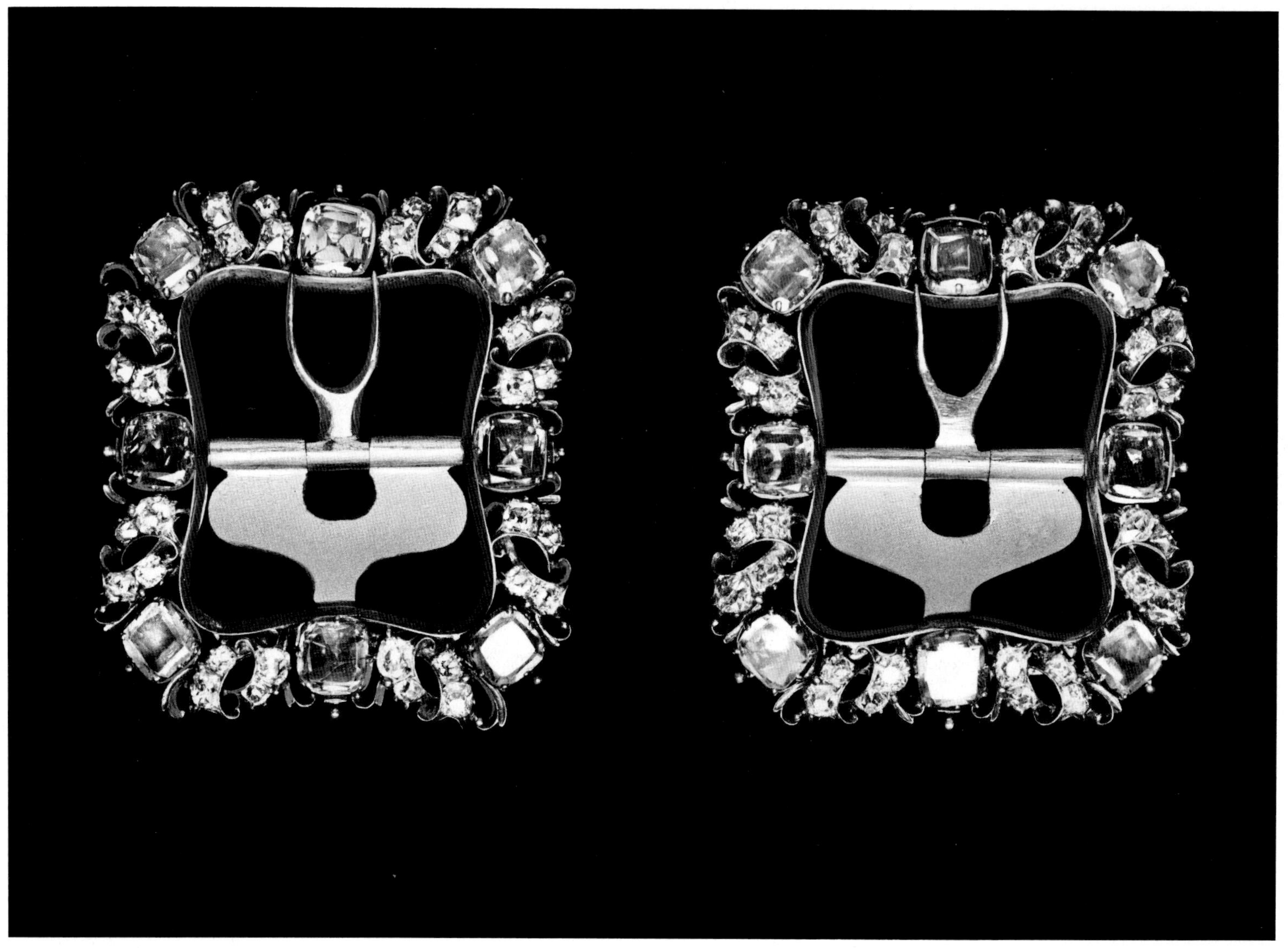

Pair of buckles: silver, diamonds and sapphires. English, c. 1720. Presented by Dr. Joan Evans. Victoria & Albert Museum, London.

provenance of its jewels would be difficult to fit into a history of western jewelry. A typical example would be the famous diamond throne acquired in 1660 by Tzar Alexei Mikhailovitch. This throne was probably made in Isfahan and included no less than 876 diamonds and nearly 1500 rubies, pearls and turquoises. It was fully worthy of the ruler whose horses' harness was garnished with turquoises, rubies and gold. Fifteen years later, the Tzar commanded his ambassador at the imperial court of China to buy him an enormous ruby. This was to form the base

Large brooch to hold a bouquet: brilliants, emeralds, gold and silver. Russian, c. 1760, Moscow.

Diamond brooch belonging to Queen Marie Caroline of Naples. Second half of the eighteenth century. Sold at Christie's in London in 1963.

of the diamond cross on the crown worn by the Empress Anna Ivanovna in which there were 2500 diamonds and several more rubies. Tzar Ivan Alexevitch in his turn left a diamond cap valued in the 1702 inventory at 15,511 rubles to the treasury. Then came Peter the Great, whose cap was a veritable monument of diamonds and sapphires bearing an enormous uncut ruby. But with this tzar, who abandoned himself to the delights of western life, the Russian style—not just a fashion but a whole way of life—was to be abruptly and harshly changed, an event which, in spite of everything, had some good results. In his description of his travels published in 1718, Corneille le Brun says: "Time has wrought great changes in this empire, particularly since the tzar returned from his travels. He first reformed the manner of dress, female as well as male, and especially that of the people who attended court and held office there, making no exceptions, not even children. Russian "merchants" and others were made to dress in such a manner that they could not be distinguished from those of our own country." (*Voyages de Corneille le Brun par la Moscovie, en Perse et aux Indes orientales,* Amsterdam, 1718, Vol.I)

To achieve his objective more rapidly Peter the Great sent for hundreds of western artists and craftsmen. He also prepared the way for one of the most brilliant sovereigns ever to rule Russia, a German princess named Augusta Sophia Frederika who took the name Catherine when she married the future Peter III and adopted the Orthodox faith. Catherine soon found herself in possession of inexhaustible resources and power, to use as she pleased. She gradually grew accustomed to the luxury of the Russian court. The marriage ceremony was held in August, 1745. "From eight o'clock until eleven o'clock the Grand Duchess was in the hands of her waiting women, her hairdresser and her jeweler, who dressed and adorned her . . . . Her gown was of silver brocade with huge panniers; all the seams, the hems and the long train were richly embroidered with silver roses. Her state robe was so heavy that the little princess felt nailed to the ground. The jeweler had been ordered to load her with chains, clasps, bracelets,

Wedding ring of Queen Maria Sophia Frederica: gold, blue enamel and brilliants. Pearl inscription reading "July 31, 1790." Rosenborg Castle, Chronological Collection of the Danish Kings, Copenhagen.

Watch and châtelaine of Queen Caroline-Mathilde: decorated with brilliants. Made in Copenhagen in 1767 by the French jeweler Jean-François Fistaine. Movement by Jodin, Paris, Rosenborg Castle, Chronological Collection of the Danish Kings, Copenhagen.

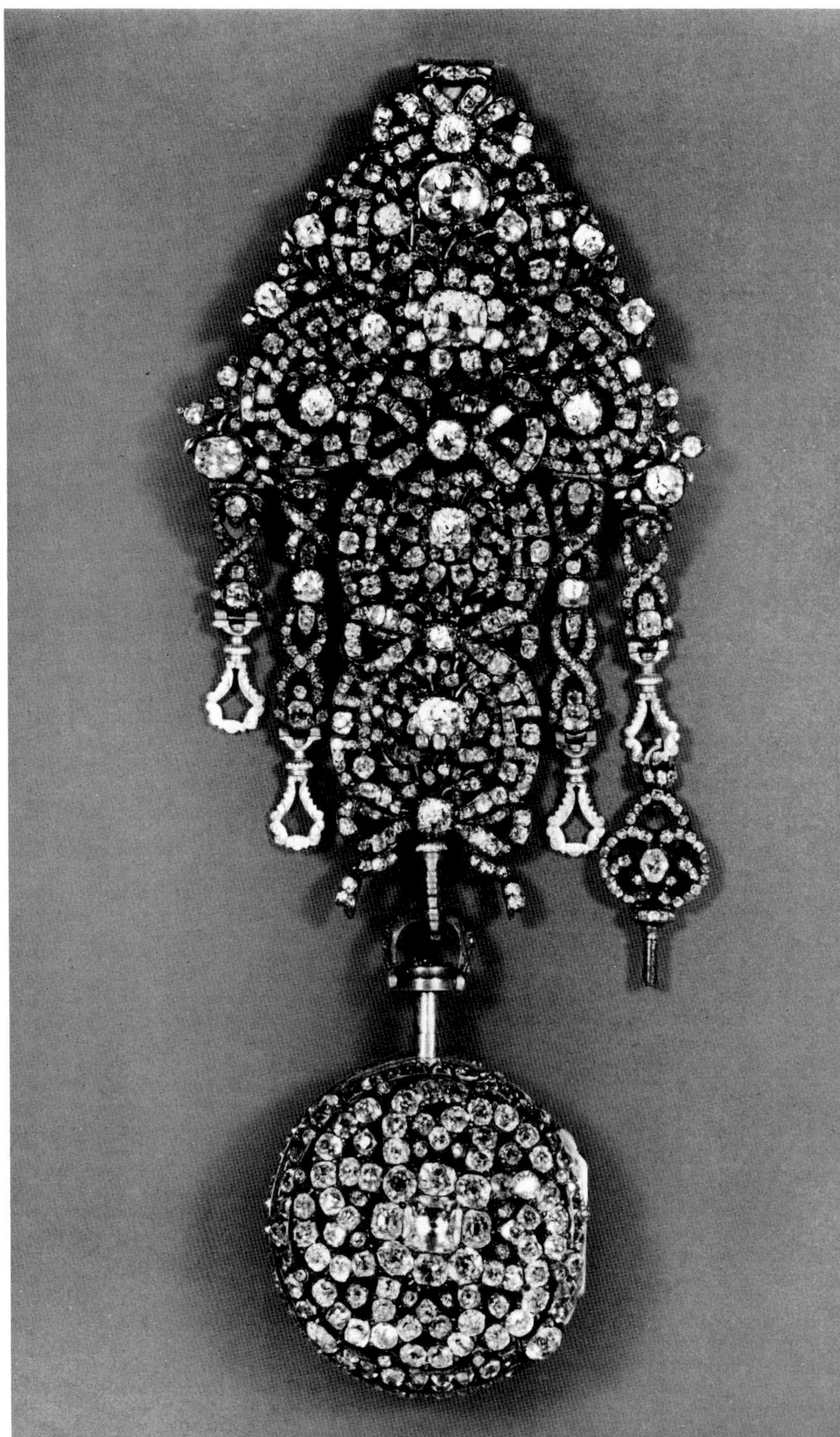

rings, earrings, buckles and everything worthy of her that the imperial treasury could furnish." (Mary Laveter-Sloman, *Cathérine II et ses temps,* Paris, 1952). Jérémie Posier, a French jeweler living in St. Petersburg, was entrusted with the creation of her famous crown, one of the most splendid pieces in the U.S.S.R. Diamond Treasury. This creation contained five thousand diamonds and pearls; some larger stones and a red spinel studded the central part, which was surmounted by a cross. The crown was fairly large (27.5 cm. high), but it gave no impression of weight. Posier succeeded in uniting great elegance with the traditional abundance of gems.

Another French jeweler, Lée Duval, worked at the court of St. Petersburg along with some German colleagues, one of whom was Pfisterer. History has not preserved the names of all the craftsmen employed by the empress and her entourage; if it had, the list would probably be extemely long. We know that the household of Potemkin alone numbered a good twenty goldsmiths and jewelers as well as five hundred servants and two hundred musicians. All the evidence indicates that people of note in the capital took whole teams of craftsmen into their service and gave them plenty to do. Indeed, every festival and ceremony was the occasion for a show of wealth unequaled even in Paris. From the bottom of the dress or the hem of the cloak to the hat, clothes glittered. They were made of cloth of gold and silver embroidered with pearls or sewn with large diamonds and sprinkled with knots, and even the smallest button was a preicous stone. The numerous anecdotes in which Potemkin figures as hero still preserve a few examples of courtly extravagance. Reviewing his life himself he said, "I always loved jewelry—there is no one in the world with a collection equal to mine." The pieces he assembled were not all of Russian workmanship. Potemkin acquired many of them abroad. He would admit no obstacles in the pursuit of his desires. In the middle of a war he entrusted two officers with a very strange mission. One left for Florence to buy perfumes, the other was sent to Paris for jewels. Towards the end of his life he gave a fefe in honor of the empress,

Spray of brilliants belonging to the Crown Jewels. Rosenborg Castle, Chronological Collection of the Danish Kings, Copenhagen.

Anonymous: design for jewelry. Florentine, first half of the eighteenth century. Victoria and Albert Museum, London.

whom he received dressed in a scarlet coat over which he had thrown a cape of lace and gold thread adorned with precious stones. He was spangled all over with diamonds and his hat was so heavy with them that he had to give it to his aide-de-camp, who followed faithfully in his master's footsteps. Potemkin did not exhaust all his treasures on his own clothes. Forty young courtiers dressed in white and wearing scarves and buckles enriched with diamonds danced a ballet in honor of their empress. At the height of the festivities the guests were led into a room richly decorated with Gobelin tapestry in the middle of which an imitation elephant covered with emeralds and rubies sat enthroned. Few individuals and no kingdoms could have competed with this powerful man. However, he did not eclipse another favorite, Gregory Orloff, who gave Catherine II a blue diamond weighing 189.62 carats valued at 400,000 rubles in 1774 to celebrate the festival of Peace. This stone, known as the "Orloff" diamond, adorned the victory sceptre and was probably the empress' pride and joy. She had to give up the idea of buying it herself as she had found the price too high.

The French Revolution was soon to bring troubled times to Europe. Russia, however, was isolated and unfriendly, and kept its traditions of splendor and luxury for several more decades. The eighteenth century continued beyond the year 1800 in Russia. Elsewhere it ended much earlier, in 1789.

Chapter 4 THE NINETEENTH CENTURY

THE NINETEENTH CENTURY

The nineteenth century, born prematurely in 1789 and extinguished by the 1914 war, was one of the richest and most eventful periods of French history. It contained all kinds of developments, revolutions and discoveries to which the French largely subscribed—a fact which they are now sometimes reluctant to admit. A parallel will perhaps be established one day between the nineteenth century and the Renaissance, and the prodigious wealth, vitality and imagination of this era, which is too frequently accused of lack of originality.

No one nowadays disparages the Italian musicians who invented opera in the process of attempting to revive ancient tragedy, but we tend to despise neo-Gothic buildings and jewelry that artlessly reproduced the style of Holbein or Hans Collaert. The men of the Renaissance drew exclusively on the wealth of Greek and Roman antiquity, but the field open to nineteenth century artists and scholars was infinitely wider in both historical and geographical terms. They found inspiration everywhere, in all countries and ages, and their investigations gave rise to something better than second-rate copies. The nineteenth century developed a style all of its own in its eclecticism. The fact that it is not always appreciated today is probably attributable to the highly subjective issue of taste.

In its limited way, jewelry, like all other forms of art, reflects the vicissitudes of its own age and perhaps all the more so in that it has always been closely allied to the fortunes of a particular social class. The balance of society throughout nineteenth century Europe was shaken to its foundations. Many countries kept their monarchies and courts but became increasingly dependent on middle-class prosperity, which expanded at a fantastic rate everywhere. There is nothing new in the spectacle of power residing with the rich; but from the end of the eighteenth century, money gradually changed hands and became the sole source of power. Little by little, the well-to-do middle classes, and to a certain extent, some of their social inferiors, abrogated a great number of privileges, among them, the right to wear the finest jewels as soon as they could afford them. It is probably too soon to speak of the "democratization" of jewelry. It should rather be said that the number of the élite increased and the demand for precious ornaments became correspondingly greater.

When the middle classes acquired these new rights they tried hard to keep them to themselves. But since the sole title to these privileges was money, they perforce had to be shared with a class of people who had hitherto been relegated to the fringes of society. Actresses, singers and "kept women" suddenly ventured to appear in public in superb jewels at least comparable and sometimes superior to those of the most virtuous wives. In the previous century, some actresses, espcially opera singers, had already had their fame and beauty immortalized by famous painters and their portraits show them richly decked with diamond drops and glittering aigrettes. This trend grew stronger in the nineteenth century, and what had once

Necklace and eardrops in the Renaissance style: gold, enamel and pearls. Hungarian, nineteenth century. Victoria & Albert Museum, London.

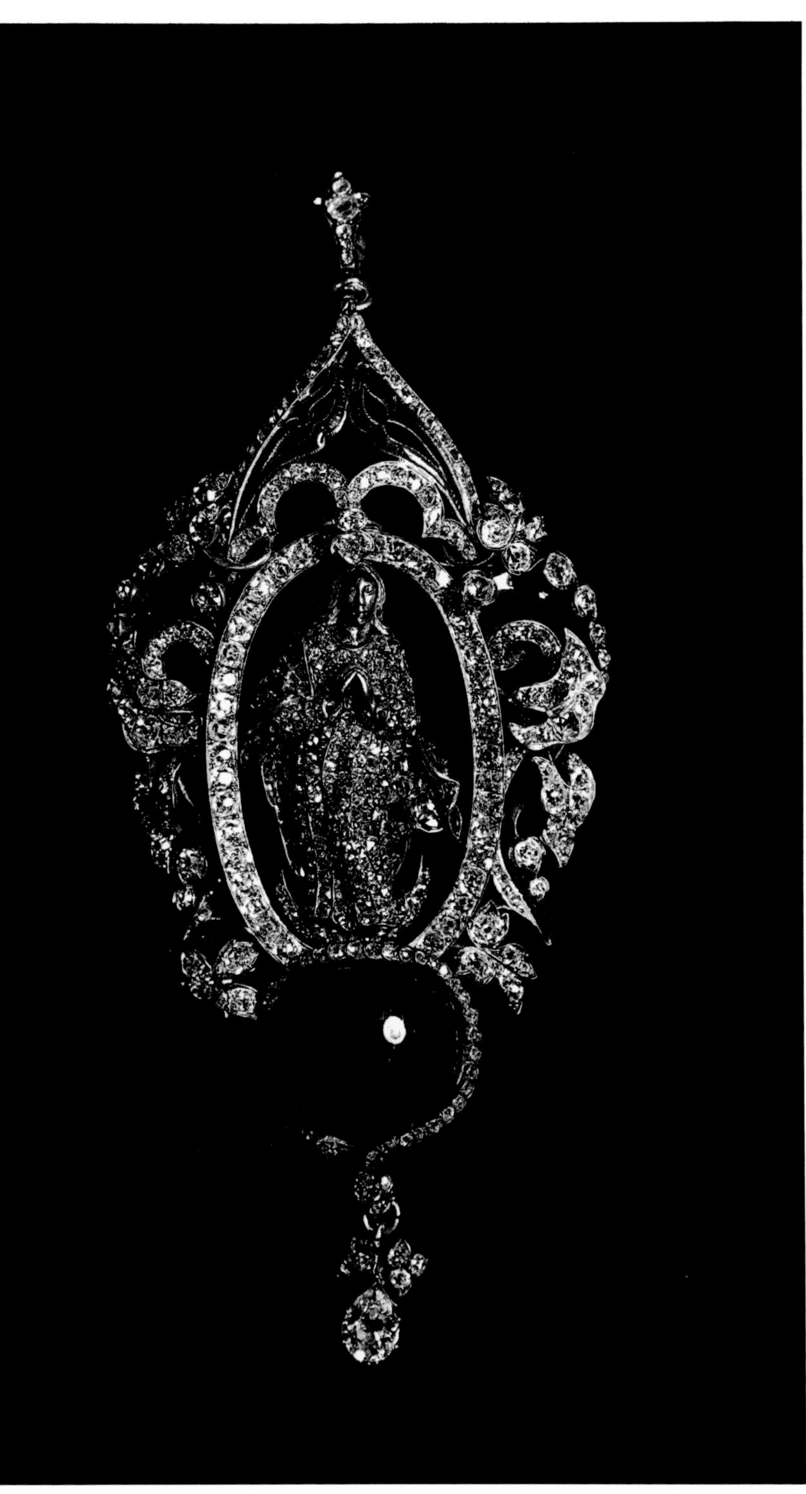

been the exception became the rule—so much so that some members of the well-to-do middle classes tried to segregate themselves by rigidly sober dress while some aristocrats, reacting to the same stimulus in the opposite way, strove to imitate the common people. Social barriers rocked and shifted, but never actually fell.

However, it is probably not enough to say that for many combined reasons jewelry became accessible to an increasing number of women. It is essential to understand the role of women in society, especially in the nineteenth century. This question is connected more closely than might be imagined with the history of jewelry and costume. Our grandparents' century might seem to be the age of female emancipation to anyone looking distantly and objectively at this recent era. During its course they gradually conquered the right to a vote, to education and independence. It seems, however, that the rise of the middle classes, particularly in the period immediately after the French Revolution, initiated and extended a merciless and unprecedented system of severe competition from which women were rigidly excluded. The position to which they found themselves was greatly inferior to the role they had filled in former times. It might seem rather specious to draw this type of comparison, but it should be clearly understood that the parallel is not between an eighteenth century middle-class woman and her daughter, but between two or three generations of women with similar incomes. In many respects, the nineteenth century woman lost her independence, and she only existed by virtue of her husband. She became his *alter ego,* his mirror. She reflected his success and he decked her with jewels for his own glorification. The jewelry worn by the wife of a rich bourgeois was too often not a personal distinction but the symbol of success and wealth in which she had only a very limited share.

Brooch and pendant: gold, enamel, diamonds, sapphire and a garnet. Portuguese, c. 1840. Presented by Mrs. H.F. Mossockle. Victoria & Albert Museum, London.

When men of achievement began to claim some share in the privileges which had formerly been only earned by birth, women became a subservient species—unless they were bold enough to defy convention. At the end of the century they rebelled against this situation and their new attitude affected their clothes, which became lighter and more practical. In the end they would no longer tolerate the array of heavy jewels that can still all too often be seen in nineteenth century portraits.

This revolution, however, did not succeed until after the first world war. In the meantime, jewelry, being no longer the mark of the women who wore it, sought other media for the expression of its indispensable symbolism. There was plenty of choice. After the end of the eighteenth century, the Romantic movement awakened new sensibilities and sentimental jewelry was a significant aspect of this trend. It flourished for a large part of the nineteenth century. Medallions with brilliants encircling a miniature were no longer only a royal gift. Fiancées, mothers, widows and wives wore them at their necks or as bracelet clasps. One of Queen Victoria's bracelets consisted of a set of medallions with all her children's portraits painted on them. Another had a clasp adorned with Prince Albert's portrait. Some jewelers specialized in mounting such relics as a first milk tooth in gold. Locks and curls of hair were sure of a place in different sorts of medallions.

When it served as a setting for mementos with neither real nor figurative value the jewel was both a sign and a fetish. Commercial and sentimental value mutually enhanced each other because the ornament has always necessarily been more than a marketable object. People of the nineteenth century understood this perfectly, and it is probably the reason why, among all the wealth of their era, they chose to pursue articles that would appreciate in value.

Design for a bracelet and eardrops. Italian, first quarter of the nineteenth century. The Cooper Union Museum for the Arts of Decoration, New York.

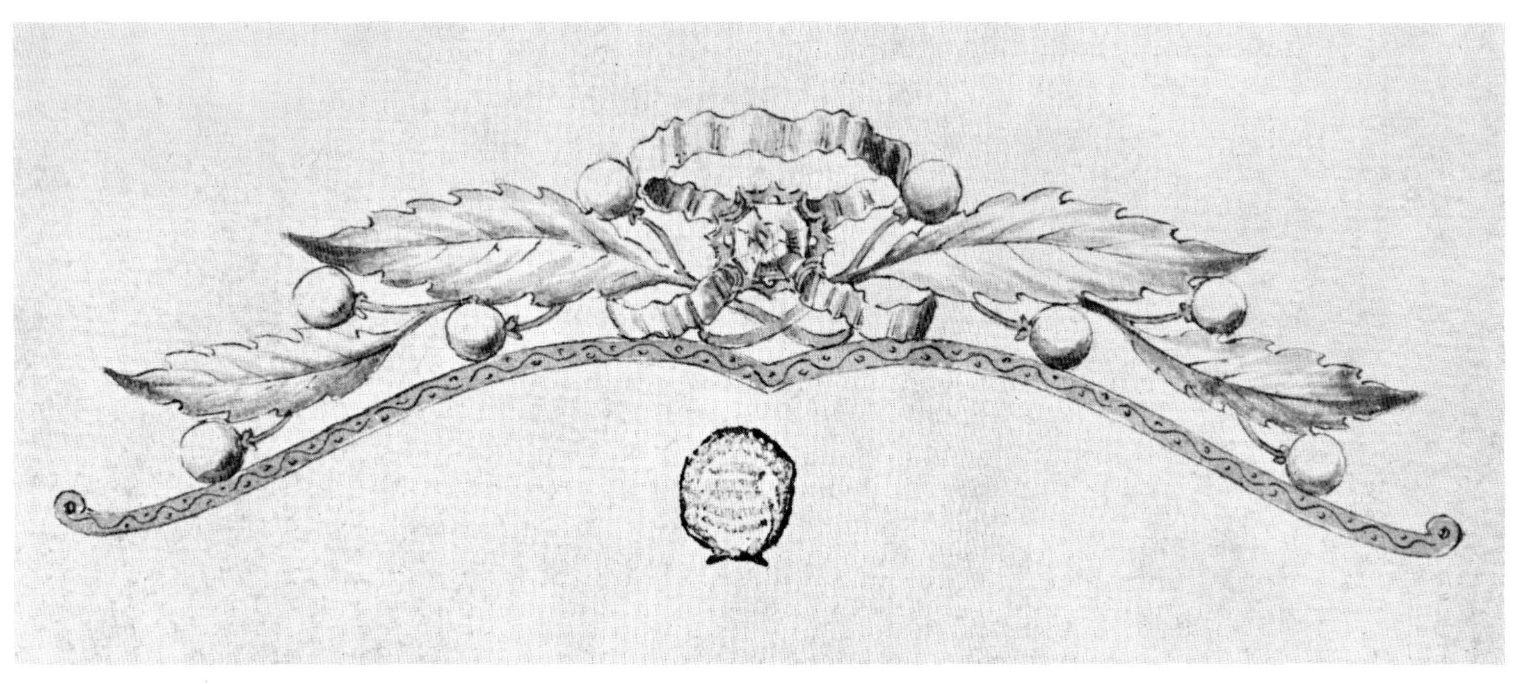

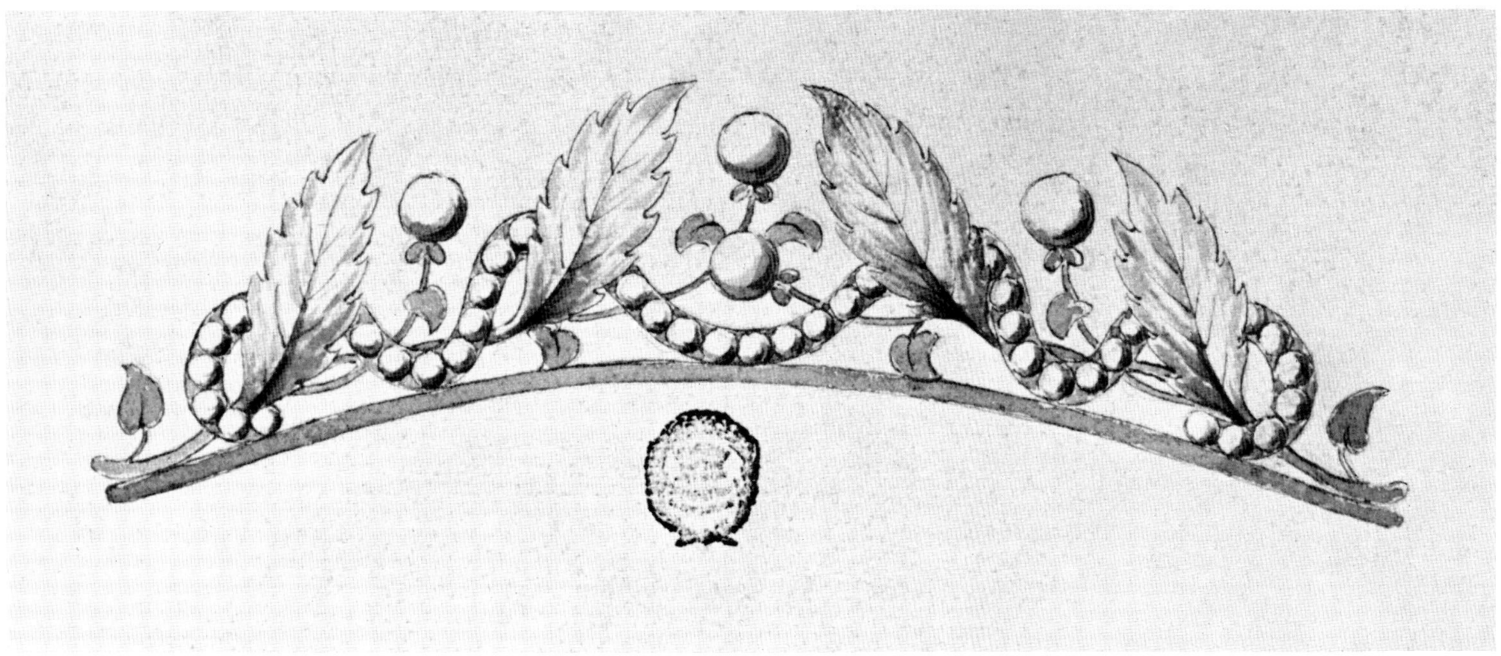

Designs for tiaras: watercolor. Italian, c. 1830. The Cooper Union Museum for the Arts of Decoration, New York.

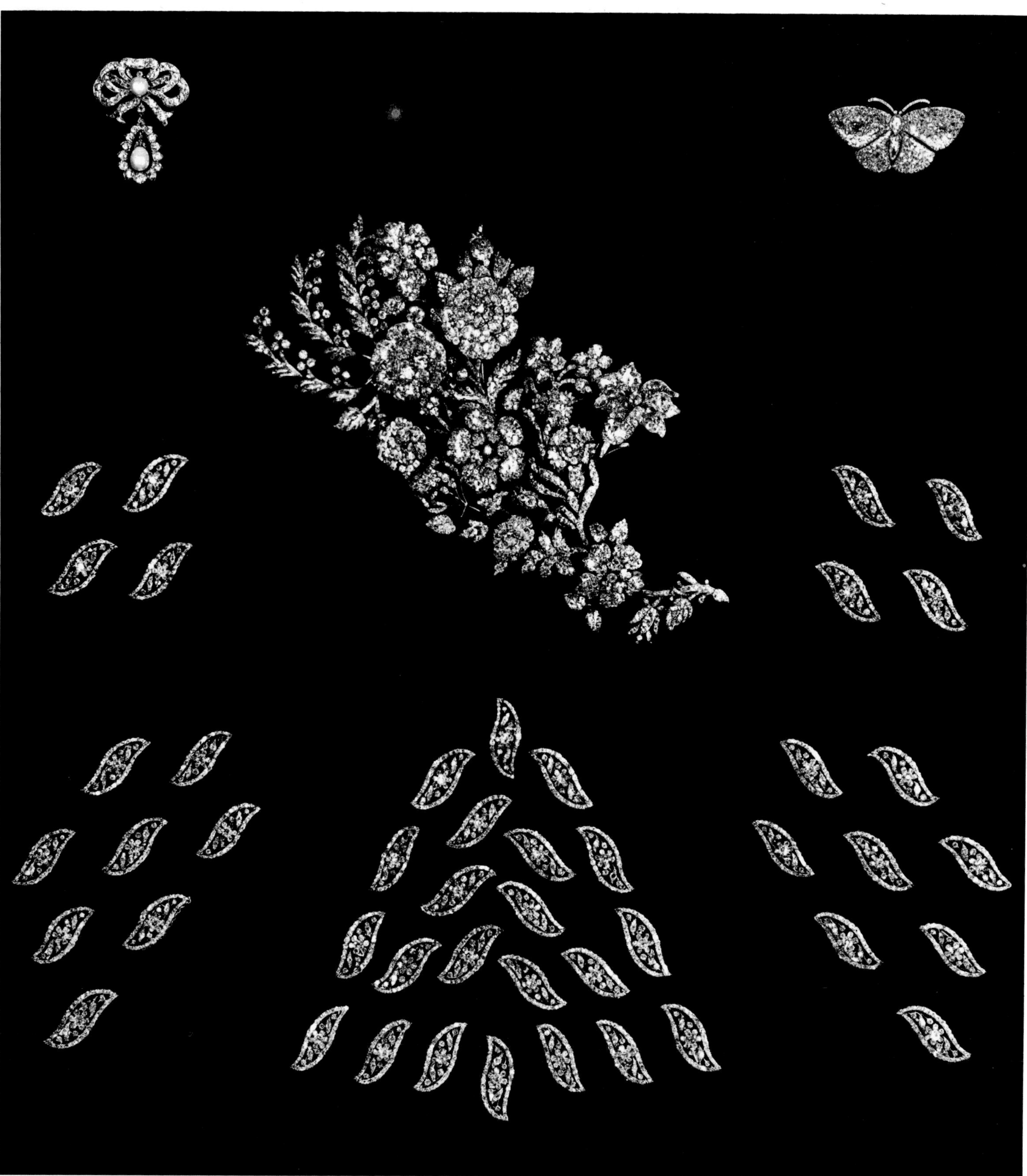

Bracelet: gold and brilliants with two hearts, one of ruby and one of sapphire. English, by Garrard, 1890. Garrard Collection, London.

The world of sentiment was by no means the only realm they explored. History, exotics and folklore also influenced jewelry for a variety of reasons in which it is difficult to define how much part was played by taste, pride, culture, illusion and of course, sentiment.

In the second half of the eighteenth century, archaeological discoveries followed in rapid succession. Cities, buildings and tombs were discovered and excavated. They yielded their treasures and generated all sorts of new trends. Historians, philosophers, artists and craftsmen fell

(top to bottom, left to right): Pendant: silver, diamonds and pearls. English, late nineteenth century. Butterfly: silver and brilliants. English, nineteenth century. Corsage ornament: gold and brilliants. English, early nineteenth century. 46 small dress ornaments: silver and diamonds. French, c. 1770. Cory Bequest, Victoria & Albert Museum, London.

Vallardi: design for a wreath with gems and cameos, comb and spray. *Dessins de joaillerie et bijouterie,* Paris-Milan, 1801-35. B.N., Paris, Cabinet des Estampes.

on these relics and sought, each in his own way, to fathom their secrets. In jewelry, this was the great age of cameos and pieces in the antique style which were chiefly adapted for combs and tiaras. Greece and Rome were all the rage and then it was the turn of Egypt and Etruria. But the more recent past was not without its charms. The eighteenth century had had little liking for the Gothic, but the nineteenth century fell in love with it and for several decades belt-buckles, brooches and *ferronnières* gave women a spuriously medieval air. Renaissance jewelry was revived late in the century. In 1870, the treasure of the Virgin of the Pillar was put up for sale (most of the best pieces were

Vallardi: design for a collet necklace, plumed aigrette and earrings. *Dessins de joaillerie et bijouterie,* Paris-Milan, 1801-35. B.N., Paris, Cabinet des Estampes.

bought by Britain and are now in the Victoria and Albert Museum). Pendants imitating sixteenth century originals could be seen in the windows of the best jewelers.

Western history was not the only source of inspiration to be explored. Africa and the eastern countries in which the great European powers had established their domination also contributed to the repertoire of forms. Indian and Algerian jewellery captivated high society and for a few years no one wanted anything else.

Another aspect of exoticism was the discovery of various folk arts which had been prized very little until that time. The rise of national feeling in countries like

Vallardi: design for a wreath of flowers and ribbons, sprays and earrings. *Dessins de joaillerie et bijouterie,* Paris-Milan, 1801-35. B.N., Paris, Cabinet des Estampes.

Poland and Hungary, which yearned for lost freedom, aroused impassioned interest in the original art of bygone ages. This phenomenon, which is quite familiar in music, also affected jewelry. It influenced all the countries in Europe, oppressed or otherwise, and was part of the historic trend. The ancestral decorative motifs of early Scotland and mysterious Ireland were borrowed, while jewelry in Belgium would later be inspired by Bruges lace.

The traditional *parure* of stylized natural motifs persisted alongside these fads and fashions, especially for court wear. Jewels were often designed in sets of tiara, necklace, earrings, brooches and bracelets all based on the same motif adapted to the shape of the various pieces.

Throughout the whole of the nineteenth century, then, there were a great many styles with very varied origins. Their history would be straightforward if they had followed one after another, but they very often coexisted. Some seemed to have vanished for good, only to reappear, brought back into fashion for some obscure reason—sometimes no more than a royal ball. In the nineteenth century, there was no shortage of balls on historical or folklore themes—Tudor, Mary Stuart and Plantagenet balls in London and Paris, and balls in traditional Russian dress at the Winter Palace in St. Petersburg. Other even more ambitious displays—notably the great exhibitions—could also completely overturn fashion by introducing new discoveries and unpredictable revivals of some forgotten style. It is very difficult to establish strict classifications among these artificially preserved styles of all kinds. Species coexisted and intermingled, fashions spread all over Europe by various routes, and all the great powers could boast that they had imposed their preferences on the rest at one time or another. As always, famous jewelers traveled and began to establish branches in some of the chief European cities towards the end of the century, which does not simplify matters.

However, it was unquestionably in early nineteenth century France that fashions *à l'antique* had the greatest success. After the upheavals of the Revolution, which lasted from 1789 to 1799 with a tragic period in 1793, it might be asked what could be left of French jewelry as either an art or an industry.

The Marquis de Laborde left no illusions on that score: "The Revolution overthrew everything in its path—national institutions and industrial associations. It destroyed every tradition, those of scholars by closing schools, those of teachers by suppressing academies and those of workers by closing the royal factories. It disrupted

Hat clasp: silver-gilt with brilliants and a few rose diamonds. By J. Staff of Munich, 1765. Nymphenburg Castle, Munich.

domestic industry and as a crowning irony that added insult to injury, it proclaimed the freedom of art and industry (which had never been enslaved) at the very time when exile and execution were decimating the generous and intelligent patrons of the arts. . . .'' With the suppression of the trade guilds, the old industrial families that supplied the practitioners of each craft lost their foundations. Henceforward, a young man might be born into a profession, but if he had the mind to do so and believed himself talented, he abandoned his craft. He rejected it to direct his hopes and labors to whatever task he regarded as superior. Artists furnished models for craftsmen on request, but without understanding their destination or the processes by which they were made. The designer and the craftsmen were poles apart, and equally justifiable complaints were raised by both sides. The artists were displeased to see their models badly executed, while craftsmen and their employees declared that the designs were impractical. This breakdown in communications produced a deplorable schism and led to a state of mutual hostility, ''the consequence of which was a break between masters and workers which, with the disappearance of jewelry and its customers, condemned the jewelers' workrooms to closure.''

When security returned under the Directory, the need for relaxation was naturally felt and luxury began tentatively to reappear. A few former masters reopened their workshops and began to recruit workers who had survived the Terror.

However, although it might have been hoped that—after a fallow period of ten long years—re-emerging jewelry would display some innovations, the style of the first pieces was that of the last years of the overthrown monarchy, typified by rococo excesses.

Comb in the form of a diadem decorated with pearls. French, nineteenth century. Musée des Arts Décoratifs, Paris.

Jewelers who opposed this tendency tried to counteract it by seeking inspiration in ancient art, but they knew very little about it. ''In 1791, when the ashes of Voltaire were removed to the Pantheon the cortège was already all in the ancient style, and the costume of ancient Rome circulated in the streets of Paris . . . .'' This trend continued during the Directory, ''then came the *Merveilleuses,* nymphs, goddesses and other elegant creatures robed in light Roman tunics with three bracelets on each arm—one near the shoulder, one above the elbow and the third

Design for a diadem for the Empress Josephine, 1807. Collection Mauboussin, Paris.

at the wrist. They had rings on all the fingers of both hands and even their thumbs, as well as big circular rings in their ears and a large girdle-clasp below their breasts. Mme. Tallien used to walk in the Champs Elysées in flesh-colored tights under a simple lawn tunic with gold rings around her thighs and legs and diamond rings on her feet, which were shod only in sandals." (Henri Vever)

This feminine craze for nudity and absence of ornaments was so widespread that it roused the medical profession to protest. In Year VIII (1799), one of them wrote in *Journal de la Mésangère,* "Nothing could be more delightful than your modern costumes, these Grecian tunics leaving the arms and bosom bare; nothing could be more alluring to your admirers or more lucrative for us doctors. . . .The fashions that pleased them in Athens are killing them in Paris. That is what the ladies are apt to forget."

Under these circumstances it is easy to see how jewelry came to be neglected, at least as far as design and innovation were concerned.

Jewelers confined themselves to relating their products to current events, with the ancient style, the Egyptian mood and head ornaments with ears of corn, gold and silver circlets sometimes set with diamonds, scarabs, sphinxes, trophies and quivers in low relief hanging from gold coronets or diamond knots.

At this time the influence of David, who was fascinated by everything having to do with the ancient world, was at its height. He was a great painter but a poor designer. This "Corneille of painting," who had once set the Academy by the ears, became the very prototype of the Academician according to the Comte de Laborde, and his style became the academic style *par excellence,* i.e., thoroughly boring and impoverished from the artistic point of view.

It was not until 1800 that luxury reappeared. The First Consul's victories and reforms reestablished confidence, industry expanded and business reached a level of prosperity unknown since 1789.

The Beaux Arts, opened in 1801 (Year IX), was the first unquestionably universal exhibition, accepting products of all kinds.

Bonaparte gave brilliant receptions, the salons reopened and jewels reappeared thanks to the workshops which, after ten years of idleness, were steadily reorganizing and rapidly coming back into normal production. As victory followed victory from the battle of Marengo on, Paris and France lived in an atmosphere of optimism and many jewelers' shops prospered again.

A leading jeweler of the period was Auguste, one of the few who dared to link the present with the past. It was he who had made the crown for Louis XVI's coronation in 1774. His new establishment employed fifty workers, but his assistants were not so skillful as formerly and his products had not the high quality of the ones he made under the *Ancien Régime.* There was also Biennais, a maker of fancy goods who had turned late to the jeweler's profession; Percier, who had collaborated with Fontaine to build the Arc de Triomphe, was his chief designer, and many of his designs are still in the Bibliothèque des Arts Décoratifs. He did not give up his former craft but added the making of goldwork and jewelry and Orders, and in this capacity he later made several state swords for the emperor.

Another great jeweler was Nitot who was entrusted with the task of resetting the Crown Jewels of France for the regalia of Napoleon's coronation in 1804. He was perhaps the most important jeweler of the first empire. It was he who set the "Regent" diamond in the hilt of a state sword decorated with some huge diamonds in 1803. The emperor only wore it from the Tuileries to Notre Dame, where he changed it for a short sword more in keeping with his Romanesque costume.

The coronation crown can still be seen in the Apollo Gallery of the Louvre. It was used again at the wedding of Marie Louise, and it too was the work of Nitot. This curious piece of symbolic jewelry, slightly archaic in style, is a floral circlet from which eight arches rise to join at the top under a globe surmounted by a cross. The whole is decorated with gemstones and cameos.

The rings—a ruby for Josephine and an emerald for the emperor, symbolized joy and divine revelation respectively. They had been blessed, as is well known, by Pope Pius VII. When the ruling pontiff came to consecrate Napoleon's power and might, the emperor wished to show reverence by presenting the Pope with a gift of great price. He asked Auguste, one of the survivors of the

Napoleon's coronation sword: gold and jasper, by Bontet. Prince Napoleon's Collection, Paris. 

Necklace given by Napoleon to the Empress Marie-Louise on the birth of the King of Rome. Harry Winston Collection, New York.

Diadem given by Napoleon to the Empress Josephine. Collection Van Cleef & Arpels, Paris.

glorious company of goldsmith-jewelers of the former monarchy, to make a magnificent tiara. Nitot was ordered to decorate the work of the former royal goldsmith and adorn it with precious stones. He set the three traditional crowns with a profusion of pearls and all the gems the liturgy allows, surmounting them with a cross of brilliants. It can still be admired today in the Papal Treasury of the Vatican.

It is probable that Nitot owed the First Consul's favor to Josephine, since he succeeded Foncier as the Beauharnais family's jeweler and it was to him that Citizeness Bonaparte turned for her jewelry. The quality of Nitot's work shows that the First Consul, subsequently emperor, was well-advised in continuing to patronize him.

Josephine was an ideal customer for both jewelers and dressmakers. She was very stylish and elegant and loved luxury, and she was wildly extravagant, spending far more than her dress allowance. Her annual allowance of 450,000 francs only covered half her actual expenses in 1809. In his book *Joséphine, Impératrice et Reine,* F. Masson gives fascinating glimpses of Josephine's wardrobe; ". . . Here is a green velvet overdress clasped around the waist with a cameo gridle; here is an overdress of purple velvet buttoned with oriental topazes and belted with a gold chain clasped with an amethyst medallion opening over a beige satin dress; and here, worn over a white satin dress, is an overdress of white corded velvet belted with gold filigree inlaid with fine pearls and a medallion, buttons and tassels of sapphires and pearls."

This extract shows how important a part jewelry played in feminine dress and gives some idea of the unparalleled prosperity of the luxury trades in general and jewelry in particular.

Napoleon was not behindhand in elegance. In 1804 and 1805, the emperor ordered, among other jewels for his personal use, some jeweled braid and a hat button worth 362,000 francs from Marguerite, who was appointed Crown jeweler in 1811. The 25-carat diamond in the button had cost 180,000 francs. Nitot and Marguerite supplied plaques and the chain for the Order of the Légion d'Honneur for the sum of 188,221 francs. In 1807, Napoleon ordered Nitot to make a ruby diadem with diamond laurel leaves of which Henri Vever wrote that it could "be regarded as the prototype of all the others of the same sort that were made subsequently."

"In Regnault's painting of Napoleon and Josephine at the wedding of Prince Jerome and the Princess of Württemburg (now in the Versailles museum) the Emperor is shown wearing a white-plumed hat in which is the famous button" (described above). "The Empress' toilette is completed by a splendid set of pearls. On her head, in her ears, at her neck, girdle and wrists and even on the sleeves and hem of her dress she wore nothing but wonderful pearls. The huge pearl of 337 grains bought in 1811 from Nitot for 40,000 francs no longer appears in this magnificent collection. This pearl, which was set in the middle of a diadem made for the Empress Marie Louise, was to be sold in 1887 by a government that was as ignorant as it was indifferent, under the meaningless name of the 'Regent,' which it had never borne." (H. Vever)

After the annulment of his marriage to Josephine, the emperor chose Marie-Louise, daughter of Francis II, emperor of Austria.

Napoleon attached great importance to the composition of his wedding gift to Marie Louise. Berthier was commanded to go to Vienna with some jewels which astounded the daughter of the Hapsburgs, unaccustomed as she was to such splendors. The wedding gifts and trousseau were worth more than five million francs.

The great square salon of the Louvre, equipped as a chapel for the occasion, was the scene of the religious ceremony which took place on April 2, 1810. According to historians, "Napoleon was as richly bejeweled as the empress. He wore a black velvet cap with eight rows of diamonds topped by three white plumes fastened with a diamond topped by three white plumes fastened with a diamond knot, in the middle of which shone the "Regent." Around his neck was the great jeweled collar of the Légion d'Honneur and at his side he wore a short

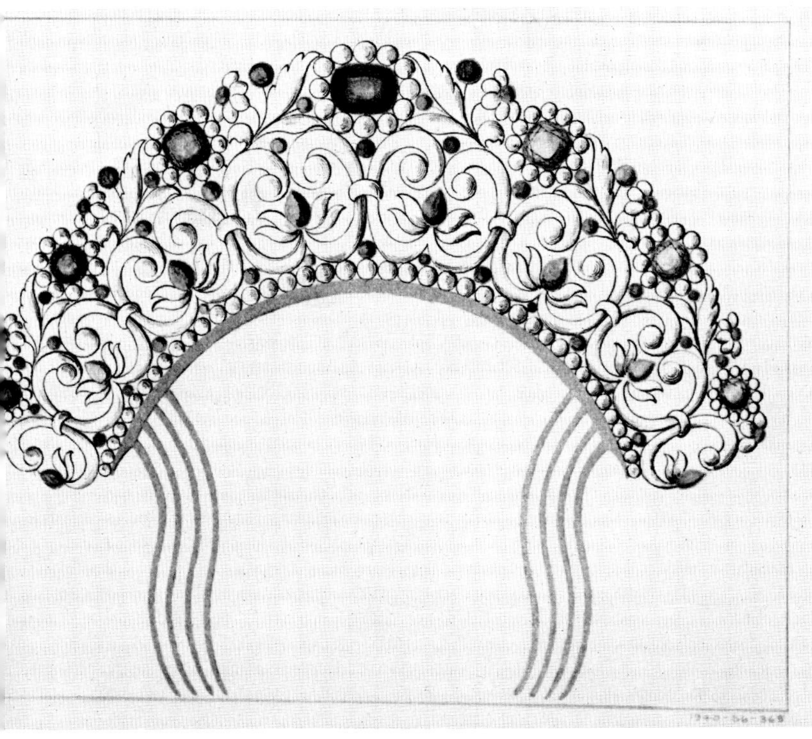

sword set with some marvelous gems." He wore diamonds everywhere, in the trimming and braid of his hat, the epaulette holding his cloak, the buckles of his garters and shoes, the collar of the Legion and the hilt of his sword. Marie Louise looked as if she were dressed in diamonds she was so loaded with them, and her dress seemed to be made of rays of moonlight." (Frederic Masson)

Luxury was the order of the day at the imperial receptions which took place up to early 1812. Court ladies were covered with diamonds and in the famous quadrille "Peruvians Going to the Temple of the Sun" danced at the Tuileries in 1812, it was said that diamonds valued at twenty million francs were worn—a very considerable sum at that time.

This was the end of the brilliant era which had begun in 1804, the last dazzling display of jewels. The new empress was not like Josephine. Her household was modest, even mediocre for her rank, in conformity with the education she had received.

After 1812, clouds gathered on the political horizon. There were no more imperial orders for jewelry. The state curtailed its expenditure and the empress found no difficulty in setting an example of moderation in her outlays. Her jewelers' accounts never exceeded 50,000 francs a year from 1810 to 1813.

Jewelry, therefore, flourished greatly in this period, and its technical quality was outstanding, particularly with regard to gem setting. But decoration was flat and there was no attempt to introduce novelty. It was always composed of the same elements—meanders, palmettes and trefoils with no surface modeling.

Cameos and intaglios had never been out of fashion since the Renaissance, but they were even more popular during the empire. The *Journal des Dames* of 25 Ventose, Year XIII (1804) said, "A fashionable woman wears cameos in her girdle, cameos in her necklace, a cameo on each

Design for jeweled combs: watercolor. Italian, c. 1850. The Cooper Union Museum for the Arts of Decoration, New York.

of her bracelets and a cameo in her tiara. There are cameos on her antique-style chair and instead of Greek objects her salon offers cameos. An Egyptian cameo on the door of a French carriage is regarded as the height of distinction."

Napoleon himself encouraged this vogue. In 1815, he instituted the Prix de Rome for engravers of fine stones, which was comparable to the other Beaux Arts prizes. He wanted to update ancient cameos by using them in modern ornaments. To this end he had several cameos of the Bibliothèque Impériale handed over to the Grand Marshall of the Palace by a decree of 1808. He chose 82 from the former Cabinet du Roi, 24 of which were set with pearls into a set of ornaments for the marriage of Marie Louise. This *parure* consisted of a diadem, necklace, comb, earrings, belt, clasp, medallion and a pair of bracelets. 2,275 small pearls completed the decoration.

People of more limited means substituted engravings "in the ancient style" on gemstones and even, in copies, on shell or moulded glass for ancient cameos.

The *Journal des Dames et des Modes de la Mésangère* contains plenty of information about this fashion. ". . . .At the Opera there were many gold nets and resillas. What the jewelers call a resilla has such fine meshes that you have to look very closely to see that it is made of wire. A thick braid of hair encircles the head and hides the edge of the resilla. When no headdress is worn a string of fine pearls is placed to the front of the hair. Fashion no longer forbids diamonds and pearls to be worn together. Necklaces of large fine stones and collet-set stones are in favor. There are all sorts of diamond earrings. We were enchanted by a vine garland with grapes of polished gold and leaves of matt gold open at the sides. This garland was supplemented by a wreath of real leaves . . . . Instead of an ancient piece, a diamond cipher or a solitaire are worn on a belt." (15 Brumaire Year X: 1801)

". . . Jewelers are showing diamonds in flat aigrettes, often shaped like sprays of jasmine. This species gives the most lightness to the spray. The whole is clear-set . . . . Jewelers are abandoning chains of palmettes in favor of round braids or cords. A great many topazes are seen. Earrings and belt clasps are adorned with diamonds . . . . These diamonds are mostly worn on cropped heads, for every day more curls fall under the hairdresser's scissors. Soon only grey-headed dowagers and conventional adolescents will not have cropped heads." (10 Floréal Year XI: 1802)

". . . . When the elegant woman is not wearing either her diadem, her feathers, her plumed hat or her wreath, she girds on her bandeau. A silver-lamé ribbon is fine; a ribbon of pearls is even better; an antique chain of palmettes and clear-set topazes is best of all. Only diamonds are superior, but they are not very suitable for this type of ornament." (30 Pluvieuse Year XIII: 1804)

". . . . Instead of coral beads in facets, they are sometimes worked all over the surface with little irregularities which make them look like strawberries" (*Almanach des Modes,* 1816). Magazines of the end of the first empire also mention "strawberry corals."

The popularity of the ancient world began to wane towards the end of the empire. Poor imitations of Greek, Roman and even Egyptian motifs slavishly reproduced by designers and craftsmen and repeated *ad nauseam* grew monotonous and dreary. The songwriter Béranger wrote, "No, even the Romans and Greeks ought not to be copied. They are our luminaries; let us learn how to use them."

When Napoleon was banished and David proscribed, other influences began to emerge. In his book *The Spirit of Christianity* Châteaubriand set everyone talking about religion. The French rediscovered their cathedrals and substituted the inhabitants of paradise for those of Olympus. However, as often happens, the style degenerated from one excess to another and the taste for the medieval and the so-called Gothic led to further imitations, more or less successful.

Another influence began to appear early in the nineteenth century. This was the Romantic movement, the devotees of which preferred sensibility, imagination and fancy to reason. In other words, individualism challenged the despotism of the rules of literary composition and the

Design for diadems: pencil drawing. Italian, c. 1815. The Cooper Union Museum for the Arts of Decoration, New York.

classical style. This set the scene for the famous controversy in the Beaux Arts between line and color as exemplified by Ingres and Delacroix, the former representing the Ecole des Beaux Arts and the Institute, the latter the independents, the poets and the young people.

The Restoration of the Bourbons changed the decorative motifs of jewelry, replacing the bees and eagles of the empire by the Bourbon fleur-de-lys, but it did not improve either the standard or the prestige of the art. The old and powerless Louis XVIII did nothing to restore a luxurious and urbane way of life. The king and the style restored by the returning émigrés both belonged to the *Ancien Régime.* Many of them had sold their jewels to keep body and soul together, and they had to be content to appear at court in ornaments which were more showy than valuable. They formed a curious antithesis to the former officials of the empire who had rallied to the Bourbons. Their contrasting clothes and hairstyles were echoed by the jewels of Nitot and Foncier alongside the surviving works of Pouget and Ménière.

When commercial relations were resumed, many less valuable stones such as topazes, amethysts, aquamarines and crystals could be imported from Mexico and Brazil. These could be set in gold to make impressive but comparatively cheap jewels. "In jewelry these second-rate stones were even used at the center of the main motif. Diamonds were set in big, striking silver settings. The setters left large strips of metal around the adjoining stones in order to get the maximum effect for the minimum expense. Wild flowers and ears of corn figured prominently in the finest pieces of jewelry." (H. Vever)

A degree of austerity was regarded as good taste. Prevailing fashion lent itself to this, with lace ruffles and high necks which made the wearing of necklaces impractical and long leg-of-mutton sleeves which permitted no more than a single bracelet at the wrist, worn over the sleeve. Headdresses consisted of caps trimmed with marabou and *esprits* (feather aigrettes) rather than hair ornaments. They contented themselves with pinning on ornaments *en pampilles* with a diamond at the top and feathers at the base. Corsets reappeared and waists grew more slender until they became positive wasp-waists by the reign of Louis Philippe.

"In 1827 Mlle. Mars, playing a medieval character, wore a girdle of goldwork with loose ends falling far down the front. The Duchess de Berry adopted this style, which can be seen in the portrait of the princess by Dubois-Drahonnet now in the Amiens museum." (H. Vever)

Most of the articles on jewelry which appeared in the magazines of this period dealt only with gold ornaments as opposed to jewels.

"Gold necklaces in the form of a snake are always fashionable." (1821)

"*Semaines* (a form of ring) are very popular. We have seen some with stones of seven different shades, the name of each stone beginning with the same letter as a day of the week." (1827)

"The chains which ladies wear around their necks are becoming so bulky that they will soon be a formidable weight. At the bottom of these chains a massive cross or a seal or some other Gothic-style ornament is sometimes suspended." (*Petit Courrier de Dames,* February 20, 1828)

The Duchess de Berry was young and elegant and she restored a degree of zest to the court of Charles X. She organized the famous Mary Stuart Quadrille at the Tuileries in which they attempted to revive the court of Scotland. "On that evening in January, 1829 the duchess wore ornaments worth more than three million specially set by Bapst with stones borrowed from the Crown Jewels. The amusing aspect of this very select occasion was the contrast between Mary Stuart's contemporaries who, in pursuit of authenticity, had sacrified their beards, and an equal number of less conscientious partners with magnificent ornaments in the purest Restoration style." (H. Vever)

"The present-day composer spectators," writes M. Henri Bouchot in his book *La Restauration* (Paris 1893), "mingled with sixteenth century nobles, and at any moment one might come upon the curious spectacle of Catherine dei Medici in the company of a colonel of the royal guard, an Ultra minister face to face with Mary of Lorraine,

Dubois-Drahonnet: portrait of the Duchess de Berry. Musée de Picardie, Amiens.

or the Connetable de Montmorency waltzing with a first empire Marshall's wife. In every direction there was a wonderfully gay panorama of white dresses tripping lightly with gold brocades, shimmering velvets and embroideries. At five o'clock in the morning, the "gallop" drew queens, princes and nobles into a fiendish farandole, mingling all ranks, breaking all the rules of etiquette and wreaking havoc with toilettes. At this moment a fringe bearing nearly half a million worth of diamonds was torn from Mary Stuart's dress by an audacious boot. What did it matter? The gallop went on. It would have been a fine thing to stop it for a mishap like this! However, it turned up next day under a seat."

From 1820 to 1830, everyone was buying ornaments of polished and faceted steel. There were also bracelets of matt gold made all in one piece like a gold ingot round the arm, which would have been thought hideous if they had not been the fashion." (1823). As for the great *parures* adorned with insipid engraving or a little chasing, they were scattered with stones of little value and had, in the last analysis, no claim to artistry." (H. Vever)

Several of the finest empire craftsmen had to retire, and their establishments passed into the hands of new owners. In 1815, F.R. Nitot, the emperor's former jeweler, was compelled for political reasons to retire from business, leaving his establishment to his foreman Fossin, who was appointed royal jeweler in 1830 by Louis Philippe.

The Almanac or the Palais Royal for 1828 mentions, among other working jewelers,

Franchet, jeweler to Mme. la Duchesse de Berry and Mlle. d'Orleans;

Daux, who specialized in "brilliants, colored stones and bracelets, and all the finest and most finished pieces of this sort;"

Janisset . . . "the most costly diamonds;"

Bernauda . . . "jeweler to H.R.H. Mme. la Duchesse de Berry," who made all kinds of jewelry in platinum and gold, fancy chains, etc.

Bernauda was not the first to use platinum, the metal which was to become so important in gem-setting. Before the Revolution a jeweler named Jeannety who studied chemistry with Lavoisier, had investigated platinum. Later on, with the cooperation of Vauqueline, he exhibited platinum jewelry and chemical instruments from his establishment at the Year X (1802) exhibition. The jury awarded him a silver medal and recognized him as the originator of a new branch of metallurgy. In 1815, the Société d'Encouragement awarded him a medal for his "valuable work, which has brought him much honor and little profit ." (Bapst-Ménière, *Joaillerie de la Couronne*)

Ménière, who had been a royal jeweler under the *Ancien Régime,* had married his daughter to his colleague Jacques-Eberhard Bapst in 1797. The Bapst family originated in Swabia but the house they established in Paris enjoyed a high reputation. Jacques's two sons Constant and Charles followed in their father's footsteps and the house took the name of "Bapst Brothers." Louis XVIII commissioned them to unset Napoleon I's ornaments one after the other, among which were one in diamonds worth 1,645,000 francs and another in emeralds, both dating to 1810. By 1820 all these jewels had been reset.

"The designs of the state ornaments were executed under the supervision of J. Eberhard Bapst aided by Seiffert, then accredited designer to the house. They were carried out by Charles-Frédéric Bapst, who controlled the workshop for more than fifty years. This was where the coronation regalia for Charles X were made, notably the crown, the sword (now in the Louvre) and a very remarkable hat-button. The crown, a real jeweler's masterpiece, was not dismantled until 1854. However, the setting without the stones was kept until the crown diamonds were sold. It is a pity that the Third Republic, less tolerant and more touchy than its predecessors, insisted on destroying this harmless setting, which is so interesting from a technical point of view." (H. Vever)

Necklace: gold and chrysoprases with brilliants and rubies. French, c. 1830. Presented by Dr. Joan Evans. Victoria & Albert Museum, London.

Here are the fashionable jewels of the last years of the Restoration, as described in the magazines of the era.

"The collection of corals of H.R.H. Mme. la Duchesse d'Angoulême offers the most interesting and elegant ornaments to the curious and to customers every day. The caskets for sale there are made in exquisite taste." (*L'Observateur des Modes,* 1819)

"We have seen necklaces known as 'sheaf' necklaces for persons inclined to embonpoint. They are made of beautifully modeled ears of corn which hang down at regular intervals. The central medallion is formed of one or more diamonds surrounded by interlaced ears."

"Several leading jewelers have set a few ornaments with coral cameos. The necklace is a row of antique heads artistically set in gold, and is so elegant that it leads us to believe that this type of ornament could well come back into fashion. At the last ball at Saint Cloud the Marquise de . . . . . wore a whole set of them." (1821)

The assassination of Duc de Berry on February 13, 1820 brought mourning back into fashion.

"Black jewelry is all the rage. Jet, iron and everything black is used in all sorts of ways. All our jeweler's shops seem to be dedicated to mourning."

"Diamonds have become the only ornament for ladies, even the young ones; but they are employed in many different ways—a butterfly poised on a wreath of real flowers, or a tiara, its simplicity emphasized by its splendid effect, or a comb with stones set along the top like a diadem, or ears of corn . . ."

"Today we noticed a headdress which combined three diadems: the first, worn on the forehead, was completely made of diamonds; the second was made of flowers and the third was of silver ears of wheat. A diamond comb was fixed at the back."

"Pearl necklaces are for elegant young ladies of twenty going to shine at the ball."

"Diamond *rivières* are for dowagers. Emeralds and amethysts for married women in good society . . ."

Garnets are for young girls, amber necklaces for grisettes."

"Steel is for concert days, jet for formal dinners and paste for actresses." (1821)

After the July revolution in 1830, Charles X, Louis XVIII's successor, abdicated and the Chambre proclaimed Louis Philippe, Duc of Orleans, King of the French. The new king's private life was more cosy than luxurious, and the fêtes at the "Château" which the Legitimists proudly boycotted bore no resemblance to those of the *Ancien Régime.* Nobility of blood was superseded by nobility of wealth. The Faubourg Saint-Honoré displaced the Faubourg Saint-Germain. Major industry replaced domestic crafts and commerce and finance went from strength to strength. Capitalism had arrived.

Lamartine had said, "France is bored," and Guizot had replied, "Get rich!" The financiers of the Chausée d'Antin greatly undermined the social and political influence of the aristocracy of the Faubourg Saint-Germain.

Queen Amélie's sober family soirées around a work-table were not without dignity and the atmosphere of bourgeois virtue which prevailed there pleased the middle classes, but the jeweler profited very little from a way of life like this.

"They confined themselves to setting brilliants in necklaces and *rivières* with big, thick, heavy settings. Diamonds were also made into insipid corsage ornaments of three adjoining brooches placed one above the other, with fringes and clusters of cascading collet-set stones hanging from outlandish flowers and thin leaves worked

(top to bottom, left to right)
Brooch: gold and topaz, c. 1830.
Pendant: gold, emeralds, rubies and an amethyst. Paris, 1838.
Brooch: gold and topaz. Bourbon Restoration period.
Bracelet: gold and colored stones. Bourbon Restoration period.
Bracelet clasp: gold and cameo. Reign of Louis Philippe.
Bracelet clasp: gold, silver and cameo on carnelian background. Bourbon Restoration period.
Bracelet clasp: gold enamel, pink topazes and pearls. Reign of Louis Philippe.
Musée des Arts Décoratifs, Paris.

without taste that were totally unknown to botany," wrote Massin. This artist and surpassing technician was the author of *Etude et Rapport sur la Joaillerie* (1890). "There was one notable product of the age, however, which had no antecedents and was to last for a long time since it was at the height of its popularity at the beginning of my apprenticeship and was still being made in 1855. Two symmetrical knots were placed on either side of the head above the temples. They were joined by a light strip running from one to the other over the forehead a little above the hairline. As always, long strings of collet-set jewels hung from these side knots and fell in showers or sheafs of lilies-of-the-valley. This fashion, which seems very antiquated to modern taste, originated in the harmony it established between the headdresses and hairstyles of the women who wore their hair in flat bands at that time."

About 1840 the taste for Viennese jewelry spread to Paris. Indeed, it must be admitted that at that time the Viennese way of executing the arrangement and construction of flowers and foliage was superior. Their method consisted of making a bunch of cold-drawn wires on which all the details of the ornament were threaded in their appropriate contours. However, this process lacked solidity, and the Paris jewelers thought of cutting out all the sprays (known as the skeleton) on a gold-plated silver plaque. Perpendicular supports were then driven in all over, and flowers, leaves and collet-set stones were all held in place like this. "The result was a sturdy piece but a deplorable effect." (H. Vever)

The art of jewelry became more international than ever. Court and town dress and customs became standardized and it would be easier to classify jewelry by the occasions for which it was worn than by its style and design. For court and high society tended increasingly to recognize two sorts of entertainments—daytime and evening. For the former, jewels were simpler and less obtrusive, except for coronations and royal weddings. For the latter, on the contrary, there seemed to be no limits. This is proved by official portraits and by the splendid ornaments which have survived. There were, however, some excesses which modern taste finds offensive.

It was not unusual for a queen to wear several rows of pearls and a necklace of huge brilliants, three or four brooches, pendants and decorations, not to mention earrings, bracelets, rings and her diadem. This was a survival of the very early royal tradition which we have traced from the fifteenth century. It was still very powerful at the end of the nineteenth century. But the profusion of gems and pearls which was an essential part of royal dress for so long is all the more striking in that, instead of extending all over the body, it tended to concentrate on the neck, hands and head. Clothes and jewelry were much less interdependent and differences in style, design, gems and settings can be seen more clearly. In the last analysis there were probably fewer gems and pearls in the outfit of a nineteenth century princess than on the costume of a Renaissance queen, but in the former case they were nearly all concentrated on her neck and head while the latter might wear them right down to the hem of her robe so that they sometimes gave the impression of overstepping the bounds of good taste.

One of the most important discoveries of this period would paradoxically accentuate the difference between day and evening dress. This was electric light. Its chief advantage, according to its supporters, was that it was as bright as daylight. But everyone soon realized that it changed some colors and brought out the sparkle of precious stones, especially diamonds, far better than daylight. When this new form of lighting was installed in some theaters of the major capitals, e.g. the Savoy Theatre in London in 1881, it was an important turning point not only in theatrical history but in that of jewelry. The diamond benefited most from this discovery at the expense of colored stones. However, this was not the only reason

Parure: silver, enamel, amethysts and pearls. French, mid-nineteenth century. Musée des Arts Décoratifs, Paris.

why emeralds, rubies and sapphires were comparatively neglected. The discovery of diamonds in South Africa, which will be discussed later, was also very influential in changing fashion. The increasingly pronounced difference between day and evening wear also militated in favor of the diamond, since the simpler type of jewels which freely combined precious and semi-precious stones was increasingly confined to everyday wear.

Throughout the nineteenth century there were two distinct categories of jewelry: formal ornaments, chiefly of pearls and diamonds and usually following traditional patterns but remarkably well made, and ornaments for everyday wear, which showed much greater variety and were more susceptible to changes in fashion. Color, obtained by using precious and semi-precious stones side by side, played an important part in everyday jewelry. The ornaments of this second category were also often extremely fine.

A third category shortly made its appearance: imitation jewelry. Once even the finest craftsmen and the greatest nobles had not disdained imitation jewelry, but now that it was being mass produced cheaply, neither the design nor the workmanship conferred any distinction upon it. With mass produced costume jewelry, the typical bad taste of the era invaded jewelry, and it was against this tendency that the Art Nouveau artists raised their standard. Apart from a few very fine sets of crystals and some pieces made early in the century, artificial jewelry does not merit any more attention than it did in the eighteenth century. On the other hand, less valuable materials such as coral, ivory, amethysts, garnet and jet, of which some very fine jewels were made during this century, deserve much more attention than in the preceding eras.

Before finishing this short study of fashion, we must briefly describe the development of male dress, even if it ended negatively as regards jewelry. Every nineteenth century author who touched on this question expressed his disgust at the monotonous ugliness of men's clothes. However, this drab and execrated costume would be universally adopted, especially after Beau Brummel had formulated his strict rules: no more color, no more fancy wear and certainly no more jewelry. Even shoe buckles were abandoned in favor of sober lacings and only sleeve-buttons, cravat-pins and signet rings were tolerated. There was a final break between man and jewelry, between male costume and fancy work, and this is fairly indicative of the spirit of the times. Never had luxury and triviality been so sharply defined, and never had jewelry and ornament been so rigidly regarded as minor arts.

Paradoxically, the nineteenth century was the age of the gold prospectors, great discoveries of diamond sources and organization of the market in precious stones. Thanks to the vast extent of their empire, the British benefited most from the new resources which opened up in the second half of the nineteenth century. Legend ran riot around these fabulous discoveries which made the fortunes of South African farmers, stockbreeders and adventurers in a few years.

In fact, these events were perfectly straightforward, and anyone who wants to believe in the intervention of the supernatural must also admit the existence of sheer bad luck.

In 1867, just over a hundred years ago, a South African Dutch farmer named Schalk van Nierkerk was quite naturally visiting his friend Jacob, who lived near the Orange River. Jacob's children were playing knucklebones in the garden and Nierkerk was watching them out of the corner of his eye while he chatted with his friend, when his attention was caught by one of the pebbles the children were using. The more he looked at it the stranger he found it, and in the end he mentioned it to his host. "Take it, by all means," said Jacob, and Schalk van Nierkerk went away with the stone that had intrigued him so much. He showed it to a merchant friend of his named O'Reilly, who took it to some experts. They turned

Ruby *parure* of Queen Theresa of Bavaria: gold, silver, rubies, spinels and brilliants. By K. Rieländer of Munich, 1830. Ordered by King Ludwig I. Nymphenburg Castle, Munich.

up their noses at it and tried to discourage the farmer. However, he persevered, and that is how Jacob's childrens' pebble arrived one fine day on the work-table of a Cape mineralogist named Dr. Atherstone. He formally identified it as a diamond worth £500 sterling; this was the price paid by the governor, who bought it.

So a diamond had been found near the Orange River. But was it an exception, a chance find, or even a hoax? Nobody wanted to count on it too much or jump to conclusions, but tongues began to wag and everyone soon knew that Nierkerk was interested in certain stones. The story soon came to the ears of a native witch-doctor who saw his chance at a good bargain. It so happened that he had a stone endowed with magical virtues with which he cured the sick and drove out evil spirits. He offered it to Nierkerk. The Dutchman did not hesitate. He gave everything he had, his horse, his ten oxen and his five hundred sheep, in exchange for the magic stone which he then sold for £11,000 to a dealer. He in his turn sold it to Lord Dudley for £25,000. It was a diamond weighing 83.5 carats, also from the Orange River district. It is now known as the Star of South Africa.

Two years passed since Nierkerk's first discovery and excitement began to seethe in South Africa. In England, however, skepticism is always the rule and an expert named Gregory declared openly that there was no reason to believe that there were diamonds in these distant lands. (For a long time afterwards a wildly mistaken decision was known as a "Gregory.") But all along the Vaal and the Orange Rivers, thousands of people arrived and quartered the ground into numerous little claims. There was soon ten thousand of them digging in the river bed. From 1870 on diamonds were found in the ground, first on one farm and then on another. The price of land soared to dizzy heights. The Kimberley region was invaded. Among the people who settled there was a young Englishman with a strong personality and an amazing capacity for work. His name was Cecil Rhodes. Two years after his arrival he founded the first company from which the mighty de Beers group arose. At the end of the nineteenth century, the Diamond Syndicate, which included the richest London buyers, established production controls to enable them to keep prices high.

Just about this time, Britain took over some equally rich lands such as Upper Burma, where the Mogok mines, which had been worked for several hundred years, produced rubies and sapphires. Another British company would dominate the market in precious stones from 1887. It should not be forgotten that emeralds are also found in South Africa and Australia, and that the latter country also produces opals and gold. British business consequently prospered immensely, and their treasury was enriched by such commandeered or presented gems as the Timur Ruby and the celebrated Koh-i-Noor, the "Mountain of Light," which weighed 191 carats when it was given to Queen Victoria in 1850. Recut by Voorsanger, who was summoned from Amsterdam and who worked on it with Garrard's help for thirty-eight hours, the Koh-i-Noor was reduced to 108 carats.

The British occupied a leading place in the history of nineteenth century jewelry, if only by virtue of their political and financial power. We shall see how craftsmen were able to take advantage of this new influx of gold and precious stones. Many other European countries discovered similar riches in their colonies, and the era was more favorable to the production of really good jewelry than any before. Innumerable forms of ornaments were made to commemorate both personal and historic events. It still remained to explore the vast realm of ancient technique, and some Italian jewelers who were soon to enjoy international fame would devote themselves to this task.

Fortunato Pio Castellani opened his shop in Rome in 1814. At first he confined himself to supplying his customers with both luxury and everyday jewels copied from

Bracelet: gold, silver, diamonds and a 7 1/2 carat emerald. English, c. 1820. Garrard Collection, London.

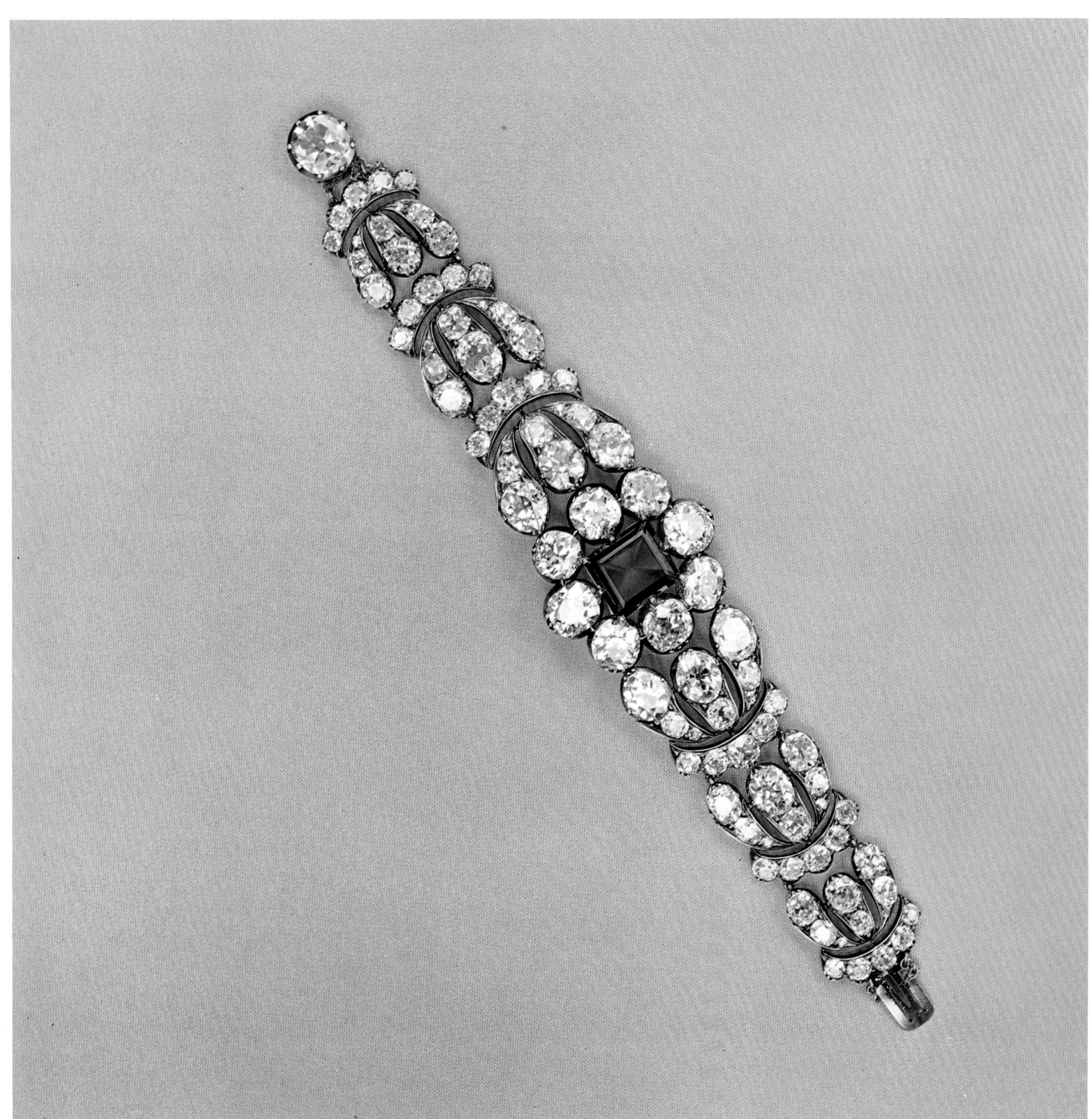

those of London and Paris. However, at that time French and English fashion decreed jewelry *à l'antique,* and in the end, Castellani realized that he was in a better position than his colleagues to draw directly on ancient models. Some Etruscan treasures which created intense public interest had just been unearthed in Italy. Thanks to these, Castellani found his own personal style and succeeded in setting the fashion for Etruscan jewels. The delicate execution of the models seemed, in fact, far beyond the capabilities of Castellani's workmen, particularly as regards the treatment of gold, and his first attempts were not at all encouraging. Etruscan art surrendered its beauty but kept the secret of its technique, and the obstacle seemed insurmountable. By a fortunate combination of circumstances, Castellani managed to find a group of craftsmen in Sant' Angelo in Vado making everyday jewelry. They were using a process handed down from generation to generation which came very close to the Etruscan method. Castellani immediately hired the whole team and took them to Rome where these country craftsmen instructed the town jewelers. The house of Castellani then produced a whole series of "archaeological" jewels in both gold and gems that rapidly became extremely popular.

In 1851, Fortunato retired and left his business to his son Augusto who had served a very thorough apprenticeship in goldworking and jewelry. Etruscan work was still produced, especially after 1858, but it was not the only specialty of the house, which also offered Greek and Renaissance jewelry and made several experiments in the medieval Scandinavian style. Augusto formed a very fine collection of ancient pieces which is now in the British Museum. He traveled a lot, not only in search of rare pieces but to show the models created by his brother in great exhibitions in both Europe and America. Thanks to his reputation as connoisseur and scholar, Augusto was appointed Curator of the Capitol Museum, where a large part of his own collection was deposited. The Castellanis were well known not only for the products of their house but also for their extensive knowledge of styles and techniques. At the beginning of the century they had begun by imitating the jewelers of London and Paris, and a few years later the process was reversed because they inspired not only Giacinto Mellilo of Naples but even Eugene Fontenay and Robert Phillips.

Carlo Giuliano, who is often regarded as the greatest jeweler of the second half of the nineteenth century, was even more famous. He was born in Naples but settled in London just before 1870. Several of his creations can still be seen in London antique shops and in the Victoria and Albert Museum. Giuliano united a thorough knowledge of technique with unquestionable creative gifts. Although the influence of Greek, Etruscan and Renaissance styles and Egyptian and oriental art on his work is obvious, he was able to endow everything he made with real originality. He saw and interpreted ancient jewelry as an artist rather than as an historian or scholar. Even when he produced pieces strongly affected by the influence of Art Nouveau towards the end of his life, he preserved the personal touch which distinguishes his work from all the other jewelry of his era.

He seems to be absolutely typical of the jewelry of the last third of the century, drawing his inspiration from all the styles of the past, from the most distant to the nearest, and attempting to create an entirely new repertoire of forms even in his last years. He paid more attention than most European jewelers to keeping his work as light as possible—and this is particularly true of his "antique" and "Renaissance" jewels. Even the most architectural settings were open work. The play of arabesques and roundels,

(top to bottom)
Castellani: bracelet. Gold and red agate scarabs.
Castellani: necklace of baroque pearls.
Gold bracelet.
Castellani: necklace and earrings. Gold, enamel and chalcedony and onyx cameos by John Brogdon of London. Exhibited in 1867.
Bolckow Bequest, Victoria & Albert Museum, London.

Giuliano: pendant in the Renaissance style. Gold, enamel, rubies and pearls with a sapphire intaglio representing a battle scene in the center. Presented by Henry L. Florence. Victoria & Albert Museum, London.

cunningly combined, gave his larger pendants and brooches an elegance and delicacy that few of his contemporaries could equal. He used shapes, colors and materials, combining spaces and masses, shiny and matt surfaces with amazing ingenuity and skill. It should be remembered that this great Italian artist (like Castellani, Mellilo and some of his less gifted earlier compatriots such as Pasquale Novissimo) found most of his admirers in England, where he settled permanently. For England, particularly during the long reign of Queen Victoria, was enjoying a period of great prosperity and brilliance in which some outstanding jewelry was produced.

For a long time, it has been considered good taste to despise Victorian jewelry, and people who have studied its history tell of some irreparable blunders which were committed because of this misconception. Margaret Flower relates the mishap of a young woman who was given a necklace of dark red stones by her mother-in-law. Believing that they were garnets, she pawned the ornament for a few pounds one day when she was short of ready money. She lost the receipt but did not worry about it until her mother-in-law asked her if she had some objection to wearing rubies. It can easily be imagined how frantically she looked for the pawn ticket and the money lender, but neither was ever seen again.

This story is significant. For a long time, people believed that Victorian jewelry was set either with worthless stones like jet, garnets, amethysts or topazes, or with precious stones in intolerably tasteless settings, in which case they were usually dismantled and only the stones kept. The jewelry of the preceding century has only recently been reinstated. Several scholarly and well-documented books

Jewelry by Giuliano (top to bottom, left to right).
Necklace: gold, enamel, pearls and diamonds.
Necklace: gold, enamel, rubies and garnets.
Pendant: crystal in an enamelled gold mount decorated with pearls and diamonds.
Necklace: gold, enamel, lapis lazuli and pearls.
Wartski Collection, London.

Pugin: bracelet and brooch designed for his third wife Jane Knill and made by John Hardman & Co. English, 1848-50.
Bracelet gold, enamel, rubies, diamonds, turquoises and pearls.
Brooch: gold, enamel, turquoises, garnets and pearls.
Presented by Mrs. C.E. Gladstone. Victoria & Albert Museum, London.

Italian and French jewelry of the nineteenth century (top to bottom, left to right).
Pendant: gold, enamel, pearls and amethysts. By Pasquale Novissimo, c. 1880.
Giuliano: small medallion.
Castellani: earring.
Giuliano: pendant. Gold, enamel, rubies, diamonds and pearls.
Giuliano: pendant.
(center) Froment-Meurice; pendant.
Giuliano: pendant. Gold, enamel, rubies, sapphires, pearls and an onyx cameo with profile portrait of Marie dei Medici.
(below center) Giuliano: ring.
Presented by Miss Linda Novissimo, the Dowager Countess of Crawford and Messrs. C. and A. Giuliano. Victoria & Albert Museum, London.

like those of Margaret Flower and Ernle Bradford have appeared, and there are a number of antique shops in London (Wartski and Cameo Corner are outstanding examples) where veritable treasures may be seen. The most reputable jewelers of Regent Street and Bond Street all have a selection of antique pieces of exceptional quality and richness, and besides this there is an extremely impressive collection in the Victoria and Albert Museum that is calculated to awaken a growing interest in nineteenth century English jewelry. Experts distinguish three styles, corresponding to the three periods of Victoria's reign: from 1837 to 1860, the Romantic period of enquiry and experiment in which sentimental and antique jewelry predominated; from 1860 to 1885, the grand period of rich and abundant production; and the closing years of the century in which the Aesthetic movement set the scene for the appearance of Art Nouveau in reaction against the preceding period.

Before embarking on this highly remarkable reign, let us briefly review the preceding years. England followed French fashions fairly closely as well as filling an important place in European jewelry. The Revolution sharply interrupted French progress, but it must be remembered that quite a number of French art treasures found their way across the Channel during these troubled times. The styles of Paris and Versailles continued to lead the way in England even when they seemed to be completely forgotten in their own home.

Then came the Romantic movement that overran all forms of art about the time of Victoria's accession in 1837. England would discover the charm of the Middle Ages, the Tudor style and the early Renaissance. Ladies wore *ferronnières* and heavy medieval belts loaded with accessories, and transfixed their chignons with daggers and arrows. Robert Phillips and Pugin were the most celebrated jewelers and designers of this period. The latter specialized in the pseudo-Gothic style probably based on architecture, stained glass and miniatures rather thanthe actual jewels of the twelfth and thirteenth centuries. He was particularly fond of necklaces and bracelets of quatrefoil medallions set with tiny stones that were perfect examples of the adaptation of the "troubador" style to jewelry. This was sometimes achieved at the expense of a degree of heaviness that was not corrected by the influence of the Frenchman Froment-Meurice, who began to affect English work about 1840, as did the German Wagner and the Italian Rudolphi who settled in Paris. The sentimentality mentioned above, which was particularly prevalent in England, was an inseparable part of this universal medievalism.

Another important feature was the increasing popularity of new styles, with the vogue for Castellani's jewels, the heavily illustrated book *Ninevah and its Remains* (1848) by Layard, and the discovery of North African art which followed the French conquest of Algeria.

In all the jewels of this type, it seems that semi-precious and gem stones were used as frequently as precious stones. This was not just because the selected models called for this kind of material but also because the French nobility who came home again after the Bourbon restoration, reacting against the *nouveaux riches* of the empire, imposed their taste for severer, heavier and less expensive jewelry inspired by a past that belonged to them alone.

For several years, the whole of Europe adopted the Parisian taste for coral, ivory, jet and topazes. When the Duchess of Aumale married the Prince of the Two Sicilies in 1845 he gave her a whole set of coral ornaments. Dark red and pale pink coral were particularly popular. It was made into ornaments and also into all sorts of other things, even toys such as rattles.

The ancient world and the Middle Ages furnished an extensive range of motifs. Cameos enjoyed such unparalleled popularity that the Italian production centers could not meet the demand. Queen Victoria, who was particularly fond of them, encouraged the art in England where Brett and Ronca were distinguished practitioners.

Reliquary brooch belonging to the Empress Eugénie. Musée du Louvre, Paris.

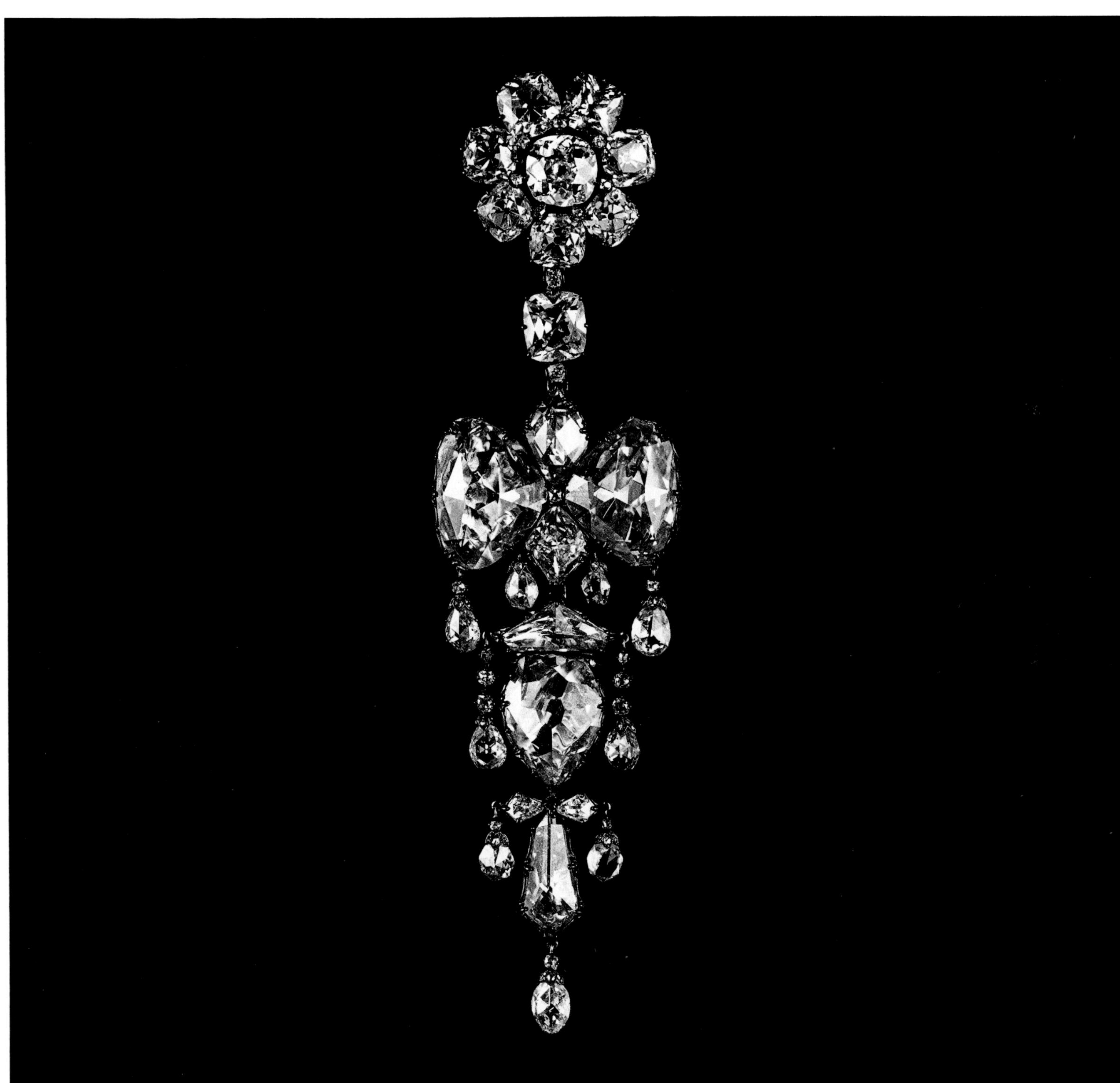

Jewelers also drew their inspiration from nature—the somewhat untrammeled nature that was so beloved at the time. Ivy, vine-tendrils and twisted branches were popular motifs, and were only surpassed by the snake, which carried all before it as far as rings and bracelts were concerned. The queen owned some very fine examples in enamelled gold set with gems.

In the first half of the nineteenth century, England was notable for the use of large cabochons allied to precious stones. Topazes and amethysts were sometimes inlaid with small brilliants or rubies which emphasized their color and effect.

Jet, chiefly found at Whitby on the Yorkshire coast, was also widely used. The founders of this flourishing industry were an innkeeper, John Carter and a painter, Robert Jefferson, who began to carve simple necklaces and crosses with very rudimentary tools such as knives and files about 1800. One day they succeeded in selling one of their ornaments for a guinea, which encouraged them to persevere and expand their business. They started their workshop just before 1810 and began to use imporved equipment. they met with such success that they soon attracted pupils and imitators. There were fifty workshops by the middle of the century and two hundred by 1873. Jet is the ideal material for mourning jewelry which was always widely worn in England. When William IV died in 1837, it was more popular than ever before, and at the death of Prince Albert in 1862 Queen Victoria made the whole court wear jet ornaments, and all her attendants had to share in her mourning.

Ten years before this sad event, England had had her hour of triumph with the Great International Exhibition, which was an important turning point in the history of the nineteenth century decorative arts and industries.

The contemporary catalogue still makes amusing and instructive reading. Each nation displayed its own specialties, e.g. America with its orthopaedic equipment and superior false teeth. Fabrics, machinery, raw materials and a great many inventions were shown. Most countries displayed jewelry, but the catalogue expatiates at length on the British section. The firm of Hardman prided itself on creations based on Pugin's designs. Morel and Co. offered a diamond and ruby floral ornament which could be taken to pieces and the various parts worn as brooches. Rowlands of Regent Street showed several sets of diamonds and emeralds and a bracelet set with diamonds and rubies. The court jeweler Garrard showed ornaments set with opals, brilliants, sapphires, pearls, diamonds and even rubies in the section reserved for him. This firm's reputation was already solidly established. It was they who made Queen Victoria's crown in 1838, that featured the famous gems from the royal treasury, the "Stuart" and St. Edward's sapphires and the Black Prince's Ruby.

Many British jewelers took part in this exhibition, and with them was Mr. Hope with his famous diamond which the queen mentions in the entry in her journal for July 12th. It was No. 73 in the catalogue; a blue diamond set in a medallion surrounded by brilliants, regarded as unique because of its weight and size.

The exhibition was opened with great ceremony on May 1, a great day for the queen who saw it as the recognition of her kingdom's wealth and glory and was delighted to associate Prince Albert, the promoter of the display, with its success and fame. Exhausted but happy, the queen noted in her journal after describing her admiration, "I forgot to mention that I wore a silk dress of pink and silver, with a diamond ray diadem and a little crown at the back . . . all the rest of my jewels being diamonds." A Winterhalter painting at Windsor immortalizes the queen's costume for the ceremony.

The 1851 exhibition was a sort of milestone marking the end of the first stage. It established Britain's reputation in the eyes of the world. About 1860, Victorian jewelers embarked upon the second period with even

Sprays of brilliants set in silver. Gold brooch set with diamonds. English, first half of the nineteenth century. Cory Bequest, Victoria & Albert Museum, London.

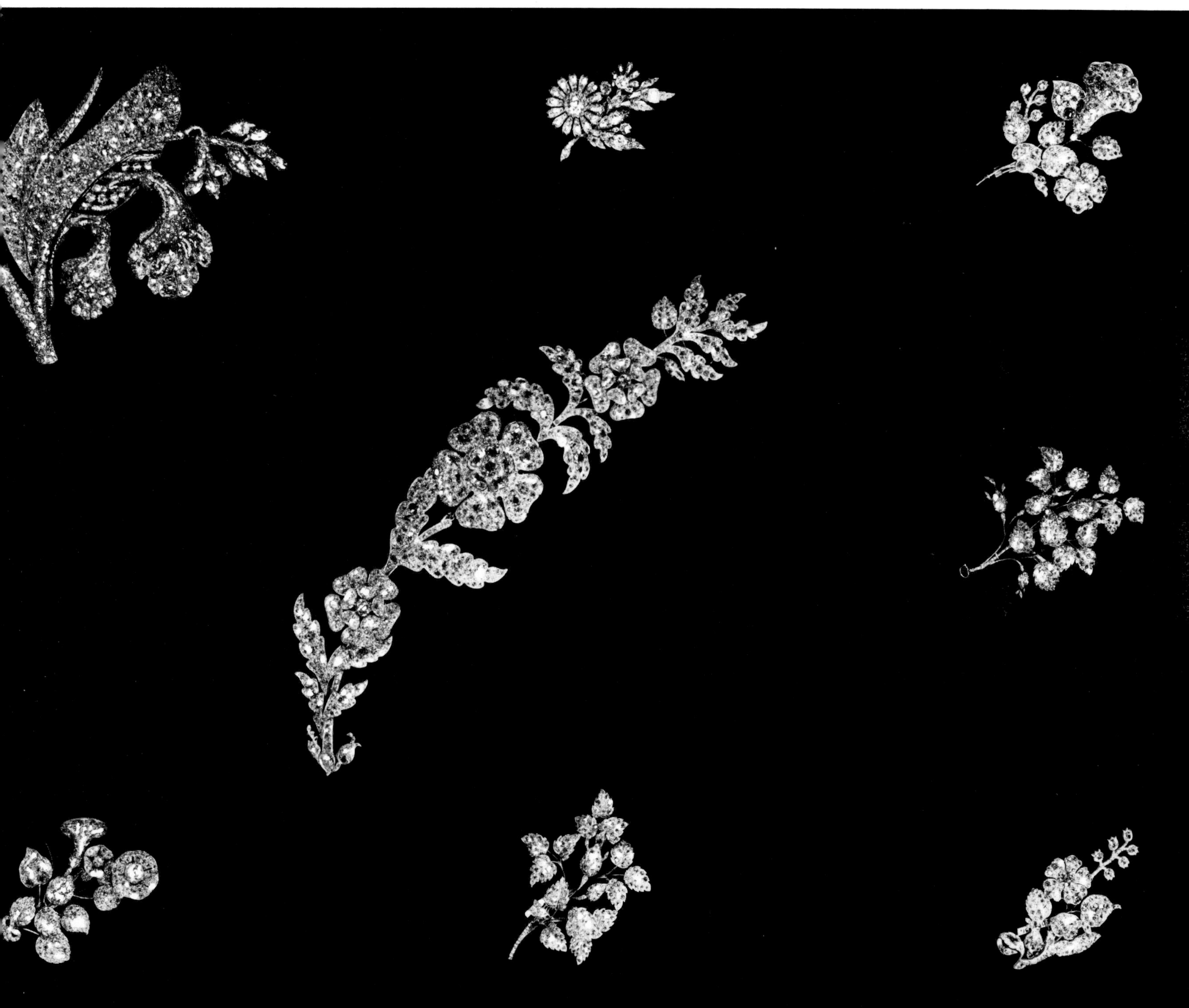

greater boldness. Output was greater and more varied than ever before. This was the heyday of Scottish and Celtic jewelry as well as pieces in the antique style (the house of Brogden specialized in these), Chinese, Arabian and Turkish jewels, and Renaissance pendants. All these pieces were mostly set in gold, silver being increasingly confined to costume jewelry. For several more years, colored and semi-precious stones were acceptable. There were a great many amethysts, topazes and chrysoberyls inlaid with tiny brilliants, and *habillées* cameos, i.e. cameos decorated with diamonds in a gold setting.

Another typically English fashion that sprang up in this period was "sporting jewelry," i.e., jewelry with motifs drawn from sports such as riding and tennis. There were little brooches in the shape of a racket with a pearl to represent the ball, horses completely covered with brilliants with an enamelled gold rider saddles, bridles and whips. During his visit to England, Napoleon III bought several pieces of this type and launched the fashion in Paris.

Then, ten years later, fashion moved very decisively toward colorless jewelry chiefly featuring diamonds and pearls. Settings became more and more light and invisible. Tiaras, which could often be worn as necklaces, were usually openwork. Abstract and natural motifs reappeared during the 1880s, violets and wild roses blossoming on every ornament. There were also many insects and beetles pinned apparently at random to shawls, tulle scarves and even parasols. This was the period when ladies at the court or the opera wore extraordinary *parures* of seven or eight matching pieces all on the same theme carried out in diamonds. Most of our information about them comes from paintings, engravings and photographs because very few have survived. A brooch or necklace can still be found but the rest of the set has usually been dismantled. Only pictures, drawings, and mementos survive of these pieces, which were unquestionably the most costly English jewels of the nineteenth century, while less expensive pieces—which are less worth modernizing—have been preserved much more frequently. However, the evidence indicates that from 1880 to 1890, fashion was dominated by diamond *parures,* which perhaps caused the violent reaction against them at the end of the century.

Indeed, it seems that people grew tired of so much wealth and perfection. This was not just minority exclusiveness. To wear diamonds during the day was regarded as a sign of bad taste, and affected trade so much that the association of British jewelers appealed in their distress to the Princess of Wales to try to launch a fashion to combat these evil tendencies. But the revolution in tastes was too deep-rooted to be reversed. The tradition of jewelry in the grand manner survived, but it was now confined to ornaments for balls, the court and the opera. Ornaments with precious stones were considered unsuitable for everyday wear.

In this period, women were adopting an aggressive attitude that sometimes went so far as to produce an impression of perversity, if not outright scandal. They claimed greater freedom and the right to control their own lives. They extended their contacts with the world at large, walked out unescorted, met people from all walks of life and were often ashamed, in the presence of the misery they found, to wear very costly jewels. This was a completely new phenomenon. Never before had anyone dreamed that the question could arise. The wealthy enjoyed unshakable rights and privileges. These were now being hotly contested and women, who for a long time had nothing to do with social problems, suddenly awoke to the fact that to advertise wealth and luxury can be an outrage.

This was not the only guilt feeling that troubled the end of the century. The people of this period, who loved the grandiose stage of their triumphs so dearly and tried so hard to convince themselves of their own success, now began to doubt the value of their discoveries and creations, and to ask themselves bluntly if, instead of creating a style, they had not rather helped to degrade everything they had borrowed by handing it over to industry. They believed that they had only preserved the letter, and killed the spirit. Did not the charm and even the value of objects

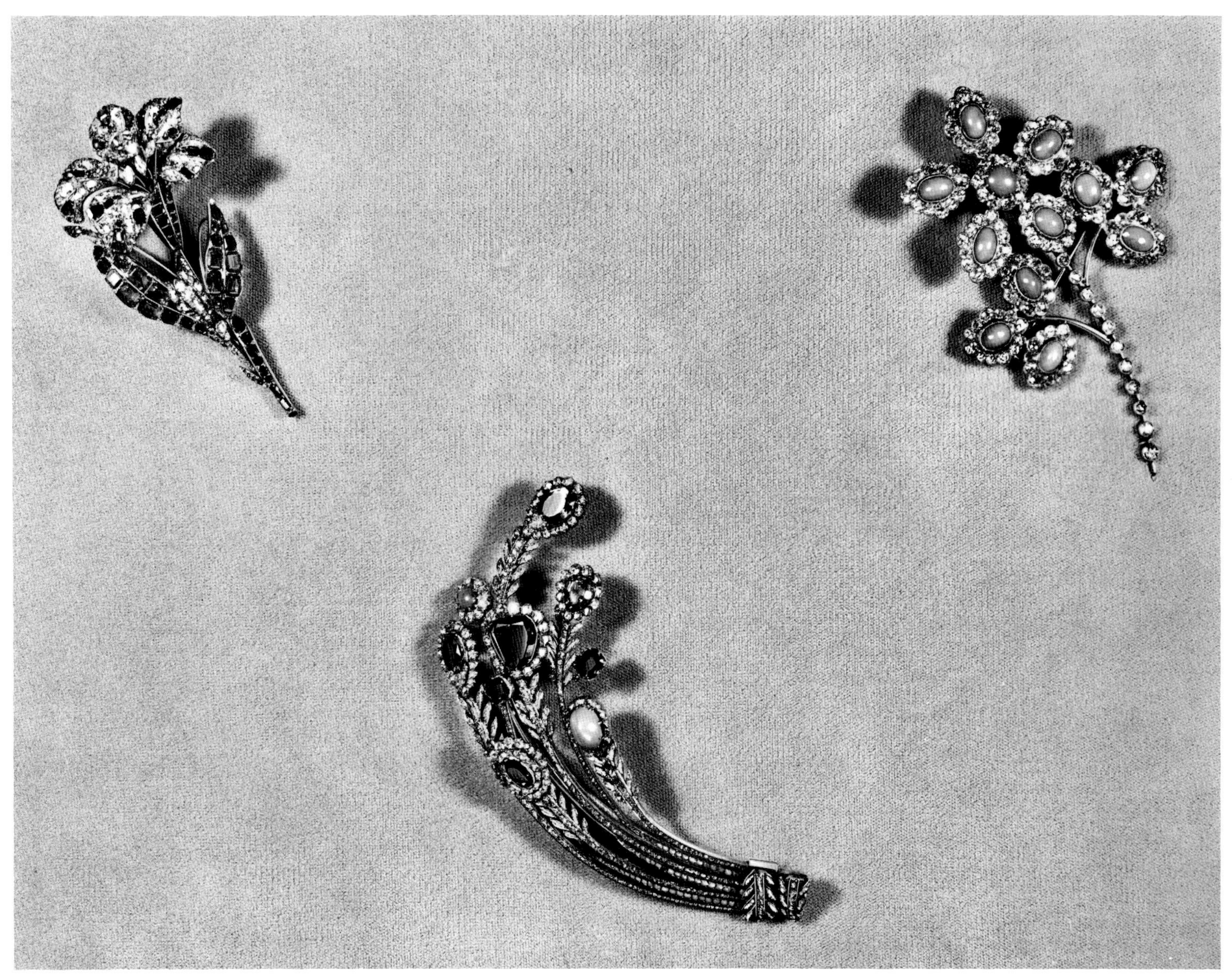

English brooches: (top left) Gold, silver, rubies, diamonds and emeralds: first half of the nineteenth century; (top right) Gold, silver, diamonds and turquoises: c. 1870. (below) Gold, turquoises, diamonds and colored stones: c. 1860-70. Cory Bequest, Victoria & Albert Museum, London.

Giuliano: brooch: Gold, a diamond, rubies and chrysoprase pendant. Late nineteenth century. Presented by Miss E. Costello. Victoria & Albert Museum, London.

from a bygone age largely come from the human errors and inadequacies that had always been recognizable in them? In the last analysis, is not the sole value of an object the amount of love that has been put into it? What are gold and diamonds if they have not been specially fashioned and supplied by one person to another? From this disgust with luxury, extravagance and inhuman mechanical perfection the Aesthetic movement was born. It was, perhaps only an exaggerated form of Romanticism, but it affected the fashion and style of the times—nowadays we would call it the environment—in an undeniable way.

The moving spirits and prophets of the Aesthetic movement were the Preraphaelites and William Morris. They were sneered at, laughed at and caricatured, but one way or another they were ultimately followed. The repertoire of motifs changed and returned to the most natural forms and the softest lines, to more spontaneous, often asymmetrical designs. Colors became delicate and subtle. Mauves, yellows and tender greens copied from fragile spring shades were popular. Cabochon amethysts, emeralds and opals were preferred to the hard glitter of faceted stones.

One of the greatest artists of this period was a jewelry designer named Charles Robert Ashbee. He was not interested in showy effects or in market prices, but in spontaneous treatment and harmonious materials and shades. His designs were floral or abstract and his favorite materials, pink topazes set in grey gold or amethysts, which he allied to silver to give a brooch or necklace a deliberately lustreless look. Then came Nelson and Edith Dawson, Arthur Gaskin and his wife, Fred Robinson, George J. Frampton and Henry Wilson. All these artists and craftsmen concentrated on everyday jewelry, rarely attempting formal design, but they affected it all the same.

Diamond and sapphire necklace, formerly the property of the Princess of Baden, Grand Duke Michael of Russia and the Duke of Harewood. Second half of the nineteenth century. Christie Collection, London.

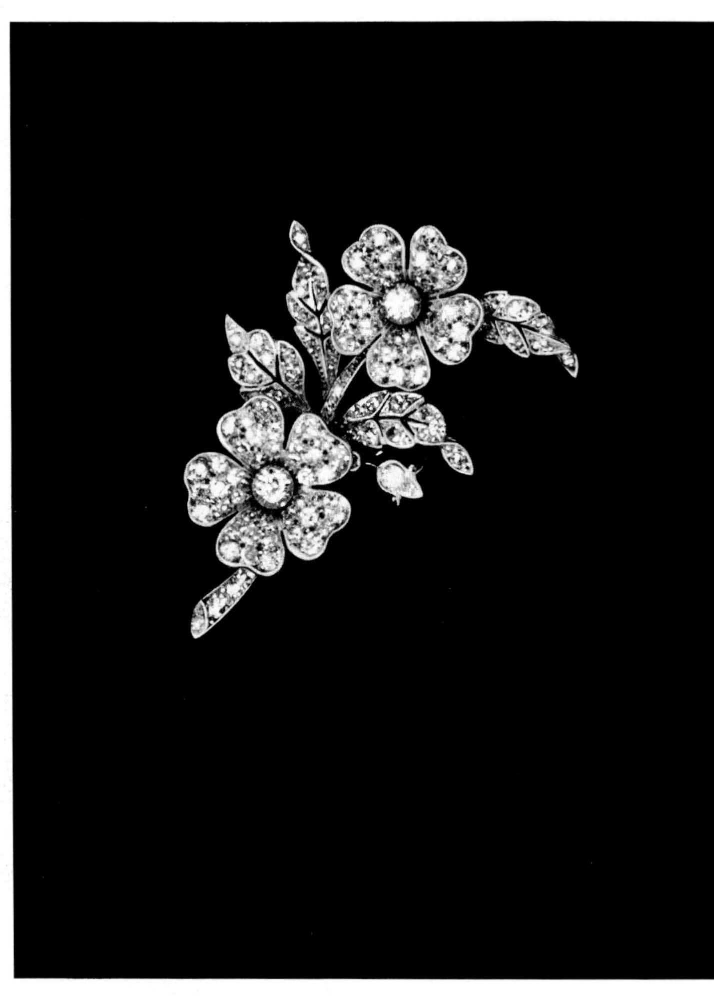

Brooch: two flowers entirely carried out in brilliants. Victorian period. Wartski Collection, London.

High society began to wear opals and moonstones. Plants, animals and asymmetric designs began to be seen in tiaras and necklaces.

In 1886, the British staged an exhibition including many Indian pieces, which caught the public fancy. A few years later, all Europe applauded Sarah Bernhardt as Cleopatra and the Egyptian jewelry she wore so lavishly helped the development of fashion and profoundly influenced taste. Art Nouveau jewelers would soon combine all these trends brilliantly and succeed in making them acceptable even in the most splendid ornaments. This is why the Aesthetic movement, for all its excesses and limitations, deserves mention right from the start.

On December 10, 1848, after the 1848 revolution and Louis Philippe's departure for Britain, Prince Louis-Napoleon Bonaparte became President of the Republic. On December 2, 1852, the Prince-President was proclaimed Emperor of the French by plebiscite. He wanted to court popularity as well as to exercise absolute power, so, to gain the approval of the laboring classes, he instituted a number of public works, encouraged agriculture, industry and commerce, created welfare institutions and reestablished credit. This policy was highly beneficial to a nation that was still suffering from the effects of June 1848.

The Prince-President gave brilliant fêtes at the Elysée Palace to which the cream of the community attended. The president's cousin, Princess Mathilde, did the honors. He was particularly anxious to promote a revival of business. After the National Exhibition of Industrial Products of 1849, he skillfully secured for France a share in the international exhibition that was to take place in Britain in 1851. French exhibitors enjoyed a great success, since they obtained 60 per cent of the prizes, Britain 27 per cent and all the other exhibitors put together 17 per cent. This great display moved the Comte de Laborde, who wrote the official report, to proclaim the union of art and industry, previously regarded as, if not actually hostile, at least strangers to each other. "Art must now give its hand to industry, not as a slave to be freed from bondage but as a wife whom one is proud to have at one's side." From this time, choice spirits recognized that there was a danger of France being abandoned to artificers devoid of inven-

Brilliant necklace which can be converted into a diadem. Victorian period. Christie Collection, London.

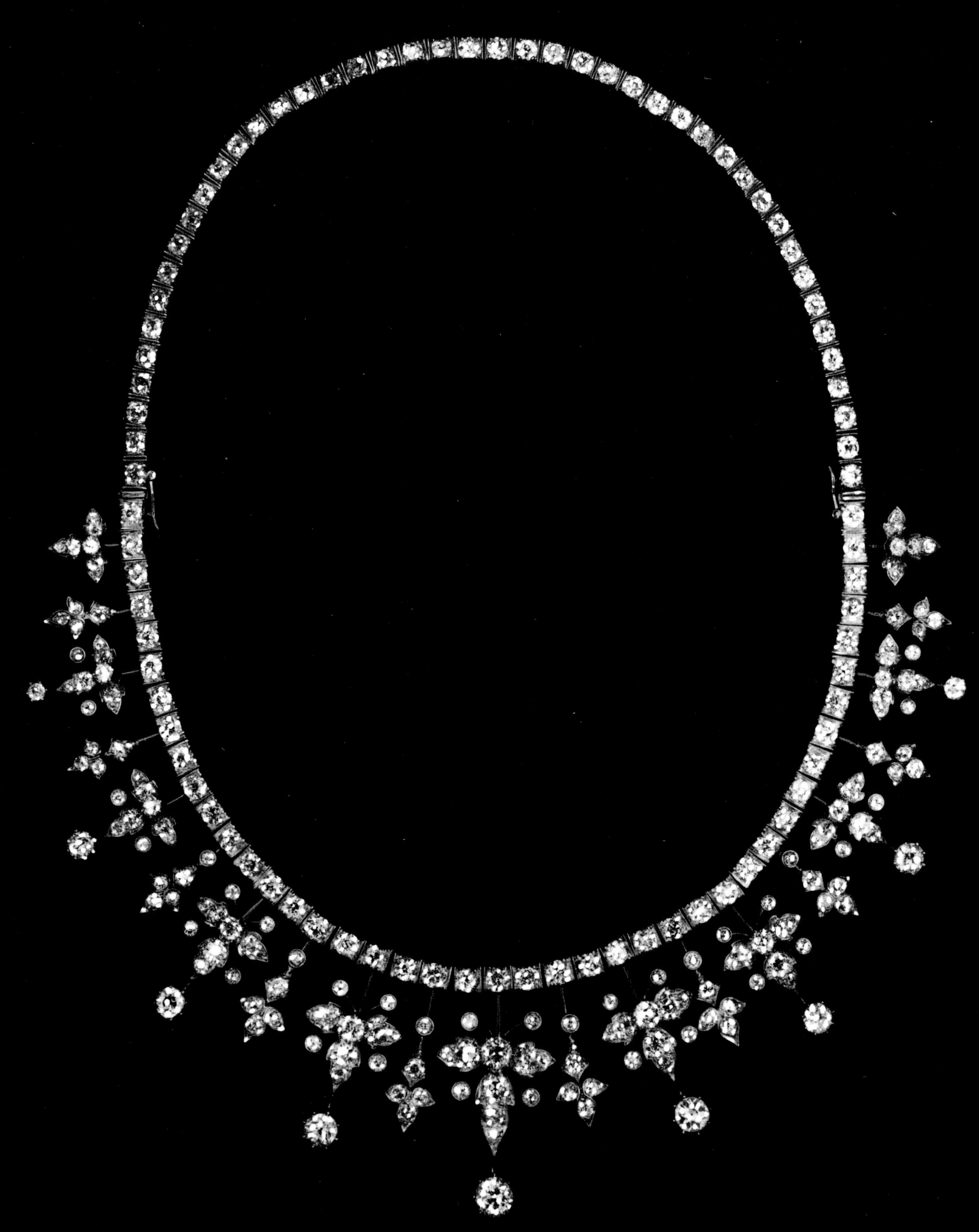

Winterhalter: Portrait of the Empress Eugénie. Musée du Louvre, Paris.

tiveness and ideas "who will deform the style and gradually destroy its originality and artistic supremacy with their facile and pretentious copies."

Jewelers who had accepted the financial sacrifices entailed in the exhibition were encouraged by the resulting orders. One of them named Lemonnier, who had a well-deserved reputation in France, was singled out for the Prince-President's favor and after 1851 was appointed jeweler to the Crown by the new emperor. He had sent several pieces to London, including two major *parures* executed for the queen of Spain which the jury's report described as showing "unerring and very elevated taste in the whole conception."

The empire was proclaimed on December 2, 1852 and on January 29, 1853, the new emperor married Eugènie de Montijo de Guzman, Contessa de Teba, in Notre-Dame.

These events, following in rapid succession, inevitably influenced public morale and business expansion. A new feeling of security initiated an era of material prosperity and extraordinary luxury.

Napoleon III's marriage was the occasion for several new creations in a very advanced style using the old Crown Jewels. "This is how Lemonnier, Baugrand, Mellilo, Kramer, Ouizille-Lemoine, Viette and Fester, all reputable jewelers, came to create the imperial crown, the empress' crown and her tiara, girdle, comb, brooches, knot, head-dress and fan." (Bapst)

The crown was entrusted to Lemonnier. The design can be seen on the cushion beside the empress in the portrait by Winterhalter and on the 50-*centime* pieces issued in 1867. It is now in a private collection, and was displayed at the Louvre in 1962.

La Sylphide, a contemporary magazine, describes the imperial wedding jewels in its issue of February 10, 1853:

"Lemonnier produced several *parures* which were positive gems of imagination and genius. One was of native pearls and rubies, and consisted of a small closed crown for the back of the head, a bracelet and a necklace of plaques. The other was of fabulously rare black pearls, and included a bracelet with three large black pearls. In addition to these outstanding *parures* there were elegantly designed bracelets of stones of so many hues that the eye could not follow them all. Then there were Louis Quinze *parures* in many-colored stones. A *parure* of sapphires and diamonds and another of emeralds and pearls . . . ."

"The empress' gown for the religious ceremony, created by Mme. Vignon, might be regarded as part of her jewelry, it contained so many gems. It was of white needlecord velvet spangled with gems and adorned with English point lace. The skirt had a trailing half-train all covered with English point lace . . . . A diamond and sapphire girdle "emphasized the slenderness of her sylph-like waist" (47 cm., they say). On her head was a diadem and a high comb with some wonderful sapphires. A splendid pearl necklace at her throat completed her jewelry."

"The emperor wore the dress uniform of a Lieutenant-General with jeweled decorations and the collar of the Grand Master of the Lègion d'Honneur which Napoleon wore for his coronation. He also wore the Emperor Charles V's Order of the Golden Fleece. He wore the diamond-hilted sword made by Bapst for Charles X which is now in the Apollo Gallery of the Louvre . . . ."

Her wedding gifts included "an oval diamond brooch the center of which was a large, very thin, flat diamond covering a portrait of the emperor. Another pendeloque diamond hung beneath the portrait." According to M. Henri Vever, the flat diamond would have been the one "that is No. 24 in the catalogue of the sale of the Crown diamonds, valued in 1891 at 11,800 francs."

"An emerald and diamond trefoil features in Pommayrac's portrait of the empress in her state robes. This was, it seems, the first jewel given by the new emperor to his fiancée, who had been enchanted by a clover leaf glittering with dew during a hunt in the forest of Compeégne. This was proably the origin of the empress' fondness for emeralds and the popularity of that stone throughout the second empire."

Empress Eugénie contributed greatly to the reestablishment of the luxury industries, especially jewelry. She was beautiful and elegant; she set the fashion and all the well-

to-do ladies of Paris tried to look like her. Fêtes and receptions followed in rapid succession at the Tuileries, the court revived and society followed suite.

In his book *Paris de 1800 a 1900,* (Plot-Nourrit, 1901) M. Charles Simon says, "After 1853 business enjoyed such great and unbroken prosperity that millions of the lucky ones believed the horn of plenty was inexhaustible. . . Everyone expected to be satisfied, and they were not disappointed: the army, the clergy, high finance, the middle classes who had already grown rich and those who would shortly do so, the working classes of town and country, not a single class or person was overlooked. Even the irreconcilables who stayed in exile to the end cried, 'the universe is taking a turn for the better,' and proclaimed, 'spring is coming back everywhere.' "

Jewelry, however, made little progress during the early years of the second empire despite the favorable economic conditions. Heavy commonplace *rivières* and *parures* of widely-spaced foliage and collet-set stones were still made, rousing Massin, the master-jeweler who was to deal a fatal blow to this regrettable style in the middle of the reign, to eloquent protest. "In 1851 when I was a journeyman I not only saw but actually made this abominable dead-alive jewelry, and when I expressed my astonishment at this sorry-state of affairs to my master Fester, he said, 'What can you do about it? As long as I make pointed leaves with round flowers or round leaves with pointed flowers and plenty of collet-set stones at thirty *sous* each, that's all they want of me.' Nevertheless, Fester was capable of better things. Pointed leaves, round flowers and collet-set stones—there is the jewelry of the era in a nutshell."

Very large gold bracelets were in favor throughout the reign. They had five or six big Panama pearls in the middle of a group of brilliants set in the gold at regular intervals round the bracelet.

Gem cameos, as they were called to distinguish them from shell cameos, were cut in gemstones such as onyx, carnelian and agates with one or more different-colored layers which the engraver utilitized to color his figures and give variety to his work. Shell cameos were merely carved on two-layer sea-shells, a soft and easily-worked material and therefore much cheaper.

It is important, however, to note that in spite of the insipidness of jewelry design, the second empire was the period when jewels once more became an essential part of dress. In the general prosperity, the luxury trades were able to create novelties which were sure of a market because of the widespread extravagance of the times.

Gold settings, formerly only common in the east, now spread to Paris. Jeweler's work grew lighter, since gold allows finer and more delicate work than silver. Diamonds took on an extra sparkle from gold, which set them off better than the thick silver setting that often disguised a cutting error or lack of size. Gold also permitted the use of enamel in jewelry. Tiaras, necklaces and bracelets were the favorite ornaments of well-dressed women of the early second empire. Hair dressed in long ringlets or bands over the ears prevented the wearing of earrings, but when earrings finally appeared about 1860 they reached a length of ten or even fifteen cm., like the "lusters" which became one of Massin's specialities and had prisms that sparkled at the least movement.

Napoleon III's cousin Princess Mathilde had some very fine jewels, particularly her collection of pearls which she pawned for her cousin's benefit, as Pauline Bonaparte had once given her jewels to her brother Napoleon I on his return from Elba.

Another fine jewelry collection belonged to Princess Metternich, who was celebrated for her spontaneous wit, high spirits and *joli-laide* charm; and others to the Comtesse Walewska, the Duchess de Mouchy, the Comtesse de Pourtalѐs and Mme. Edouard André. Alongside high society there developed the class which Dumas *fils* called the *demi-monde,* the queens of which were extremely well-provided with jewels. Mme. Musard, whom Henri Vever saw at the opera during the last years of her life, had some splendid ornaments. "This former adventuress of the Texas Inn, favorite of William II of Holland, had

Brooch: gold, enamel, diamonds, amethysts, emeralds. By Froment-Meurice. Exhibited in 1855. Victoria & Albert Museum, London.

been given a bundle of deeds to American oil-bearing lands by her royal protector. At that time their value was nominal, but one fine day they were suddenly worth a considerable fortune. She was famous for her princely household, the luxury of her carriages and her marvelous toilettes. Among others she had a dress on which more than three thousand perals spread their milky shimmer. In the evening she sometimes wore dazzling sets of enormous diamonds worth more than a million francs, one of which was a historic, slightly lozenge-shaped stone weighing 41 carats that had once belonged to the Crown of Naples and was known as the "Cross" dimaond because of its very curious shape, with a cross instead of the usual flat table of the brilliant. Thérèse Lachman, later Comtesse de Paiva, had a set of magnificent emeralds. Cora Pearl, Hortense Schneider, Caroline Letessier "of whom it was said that she was rolling in diamonds," Léonide Leblanc and the notorious Comtesse de Castiglione adorned themselves with famous jewels, preferably multiple ropes of pearls.

The popularity of jewelry was consolidated by the 1855 exhibition at the Palais de l'Industrie which the emperor opened in person. The Crown diamonds were on display for the first time in their new settings, showing how keen the sovereigns were to encourage the luxury arts in general and jewelry in particular. Among the exhibitors who received prizes were Marret Frères et Jarry, who displayed, among other pieces, a very fine ruby corsage ornament; Mellerio, with jeweled flowers and knots; Viette, with combs and knots in brilliants; A. Paul et Frères, "with a knot of oats in green enamel and diamonds which had a most enchanting effect;" and Marret et Baugrand, to whom the reporter ascribed, "a very pretty ornament in the form of a wreath of blue flowers of very fine workmanship to be worn on the head, and a necklace of black pearls in fine, simple and elegant work."

The ending of the Crimean War and the birth of the Prince Imperial in 1856 following the success of the 1855 exhibition helped to confirm the new business prosperity. So many orders were placed that the price of diamonds soared, and this perhaps interfered with the empress' cherished project of giving her ladies-of-honor a badge consisting of a knot of blue ribbon fastened to the shoulder by two interlaced rings of diamonds.

The christening of the little prince was the occasion of a great fête given by the city of Paris at the Hôtel de Ville. The empress, as always, was a rare picture of elegance and beauty. "She wore a gown of white tulle scattered with silver stars and her diadem and the double necklace which covered all the top of her corsage were made of remarkably large diamonds and amethysts. She wore a broad diamond girdle and a big comb *en pampilles* set specially for the occasion with several 'Mazarin' diamonds and that admirable pentagonal diamond with its soft pink color, the 'Peach Blossom,' which is now in the Apollo Gallery at the Louvre." (H. Vever)

This comb was made by Bapst, who carried out many more imperial orders because he knew the gems of the Crown Jewels better than anyone else. Among the jewels he is known to have made was a large Grecian-style diadem all of diamonds after a very fine design by Alfred Bapst, which the empress wore to the opera on the day of Orsini's assassination attempt. It was subsequently adorned with the "Regent" diamond for the reception of the Siamese ambassadors at the Fontainbleau in 1861.

In 1860, the administrators of the Beaux Arts acquired the Marquis de Campana's celebrated collection. He was Director of the Monte di Pieta di Roma, and a most knowledgeable antiquarian and collector. It included more than ten thousand pieces including twelve hundred invaluable ornaments which were specimens of Greek, Roman and Etruscan art. Napoleon III took part personally in the discussions and the collection was bought on his advice for 4,500,000 francs. This was far less than it was worth and far less than it had cost the marquis. It was displayed at the Palais de l'Industrie before being deposited in the Louvre in 1862 under the name of the Napoleon III Collection. It moved the public and the experts to lively admiration by revealing new aspects of the ancient arts, even to experts as knowledgeable as Ingres, who said of it, "There are some articles of an entirely new type that will surprise a lot of people who thought they knew all about the ancient world."

Two names to be remembered are those of Fontenay and Massin, who influenced the gold and jewels of this period profoundly. They had two things in common: their artistic temperament and their thorough knowledge of their craft, which enabled them both to carry outsingle-handed any piece from the drawing board to the jewel case. Fontenay, who was six years older than his colleague Massin, was enchanted by the masterpieces of the Campana collection, but he was not content to be merely a skillful copyist. His new and ingenious compositions proved that he had excellent style and unerring taste, and that he was an original and truly creative artist. In 1855, he made his reputation as a jeweler with a diadem that boldly broke away from the traditional style. It was a spray of wild blackberries trimmed with its own fruits and flowers, the design of which showed close observation of nature and the execution, a degree of lightness and taste very rarely found in this period. One of his most remarkable productions was a table service for Said Pasha, Viceroy of Egypt, which he describes as follows: "This service consisted of forty-two place settings of gold and enamel all covered with brilliants, each one of which was 60,000 francs (in 1863). It was completed by a big fruit stand for the centerpiece with two six-branched candelabra studded with brilliants, pearls, rubies and emeralds of enormous size, each worth 900,000 francs, and six fruit bowls decorated with the broad natural leaves of palms, chestnuts, and others. Along with these objects there were ewers and basins for washing, serving trays and toilet trays. One of the latter alone was valued at one and a half million francs."

Lemonnier: large brooch. Brilliants and pearls. In the center is pearl weighing 337 grains, inaccurately known as "La Régente." Made for the wedding of the Empress Eugénie. Bibliothèque Forney, Paris.

Said Pasha placed this order during his trip to Paris in 1863. He stayed at the Tuileries, where he entertained the emperor and empress at dinner and did the honors of his splendid service. Splendid it certainly was. Whether it was practical is quite another matter. One wonders what effect sauces might have had on this kind of jewelry.

Massin was a great artist who influenced the jewelry of his time considerably, both in France and elsewhere. He was the epitome of the accomplished jeweler and—when Fossin was no longer competing—the best of his period.

He was a Frenchman born in Liege in 1829 and apprenticed at twelve years of age. He went to Paris as a journeyman jeweler taking little with him but the bare necessities of his craft as he had studied it in the provinces, where he had to know something about everything, including making, designing, setting and polishing his pieces and sometimes engraving them. He was twenty-six years old in 1854 when he became foreman of the Rouvenat establishment, one of the leading Parisian jewelers. In 1856, he went to London, where he spent eighteen months studying the work of British jewelers, whose craftsmanship was reputedly highly skilled but very heavy. On his return to France, he began to make the lighter and better designed jeweled flowers and sprays that only Fossin had made before. He then applied himself to the study of form—how flowers and leaves were joined on, their structure and their appearance—and this was his chief innovation.

In 1863, he refused offers from London and from Tiffany's in New York and set up on his own account in Paris. "At that time he began to adopt as his model the wild rose with its heart-shaped petals and strong, simple lines, and this type of flower was subsequently imitated by everyone in innumerable copies without modification right up to 1880. He also produced new types of knots and aigrettes, heron feathers in cross shapes combined with *pampilles* and mobile collet-set diamonds that had first been introduced by the jewelers of the eighteenth century." (H. Vever)

The most successful of these aigrettes was the one which was made for the Duchess of Medina-Coeli, a great Lady of the court of Madrid. It was ordered from Lemonnier, royal jeweler and supplier to Queen Isabella II. From the various designs submitted by several jewelers, Massin's was selected. "It consisted of five aigrettes shaped like three-sided pyramids with mobile diamonds on each face invisibly attached to clusters of very fine-drawn wires set with thousands of tiny brilliants and roses. The aigrettes sprang from a rich flowered base. They were light and shimmering, the space between the main motifs filled with collet-set diamonds falling in a "rain." They were arranged round the head and held in place by a wide corrugated ribbon which made a firm, comfortable base fastened at the back in a knot with big loops leaving long floating ends hanging down the back of the neck."

"At a fête which took place shortly after the ornament was delivered by Lemonnier, the Duchess was passing under a hanging when she was caught by her headdress, and the aigrettes got so firmly entangled that they could not be undone without severe damage. The broken fragments, fallen gems and the bent and inextricably muddled remains were picked up. It was, in short, a total disaster, which it was vital to repair as Queen Isabella was shortly to give a great reception. As there was no time to send the ornament to Paris, Lemonnier was asked to send someone to carry out the repairs in Madrid. When Massin was consulted he said, 'There are broken parts to be remade—you'll need a jeweler. Stones to be reset or replaced—that's a stone-setter's business. And pieces to be polished and finished off—that needs a polisher. You need a team of three people. I haven't anyone in my workshop and I don't know anyone outside it who combines all the skills needed for this operation." In the end, Massin went to Madrid himself with an assortment of stones, some prepared material and plenty of equipment. He himself told Henry Vever, "When I reached the duchess' palace in Madrid, I was given a splendid drawing room to work in. I had a beautiful Louis XIV gilded table for a work bench." It was in this gorgeous but dread-

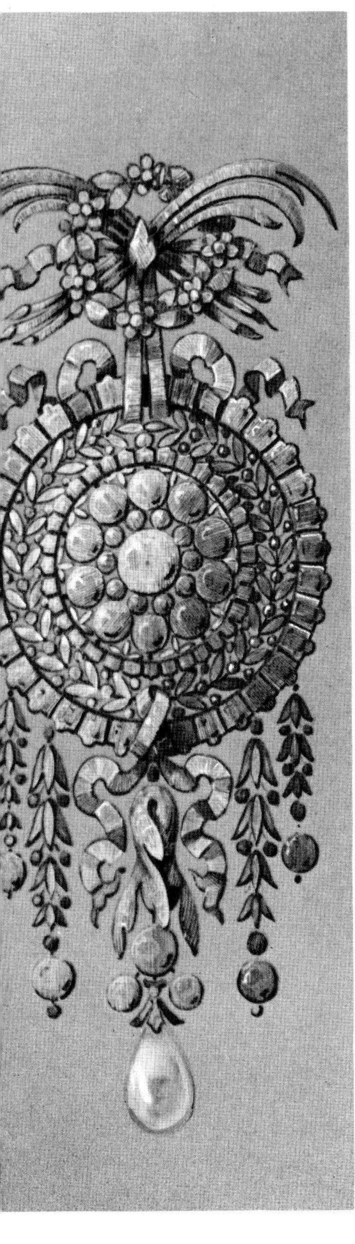

Gustave Baugrand: Design for brooches. Watercolor, tempera and pen. French, c. 1867. The Cooper Union Museum for the Arts of Decoration, New York.

fully inconvenient setting that Massin was able to restore the aigrette to its pristine perfection in ten days of unremitting toil. He showed it to its noble owner, who was quite dismayed to find her salon full of pots and pans which had been used for washing the ornament and drying it in sawdust.

An amusing incident occured during the work. When he came to do some soldering, Massin discovered that in rushing his departure, he had forgotten his blow-pipe. In this difficulty he went out, planning to throw himself on the mercy of any helpful colleague. On the way he saw some clay pipes in a tobacconist's window. Light dawned. The problem was solved. Massin bought a pipe, broke off the end, tried blowing through it, and carried out all his soldering with this makeshift blow-pipe. Necessity is the mother of inventionı When his work was finished and he was about to leave Madrid, Massin paid his respects to the duchess, who tried to thank him and invited him to visit the palace the next day to see the wife of a Spanish Grandee in full court dress going to a royal reception. Massin was punctual, and admired the richness of a magnificently equipped, entirely gilded chariot, but was even more impressed by the beauty and grace of the noble lady. "You see, Monsieur l'artiste, that I am wearing your diadem on my head," she told him. "I never knew it was beautiful till I saw it there, Mme. la duchesse," he cried. "But beware of fringes of hangingsı" "Thank you, Monsieur, and goodbye." "Farewell, Madame." (Vever, after Massin)

From 1851, advertising grew more common. Jewelers such as Fossin, Fontenay and Massin made use of it and it gradually spread the universal taste and discrimination that became the foundations of the art throughout the country. In this period, Ruskin was publishing his theories of art in Britain and directing taste towards the ideal. In France, Michelet launched his motto "Discover or die!" The Duc de Luynes, Vogüé and the Comte de Laborde condemned imitations. In his report on the art in industry, the Comte de Laborde proclaimed, "Do you realize that art has been killed by two generations of grave-diggers who have followed each other in rifling the tombs of past generations and blindly, servilely and undiscriminatingly copying them as if they were impelled by some fanatical idolatry?"

These exhortations were now slow to bear fruit. A new spirit seemed to be enlivening industry. The first signs of it appear in a report by Fossin and Baugrand in 1867 on goldworking and jewelry, in which they advise, "Stimulate the artist by rewards, secure the ownership of the design, and give the craftsman a stake in the results of his labors by making him jointly liable for the prosperity of the trade."

The Universal Exhibition of 1867, which was even more spectacular than that of 1865, was a milestone in the evolution of jewelry. Even more jewelers took part, and the work they exhibited showed that substantial advances in lightness and composition had been made.

A new fashion, the Egyptian style, was introduced by the Suez Canal project. However, there were also survivals of the Etruscan style launched by the Campana Collection, the Louis XVI style which the empress preferred, and even the Renaissance style which had been revived by the work in progress at the Louvre.

Among the exhibits, that of a jeweler named Rouvenat was particularly admired. He showed a life-sized spray of lilac made of diamonds which was bought by the empress. The report by the delegates described it as follows: "This is an article of real merit. The craftsman who executed it had a natural spray before his eyes while he was working and he has made a perfect copy. Its only fault is that it is a shade too thick . . ." He adds, "This is the first time anyone has tried to carry out this motif in jewelry."

His showcase also displayed "Kashmirians," i.e., brooches for pinning the Kashmir shawls which were fashionable at the time, and humming birds, thirty-eight of which were bought by Ismail pasha, Viceroy of Egypt.

The 1867 exhibition was also the scene of the first appearance of a young jeweler named Boucheron, then on the threshold of his career. He set to work to remodel cur-

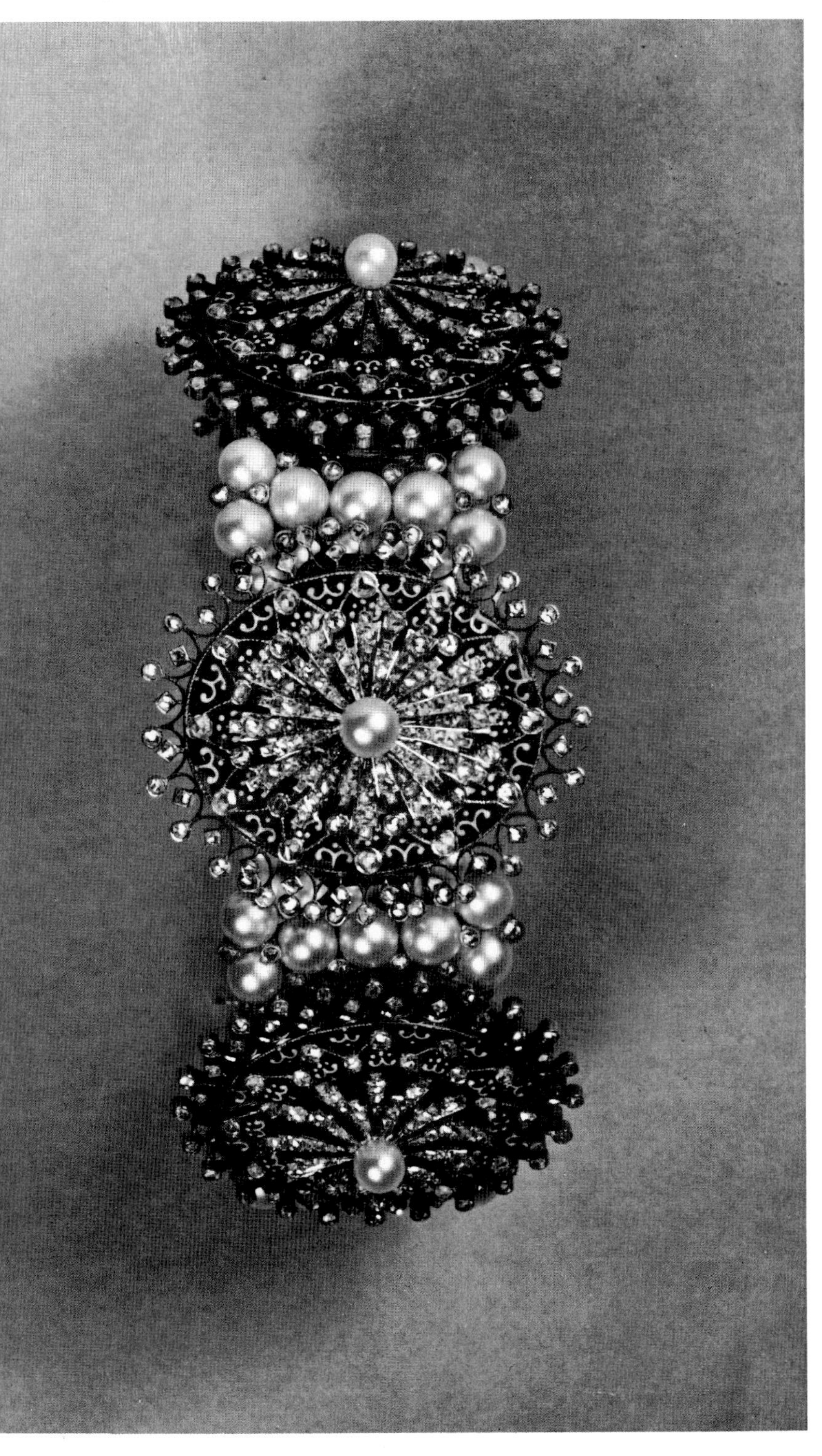

rent styles with new interpretations and ornaments, e.g., Florentine pierced work, translucent enamels and a judicious use of color.

Boucheron put a marble plaque in his showcase bearing the names of his chief assistants, a gesture they greatly appreciated and which was subsequently imitated by others.

Massin himself held a personal exhibition described in a report as extremely interesting. "A few specimens of jewelry scattered about a showcase prove that nowadays real talent will always triumph, regardless of capital interest. His waterlilies, sprays of wild roses and daisies, and the little wreath of pink pearl buds extinguish all the blaze of the millions of gems glittering around them, and do convincingly demonstrate that the purity, grace and elegance of design and the sense of poetry which pervades the collection and the delicacy and lightness of the craftsman's hand are the most important qualities of the jeweler."

This eulogy of Massin winds up the progress made by the jewelers of the second empire, for which he was largely responsible."

After the twofold trials of the Franco-Prussian war and the struggle against the revolutionary Commune in Paris in 1871, the French courageously returned to work under the government of the Third Republic. When calm and security had been re-established, France healed its wounds and embarked again on the industrial and commercial program which had flourished there during the last years of the second empire. After 1871, France took part in the exhibition in the South Kensington Museum in London. French jewelers and goldsmiths created quite a sensation at the 1877 exhibition, and repeated this triumph in Vienna and Philadelphia in 1876.

Boucheron: bracelet. Gold, translucent enamel, pearls and diamonds. French, late nineteenth century. Bolckow Bequest. Victoria & Albert Museum, London.

French visitors could not but learn a lesson from this succession of exhibitions, from Paris in 1855 and 1864 to London in 1862. The Comte de Laborde, the Duc de Luynes and Prosper Mérimée sought to stress this point in their reports by denouncing "the precarious situation of the arts and professions which once established the superiority of French workmanship wherever taste and luxury were appreciated. Contemporary French products are only too often merely curious combinations of different styles thrown together at random, proving nothing but the maker's lack of ideas and illogicality," added Mérimée.

Perhaps the British example and Prosper Mérimée's evidence did not reach the public at large, but they were at least heeded in artistic and industrial circles, and a large share in the movement of ideas taking place in France after 1863 that was brought to fruition during the Third Republic can reasonably be attributed to them.

After the 1863 exhibition in London, promoters of the French industrial arts were worried about the progress of their rivals, and decided to take stock of their own assets at the National Exhibition of Fine Arts in Industry which was planned during the summer of 1864. The participators were wise enough not to let themselves be impressed by its sensational effect nor by the optimistic reports of Philippe Burty. They realized that the increase in prestige it had produced must be supported by a sustained and fruitful effort, especially as regards creativity. "Training in design was deliberately abandoned at the fall of the monarchy, when art became synonymous with luxury overnight, and consequently the object of virtuous disapproval, and it has never been seriously revived." (Emile Sedeyn)

The Central Union of the Fine Arts in Industry was founded on January 13, 1864, with the object of carrying out a program of training and publicity. It ultimately succeeded in disseminating the study of design throughout all the schools in France and establishing the Museum of the Decorative Arts in the Pavillon de Marsan in the Louvre, where it is still located. The public could educate themselves and the artists could find the records they needed for their studies and work in its collections and exhibitions.

In the book *La Bijouterie et Joaillerie* (Georges Fouquet, 1934) Emile Sedeyn discussed, among other matters, "the historic and human interest of jewelry." He says, "A necklace, ring or bracelet often evokes a date and sheds light on an era more forcefully and expressively than a painting because it is closer to human life. . . Thus the only jewels which matter to posterity are those which are clearly dated. . . Young people have always remodeled their grandparents' jewels, and with a few rare exceptions we only know ancient pieces from paintings and engravings. But surely the fact that each generation destroys the jewels of the preceding era to make new ones proves that evolution is always going on, just as we stated in the beginning."

The ephemeral nature of jewelry and ornaments links them closely to contemporary taste and this trend has continued unchecked from 1875 to the present.

In 1872, an unforeseen circumstance influenced the technical development of jewelry and increased jewelers' output. In 1869, a few samples of South African diamonds had been seen, but as no one realized how plentiful they were, business was not affected. It was not until about 1872 that Cape diamonds began to appear on the Paris market. The first specimens were fairly big but rather yellow. When they first appeared prices in general fell, but the number of sales soon rose rapidly because of the increased demand. The art of jewelry soon consisted of making the most of bigger and more plentiful diamonds rather than giving them weight by using settings designed to lend them an illusion of size. Massin took the first steps in this direction with his flowering sprays and invisible settings which gave great suppleness to necklaces and bracelets.

Parts of the "currant leaf" *parure,* after a design by Alfred Bapst, 1856. Bibliothèque Forney, Paris.

The Paris exhibition of 1878 attracted a great many foreigners. Jewelers and goldsmiths figure prominently, but their work showed that they were reluctant to break with the traditional earlier styles, either owing to respect for their own brotherhood or to lack of confidence in their own ability to use their technical skill in freer creations.

One of these jewelers was Alphonse Fouquet, "a former apprentice who had worked his way through to the rank of master by perseverance and talent and who, exhibiting for the first time in 1878, showed himself to be a skillful craftsman and an imaginative and individual designer." (Sedeyn) Several pieces from the 1878 exhibition are preserved in the Museum of Decorative Arts.

Ernest Vever, son of a jeweler from Metz who settled in Paris in 1870, was also noticed by a reporter of the exhibition for his "wide bandeau, all the pieces of which are joined without solder; a necklace in the purest Greek style fringed with brilliants and pearls, of admirable suppleness; some elegant jeweled knots, a fine Assyrian necklace of engraved gold and a set of ornaments in the classic style, of magnificent emeralds of rare quality and size."

It is interesting to learn that in 1867-78, jewelry showed more initiative and imagination than the other industrial arts despite the value of the raw materials and the risks involved. It was the only art which seemed anxious to keep closely in touch with new trends and their application.

It seems that a similar transformation was brewing all over Europe. It was initiated by French artists and by the moving spirits of the "Arts and Crafts." Its antecedents, unobtrusive but none the less far from negligible, can be recognized in some of Fabergé's work.

When young Carl Fabergé succeeded his father in St. Petersburg in 1870 he was not very interested in designing or making ornaments. He much preferred precious ar-

Brooch: gold, diamonds, rubies and emeralds. English or Russian, first half of the nineteenth century. Victoria & Albert Museum, London.

Necklace and earrings: gold, enamel, rubies, diamonds and pearls. Hungarian, c. 1840. Victoria & Albert Museum, London.

ticles like knots and Easter eggs, and the whole range of gold and jeweled luxury toys which won him his worldwide reputation. But at this time he acquired the patronage of the court, which had previously been supplied by Nichols and Plinke, two Englishmen whose establishment was called "The English Shop." An amusing exchange of compliments was then taking place: the British professed great admiration for Russian jewelry, which had been praised to the skies at the 1851 exhibition, while the nobility of St. Petersburg adorned themselves with British-made jewels. Nevertheless, the house of Fabergé prospered until 1870. Gustave Fabergé, Carl's father, settled there in 1842 and made his fortune by selling traditional but good-quality jewels. Thinking that his thirty years in the business was enough, he retired to Dresden where his son was to visit him frequently—an important detail in view of the treasures of the Grünes Gewölbe and the work of Dingliner which is displayed in it. Carl Gewölbe served a long apprenticeship with Pendin, his father's colleague. He traveled in Italy, England, France and Germany. Then this young man, only twenty-four years old, shouldered the heavy responsibility for his father's firm, accepting it with his eyes wide open and with the fixed determination of achieving his goals. He had not abandoned jewels in favor of his almost exclusive interest in *bibelots.* He continued to give his clients the traditional pieces they wanted, designed many articles for the royal family and when asked, did not refuse to create original, subtly composed ornaments for which he favored rose-cut diamonds, moonstones and garnets. He adapted the objects on which his reputation was based to jewelry, and specialized in necklaces of tiny enameled and bejeweled gold eggs. In his more traditional pieces, he used pearls, emeralds and diamonds, e.g., the beautiful necklace of 1898 now in the Kremlin, made for the Russian-dress Ball, and some brooches reproducing ancient models.

Although he was comparatively limited and most of his work was destroyed or lost in the Revolution, Fabergé's ornaments were rich and varied. Some pendants and brooches with lines and materials belonging to the most

Pendant: gold, enamel in blue and white. In the center is a garnet surrounded by rose diamonds and eight half-pearls. American, mid-nineteenth century. The Cooper Union Museum for the Arts of Decoration, New York.

Necklace which can be converted into a diadem: diamonds. Victorian period. Wartski Collection, London. 

modern *fin-de-siècle* styles are more memorable than the court pieces, which were still very traditional. The arrival of the new style was foreshadowed here too, and Fabergé played an important part in its development.

This short-lived *fin-de-siécle* style was not an exclusively European creation. The U.S.A. will now play an increasingly important part in the history of jewels. From 1850 on the countries of Europe and especially Britain had to allow for their transatlantic customers' tastes and traditions. A diamond ring was the customary gift from husband to wife and this custom brought the solitaire or the ring with a perfect pearl into fashion in Europe.

However, jewelers would find more in America than rich customers who knew exactly what they wanted. They were soon to see the emergence of a new power in the person of Charles Lewis Tiffany, who paid extensive visits to Paris and other capitals and quickly acquired a well-deserved reputation as a knowledgeable expert on the subject of ancient jewelry. His establishment was founded in the U.S.A. in 1837 and a branch was opened in Paris in the 1850s. In 1887, Charles L. Tiffany was one of the leading buyers when the French Crown Jewels were sold. When he died in 1902, he bequeathed his business to his son Louis Comfort Tiffany, who was best known for his work in glass but was just as skilled in jewelry.

Like many artists of his time (Tiffany started out as a painter), he abandoned the fine arts in favor of the decorative arts, and was particularly attracted by the innumerable possibilities offered by the working of even the least valuable raw materials. He was deeply influenced by the theories of Ruskin and William Morris, and he strove to preserve the quality of spontaneous craftsmanship in the jewels he designed. The metal was always worked by hand and the stones he set were preferably cabochons selected for their color and shape rather than their market value. However, Louis C. Tiffany was one of the adepts of Art Nouveau, a movement as shortlived as it was remarkable. As far as jewelry is concerned, a single artist, Lalique, springs to mind, as if he were the only distinguished practitioner. It is true that he was one of the greatest, but he did not wholly eclipse a number of Belgian and German jewelers and creative artists like Ashbee and Tiffany, who produced original and beautiful pieces which were often just as good as those of the famous French artist.

Art Nouveau

Art Nouveau flourished extremely briefly—so much so that some critics refuse to recognize it as a style in its own right while others speak of the Modern Style or the Jugendstil. Some regard it as a few years' interlude, a sort of brief crisis in which all the trends of the century were carried to excess and which soon faded away for lack of resources and means, and therefore had neither consequences and descendents. But it might be asked whether Art Nouveau did not contribute something absolutely new to its own era and to ours, the effects of which are still being dimly felt. For, if we do not let ourselves be put off by a few excesses which sometimes overstepped the bounds of taste and reason, and try to analyze the spirit of the time in depth, a resolutely modern character can be discerned in it. Like all movements, Art Nouveau adopted some traditions and rejected others. Its artists were particularly opposed to what they called the absence of style of the era, and they turned to the more distant past—the Middle Ages and the Renaissance—the lessons of which they believed had been insufficiently learned. They nevertheless aimed to produce environmental art for the new world society in which equality and justice were to reign—principles which were notoriously foreign to the periods with which they claimed kinship.

Indeed, the theoreticians and practitioners of Art Nouveau give the impression that they were not entirely clear about their ideology, and among the volumes of their writings and the diversity of their works it is sometimes difficult to discern the objective of their experiments and achievements.

It is possible, however, to recognize a number of characteristic features that can help us to understand the

Philippe Wolfers: diadem ("Salisburia"), 1901. Enamel and brilliants. Wolfers Frères Collection, Brussels.

new jewelry better. In the first place, the accent was more than ever before on the importance of the decorative arts—and except for architecture, Art Nouveau only minimally affected the fine arts. Consequently, many artists who were trained as painters or sculptors and sometimes started out like this abandoned or neglected their first profession in favor of what is now known as "design." Tiffany has already been mentioned, and others of the same type were Van der Velde and Philippe Wolfers. On the other hand, architects like J. Hoffmann or Koloman Moser, who regarded themselves as creators of environment rather than mere builders, pursued several careers at once.

Many artists, therefore, applied their talents to creating jewels and tried to revive the aesthetic value of jewelry. However, they were not exclusively interested in design. They loved the raw materials, stones and metals, for themselves, and made many technical experiments which led to revival of or progress in a great many techniques. The art of enamelling, for instance, returned to favor and some artists performed great feats in it. To say that these *fin-de-siècle* jewelers loved raw materials "for themselves" is only repeating their own words, but it is probably necessary to realize what this implies in order to appreciate its full meaning. This interest in raw materials, valuable or not, can apparently be explained by two factors—the progress of physics and chemistry, and the new inventions and possibilities of more advanced studies opened up by new apparatus, which revealed hitherto undreamed of secrets of secrets and richness in the simplest things The smallest stone seemed to harbor extraordinary treasures of beauty which no one had previously been able to see, and which came to be preferred to the valuable materials once considered beautiful.

This, no doubt, is the second reason for Art Nouveau's preoccupation with reputedly commonplace materials. It was a reaction against the age-old conventions of jewelry which too often led the nineteenth century bourgeoisie to mistake market value for aesthetic quality. An object is not necessarily beautiful because it costs a lot, and this was what these artists wanted to prove.

Other factors also came into play. If the beauty of a jewel resides chiefly in its quality and originality, it must owe its price to the signature or mark it bears rather than to the value of its gems. The revival of craftsmanship was death to anonymity. Artists wanted to make even the most utilitarian object into a recognizable work of art.

The last factor was the clientele for whom these new jewels were designed. Artists turned to womankind, or rather to an ideal of womanhood as ephemeral and novel as themselves. She was seen as delicate, mysterious, perverse and sensitive, a victim or a subtle tormentor, a dream-creature having deep secret affinities with flowers and water, ancient legends and night creatures. They therefore adorned her with water-plants, climbing plants, reeds, simple wild flowers or rarer, more treacherous exotics. Snakes coiled about her wrists, writhed in knots on her corsage and even gaped their menacing jaws on her shoulders and hands. Flora and fauna dominated jewelry as never before. Woman herself, however, as model or reflection, played an important part in jewelry—flower-woman, dragonfly-woman or just woman, a gracious creature floating and swirling in a billow of light, sinuous lines.

Many new elements were added to the decorative repertoire, themes which jewelry had rarely touched on before. Especially typical was the interplay of lines which occurs on all the objects of this period, to which metals such as bronze, gold and silver give very great beauty.

The new style of jewelry was favored by dress fashions. Long dresses with tight waists and wide low necks and all the accessories of the feminine toilette offered many opportunities for creating ornaments. Owing to the low waist, the corsage was quite expensive enough for large brooches and pendants. The neck was left uncovered by evening dress and could be adorned with either a made-to-measure necklace, which followed its contours closely, or with several rows of chains hanging right down to the waist. It was quite acceptable to wear both at once. Women still wore their hair long, and their heavy chignons were held in place by jeweled combs. Jewelers also showed all sorts of pins for hats, hair, scarves and cravats.

(Left to right, top to bottom)
Vever: signed pendant, "Sylvia." Gold, brilliants, rubies, agate and enamel. Paris, 1900.
Vever: belt buckle in the form of a peacock. Gold, enamel and gems, signed. Paris, 1900.
Vever: signed brooch, "Apparition," after a composition by Grasset. Gold, ivory and enamel. Paris, 1900.
Vever, signed brooch, "Syracuse." Gold, enamel and a cabochon emerald. Paris, 1900. Musée des Arts Decoratifs, Paris.

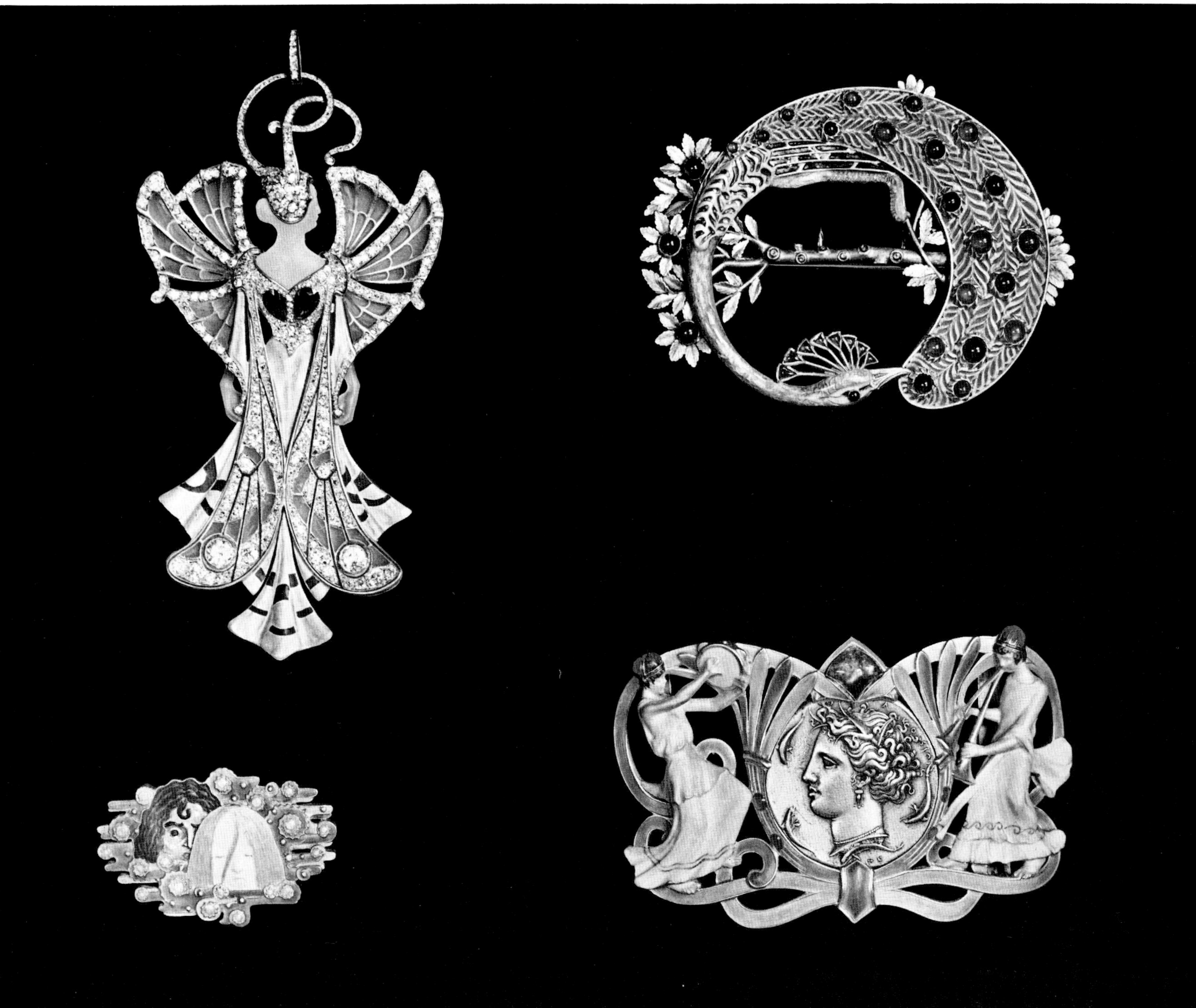

Three ornaments by Georges Fouquet.
Comb: horn, gold, enamel and diamonds. Designed by C. Desrosiers, signed.
Pendant: opal, gold and enamel.
"Blackberry" necklace: gold, enamel and pearls.
Musée des Arts Decoratifs, Paris.

Many accessories, from handbags to parasol handles and from lornettes and fans to cigarette cases were treated as real jewels.

The 1889 exhibition was another triumph for jewelry, but it was not distinguished by any notable advance in artistry. Imitations of nature, even the most ingenious and accurate from the technical point of view, are still, as Sedeyn puts it, "only a fancy, and fancy must beware of exaggeration." A new breath of fresh air was not to pass over this delicate art until Lalique appeared at the French Salon des Artistes in 1894.

Jules-René Lalique was born in Ay (Marne) in 1860 but soon moved to Paris. All his life this designer was enthralled by nature, but he always sought to find new forms. To begin with, he merely supplied designs to other jewelers such as Jacta, Aucoc, Cartier, Renn, Gariod, Hamelin and Destape, but in 1905, he finally became a jeweler in his own right by acquiring the Destape establishment. From year to year his venture prospered as he grew more skilled in his craft. He produced increasingly daring and popular work, extending his curiosity to every material and subject. This was how he came to introduce the human form (or the female form, to be more precise) and animals into jewelry, and to make use of hitherto rejected or ignored materials such as horn, rock crystal and coral, and gemstones such as agate, jade, carnelian and onyx. He was also fascinated by enamel and glass. He was both a skilled craftsman and a gifted artist, and brought the same spirit of curiosity to all his enterprises, using, for instance, a reducing machine for medals. This process produced very fine details and relief from a large wax model without the collaboration of an expert engraver. He obtained striking success and started a school. Interpreting nature in all its guises through the medium of his own imagination with a freedom which occasionally got out of hand, his attitude was novel and productive.

He was soon emulated by other jewelers, and closer collaboration was established between decorators and crafts-

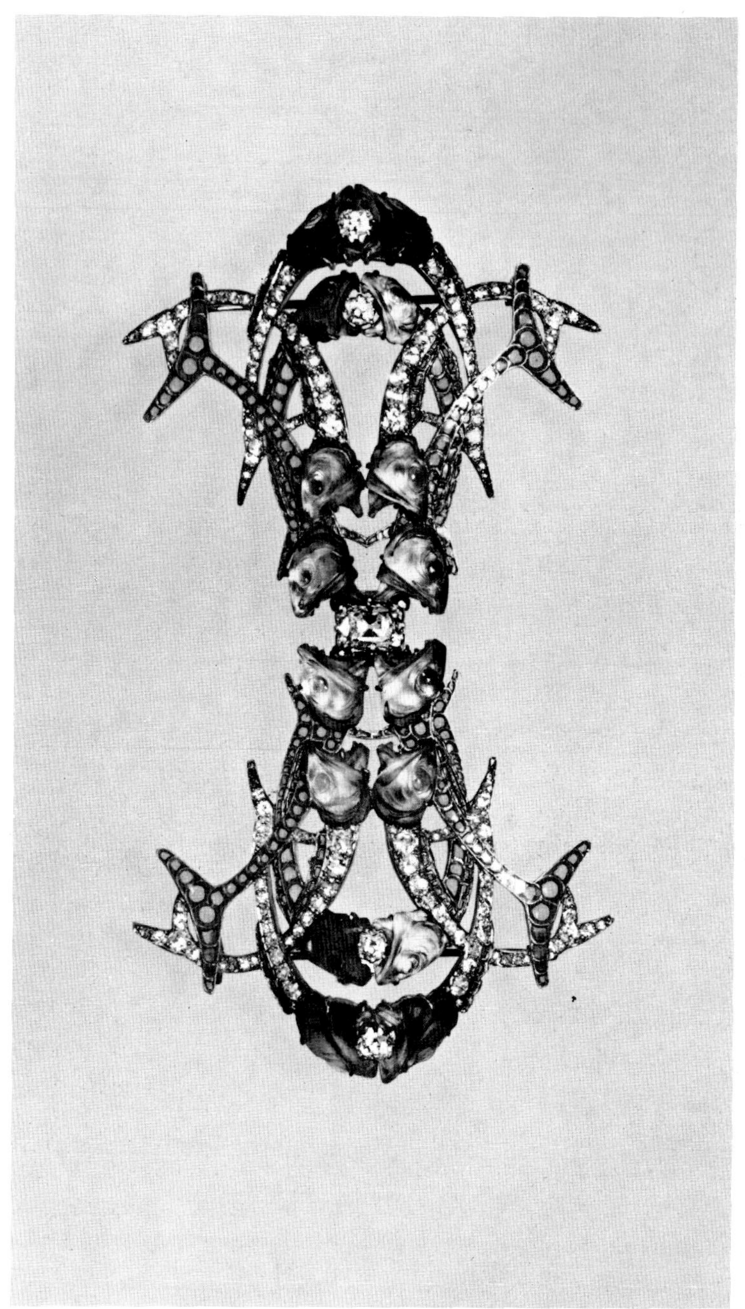

Jules-René Lalique: brooch. Green gold, enamel, diamonds and glass. Bequest of Mary Kellog Hopkins. The Metropolitan Museum of Art, New York.

men, each making new discoveries in his own field. This was true of Vever and Grasset and of Fouquet and Mucha. All these experiments culminated in the 1900 exhibition.

The 1900 exhibition was the inauguration of Art Nouveau. In the vast, ambitious program covering both past and present, technical media and their end products, the three aspects of jewelry (museum pieces, craftsmen and specimen jewels) were split up, but Paul Soufflot's report picks out the salient points. He stressed the value of the influences inherited from products displayed in the various earlier exhibitions since 1894. In this respect, jewelry followed the general trend of the other industries such as furnishing, pottery, bronzeworking, etc. Modern taste condemns the excessive use of human figures, dragonflies, irises and snakes. Perhaps we do not agree with Boileau and probably with Lalique himself that:

> "There is no snake nor any monster,
> however hideous
> Which art cannot turn into a thing of beauty."

An ornament consisting of field mice, a cock's head with a big yellow diamond in its beak, snakes vomiting cascades of pearls and all those birds and butterflies, even when very prettily stylized in the Japanese manner, may perhaps make us smile, but they embody some highly practical and lasting innovations, such as the extended use of patina on gold and silver and the adaptation of jewelry to dress. Georges Fouquet was the most successful designer in the latter respect. Handling the metal positively architecturally, he fashioned enormous, slightly theatrical jewels which were both functional parts of the clothing, as we would say today, and aesthetic. We should be grateful to jewelers such as Vever, Boucheron, Aucoc, Falize, Sandoz and Templier, who had the courage to venture forth into the unexplored realm of Art Nouveau instead of staying safely in the dead-end path of traditional design.

A lot of faith and courage were needed in 1883 to speak of a revival of the decorative arts, but by 1889 and 1895 all the art industries undeniably made a strenuous effort to throw off conventional and obsolete forms. The grandiose and spectacular exhibition of 1900 crowned and consolidated the work of sowing in the public mind "the good seed, only too often mixed with tares," as Henri Vever so rightly puts it. The things which finally destroyed the prestige of Art Nouveau was not only the runaway imaginations of reputable artists but the excesses of artists and craftsmen from the professions who exaggerated the characteristics of the style in badly executed pieces. When the style was no longer a novelty which only appealed to the progressive few, everyone enthusiastically surrounded themselves with all sorts of Art Nouveau objects with a capital A, especially furniture. The highly sinuous lines and, one might say, intense "expressiveness" of the style became tiresome. At this stage, some designers were already beginning to yearn for the straight, cool lines of the style which triumphed in 1925. The coldness of this style left it open to abuse in its turn, and this is the recurrent history of every art movement and its applications.

In his contribution to Georges Fouquet's book *La Bijouterie et la Joaillerie au XX Siecle,* Emile Sedeyn concludes, "Immediately after the 1900 exhibition, jewelry entered into a remarkable period. Everyone set to work to design jewels. Painters, sculptors and energetic young ladies who had discovered the joys of pokerwork and embossed leather the year before now competed with spirit and imagination in creating model brooches, pendants, rings and necklace beads. Nymphs, sirens, seaweed, thistles, snakes and insects were put to work in all kinds of ways, in enamel, horn and ivory, and craftsmen could even be found to carry out these foggy dreams and wild notions. Not only did "art jewelers" proliferate in all the

L. Gaillard: necklace and pendant. Gold, enamel and brilliants. French, c. 1900. Victoria & Albert Museum, London.

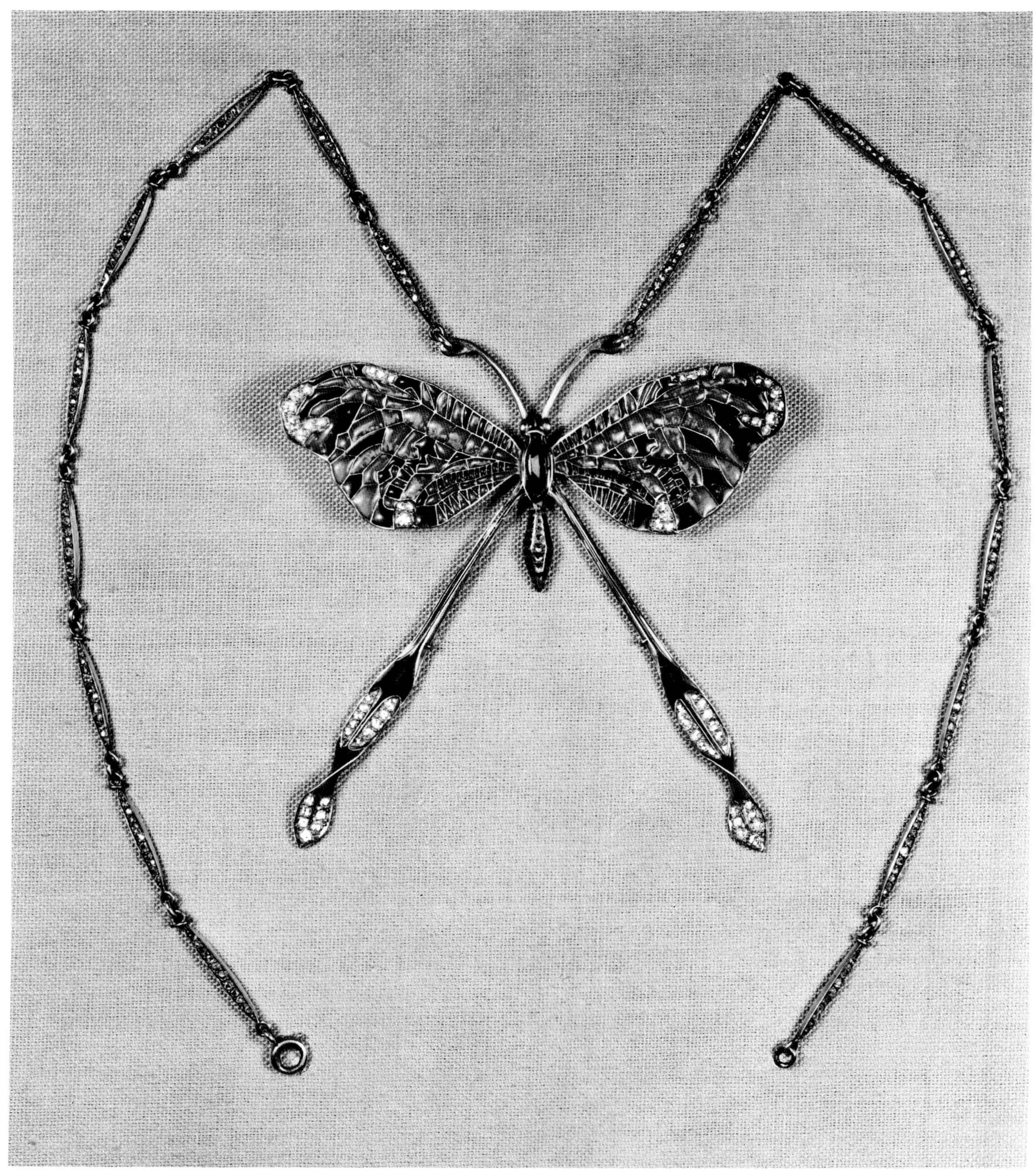

L. Gautran: pendant. Gold, enamel, diamonds, opals and emeralds. French, c. 1900. Victoria & Albert Museum, London.

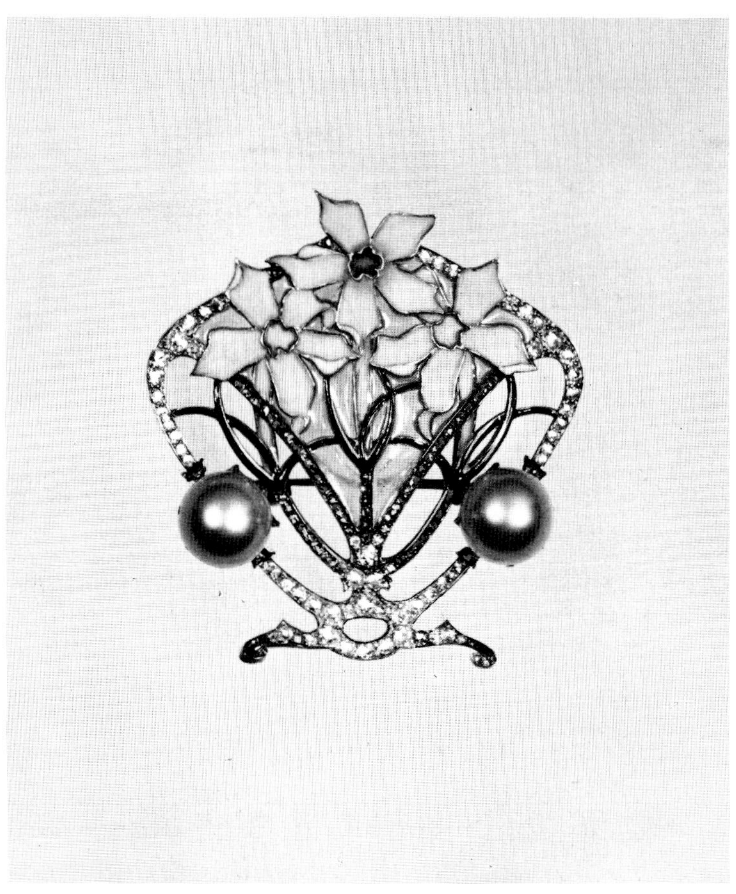

Jules-René Lalique: brooch. Gold, enamel, diamonds and cultured pearls. Bequest of Mary Kellog Hopkins. The Metropolitan Museum of Art, New York.

exhibitions, these art jewels were to be seen in all kinds of shops. Art dealers and print sellers displayed and sold jewelry, and tried to claim that they were the only ones who provided original artistic ornaments."

The new style had offshoots all over Europe and America. After his triumphant success at the Salon du Champ de mars in 1895, Lalique attracted admirers and imitators all over. However, it would be misleading to suggest that he alone influenced the vast number of ornaments which were produced during this period. Some artists absorbed his influence only to discard it later, and their work is quite different from Parisian pieces. The British and Austrians in particular often stayed clear of the main current and worked towards geometric forms which foreshadowed the Aesthetic style of the thirties.

Five ornaments by Lalique.
Pendant in chased gold: white stone, baroque pearl and enamel.
Dog-collar: gold, enamel, baroque pearl, signed.
Brooch: gold, enamel, baroque pearl, signed.
Comb: carved horn, gold, enamel, signed and dated 1900.
Ring: chased gold, pearl, signed and dated 1900.
Musée des Arts Decoratifs, Paris.

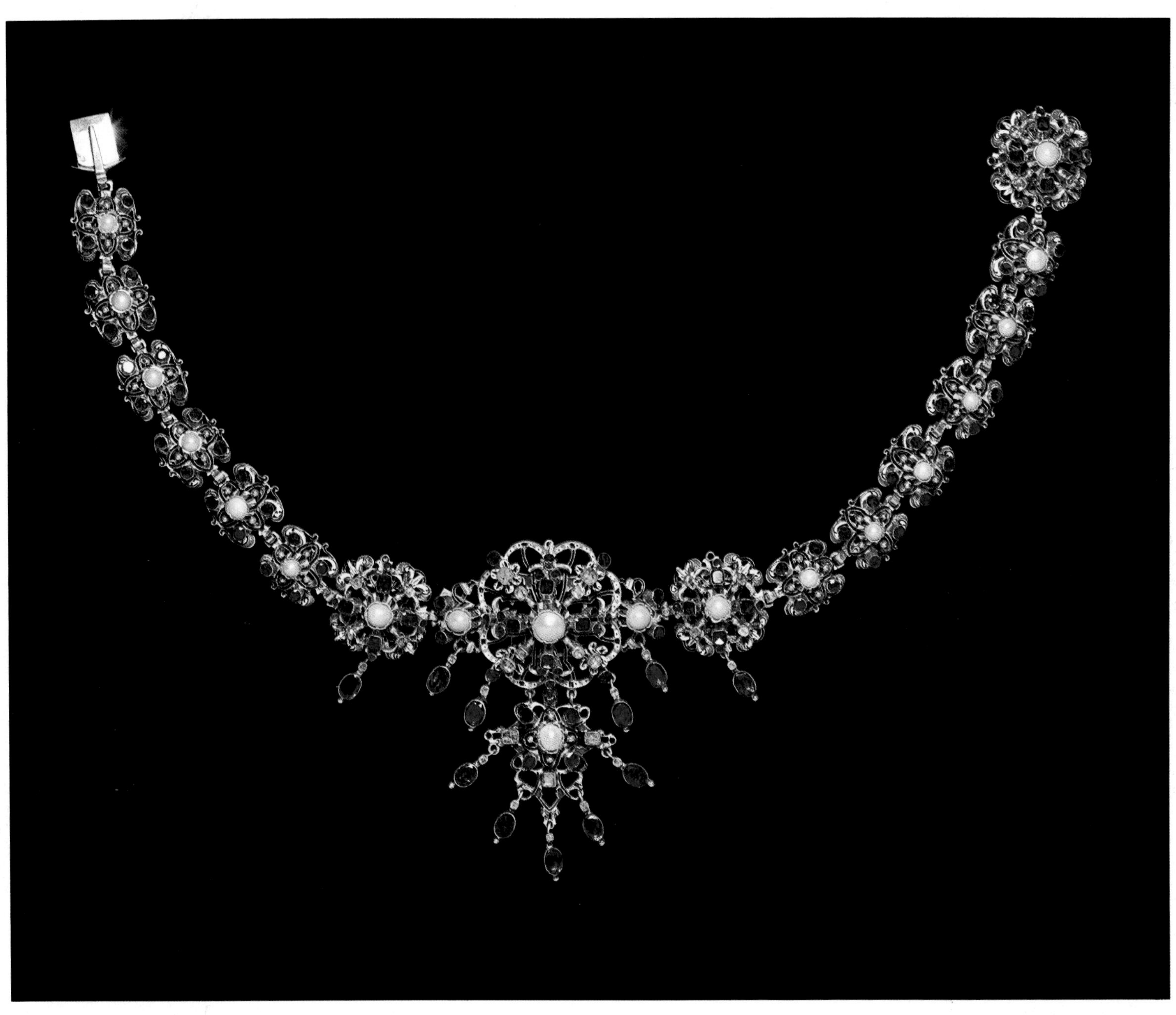

Parts of the "currant leaf" *parure,* after a design by Alfred Bapst, 1856. Bibliothèque Forney, Paris.

Necklace: silver gilt, enamel, pearls, garnets and green garnets. By Schlichtegroll of Vienna. Victoria & Albert Museum, London.

Indeed, two widely different styles seem to have coexisted. One, partly originated by Lalique, could be regarded as the *fin-de-siècle* style in that it carried the experiments and innovations of the past hundred years to the ultimate limit. The other heralded the future. The Aesthetic movement had profound effects on England and Scotland, and the Germans and Austrians of the time of the Secession followed the same lines of development. Between these two main streams, however, there were a number of independent creative artists who drew on both at once, adopting French lightness and flowing line and Anglo-German abstract motifs and unusual materials. Others again moved with the times from the nineteenth to the twentieth century.

Phillipe Wolfers of Belgium seems to have been one of the latter. He was born in Brussels in 1858. He studied sculpture at the Académie Royal des Beaux-Arts and then served a thorough technical apprenticeship in the workshop of his father, "a master goldsmith and dealer." He sought from the first to eliminate the excess decoration of the rococo style which was currently enjoying a revival. His first designs, pieces on floral motifs with pure lines, show this preoccupation. His works were soon to be displayed in the great exhibitions which were frequent at the time, but he hardly produced anything after 1908, preferring to devote himself to sculpture.

Flowers, dragonflies and butterflies were his favorite motifs. They are always full of natural freshness and grace translated into jeweled ornaments. They seem quite original and show remarkable mastery of design and technique. The delicacy of his colors and the variety of his raw materials are also striking. He was skilled in combining opaque and clear enamels, turned and chased gold, brilliants, precious stones, baroque and regular pearls and

Philippe Wolfers: pendant, "Scarab." Gold, translucent enamel, a large opal, pearls and brilliants. Monogram P.W., 1900. Private collection, Brussels.

Philippe Wolfers: necklace and pendant. Gold, enamel, brilliants and pearls, c. 1900. Wolfers Frères Collection, Brussels.

Philippe Wolfers: pendant, "Libellulu." Gold, enamel, pearls and gems, c. 1900. Wolfers Frères Collection, Brussels.

Combs, bracelets, belt buckle, eardrops: amber, feldspar, green onyx and opal, c. 1904, Georg Jensen, Copenhagen.

semiprecious stones. He used a lot of opals, peridots and amethysts, and took advantage of different colors of gold and cuts of gem and varying shades of enamel. During the few years he devoted to jewelry, he was almost as famous as Lalique, and like him, he was one of the few adepts of Art Nouveau whose reputation and whose firm have survived all the subsequent fluctuations of fashion.

He was not the only Belgian to produce Art Nouveau jewelry. Paul Dubois, Leopold Vanstrydonck and Henry Ven der Velde were also notable jewelers. The last-named, who was also a painter, decorator, writer and artist, has left very few ornaments, but he deserves to be singled out for his great originality. It is true that his work has more to do with the goldsmith than the jeweler, but the dividing line was far from clear in this period, and these jewels show the extraordinary mastery of line which is the mark of the true artist. Van der Velde was an international artist by virtue of both his career and his style. His reputation earned him an invitation to Weimar, where he founded a school of decorative arts. He traveled to Holland and Switzerland and died in Zurich in 1957. He met artists from many different disciplines and seemed to absorb many trends and to unite them all in a pleasing synthesis. His work shows typically British simple purity, a taste for geometrically balanced shapes which he could only have learned from the Germans, and fertile creative powers which belonged to him alone. He was one of the artists who began his career in the nineteenth century and rapidly became one of the precursors of the twentieth.

The great artists of Austria and Germany were also a long way ahead of their times. They were the moving spirits of the great centers of Vienna, Pforzheim and Darmstadt where the new aesthetic movement developed. Cranach, Czeschka, Ferdinand Hauser, Müller, Koloman Moser and Joseph Hoffmann were not just skilled jewelers, but architects and decorators who took as much interest in jewelry as they did in the other arts. They aimed to bring a touch of style to every aspect of the environment. This phenomenon, which is typical of Art Nouveau, was especially pronounced in Austria and Germany. A group

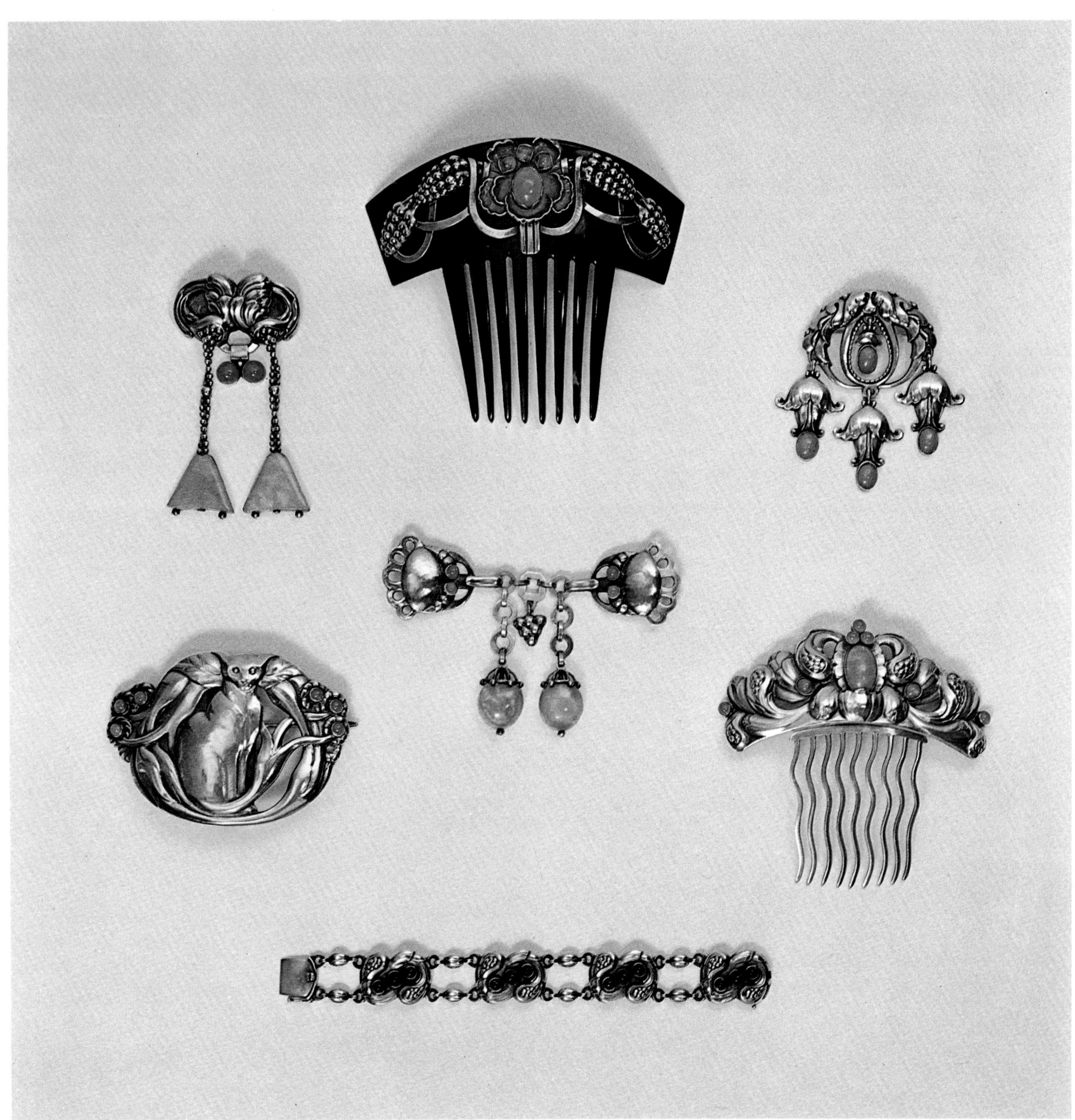

of architects started the movement. Their influence had profound effects on their disciples, and this is perhaps the origin of the movement towards straight lines, clean angles and finally defined geometric forms. It may also have been a reaction against the contrasting tendencies of Belgian and French Art Nouveau which, compared with their work, sometimes seems like the last flowering of the rococo movement.

Joseph Hoffmann's jewels are typical of this style. They make use of curved lines and concave and convex surfaces, but they also follow a very simple uncluttered line the deliberate severity of which is not without grace. Hoffmann was particularly fond of square pendants with rectangular or triangular cabochons, and whenever he adopted a floral motif he stylized it as much as possible. Ferdinand Hauser too made no concessions to naturalism, and Koloman Moser decorated his highly abstract jewels with big cabochons and semiprecious stones, with precious stones to add brilliant touches of color.

It could be said that nearly every artist and decorator made jewelry at the end of the century. It would therefore be impossible to give a complete list, especially as some of the surviving works are anonymous while others are signed with initials which we can no longer identify. In the face of ths profusion, one might be tempted to pass on to the twentieth century, but it must be stressed that these pieces are far more than costume jewelry, even though they were not made or distributed by recognized jewelry firms. They are sometimes criticized as being *objets d'art* or show pieces rather than jewelry—this criticism was even leveled at Lalique—but it cannot be denied that they were ultimately accepted and that they contributed substantially to the formation of the early twentieth century style.

England and Scotland also made important contributions to creative jewelry. The work of Ashbee and his contemporaries has already been mentioned. Other outstanding designers were the MacDonald sisters, interior

Philippe Wolfers: belt buckle, "Peacock's feather." Chased gold, opal with rubies, a brilliant, 1898. Wolfers Frères Collection, Brussels.

decorators whose studios produced objects with characteristically etiolated, elegant fragile shapes and Alexander Fisher, a goldsmith who sometimes made jewelry. British artists, too, were preoccupied with shapes, materials, curves and colors, and did not care whether a stone was valuable or not. This style did not take root and spread without affecting traditional jewelry in England, too. Its influence can be assessed simply by consulting the catalogues of the best London jewelers.

Two currents can be discerned in the two contrasting trends in the decorative arts which we have traced. One might be called the Latin style. It is dominated by the pursuit of grace, elegance and ornamental suppleness. The other, which is particularly prevalent in the Anglo-Saxon and Nordic countries, is characterized by great simplicity of form.

Two artists could be taken as typical: the Spaniard Luis Masriera and the Dane Georg Jensen. The former was born in Barcelona in 1872 and was a painter, goldsmith and playwright. He studied in London, Geneva and Paris, and seems to have been strongly influenced by the French style. The influence of Lalique, Vever and Fouqet can be recognized in many pendants and medallions of his workmanship, and like them, his favorite motifs were flowers and women, often graceful creatures with enamelled wings flying over a background starred with brilliants. He liked circular frames, soft angles and a cunning interplay of curved lines. A pendant with St. George transfixing the dragon and another with a profile of Iseult on a cloisonné enamel background like stained glass have motifs belonging to the trend which was current more than fifty years earlier, but their treatment is undeniably that of Nouveau Art.

Georg Jensen was quite different. He is best known as a goldsmith. He opened a workshop in Copenhagen in 1904. He chiefly worked in silver, and his silver tableware still has a modern look. However, Jensen also produced ornaments decorated with enamel and stones (particularly amber, turquoise, onyx, and opals). These owe a lot to contemporary styles, but they are distinguished by greater

Philippe Wolfers: pendant, "The Charmer." Carved ivory, carved rainbow quartz stone, pear-shaped opal, pink topazes, native pearls and small brilliants. Chased gold. Wolfers Frères Collection, Brussels.

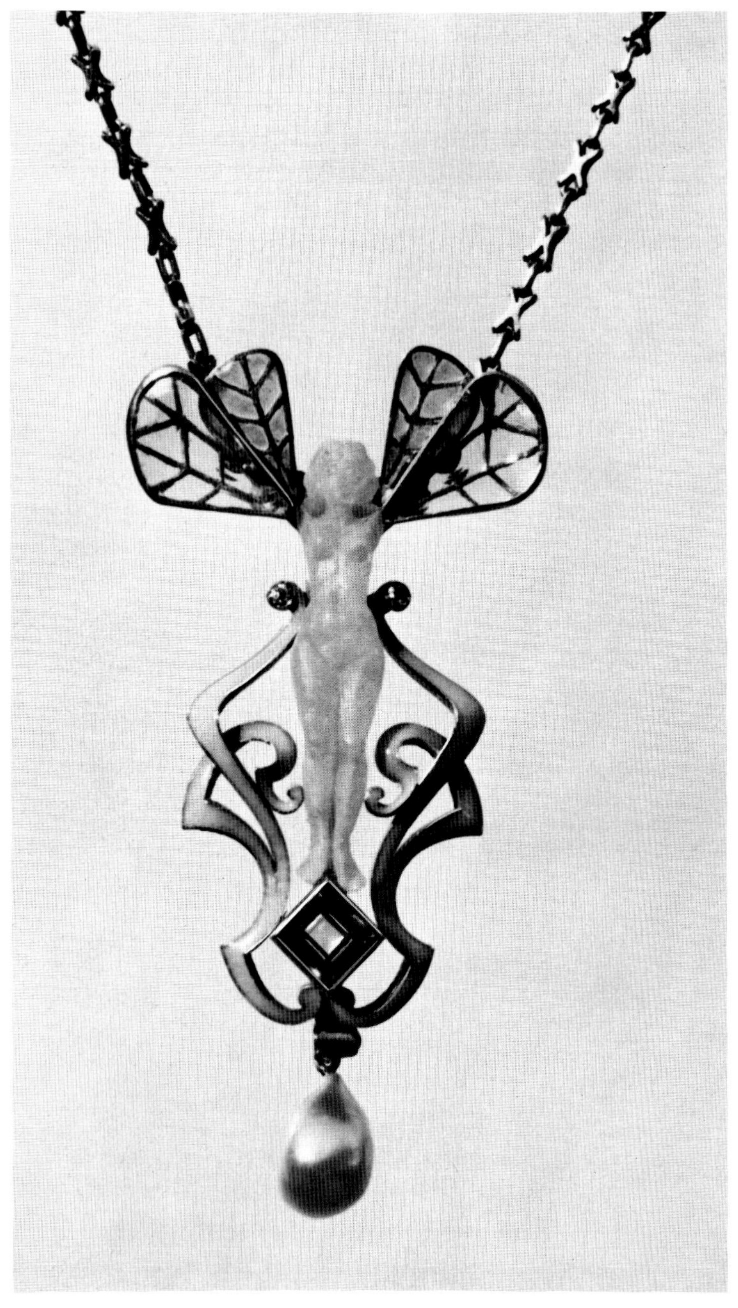

simplicity and some have a deliberate stiffness which seems to be derived from the folk art in which Jensen was becoming interested. His animals and flowers were highly stylized and he preferred abstract motifs. It must be remembered that Scandinavian decorative arts in the late nineteenth and early twentieth century achieved a really original style which is just as important today.

Some aspects of Art Nouveau therefore contributed quite substantially to modern style by freeing the decorative arts of petrified traditional formulae and reviving the quality of inventiveness. The whole living environment was altered by it, and jewelry was perhaps affected even more than interior decor. By seeking a new significance in the interplay of lines, colors and materials, the creators of Art Nouveau partially revived the former symbolism of precious ornaments, not only by virtue of the fact that some of their jewels, like some of Gallé's vases, bore a title or an inscription, but because they sometimes aspired to a value which had nothing to do with the market price. Some overzealous craftsmen refused on principle to use gems in order to preserve the "purity" of the artistry of their work. In this respect they passed from one extreme to another, but if time has softened these excesses, it is nonetheless true that the old spirit had been revived and a new stimulus infused into jewelry. Another characteristic of this period was the way sculptors and painters participated in the minor arts. We saw that during the Renaissance many goldsmiths became painters. In the late nineteenth century, the reverse is true. Artists turned back to goldworking and jewelry, designed ornaments and studied technique. This trend began about 90 years ago and is still very active today. We shall have occasion to mention it again.

Philippe Wolfers: pendant, "Butterfly." Carved rainbow quartz stone, enamel, emerald, pearl, brilliant, gold. L.-R, Feldheim Collection, Brussels.

Georg Jensen: pendant. Opals, turquoises and enamel, 1914. National Museum, Stockholm, Sweden.

Surely, this long century pointed out the way for the twentieth, although some people would like to deny it. We have followed its archaeological discoveries and innovations of processes and motifs, and by the time we leave it with the approach of the first world war, it might seem that the die was already cast. We cannot avoid recognizing many connections with it, and these common points are emphasized by the fact that many of our greatest contemporary jewelry firms and dynasties were started in the nineteenth century. Garrard, which is probably the oldest since it was founded in 1721, has consolidated its leading position in London. Houses like Wolfers, Tiffany and Jensen prospered greatly towards the end of the century. There would certainly be some newcomers in twentieth century jewelry, but many of our famous jewelers were already well known before 1914. From this time forwards, names will be more important than countries, a trend which grew stronger all through the nineteenth century in fashion and jewelry and must be emphasized before we embark on the twentieth.

Philippe Wolfers: pendant, "Swan and Hyacinth." Gold, enamel, brilliants, baroque pearl, rubies and semi-precious stones. The swan is a rainbow quartz stone carved in the round; the three hyacincths are carnelians and pink and green tourmaline. Mr. and Mrs. Wittamer De Camps Collection, Brussels.

Philippe Wolfers: necklace and pendant. Gold, enamel, brilliants and pearls, c. 1900. Wolfers Frères Collection, Brussels.

Chapter 5

THE TWENTIETH CENTURY

THE TWENTIETH CENTURY

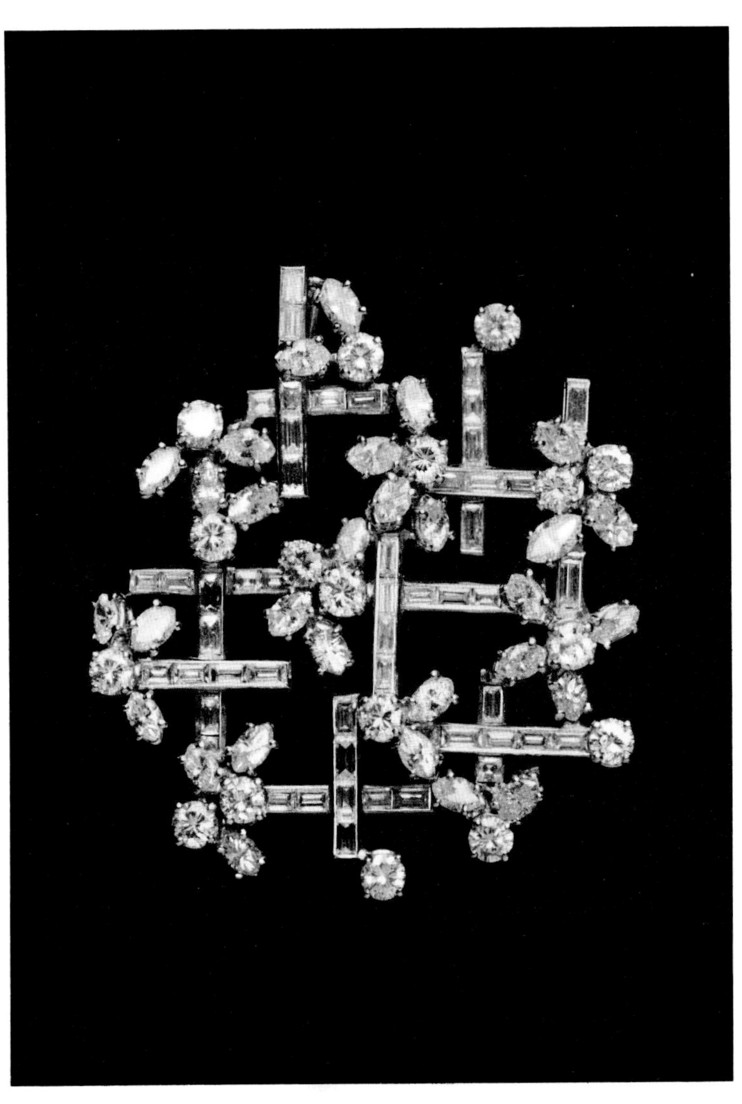

It is always harder to evaluate one's own contemporary period than a previous age. We have discounted the first ten years of the twentieth century because they seemed historically to belong to the nineteenth, the final break not occurring until just before the first world war, but even in this attenuated form the present century still includes more than fifty years of discoveries and disturbances, the stages of which we must now attempt to define. Some chronological divisions spring immediately to mind, but it is sometimes all the more difficult to analyze trends of the past fifty years because many of them are still influencing our fashions and tastes, and people of every era tend to regard their own likings as an unprecedented and sharply defined advance on everything that had gone before.

This problem is especially relevant in the case of the decorative arts, since we inherited from Art Nouveau a tendency to love the object for itself, and to be perhaps a shade too ready to divorce it from its function. This apparently unprecedented phenomenon leads us to elevate things which were primarily meant to be utilitarian to the rank of *objets d'art,* and there they stagnate. Our viewpoint has changed. We love shapes, colors and materials, sometimes without reference to the function for which the object was designed.

Brooch: baguette and navette brilliants in a platinum setting, 1967. Garrard, London.

However, we are also more conscious than ever before of the functional aspect of an object, which we believe should be a source of beauty in itself. All superfluous ornament should therefore be eliminated and we should concentrate on the interplay of very pure lines, although some people might regard this as rather cold.

The previous century has bequeathed other tastes to us. Primitive and folk arts revealed the charm of spontaneous, unpolished articles made of rough materials, and we now attach far less importance than they did a hundred years ago to the apparent "finish" of a work of art. Each in its turn or simultaneously, these trends deem to dominate our decorative arts and determine the style of our ornaments more or less directly.

It is nevertheless possible to distinguish several periods. The first is the "1925" style, which began to appear early in the century and persisted till just after 1930. From 1929 on, in fact, jewelers in France and abroad pursued an effect of lightness which had been lost and partially abandoned color. The second world war appreciably slowed down production practically everywhere, and it was followed by an entirely understandable period of reaction. After years of privation, everyone wanted abundance, and for a few years heavy geometric jewels which needed a lot of gold were worn. However, jewelry gradually reverted to a light, harmonious style, and these are the characteristics of contemporary jewels.

We shall not devote much space to the ornaments of 1940-45, but we must discuss the original style which developed about 1910 in greater detail. Many international exhibitions heralded what might seem to be an aesthetic revolution. It was perceptible in every art form all over the world. Its progress can be followed in the work of leading French jewelers, especially Lalique.

After a rather lean period for French jewelry, an increasing number of artists including Raymond Templier, Jean Fouquet, Gerald Sandoz and many other enthusiasts, continued the work of renovation started in 1900. Interesting creations reappeared in jeweler's windows. Even Lalique sobered down, though he still continued to produce charming work.

The production of Sergei Diaghilev's Russian Ballet in 1910 had repercussions on all the arts. It was a triumph of glowing color, bold contrasts and many geometrical lines. Jewelry followed suit, using precious and semiprecious stones in voluminous jewelry—pendants and rings designed to harmonize with high fashion and theatrical costume, as we have already seen in the case of Georges Fouquet. Enamel reappeared in ornaments by Lalique and Vever.

Technical considerations initiated a return to creations essentially belonging to the jeweler's art. The years 1910-14 were a time of purification. It was also in this period that work was started on an exhibition planned for 1916 which, owing to the 1914-18 war, did not take place until 1925. Only models and articles of new inspiration and real originality were to be accepted, to the exclusion of all copies based on or imitated from ancient or antique styles.

Many critics dismissed the results of all this activity and invention by saying most disparagingly that everything "had gone Cubist," and it is true that some artists claimed kinship with this movement. Cubist painting, however, did not engender the whole style by itself. In their buildings and furniture German and Belgian architects introduced an ideal of cut-away, clearly defined volumes and clean breaks and articulations in which there was no room for ornament. Artists sought more eagerly than ever before to create a total environment, a harmonious ensemble, and the importance of the art of "design" which, as we have seen, emerged in the late nineteenth century, was confirmed. On the eve of the 1914 war the stage

Boucheron: brooch. Onyx, coral and brilliant in a platinum setting, after a design by Masse, 1925.
G. Fouqet: gold clip.
Raymond Templier: brooch. Platinum, brilliants and enamel, 1925. Musée des Arts Decoratifs, Paris.

seemed to be set for a new style, not only among artists and craftsmen, but among the public, whose viewpoint was gradually being altered. After the war, all the tendencies which had been germinated burst into flower.

The birth of the new style was favored by another psychological factor which is common to most post-war periods. Years of misery and privation are nearly always followed by a few years of extravagance. Everyone wants novelties and things they have never seen before. They must forget the past, wipe out everything that reminds them of it, and create a bright new world. For six years, all the artists of Europe and America worked towards this end, and so abundant and original was the output of this short span of time that many people regard it as an entire generation.

Changes in fashion must also be taken into account. It is obvious that the nearer a period is to the present, the better its differences can be appreciated. The history of costume in past ages is described by defining the stages every twenty or thirty years, but nowadays, every season seems to bring a comparatively new way of dressing. Evolution was probably just as rapid in the past, and it would be hopeless to try to follow it. However, the advent of short, light clothes which totally changed the female shape was very important. Another revolutionary feature was the fact that never before, except perhaps during the Directory period in France, had women's clothes been so simple. The skirt and bodice which had been through every possible variation disappeared in favor of the "little dress," which the most eminent critics unhesitatingly compared to the Greek *chiton.* Fashion plates are an invaluable source of information, as they show not only what was worn but the new type of woman for whom these dresses and outfits were designed. The so-called Cubist influence can be recognized in both. The silhouette had never been so long and flat. Short, shingled hair, tunic dresses and tailored tweeds were worn by slender, athletic women. Couturiers' models were called "100 m.p.h.," "Wireless telegraphy," "Top speed," and needless to say, these dynamic clothes called for an absolutely new style of jewelry.

This new style owed a good deal to various artistic movements like the Bauhaus, which was founded in 1919 by Gropius in collaboration with masters like Klee and Kandinsky. The aesthetic revolution initiated by the Bauhaus did not perhaps affect jewelry immediately, but its influence would be obvious a few years later, as would that of the groups such as Valori Plastici, Neue Sachlichkeit, November, de Stijl and Neo-Plasticism which were springing up all over Europe.

This was the spirit of the program for the 1925 exhibition of decorative arts. It was thought advisable to hold a preliminary exhibition in 1924 in the Pavillon de Marsan at the Louvre, and this rehearsal greatly improved the quality of the final product.

The jewelry exhibition of 1925 took place in a highly elegant modern setting by the architect Eric Bagge. It produced an impression of harmony and unity as well as novelty. The feature which characterized it in contrast with other earlier shows was the close collaboration between the decorator-designer and the craftsman, whether the designer belonged to the craftsman's workshop or whether he worked freelance. Each house preserved its individuality by its selection from the common repertoire, but all the exhibitors agreed in accepting the broad outlines of the new aesthetic movement—the priority of linear qualities, contrasting colors a hitherto unequaled technical standard, and the discriminating use of materials chosen for their ornamental properties rather than their market value.

The report on the jewelry section says, "Stones like topaz and aquamarine which have been out of fashion for a long time have reappeared. They are big enough to supply transparent masses in which the light plays as softly

Raymond Templier: jewelry in brilliants and onyx, 1925. Musée des Arts Decoratifs, Paris.

as in calm, tinted water. Enamel, mother-of-pearl, coral and onyx have returned to favor, and Chinese jade is also used, and not just for necklaces and pendants. Their opaque or matt surfaces allied to cut stones which reflect the light offer novel contrasts."

This was the definitive arrival of color, foreseen since 1900 by some, confirmed in 1910 by the success of the Russian Ballet, but subsequently retarded by traditional, if not commerical considerations. This trend was supported by new technical improvements which favored its survival.

Even diamonds achieved new effects. Table and baguette cut stones were set alongside the classic cuts, producing a play of light in the scintillating surface of the ornament, which was even more subtly pleasing to the eye in that the reason for it was not immediately apparent. Colored stones often picked out a motif in this luminous background. Such combinations with no gaps to be seen were only possible because platinum was so easy to work. "While fifty years ago colored stones had been isolated by their surroundings by visible gold claws and brilliants had been given a thick and soon tarnished silver setting to avoid having gold near them, the brightness and strength of platinum now make invisible settings possible. Platinum mounts can be divided into a great many sections linked by tiny joints. A bracelet becomes as flexible as a ribbon; no roughness can be seen and the support holding the stones together is scarcely visible beneath the mosaic of gems." (*Rapport general* C1.24, French section)

Critics, who were perhaps less knowledgeable about technical problems, were particularly aware of the aesthetic and sociological significance of the new creations. Guillaume Janneau writes, "It was the overt expression of the sensibility 'conditioned' by new psychological stimuli, which the 1915-25 generation were trying to give a permanent form. These stimuli have been named by the artists themselves; they are the products of science, with its relativity and fascination, sure as the cinema, electricity, speed and the great creations of modern mechanical equipment." Analyzing the new style, he concludes, "these forms, determined by specific conditions, express the real modern aesthetic—the aesthetic of cleanness."

France, as we have seen, continued to lead the world in jewelry and was followed, as always, with varying degrees of success. However, some European countries kept their individuality, although they were drawn along with the current. Unfortunately, we must confine ourselves to naming jewelers and describing their work, since photographic records are extremely rare.

It is recorded, for example, that the Catalan Pavilion provoked amused or horrified reactions with a series of Cubist jewels which, to say the least, showed a great deal of imagination and boldness. Critics agreed in finding them rather ugly, but more interesting than the false ivory cameos heavily decorated with gold which Spain displayed, along with other jewels of antiquated appearance, mostly enamelled in pale colors.

The Austrians distinguished themselves everywhere by their gaiety and the imagination and richness of their designs. The name of Dagobert Peche, who had recently died and who had been one of the most brilliant artists of the Wiener Werkstätte, was particularly acclaimed.

As far as the Swiss were concerned, the watch seemed to be more or less closely connected with jewelry, but from a completely different point of view from earlier times. While in the eighteenth century, the watch, châtelaine and pendants had provided large surfaces to be decorated with enamels, diamonds and gems, the reverse was now true. "Prodigiously tiny" watches were integrated into ornaments which hid them and eclipsed them completely.

Belgium, too, achieved great distinction in this exhibition, with the work of the Leyssen brothers and Coosemans. Parisian influence was quite strong in Brussels, but it did not obscure a certain originality of form. Wolfers is quoted in all the accounts, but more for his interior

Wolfers: design for a necklace, c. 1925. Wolfers Frères Collection, Brussels.

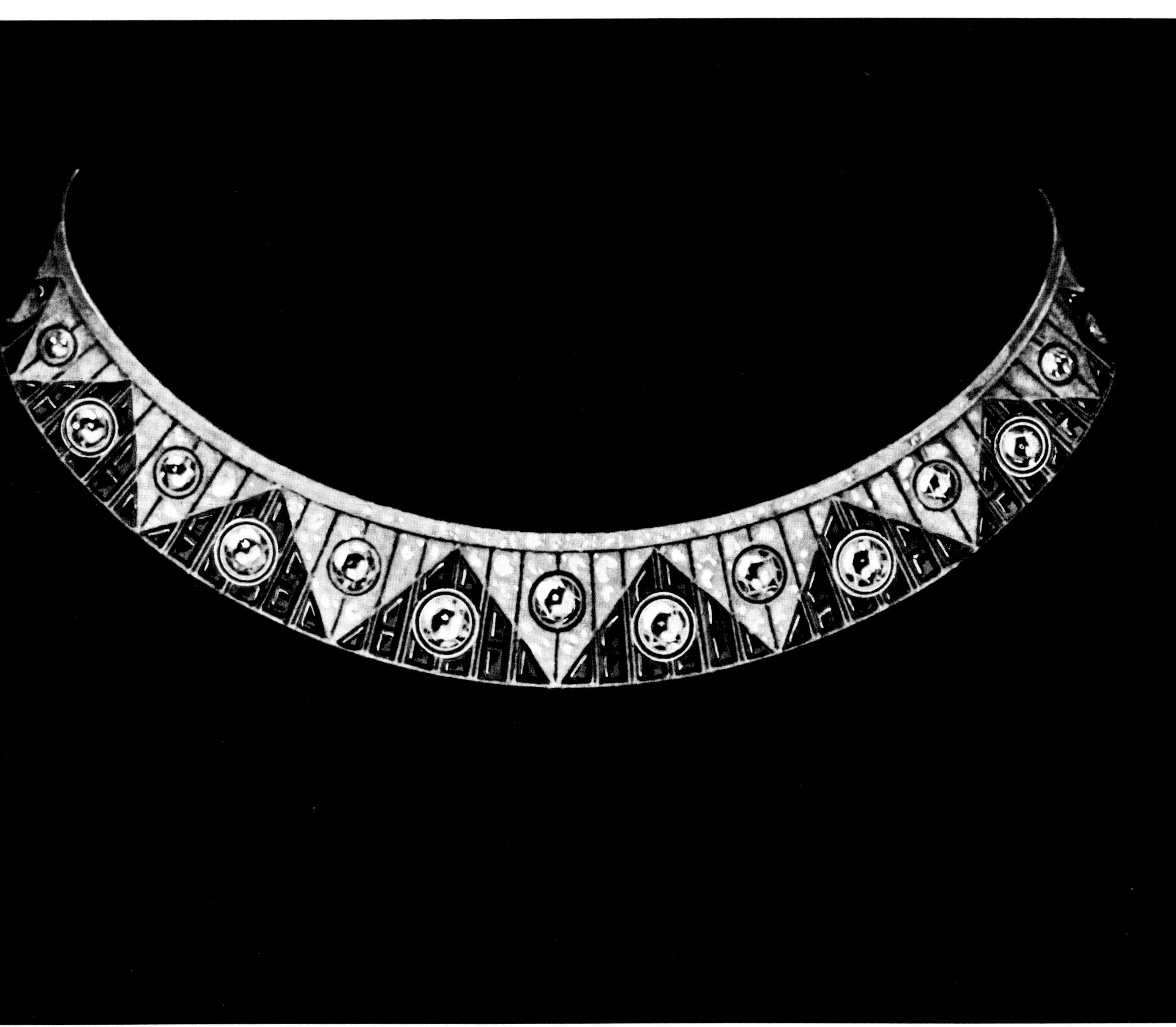

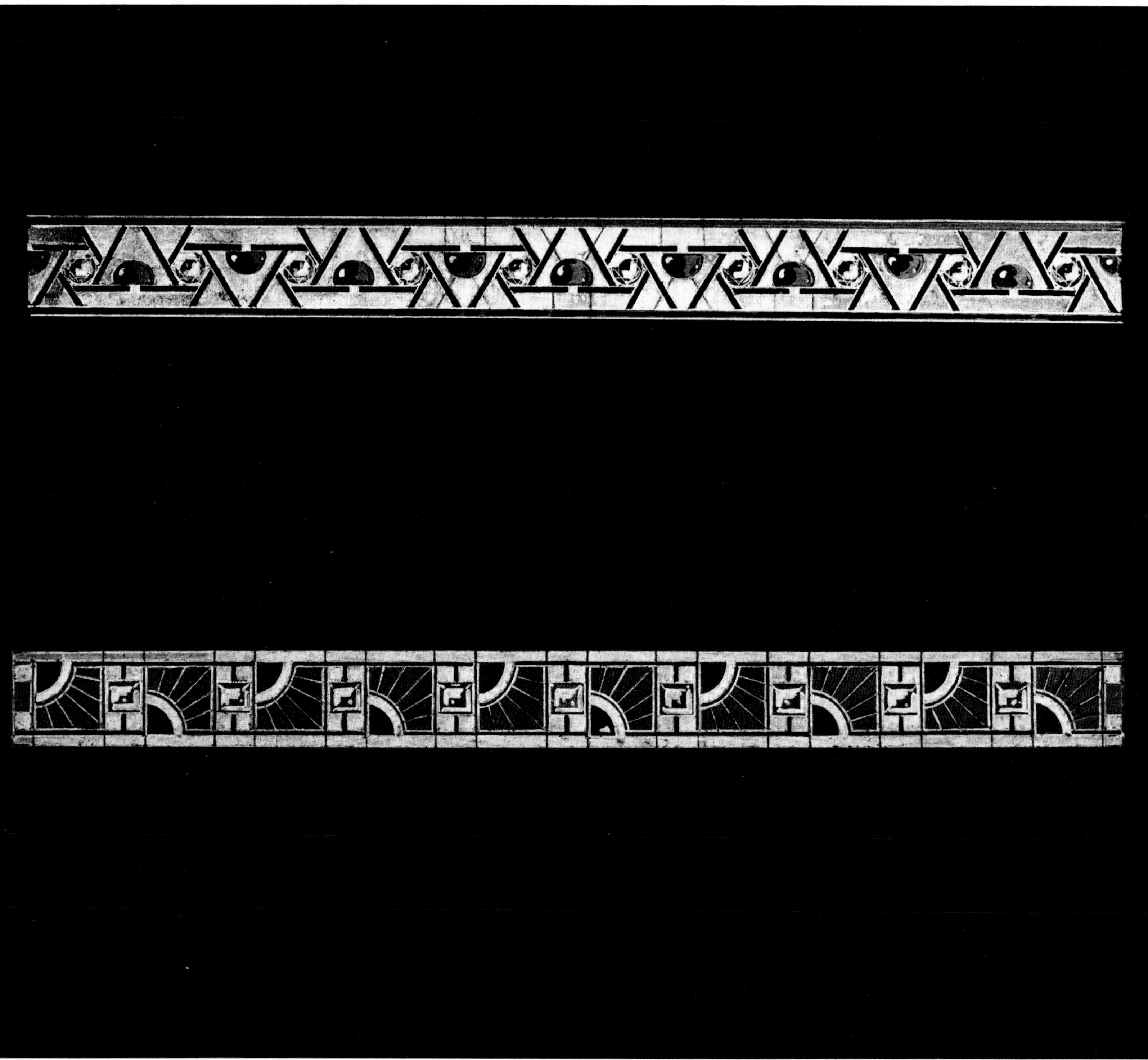

Chaumet: double clip. Platinum and diamonds, 1935. Chaumet Collection, Paris.

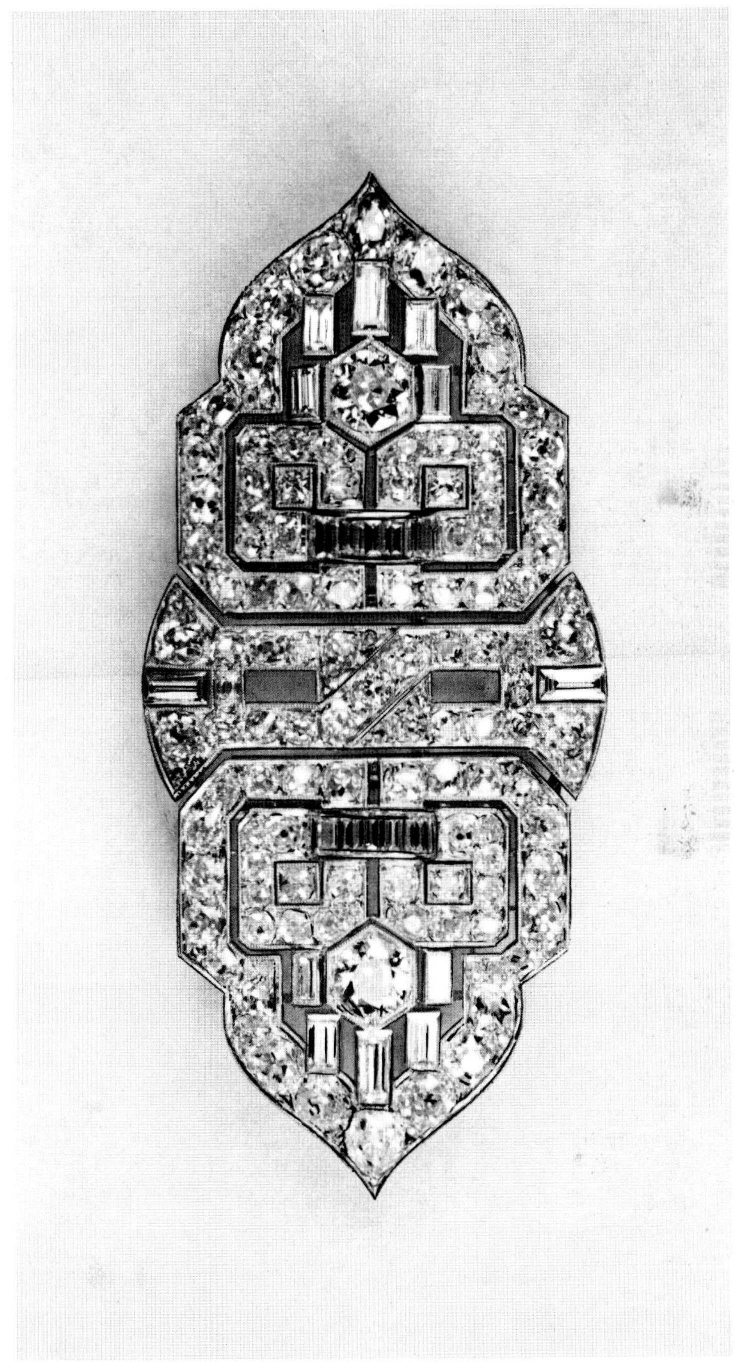

Chaumet: double clip. Platinum and diamonds, 1935. Chaumet Colletion, Paris.

Mauboussin: necklace. Twist of sapphire beads, emerald leaves, brilliants and rubies with a cabochon sapphire in the center. Mauboussin Collection, Paris.

Chaumet: double clip. Platinum and diamonds, 1935. Chaumet Collection, Paris.

Chaumet: clip and eardrops. Platinum and diamonds, 1938. Chaumet Collection, Paris.

Mauboussin: convertible clip, "Cascade." Baguette and round, pear-shaped and navette brilliants. Mauboussin Collection, Paris.

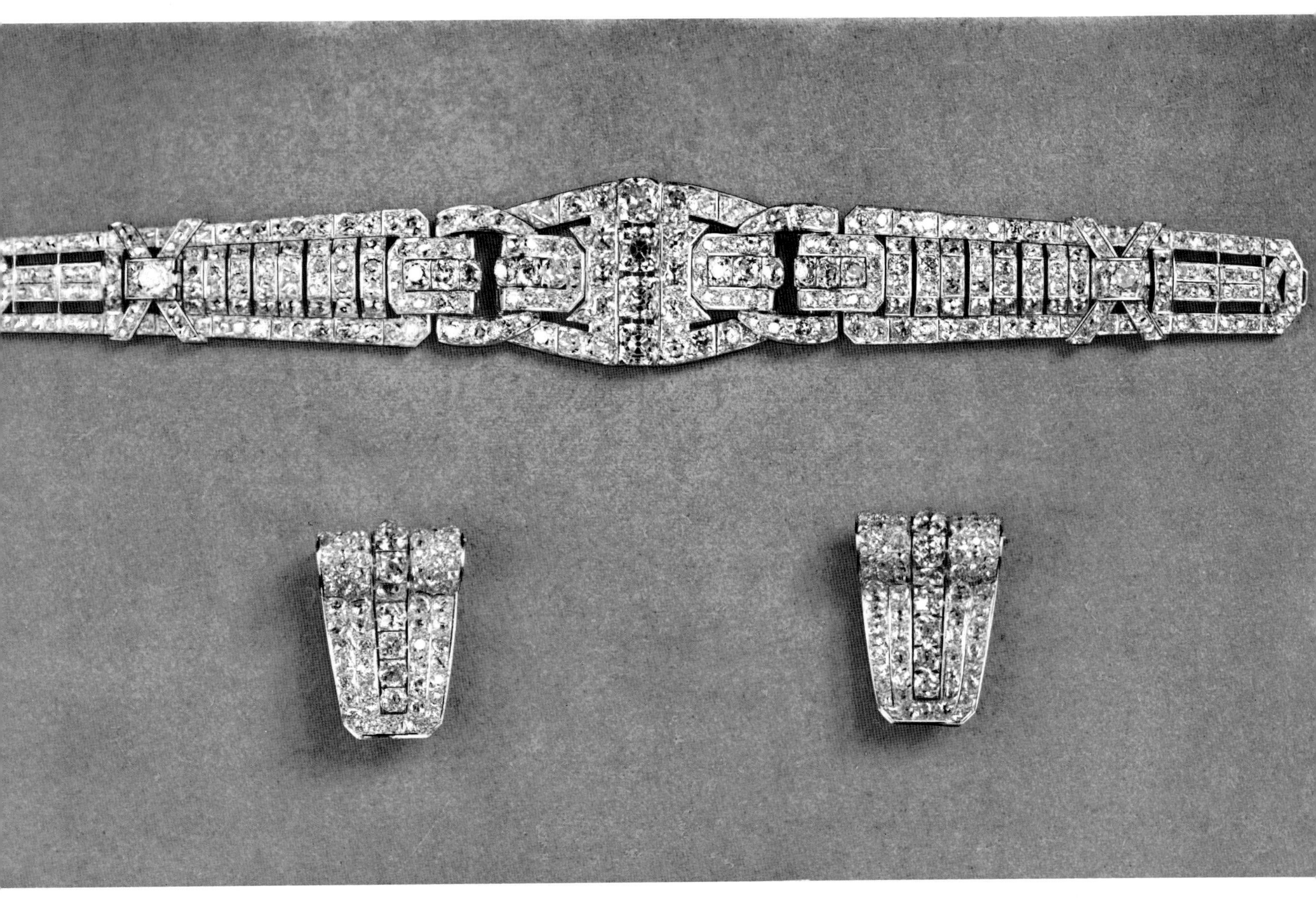

Chaumet: clips and bracelet. Platinum and diamonds, c. 1940. Chaumet Collection, Paris.

Wolfers: brooch. Gold, diamonds and gems, c. 1940. Wolfers Frères Collection, Brussels.

Chaumet: clip, "Flower." Platinum and diamonds, c. 1940. Chaumet Collection, Paris.

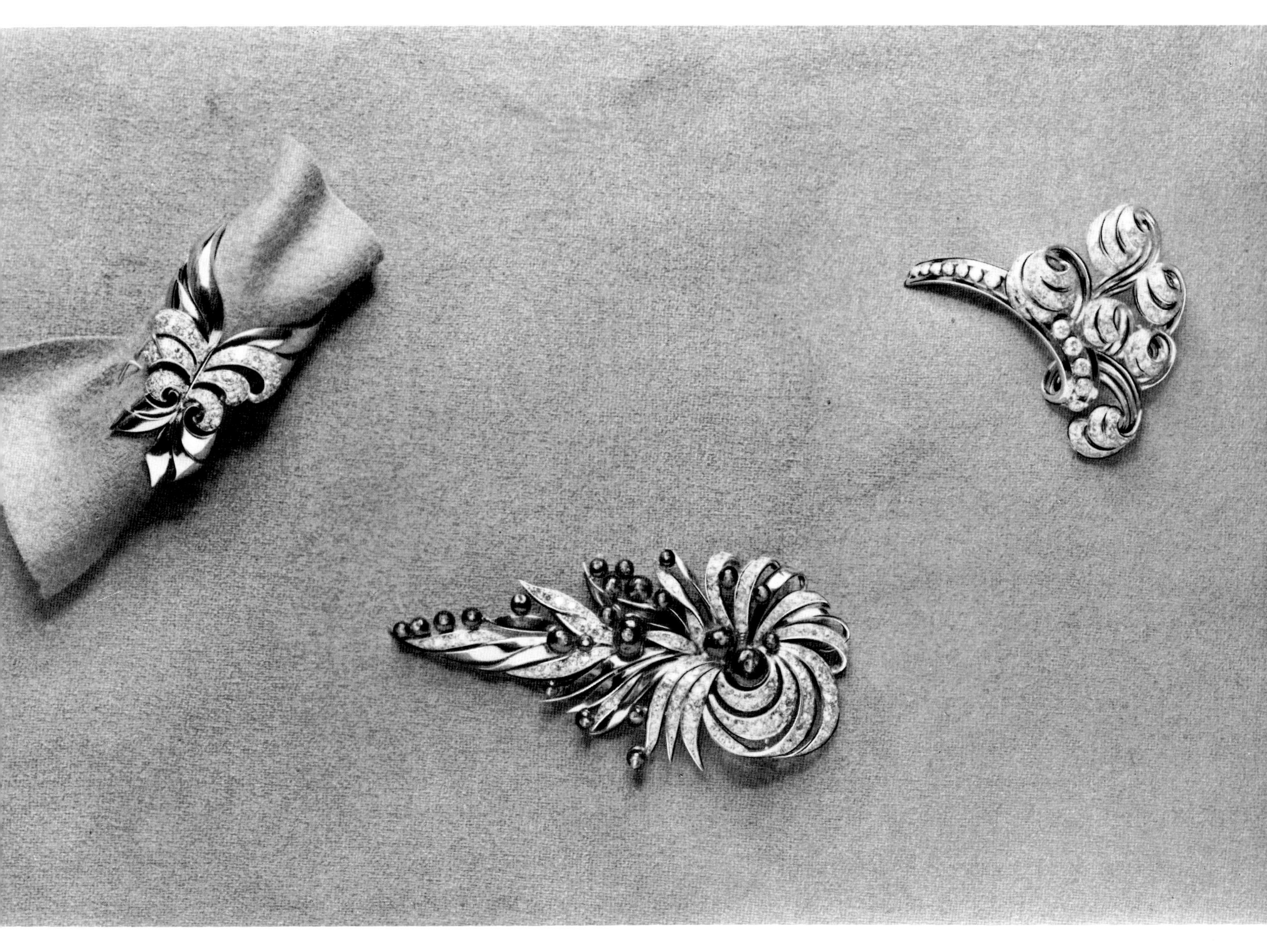

Chaumet: clips. Platinum and diamonds, 1949. Chaumet Collection, Paris.

decorations than his jewelry, although the firm was producing some extremely interesting pieces during this period. The geometric designs of his bracelets were remarkably varied. Shapes and colors alternated, set off by black onyx and *pavé* backgrounds of tiny brilliants. The same inventiveness is found in the necklaces and many colorful brooches which the firm of Wolfers produced at this time. They show constant eagerness to adapt the new repertoire to the art of jewelry without relinquishing either delicacy of execution or richness of material.

The jewelry of the 1920s, whether it is regarded as an aspect of a movement or simply as a caprice of fashion, was very significant, either because it had succeeded in freeing itself completely from obsolete forms or because it marked an important milestone in technical progress. Even critics who find its color tiresome and its stiffness excessive to the point of heaviness cannot deny the great wealth of the contribution of the decade after the first world war.

The 1925 exhibition, especially the jewelry section, was an unquestionable success. A few jewelers and goldsmiths, urged and led by Georges Fouquet, decided to organize a select exhibition in an essentially Parisian setting in order to continue the good work and point out the future path to foreign clients, artists and collectors.

Under the auspices of the city of Paris and Henri Clouzot, the curator of the Galliéra museum, the exhibition took place in the Galliéra palace in June and July 1929. Designed once more by Eric Bagge, the interior of the palace was transformed into a setting which was both sober and elegant, and perfectly suited to the magnificence of jewelry. "After crossing the threshold you entered a vast grey, gold and silver casket. The light seemed to come entirely from the objects on display. Forgetting the walls,

Wolfers: clip. Baguette, navette and round brilliants, 1958. Wolfers Frères Collection, Brussels.

Chaumet: necklace. Platinum and diamonds with three large pear-shaped emeralds, 1950. Chaumet Collection, Paris.

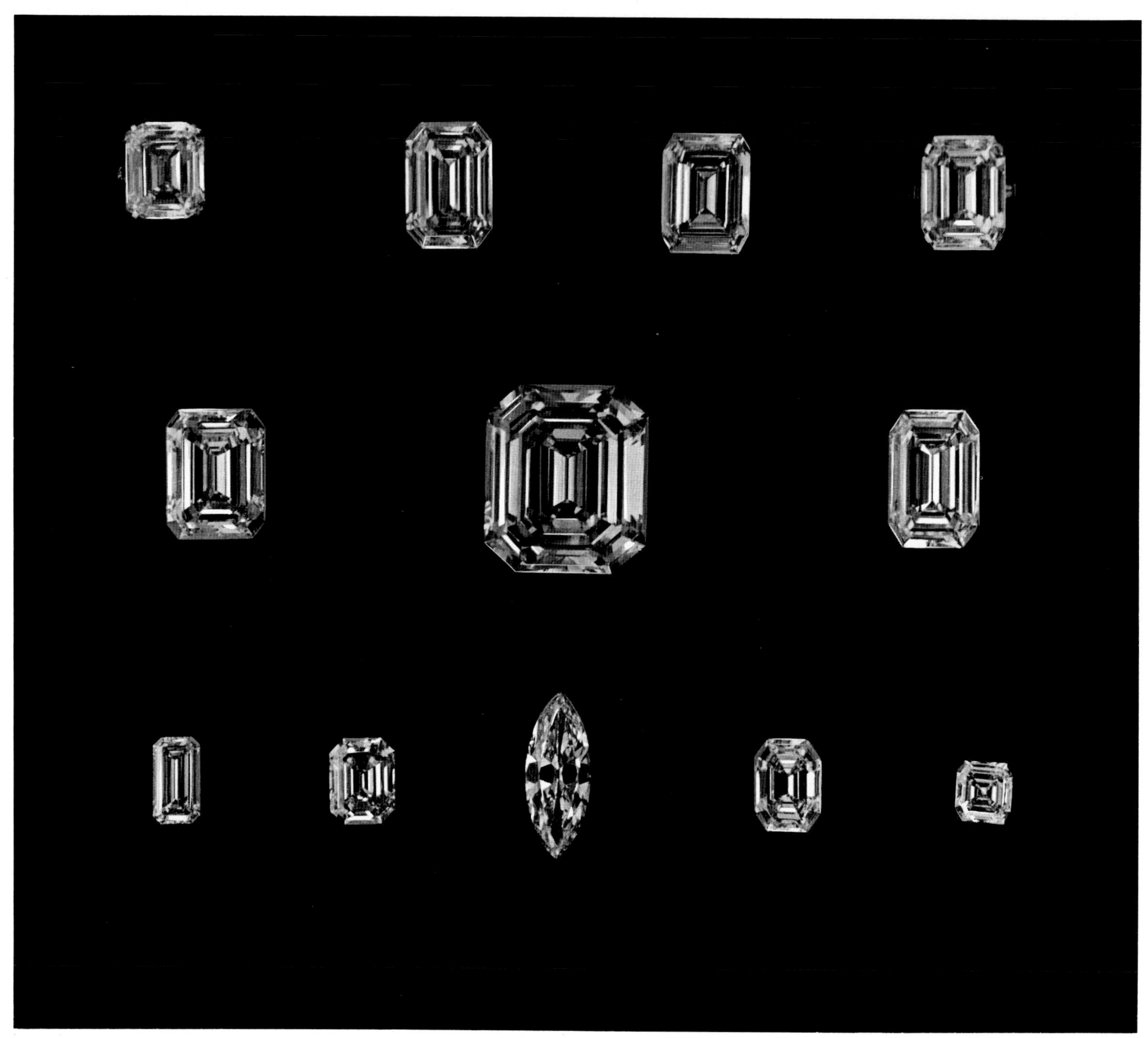

Harry Winston: twelve diamonds cut from the "Jonker." The biggest weighs 126 carats. Harry Winston Collection, New York.

Harry Winston: clip, rings and eardrops. Diamonds. Harry Winston Collection, New York.

Chaumet: necklace. Platinum and diamonds with a large cabochon emerald in the center, 1958. Chaumet Collection, Paris.

Harry Winston: necklace. Platinum and diamonds with an emerald-cut diamond weighing 127 carats in the center. Harry Winston Collection, New York ⇨

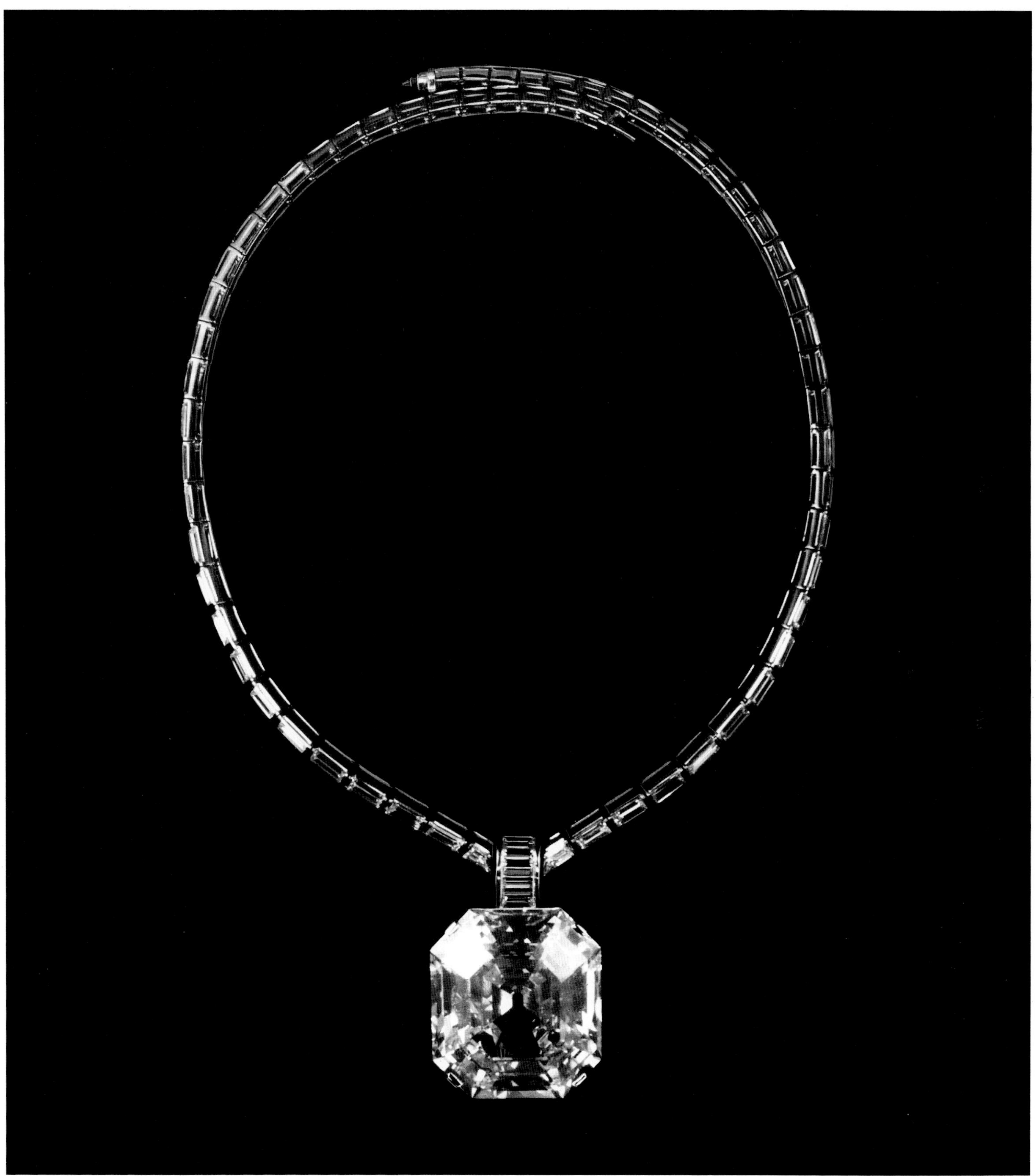

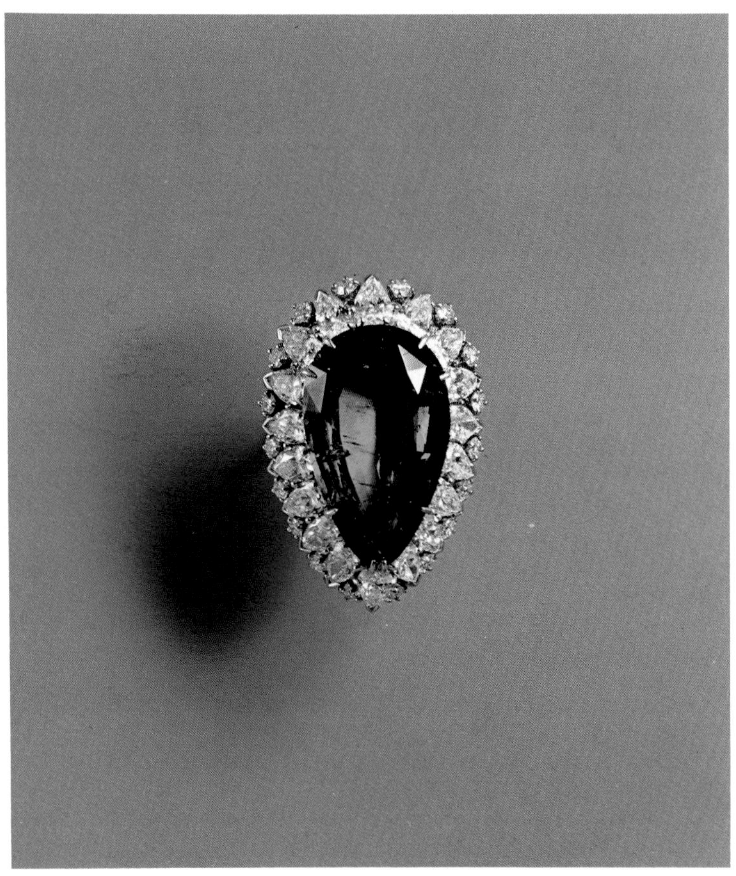

Harry Winston: eardrops with pear-shaped diamonds. Ring: 25-carat emerald and brilliants. Harry Winston Collection, New York.

the guards and the street outside, he visitor saw nothig but a glowing museum of artistically wrought ornaments, each one of which was a miracle of taste, invention, technical skill and talent, and an admirable fragment of the beauty which nature first produces and then disguises.''

An interesting retrospective section on the theme of ''the French *parure* of the past hundred years enabled the visitor to follow jewelry since the second empire and to compare the slightly affected graces or heaviness of former jewels with the sobriety of those of his own day, with their impeccable technique, which were so suitable for a different way of life—practical, active and sporting.

After the success of color in 1925, the keynote of the Galliéra exhibition was the triumph of the diamond, ''the white note.'' Its variety lay in the many different cuts produced by lapidaries. The baguette had already appeared in 1925, and the trapeze, the torpedo, the shell and the square with sharp corners were now introduced. ''A new harmony was achieved by means of a judicious use of a mixture of baguette and round brilliants. Varied, one might almost say colored, effects were obtained by successful

Harry Winston: necklace. Platinum and diamonds, with the ''Hope'' diamond in the center. Harry Winston Collection, New York.

combinations of these different cuts and styles of stones." (Georges Fouquet)

The art of jewelry now included intresting combinations of diamonds and metal such as smooth or matt-finished platinum. This process gave place to pieces which might be described as Surrealist, which consisted of plates of platinum encrusted with round or baguette diamonds with the motif suggested rather than clearly defined. This new interpretation of the ornament made it a true part of clothing. It put the final touch to a dress, not so much as an independent detail, but as an integral part of the dress itself, in the form of a clip, brooch, clasp or belt buckle, on the shoulder or at the waist, holding a fold or a drapery. The jeweler became the couturier's collaborator. Their creations were henceforth inseparable in the minds of women of taste, who wanted new ornaments every season and ordered matching dresses and jewels. This was Georges Fouquet's idea, which he put into practice with the help of Jean Patou, an eminent couturier who decided in 1927 to show his dresses with jewels chosen to match them.

After the success of 1925 and the Galliéra exhibition of 1929, there was no new international show until 1937, the year of the two-fold Arts and Technique exhibition. This title was completely accurate as regards jewelers, for they had been ceaselessly pursuing their researches in these fields since 1925.

The program of the 1937 exhibition was the same as that of 1925, but even more rigorous, since it required not only new creations, but that these must be submitted to a special jury and passed before being displayed.

1937 saw a revival of color, especially rubies. A great advance in gem setting consisted of concealing the cells between the stones so that they seemed to be cohering together in a solid mass. A new brilliant cut known as the "moderne" was tried. It increased the shine of the gem but appreciably diminished its weight.

Bracelet in brilliants and sapphires, with gold. Boucheron, Paris

Generally speaking, the jewels on display were remarkable for their decorative composition and skilled craftsmanship. They thus attained the goal of the previous exhibitions and carried on the good work.

Jewelry was reacting to the same stimulus all over the world. The oldest houses confirmed the soundness of their reputations by their experiments with new forms and their technical feats. The widespread use of platinum and palladium, especially in the U.S.A., allowed collapsible jewels to be made. A necklace could be made into a bracelet and a pair of clips according to taste and occasion.

Most of the leading firms of Belgium, Britain, Germany, Switzerland, Italy, Denmark and the U.S.A. have already been named and are still famous today. Garrard, Wolfers, Jensen and Tiffany have been discussed. Bulgari of Rome, a great specialist in colored stones whose establishment, founded in 1881, is famous today for the originality of its creations, and Gübelin of Lucerne, a former clockmaker who made a brilliant debut as a jeweler in 1925, should also be mentioned. The Gübelin family currently includes an eminent gemologist among its members. This means that the stones selected for their jewelry are always of the highest quality.

Among the newcomers of the twentieth century there was one whose personality and working methods set him apart from traditional jewelry—which sometimes startled his colleagues—but whom everyone recognized as a remarkable expert. Harry Winston is a jeweler and a fanatical collector of fine stones, especially diamonds. His beginnings were very modest. At the end of the first world war, he was a young man scarcely twenty years of age. He set up in business on his own account with rather scanty means but, thanks to his boldness and self-confidence, he obtained the support of some important banks and began to buy collections of ornaments and the stones he loved, and to mount them in the most up-to-date style and resell them—not without regrets, since he was so fond of fine diamonds. He is universally known, and many people regarded him as the leading purveyor of precious stones

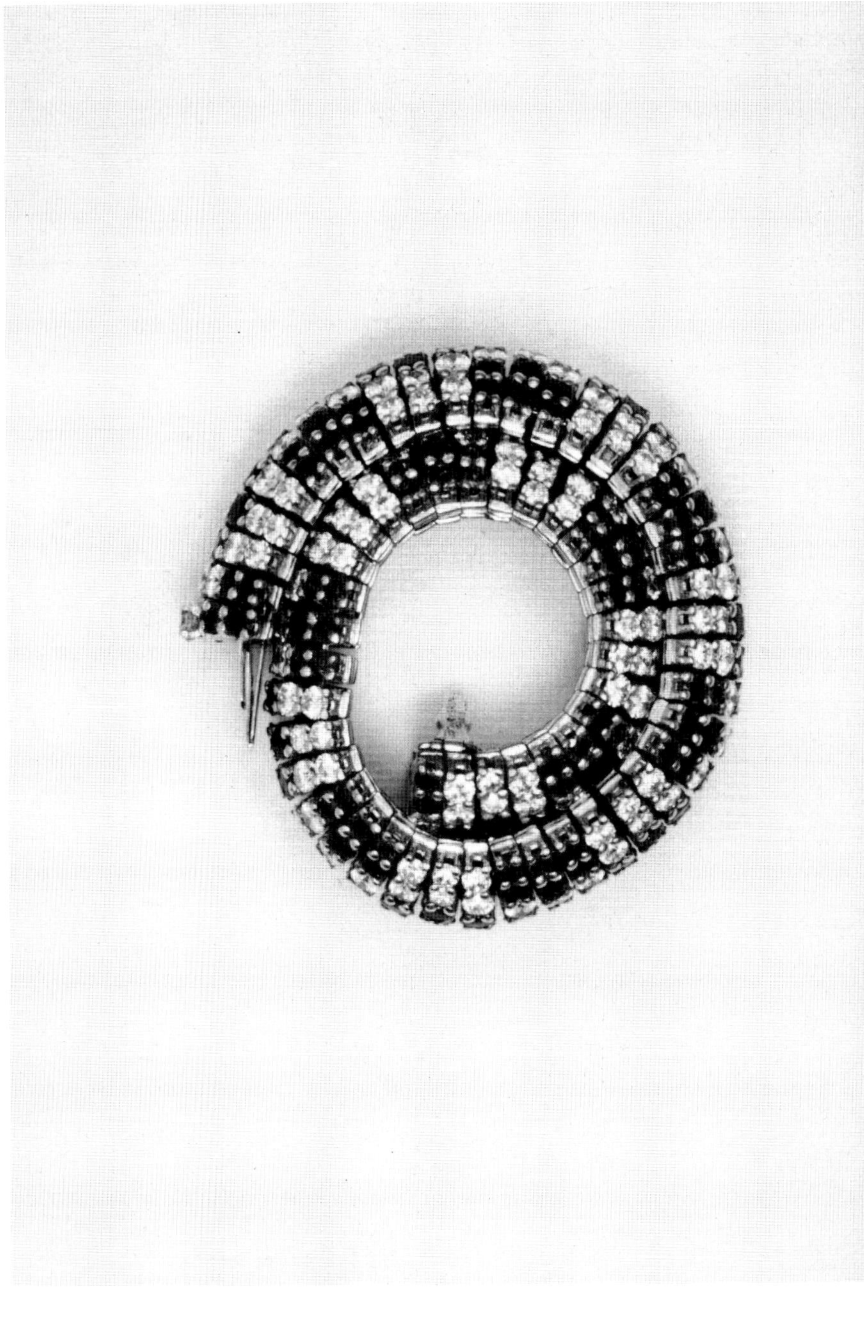

This recent piece shows a certain suppleness in jewelry of the last fifty years. Boucheron, Paris

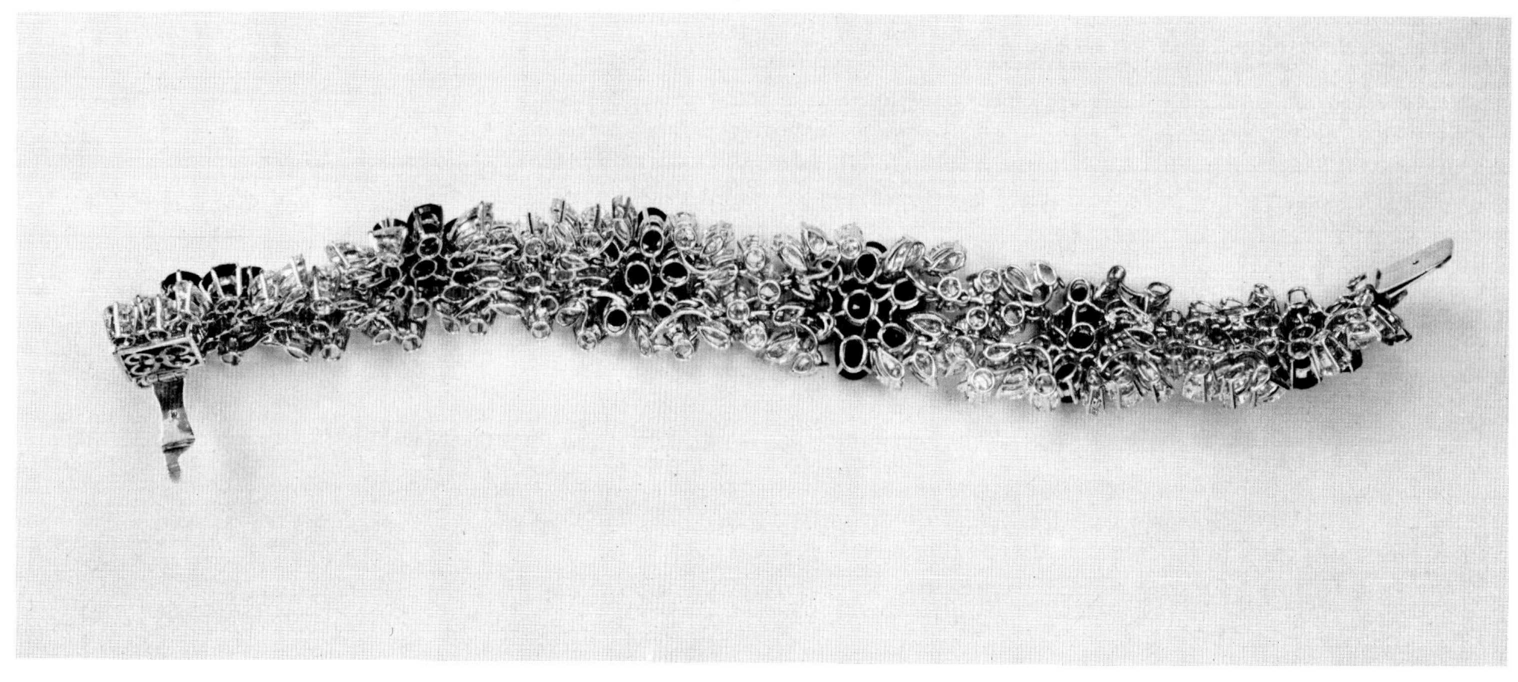

Reverse of a bracelet of the same type as 249 Boucheron, Paris.

of outstanding size and value. It is true that most of the biggest diamonds in the world passed through his hands.

However, this is not what fires the imagination, and it is easier to remember the marvelous gems that have passed through his hands—the Jonker (126 carats) and the Star of the East (94.8 carats), both bought from King Farouk; the Hope diamond (44.5 carats) presented to the Smithsonian Institution in 1958; the Eye of the Idol and the Liberator, a diamond of 155 carats found in Venezuela in 1942, and the President Vargas found in Brazil three years earlier. Harry Winston also bought Catherine the Great's sapphire and some of the finest emeralds in the world, which he set in a necklace adorned with 752 diamonds, which could be changed into a bracelet, brooches and ear clips. Among his latest purchases was the Lesoto diamond (601 carats) found recently near the village of Mafeteng in western Lesoto in South Africa.

As owner of some of the finest diamonds in the world as well as some historic jewels, Harry Winston resets them in the modern taste, but he has to give the stone the place of honor. This is why the metal in his creations is only a support and is as thin and unobtrusive as possible. He

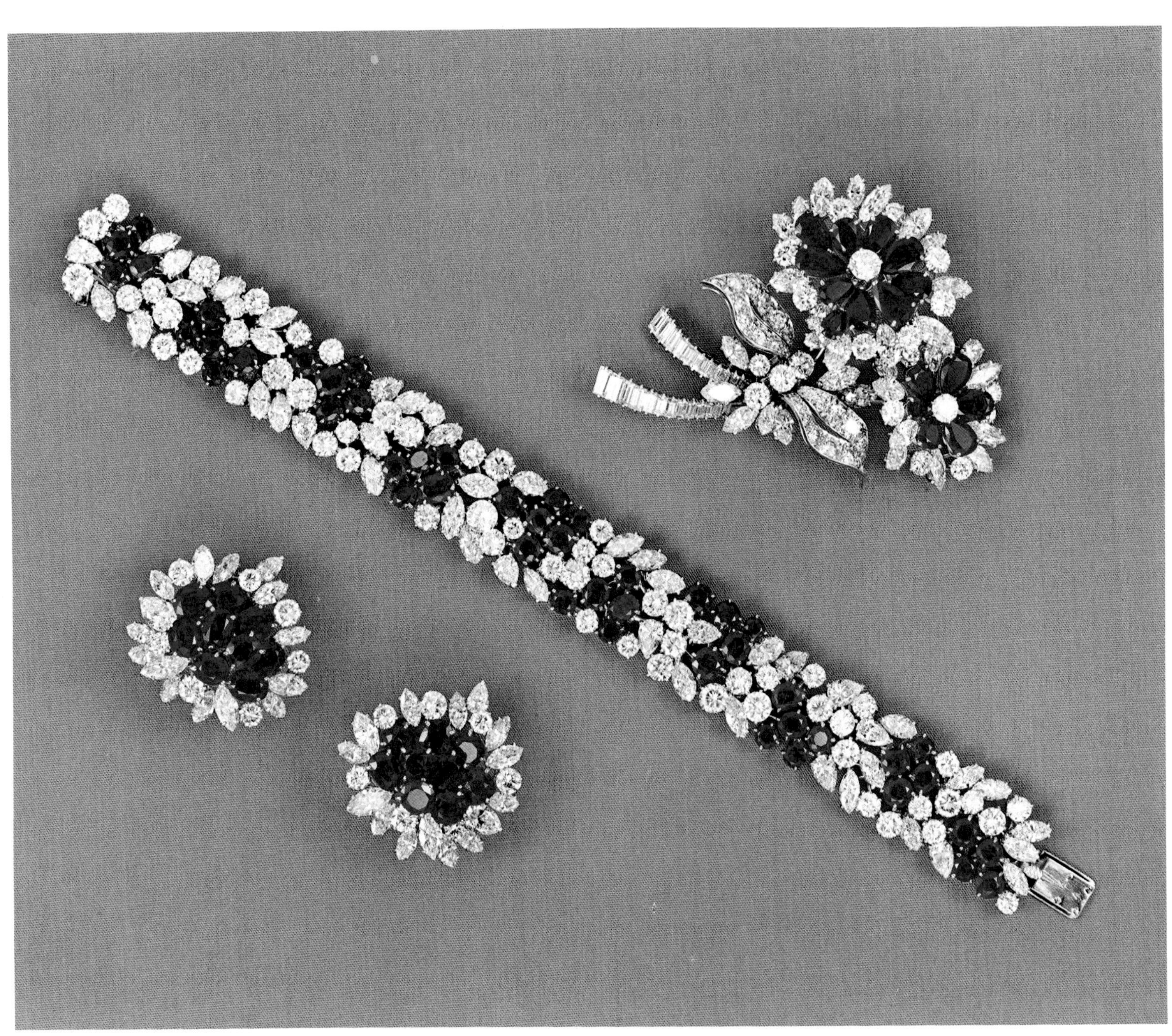

Bracelet, earclips and brooch: round, navette and baguette brilliants, rubies, platinum setting. Boucheron, Paris.

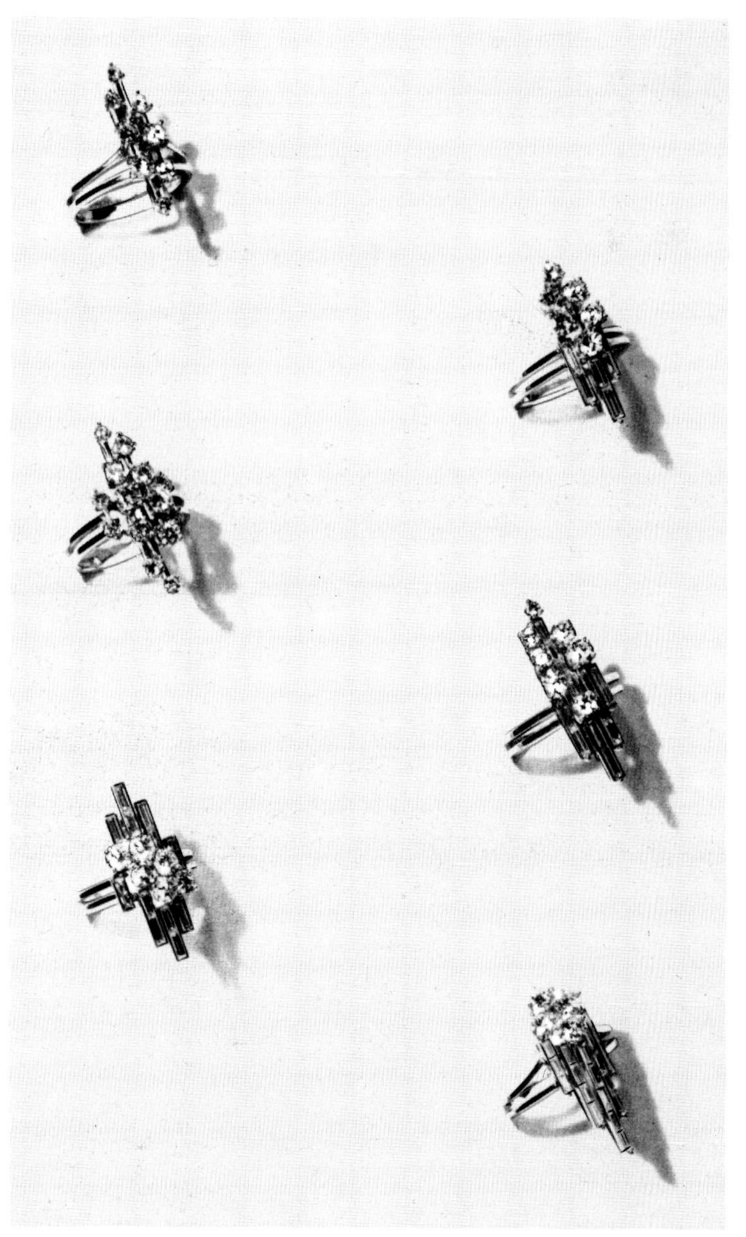

Rings in the "flowing line:" platinum and brilliants, 1969-70. Mauboussin, Paris.

Necklace: baguette, navette and round brilliants and a pear-shaped brilliant pendant. Boucheron, Paris.

Necklace: gold, emeralds, rubies, sapphires and brilliants. Mauboussin, Paris.

Necklace: baguette, navette and round brilliants, three pendant pear-shaped diamonds. Cartier, Paris.

Diamond Necklace. Van Cleef & Arpels, Paris

does not like gold, and uses only platinum. He is, in fact, only interested in jewels, and designs his creations with an eye to the color, light and cut of the gems. His most remarkable ornaments are not dictated by fashion, and it is obvious that the value of the stones demands this kind of treatment.

This brings us to one of the chief characteristics of contemporary jewelry. Technical advances in the last fifty years have permitted the making of jewels of unequaled lightness and suppleness which assign to gems not only the most important but virtually the only place. This is the reason for the unreal look of some ornaments which seem to have no settings. Settings of necklaces, bracelets and earrings of platinum wire have succeeded in uniting flexibility with strength. Nothing but stones can be seen on the front of the jewel, while on the back one can admire the delicacy and accuracy of work which may have taken hundreds of hours. Every setting on a Boucheron bracelet has seven or eight solders, and the whole piece includes more than a thousand.

Every firm has its secrets, but they all seek to produce a light, flexible effect in their jewels. Van Cleef and Arpels have named one of their processes the "mystery setting." It actually allows ornaments to be fashioned in which not a single claw can be seen; the jeweler, then, plays on the shape, color and cut of the stones. The glitter and reflections vary between the different planes of the ornament.

The execution of a flower in the "mystery setting" requires a lot of time. Not only must a mount be fashioned of gold bars, which allows the metal to be kept out of sight; it is also necessary to find a considerable number of sapphires and rubies of the same shade, which are then cut according to the place they are to occupy on the corolla. The stones outlining the outer contours all have a curved edge, which calls for work of the utmost precision.

Jeweled flowers are not Van Cleef and Arpels's only specialty. The house is known for its very fine colored stones,

Flower in the "mystery setting:" sapphires, diamonds, gold and platinum. Van Cleef & Arpels, Paris.

often set in gold. They are sometimes accompanied by a surrounding of brilliants to heighten the color.

Very magnificent *parures* cannot be worn on all occasions, so the rich jewels of Van Cleef and Arpels are always collapsible. The little pendants can be removed from a necklace, or it may be transformed into two bracelets and a clip. the pursuit of versatility affects more than the shapes and materials of *parures;* it has encouraged the creation of these collapsible jewels, at least one part of which can be worn on many different occasions.

The house of Van Cleef and Arpels is one of the newest of the big French jewelers, since its foundation only dates to 1906, while Boucheron has been in existence since 1858, Chaumet was founded in 1847 and Mauboussin in 1827. But this young establishment has succeeded in gaining as much prestige as its elders in a few years, since it was chosen to create the crown for H.I.M. Farah Pahlavi. The task was complicated by the fact that the stones used for it could not be taken away from the Imperial Treasury. Pierre Arpels had to go to Teheran twenty-five times to choose the stones and adapt the design for the 1,469 brilliants, 36 rubies, 36 emeralds and 105 pearls selected. The design was worked out in Paris, but the first wax model was made in Iran, and an exact cast taken of every stone. Thanks to the replicas obtained in this way, the Paris studio could work on the gold and platinum mount, the stones being subsequently set on the spot in Teheran.

Not all the great jewelers have had opportunities to carry out such spectacular masterpieces, and many of them regret the passing of the formal galas, great balls and brilliant receptions at which all the ladies who attended covered themselves with diamonds, and where evening dress permitted the wearing of the most valuable ornaments. However, although customs and fashions are changing and jewelers' customers do not order so many tiaras, modern needs and requirements are still just as important.

Modern life calls for more modest jewelry, and brooches and clips answer this need. All the jewelers in the world

The crown of H.I.M. Farah Pahlavi: height 16 cm; weight 1.600 kg. Van Cleef & Arpels, Paris.

Van Cleef & Arpels: stages in the making of the crown for H.I.M. Farah Pahlavi.

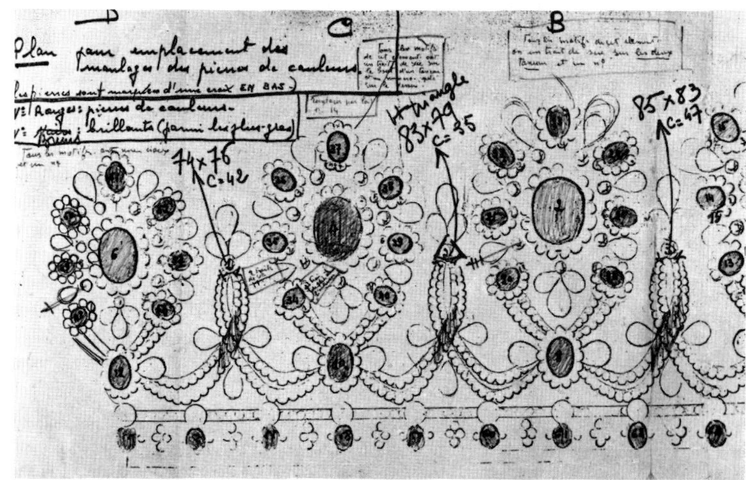

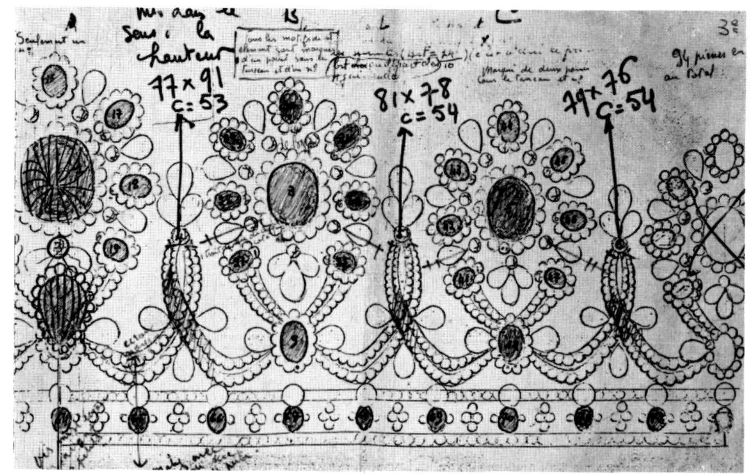

One of the many working copies made in the course of the work.

Design for the crown.
Part of the wax model made in Teheran with the stones chosen from the Treasure Room.

Wax model made in Teheran. Casts made from the imprints of real stones can be seen on it.

have produced a great variety of designs, the motifs ranging from floral to abstract and the treatment from stylized natural elements to geometric forms. A great variety can be seen at the house of Boucheron, for example, where they are matched with earclips. Some jewelers adopt the modern trend with straight lines and abstract motifs. Others are more traditional, utilizing different cuts and allying baguettes with navettes. Floral motifs on a very openwork gold mount with minute claws holding hundreds of little brilliants have appeared very recently.

Like all great jewelers, G. Boucheron attaches great importance to the quality of the stones and the workmanship of the setting, which has to be both flexible and strong. His bracelets coil like corkscrews, and his eardrops are made very mobile to increase their glitter while following all the movements of the head and neck freely. Nevertheless, he rarely uses very small gems or tiny brilliants. He achieves flexibility and lightness with fairly large diamonds, but this does not detract from the restraint and sobriety of his ornaments. Boucheron's theory of jewelry can be expressed in a few words: "Certainly it must be beautiful, but it must also be pleasant to wear. No carcans or heavy bracelets and eardrops, and no more ostentatious jewels which the owner seldom dares wear. I want women to feel at ease wearing my jewelry in every sense of the word." This principle dominates all his pieces, including watches made in the house, some of which are entirely made of coral or lapis lazuli and are miniature masterpieces of lightness and originality.

The Place Vendome and the Rue de la Paix are the centers of high fashion and jewelry in Paris. Jewelers' shops occupy almost all one side of the Place. Shops and boutiques stand side by side, one great name after another, but each with its own individual style and clientele. We have already mentioned the house of Mauboussin, which

Bracelet: brilliants. Boucheron, Paris.

Necklace, bracelet, earrings, clip and earclips, ring: sapphires, rubies, emeralds and brilliants. Boucheron, Paris.

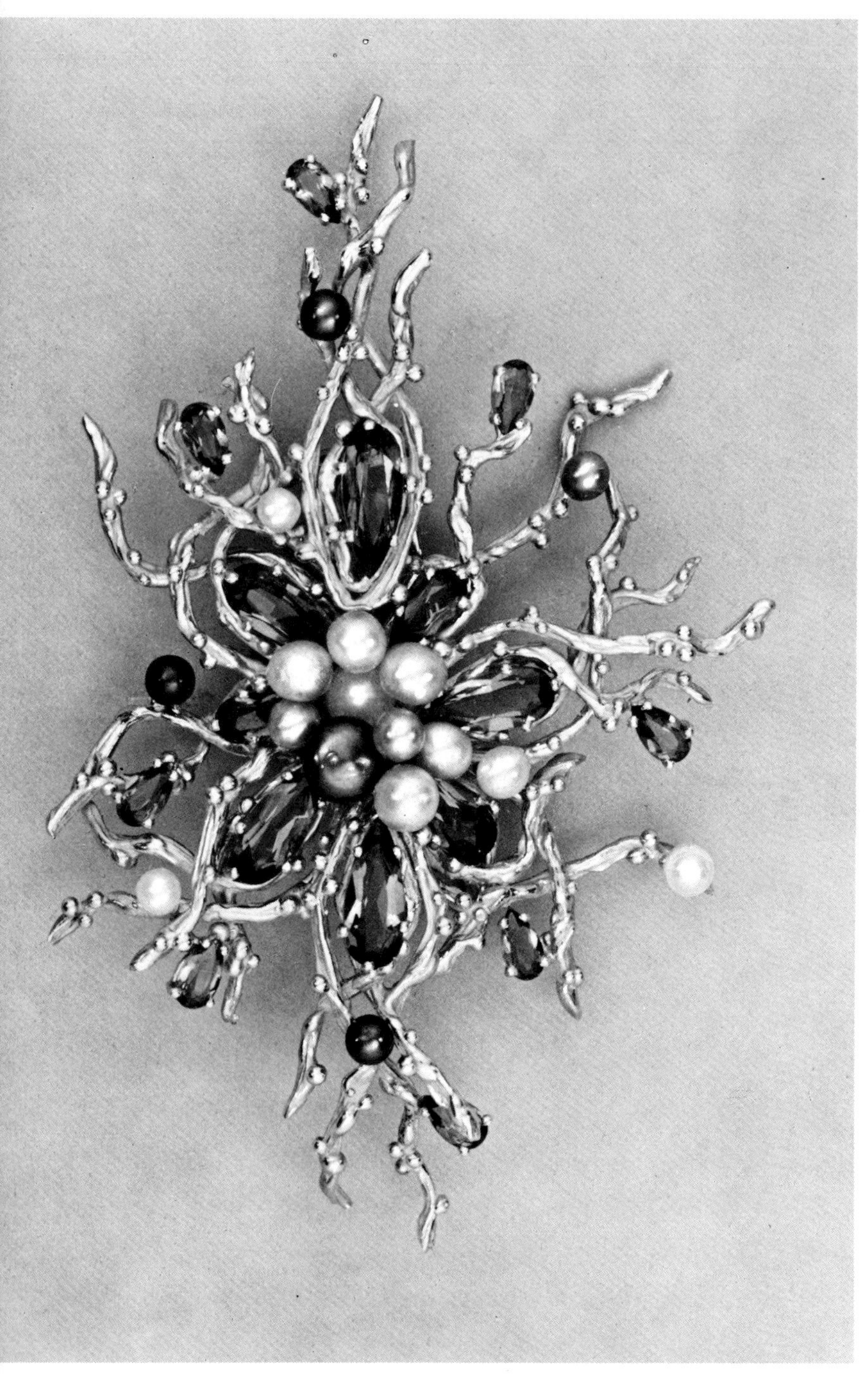

Brooch-pendant: gold, citrines and pearls. Designed by Mme. Pera. Wolfers Frères, Brussels.

Clip: gold, citrines and pearls. Designed by Mme. Pera. Wolfers Frères, Brussels.

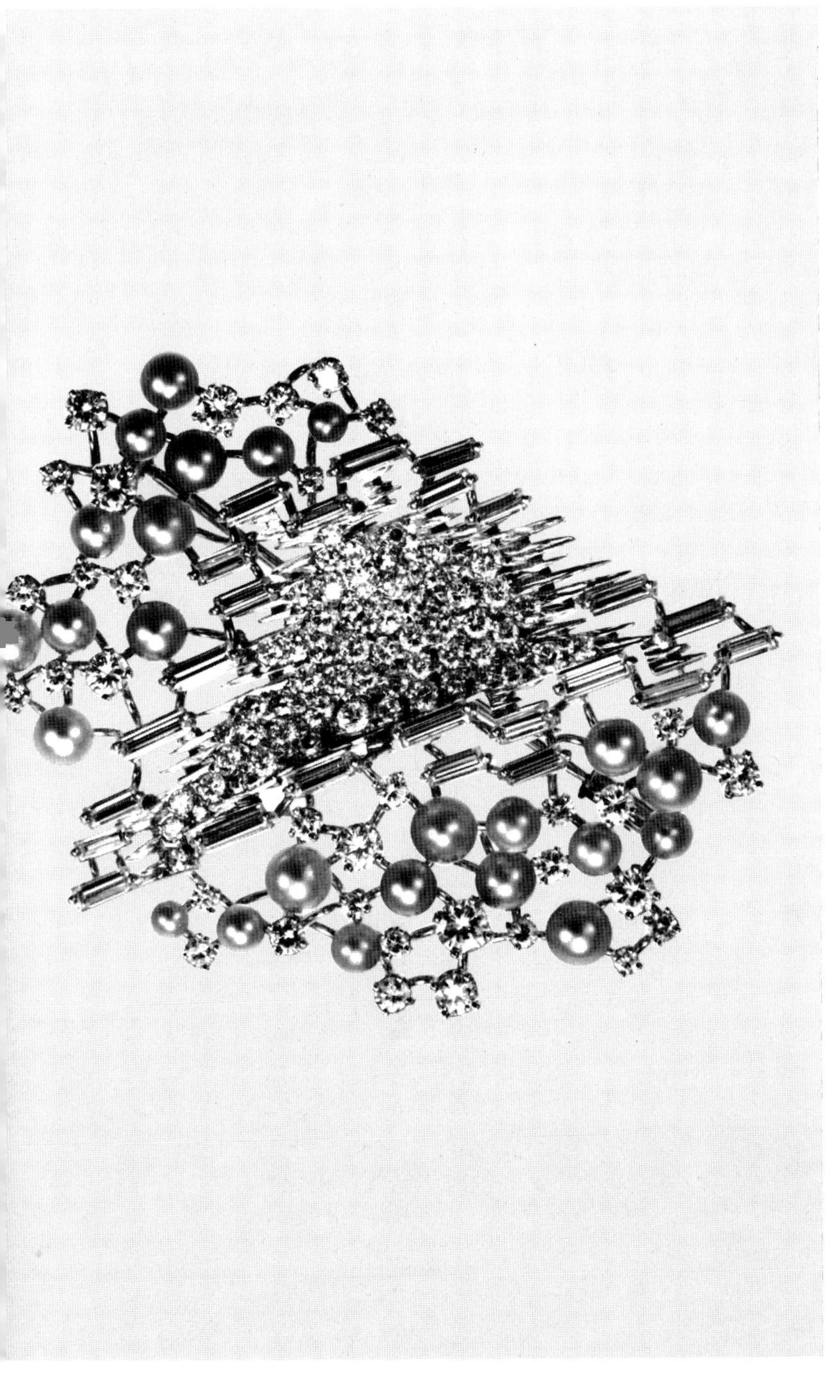

Clip: pearls, brilliants and baguette diamonds. Gübelin, Lucerne.

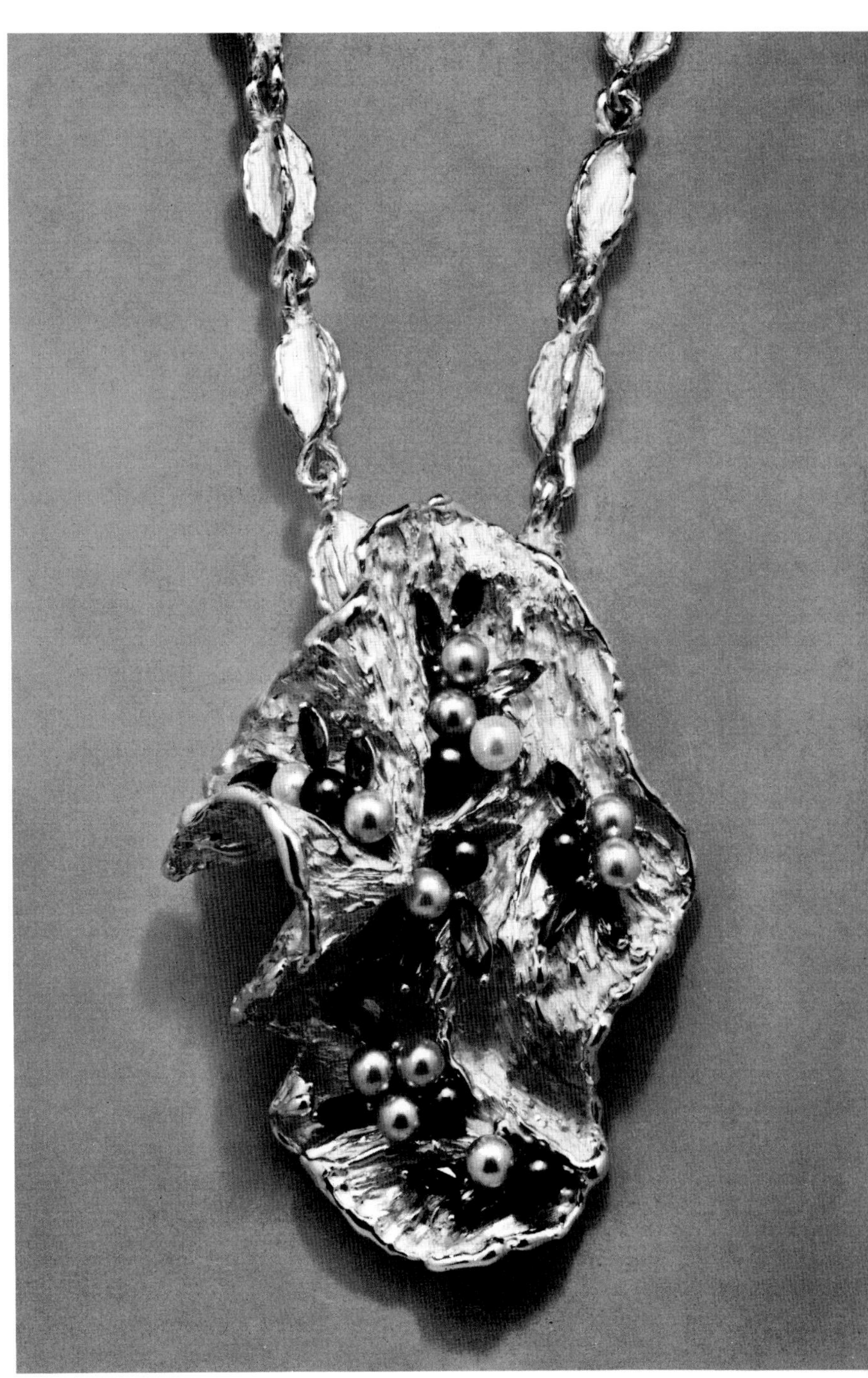

Pendant: gold, citrines and pearls. Designed by Mme. Pera. Wolfers Frères, Brussels.

Necklace which can be converted into a diadem: brilliants and rubies. Cartier, Paris.

is unquestionably one of the oldest. Its reputation is not founded solely on the quality of its ornaments. The Mauboussin family have a long tradition as great connoisseurs of stones and pearls, and many famous diamonds have been bought and set by them. Carefully selected colored stones are cut and used in every possible way, including spherical beads, several ropes of which form brilliant cables. Color combinations have been a specialty of this house for several years. Sapphires, rubies and emeralds are set in the same ornament, and a variety of shapes as well as colors are used. With such designs the most formal *parures* have an atttractive freshness and gaiety. Most Mauboussin jewels show similar daring. About 1930, for example, Mauboussin made a necklace which was like nothing else in the world. It consisted of thirty-five diamonds shaped in faceted spheres separated by baguette brilliants. The house has very recently launched the "flowing" line, which is a new style of rings and clips. The arrangement of round, navette and baguette diamonds down the length of the finger on the rings is a completely new idea. The uncluttered line of clips gets its effect from the shape and size of the diamonds on different planes.

The house of Cartier also has traditions going back more than a hundred years. His studio, shop and boutique are famous all over the world. The house was established in the Rue de la Paix in 1898, and it was there that he executed *parures* for a great many sovereigns, nobles and leading families for all nationalities. At the beginning of the century, his customers included the imperial family of Brazil, the King of Portugal, the Prince of Saxe-Coburg-Gotna and the Prince of Wales, the future Edward VII. Cartier created invisibly-set jewels in which he was one of the first to use platinum, freely inspired by the shapes and colors of oriental jewelry. Cartier showed many jewels with stylized motifs and flowers interpreted in navette, baguette and round brilliants with occasional touches of color. Even valuable jewels might use animal motifs. Wild

Necklace: brilliants and a cabochon ruby, gold setting. Chaumet, Paris. ⇨

Necklace: baguette and navette brilliants. Cartier, Paris.

Design for a diamond necklace. Wolfers Frères, Brussels.

Wolfers: the finished necklace. Private collection, Brussels.

and tame creatures, island birds, butterflies, lions and leopards covered with the rarest gems add a note of color and gaiety to the splendor of his jewels.

It is admittedly very hard to give an account of such a varied and abundant output, in which great ingenuity is exercised to please different and sometimes contrasting tastes without relinquishing the traditional aesthetic and technical standards. Along with the jewels which might be called classic have been described, others are more closely related to the modern way of life. Indeed, a trend emerged which gradually renewed the decorative repertoire, created new forms and drew on all the elements of modern life from abstract and Op art to Indian and Mexican jewelry.

In Paris, the house of Chaumet seems to have started a revival of the jeweled *parure*. Jacques Chaumet, in fact, believes that the new fashion (very short dresses or trousers) has altered the feminine silhouette as radically as the "little dress" of the twenties. It is not just the lines but the volumes which have changed. Chaumet strongly emphasizes the importance of the third dimension of the ornament—the wearer. Recognizing that jewelry is somewhat static in spite of a degree of evolution, he wants the jeweler to be always creating and trying to renew or reshape the twentieth century woman's jewels. The new ornament must suit not only her clothes but her way of life and background. Such innovations cannot be introduced without raising a lot of problems, but the progress shown by the most recent creations is encouraging.

Jewelers' clientele, in fact, has changed and expanded. Parisian jewelers have opened "boutiques" selling more informal jewels which are better suited for everyday wear. Gold, accompanied by precious stones, semi-precious stones and gemstones, features prominently. Elsewhere in Europe and America, jewels of a very different type, traditional necklaces, bracelets and brooches, are displayed alongside jewels of a newer style in the same shop.

The house of Wolfers, jewelers to the Crown of Belgium, shows a great many pendants with gold, precious stones and semi-precious stones interpreting the medal

Necklace: brilliants and seven historic emeralds of rectangular shape. Cartier, Paris.

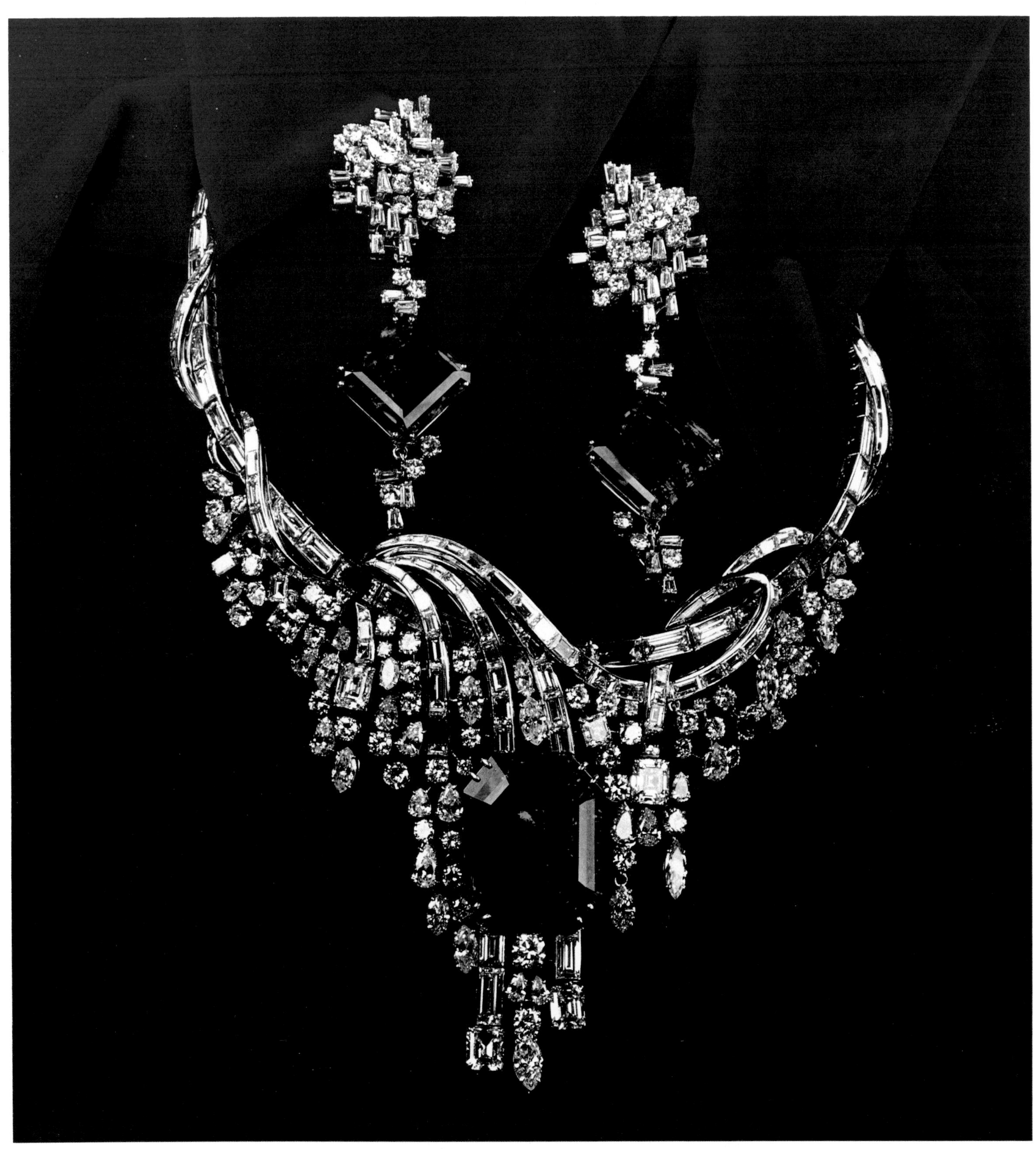

Necklace and eardrops: brilliants and emeralds. Chaumet, Paris.

Bracelet: grey gold, sapphires and brilliants, 1968. Gübelin, Lucerne.

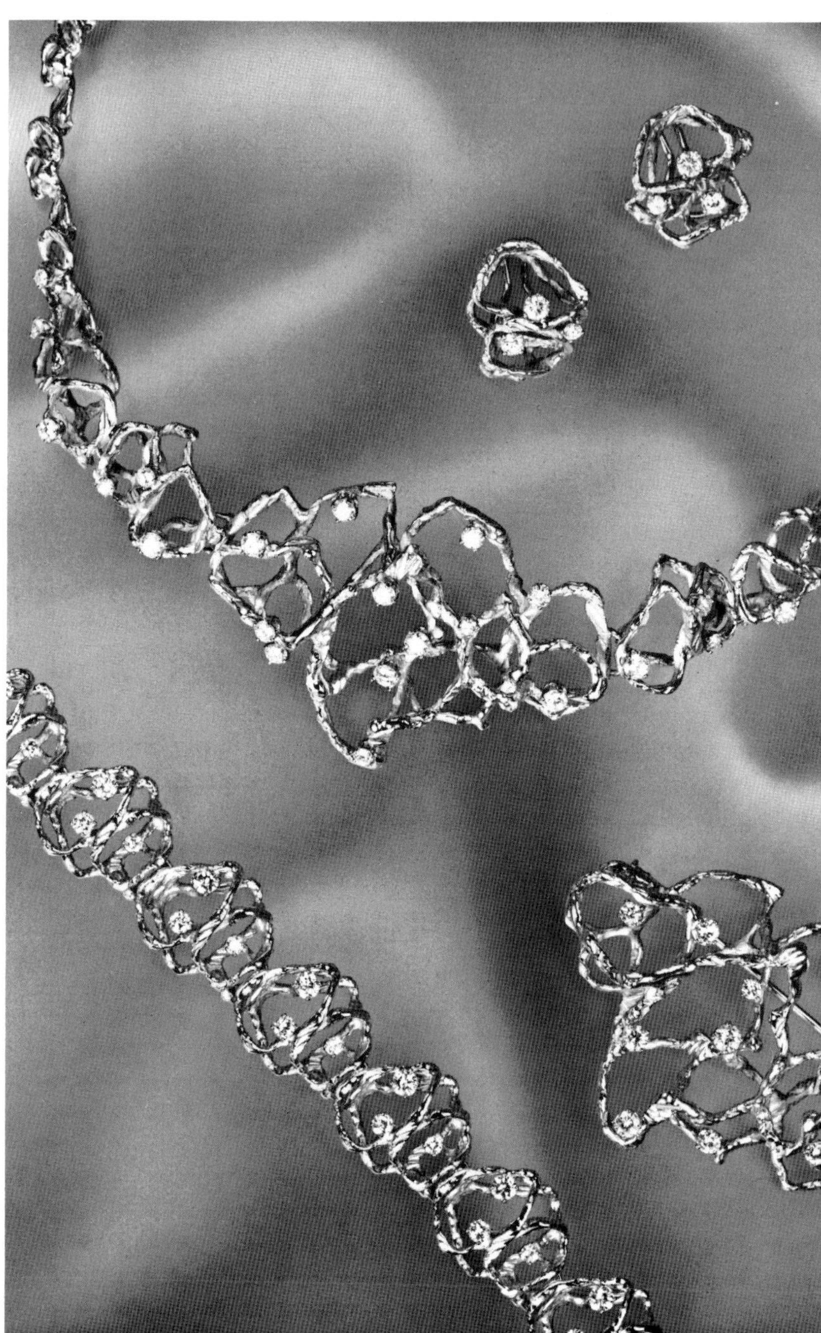

Parure: yellow gold set with brilliants. Gübelin, Lucerne.

Clip: yellow gold with cabochon chrysoprases, 1967. Gübelin, Lucerne.

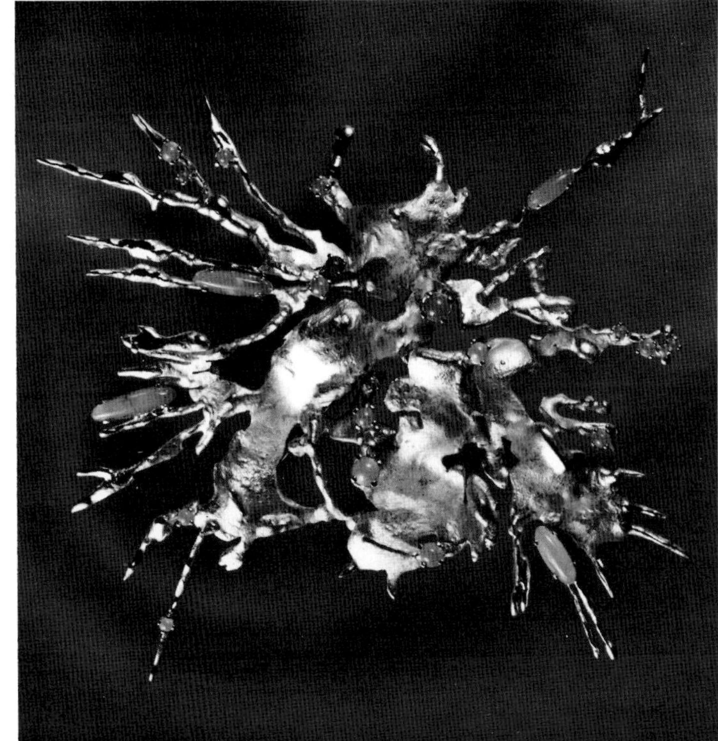

or amulet so many young people are wearing around their necks. The gold looks rough, even twisted. Amethysts are sometimes handled as chunks of crystal. Rings and brooches have bold outlines, while other jewels are designed for the more moderate tastes of other customers.

The same variety is to be found at Gubelin's. He offers his young customers "ballerina-style" jewelry, in which imaginative design is combined with very pure lines. His high-quality jewels included a watch-bracelet entirely carried out in diamonds, attached to a ring by a fine chain of brilliants running down the back of the hand. Besides these experiments, some very fine pieces in a more classic style carry on the tradition of jewelry in the grand manner.

In the U.S.A., the house of Tiffany & Co. is probably one of the oldest and can therefore pride itself on its history and its glorious tradition, but it has undergone many changes in nearly 150 years.

When Walter Hoving took over the management of the house, New Yorkers witnessed a radical change, the first signs of which were a series of sales. The new approach entailed not only a change in business policy but a new aesthetic bias. The house of Tiffany decided that they were no longer going to produce anything but articles reaching a minimum artistic standard. They would no longer pander to public taste which, if it existed at all, was hopelessly reactionary, but would educate and form that taste even at the cost of losing clients or refusing orders which did not meet the standards of the house.

While the articles which were regarded as substandard were being sold off from their stock, they set to work to create others and devise a new form of display, because it was equally important to stress the originality of style even in the smallest details. The boxes, cases and caskets in which jewels were delived were the objects of as much care as the pieces inside. Tiffany's windows did not show

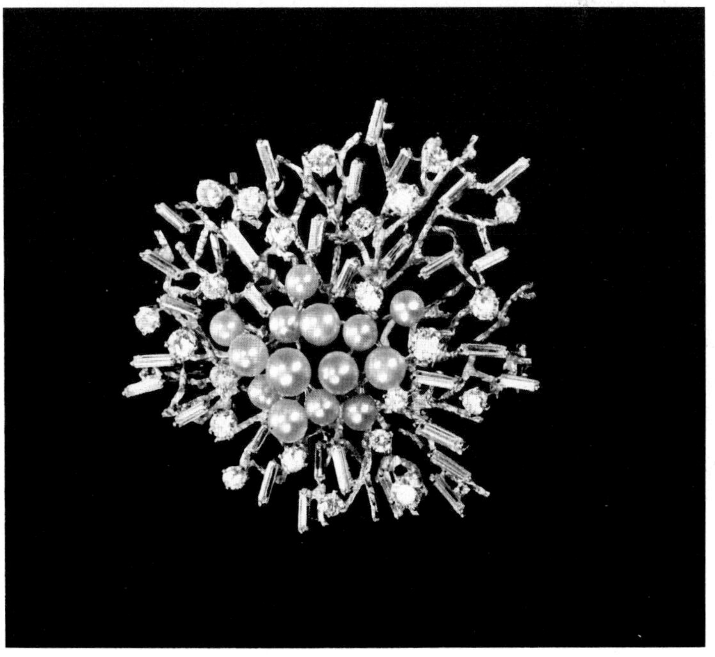

Clip: grey gold with baguettes and collet-set brilliants and pearls, 1967. Gübelin, Lucerne.

Brooch: platinum and brilliants. Garrard, London.

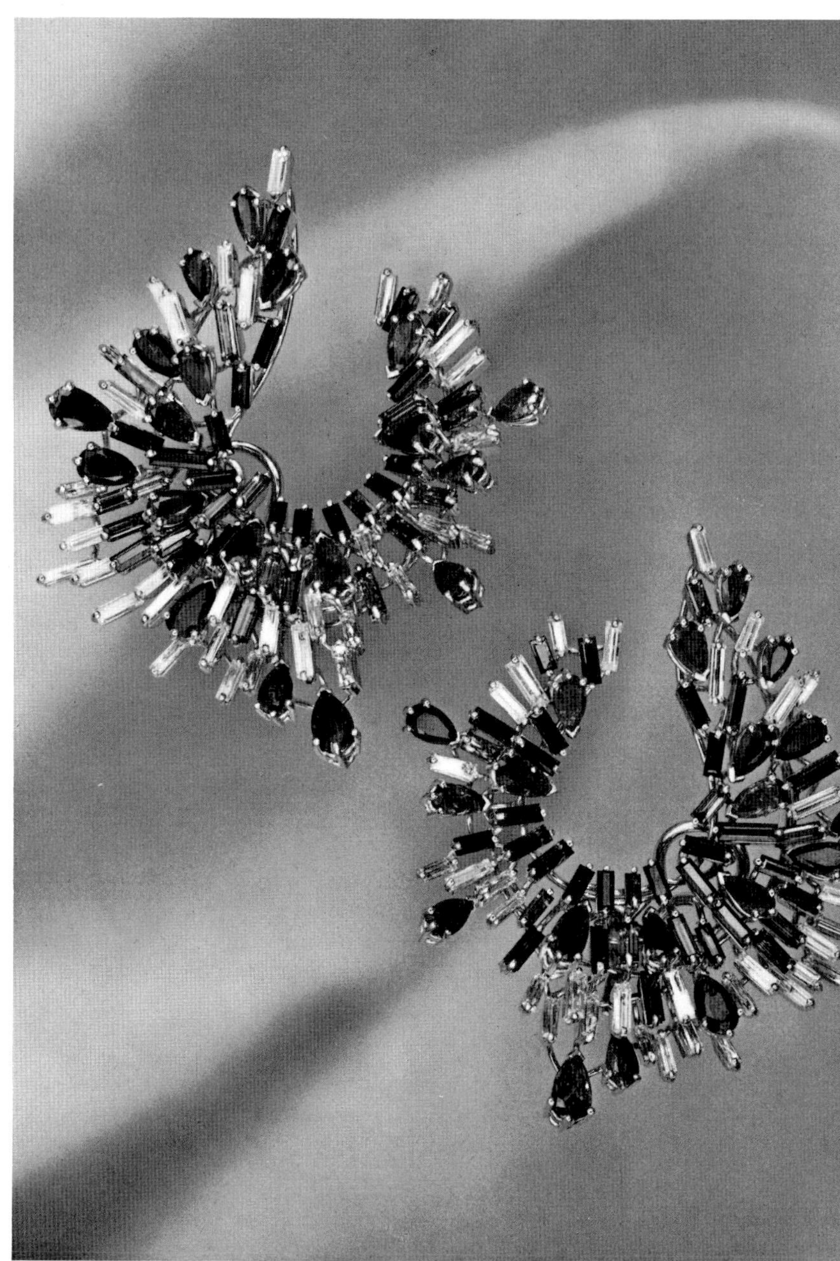

Earclips: platinum with baguette diamonds and sapphires and Sandawana emerald drops, 1967. Gübelin, Lucerne.

Necklace: brilliants and seven pear-shaped diamonds. Chaumet, Paris.

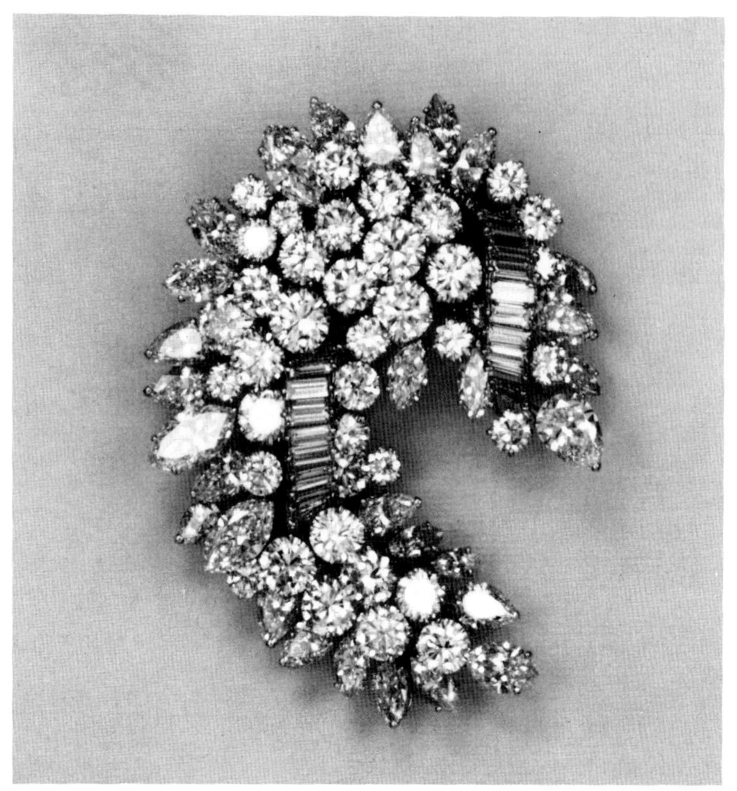

Clip: baguette, navette and round brilliants. Boucheron, Paris.

Eardrops: brilliants. Boucheron, Paris.

the traditional display of jewels, but were an original decor by Gene Moore designed to attract attention and publicize the style rather than to show off the best pieces.

The house of Tiffany benefitted by the collaboration of artists and designers, the best-known of whom is a Frenchman named Jean Schlumberger, whose interest was in costume jewelry before he turned to high-quality jewels. What he seeks in the pieces he creates is beauty of line and volume and the artistic quality which makes an ornament much more than a sign of wealth. Drawing on Renaissance floral motifs or combining forms and materials in the most modern way, Jean Schlumberger creates ornaments of brand-new design and very delicate workmanship.

For several years now, the palette of Tiffany's jewelers has been enriched with a new stone, tanzanite, which is usually a dark blue color like that of the sapphire. The firm has secured virtually exclusive rights to this stone by reserving the first choice of world production.

All these elements confer a highly individual youthfulness and originality on this old establishment. The creation of jewels is not their only line. They also produce goldwork and porcelain. But in everything they touch,

Necklace, eardrops and bracelet: brilliants and emeralds. Van Cleef & Arpels, Paris.

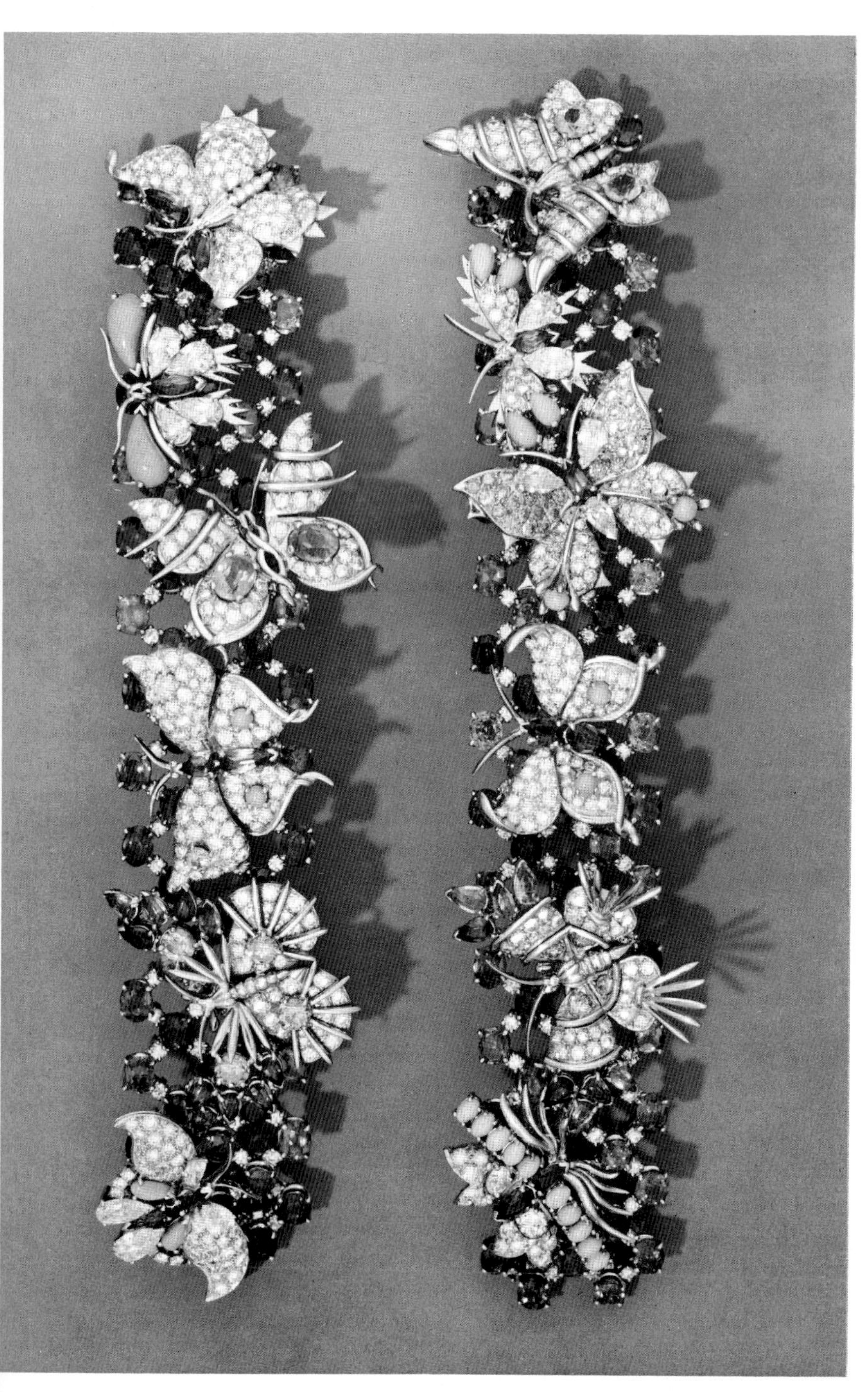

Bracelets which can be joined together to make a necklace: diamonds (white and yellow), green peridots, turquoises, blue-grey spinels, amethysts and sapphires. Tiffany & Co., New York.

Clip: sapphires, diamonds, gold and platinum. Designed by Jean Schlumberger. Tiffany & Co., New York

Necklace: yellow gold, white brilliants. In the center is the "Tiffany" diamond, a yellow stone weighing 128.51 carats with 90 facets. Tiffany & Co., New York.

Clip, "Bird:" sapphires, diamonds, gold and platinum. Designed by Jean Schlumberger. Tiffany & Co., New York.

they have attained a reputation which ranks them among the first in the United States.

During the past twenty years, a few new firms, among which is the house of Kern, have appeared. René Kern has been a jeweler since 1946. He began with a very small workroom which he soon had to expand as his fame spread. He now has a very fine house in Düsseldorf and another in Munich, and employs a staff of sixty. Since 1960, he has worked with Jacques Desnoues, a French designer who creates all his models. The little workshop of his early days is now completely transformed. The house of Kern is entirely self-sufficient, creating jewels and other articles and accessories. A gemology laboratory is attached to it, and is empowered to issue the certificates of authenticity required by law. All Kern's creations are photographed and classified by means of a fast, efficient organization. Three workrooms supply Kern, one in Munich with twelve craftsmen, a much larger one in Düsseldorf with four times the labor force and another in Paris. Founded by a dynamic personality who is interested in all kinds of innovation and readily goes with his designers to see the Cairo Museum or to visit old Viennese or

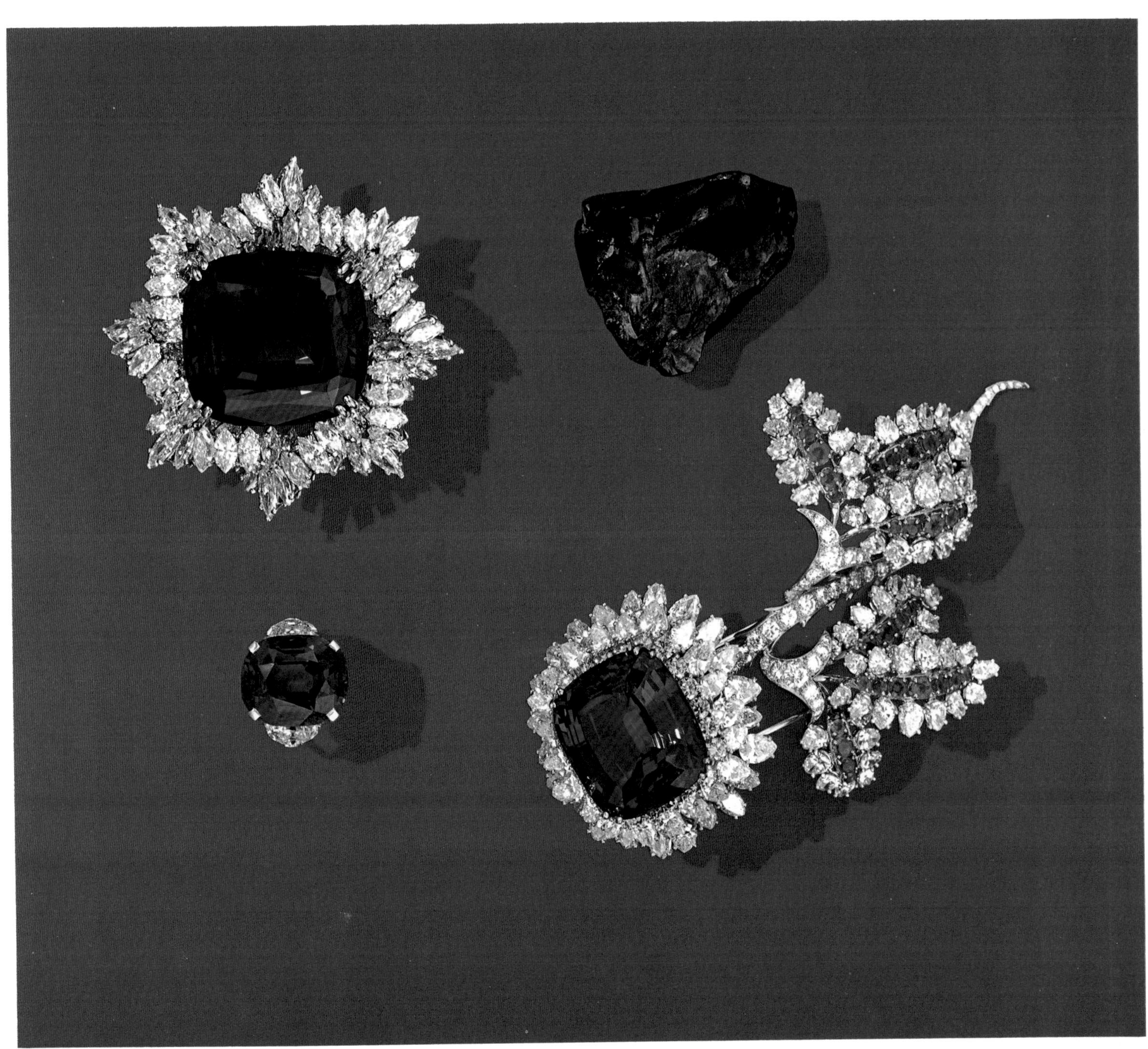

Brooches and ring: gold, platinum, diamonds, emeralds and tanzanite. Tiffany & Co., New York.

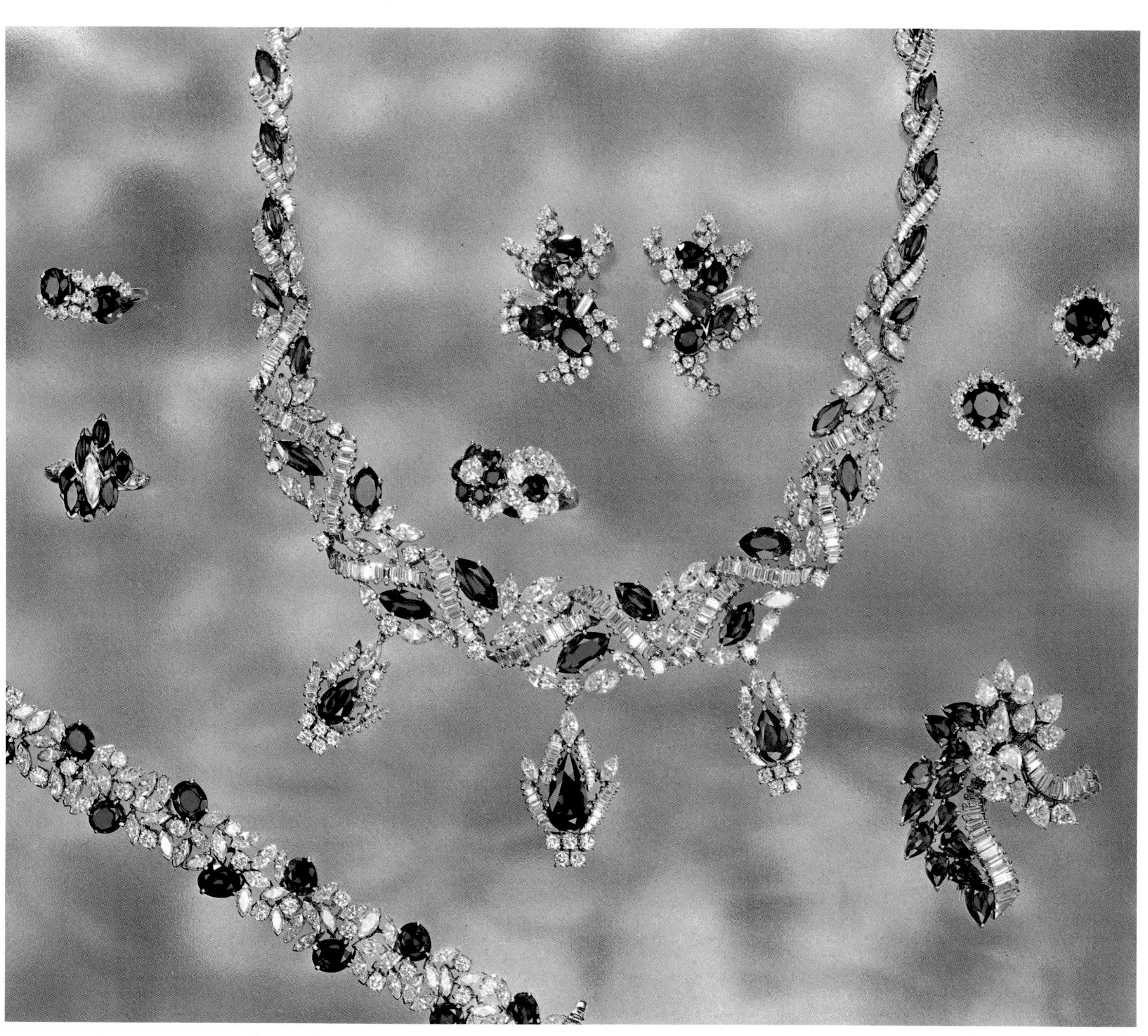

Necklace: gold, platinum and diamonds. Designed by Jean Schlumberger. Tiffany & Co., New York.

Necklace, bracelet, clip, earclips and rings: sapphires and brilliants. Garrard, London.

Spanish craftsmen, the house of Kern is a truly modern enterprise. This quality of youth is also apparent in its highly colorful style. Birds, flowers, butterflies and fish are decorated with translucent enamel in glowing shades and studded with precious stones. The great *parures* are designed in the same spirit, with a combination of rationalization and imagination.

It could be said that the greater jewelers nearly everywhere in Europe and America have the same desire to please young customers and to keep in touch with modern movements in art. They also refuse to confine themselves to traditional formal work, although it is so profitable. Many of them have given young designers a chance and carried out their designs. In England, for example, Garrard's often shows a very modern style of jewelry designed by young artists. Garrard's, who have been Crown jewelers since the eighteenth century, preserve the ancient tradition of craftsmanship on which their fame is based, but they also try to be in the vanguard of all the new jewelry trends. In Denmark, Jensen has assembled artists such as Henning Koppel, Erik Herlow, Nanna Ditzel and Torun Bülow-Hübe, who are already well-known in Europe.

Bracelet: platinum and baguette brilliants. Designed by Jacques Desnoues. Kern, Düsseldorf.

Necklace: emeralds and brilliants. Designed by Jacques Desnoues. Kern, Düsseldorf.

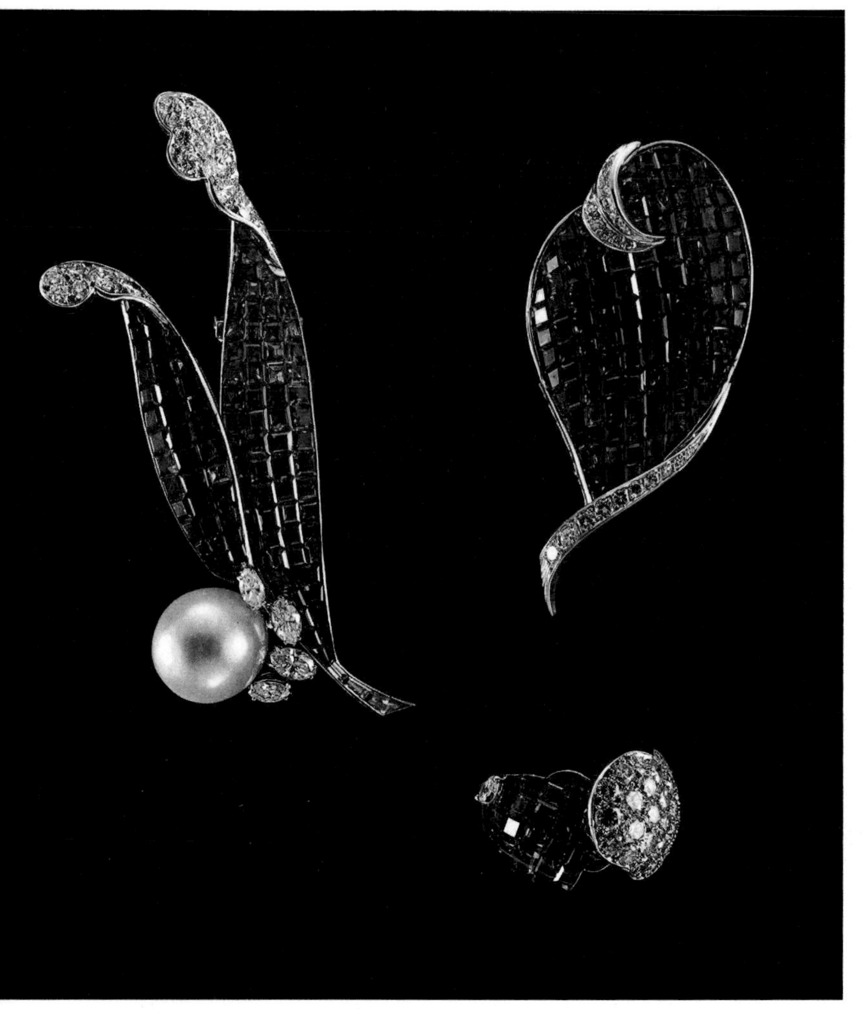

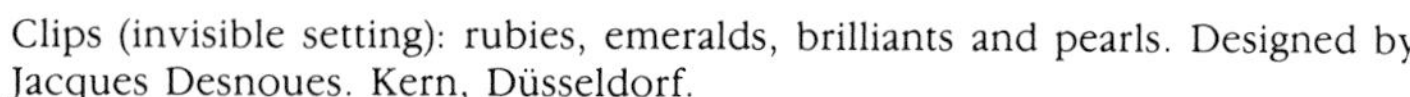

Clips (invisible setting): rubies, emeralds, brilliants and pearls. Designed by Jacques Desnoues. Kern, Düsseldorf.

Clip and earclips: brilliants, emeralds and pearls. Designed by Jacques Desnoues. Kern, Düsseldorf.

This sort of patronage, exercised by each firm on its own account, is continued on a world scale by an annual competition, the Diamond International Award, which was introduced in America in 1954 and expanded to include the rest of the world in the following year. This innovation is the work of the de Beers group, and the jury includes some eminent jewelers and art critics. Every year, thirty prizes are distributed among thousands of competitors, the criteria of judgment being not only beauty but also originality of design, treatment and material. The jury also attaches very great importance to the function of the ornament and requires it to be really wearable. To win an award is not the only encouragement for beginners. It also brings a degree of fame and a chance to see one's jewels displayed in New York and other big cities. Jewelers who are already well known in Germany, Brit-

Necklace: rubies and brilliants. Designed by Jacques Desnoues. Kern, Düsseldorf.

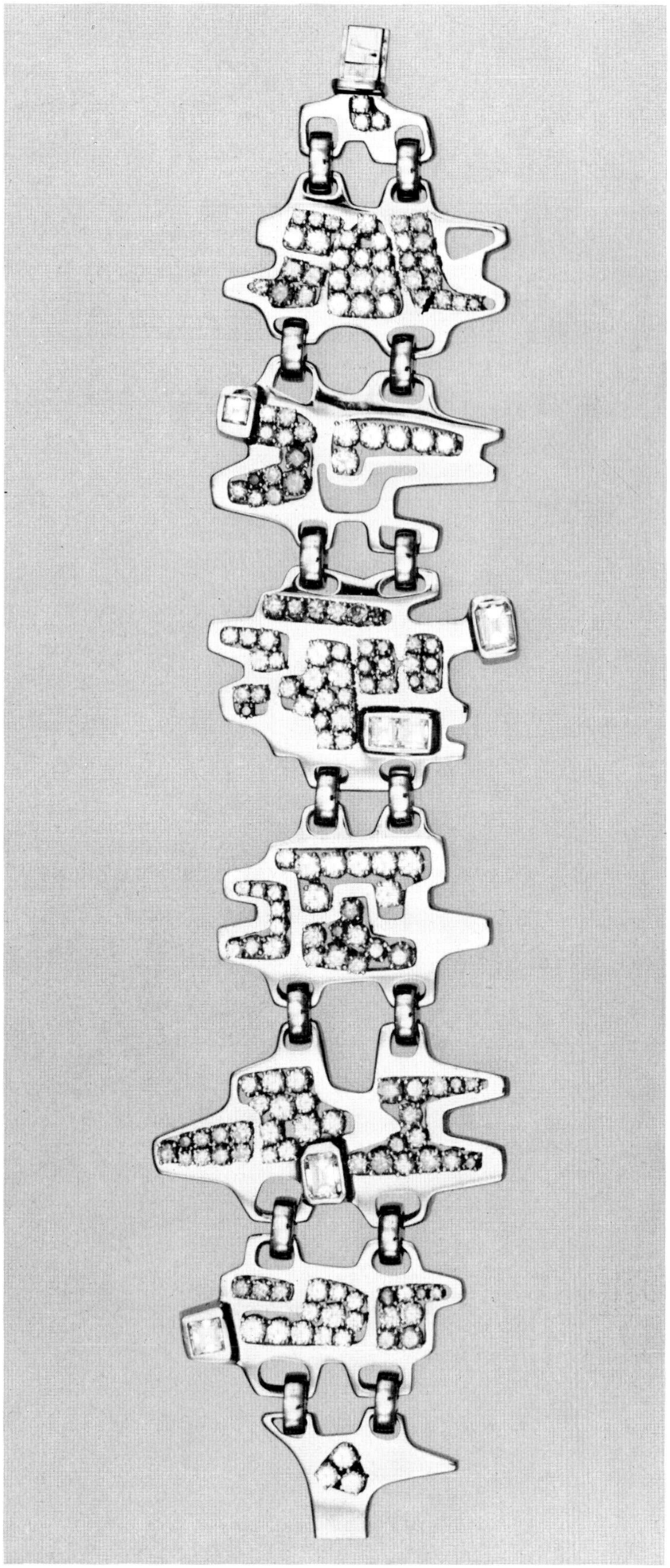

Bracelet and brooch: citrines. Ring: amethysts. Designed by Erik Herlow, 1960. Georg Jensen. Museum of Decorative Arts, Copenhagen.

Bracelet: white, yellow and brown brilliants and white gold. Designed by Henning Koppel. Georg Jensen, Copenhagen.

Bracelet: gold, coral and brilliants. Designed by Maurice Asprey. Asprey & Co., London.

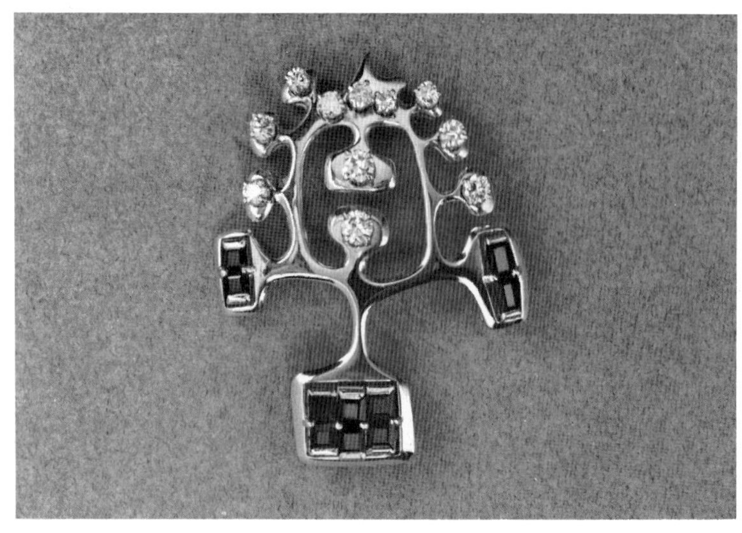

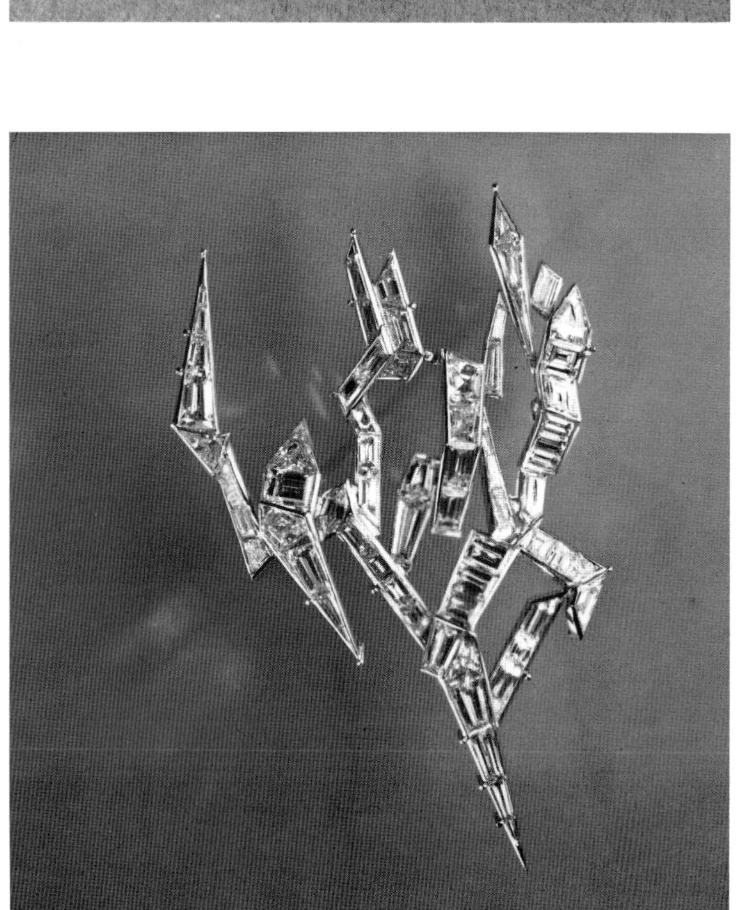

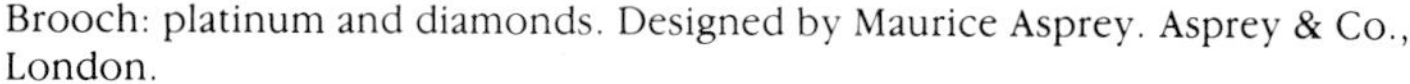

Brooch: platinum and diamonds. Designed by Maurice Asprey. Asprey & Co., London.

Brooch: gold and brilliants. Designed by Robert Johnston. Asprey & Co., London.

Clip: platinum, brilliants and rubies. Gilbert Albert, Geneva.

ain and Denmark do not disdain to submit a few of their creations to the jury. Jensen, Asprey of London and young designers from Garrard's and René Kern's have featured among the winners in recent years.

When a jeweler's work has won a few "Oscars," he is enrolled in the Diamond International Academy. This happened in the case of Gilbert Albert, who was subsequently promoted to the rank of jury-member.

This young jeweler began by working for Patek Philippe and Omega. In 1962, he opened his own establishment in Geneva, and already enjoys a world-wide reputation which extends to Japan and America.

It is always hard to define a style, and Gilbert Albert's, being in a continual state of evolution, is particularly difficult to confine in definitions. It has, however, some constant features, the chief of which are lightness and transparency. Precious stones often adorn broad-meshed setting, a fine net through which the skin can be seen. Pearls and diamonds are thickly spread on this web, but even sapphires, emeralds and rubies contribute their color and glow with what might be called modesty, as though conscious that their value needs no emphasizing. Another typical feautre of Gilbert Albert's jewels is that they are often decorated with meteorites, the name, history and source of which are so fabulous. Strange, mysterious cabochons are surrounded with gold, diamonds and colored stones. They are all precious in Albert's eyes, even if meteorites are not classified as such. Not yet, at least, he says; and who can judge the furture? As to rarity, that of meteorites is just as great as that of precious stones. In them, he introduces a new material for ornaments, for which he incessantly seeks new forms. "In the enchanted world of jewels," he said to Henri Poulaoin, "everything has to be renewed and remade. It will always be like that."

Clip: meteorite, gold and brilliants. Gilbert Albert, Geneva.

Cross: indochinite, rubies, gold and platinum. Gilbert Albert, Geneva.

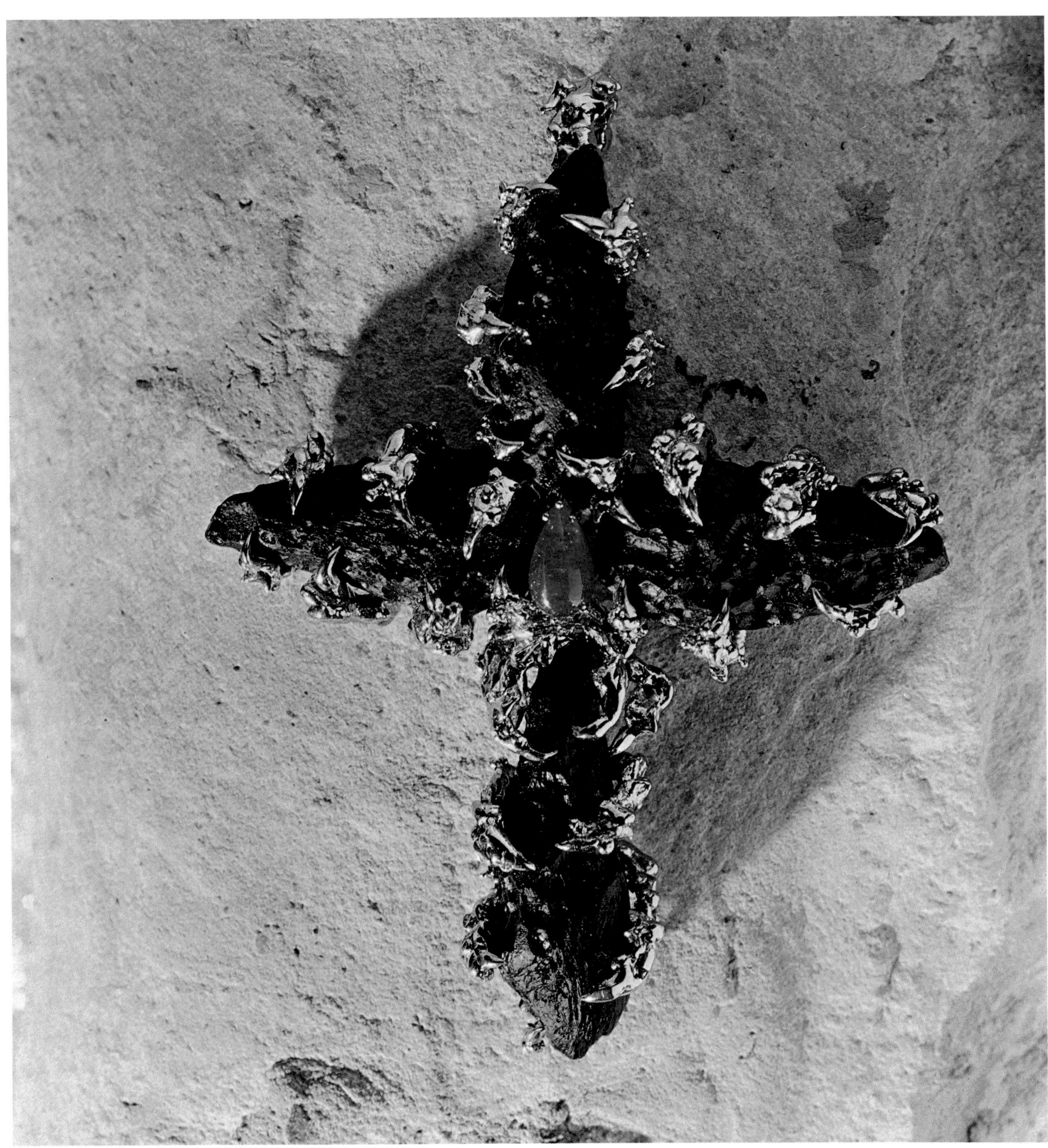

The Diamond International Academy also numbers Klaus Bohnenberger among its members. He won awards in 1965, 1966 and 1968.

Klaus Bohnenberger learned his craft at a very early age in different famous workshops. He spent a few years in Pforzheim, creted many models for the firm of Daub and, before opening his own establishment, studied jewelry in various European countries and America. In just over ten years, 31 prizes were awarded to him, including that of Geneva in 1964. Three years later, one of his rings won the title "jewel of the year."

Klaus Bohnenberger's jewels are outstanding for their lightness and the interplay of color and relief. Modern without being aggressive, their originality and grace explains their success.

Fascinated by his craft and by the possibilities of contemporary jewelry, Bohnenberger likes to explore all the paths of artistic creation with a group of pupils. His love of teaching and his willingness to let his apprentices share in his experiments bear witness to his enthusiasm and to the vitality of the art of jewelry.

Clip: gold, baroque pearls and moonstone. Gilbert Albert, Geneva.

Brooch, "Starlight:" white and yellow gold and brilliants. Klaus Bohnenberger, Schwäbisch Gmünd.

Necklace: australites, brilliants and pearls. Gilbert Albert, Geneva.

Necklace, "Revery:" white gold, brilliants and emeralds. Klaus Bohnenberger, Schwäbish Gmünd.

Chapter 6 ARTISTS' JEWELRY

ARTISTS' JEWELRY

Braque: "Phoenix:" gold, enamel and brilliants.

In addition to professional jewelers and a number of up-and-coming learners, many artists are also amateur jewelers. For two hundred years, as we have seen, sculptors, painters and architects have taken an interest in the decorative arts in general and jewelry in particular. they are thus reviving the very ancient tradition of the artist as a creator of ornaments. Even today some artists devote a large part of their time and output to designing and making jewelry. Although this book does not claim to be exhaustive, it seemed indispensable to discuss a few artists' jewels as well as those of jewelers in order to give some examples of all the trends of contemporary jewelry.

It must be stated at the outset that this fortuitous association of jewelers and artists in no way reflects the real state of affairs. They appreciate each other, but only with reservations, jewelers claiming that artists' products are not really jewelry, and painters and sculptors criticizing contemporary jewelry design. This is not so much a controversy as a fundamental difference of opinion on the basic theory of jewelry which prevents an exchange of views, each keeping obstinately to his own ideas. Many artists take pleasure in expressing extreme disgust for precious stones.

It would therefore be useless to try to reconcile these antagonists. They have no common ground and customers buy from one or the other, or sometimes both, according to their tastes and temperament. This is the attitude we shall adopt, leaving the reader free to make his own choice.

The first difficulty encountered by the collector of artists' jewelry is the rarity of the specimens. Metalwork always seems to appeal more strongly to sculptors and even painters. Calder, Picasso, Giacometti, Cocteau, Mathieu and Fontana do not use precious stones. For them, jewelry is a self-sufficient shape or volume needing no assistance from gems. Furthermore, to "think" in terms of jewels is a form of creativity which is only achieved after a long technical apprenticeship, and it only occurs among people who have devoted a large part of their working lives to creating ornaments. Finally, there is another very simple consideration: the cost of the material. Few artists have the financial means to buy a large selection of gems and even fewer can afford to risk experiments that might turn out unprofitable.

Gold is easily worked and fashioned. It is a soft material which is suitable for all kinds of treatment and can be shaped into any desired form. It is much more difficult to set a stone and an artist might find this much less interesting, since the cut of diamonds, emeralds, rubies and sapphires gives them a predetermined shape and design. A cut stone is beautiful in itself, and this, in a sense, gives less scope for the creative powers of the artist. It can easily be understood why some artists refuse to use stones. Others, as we shall see, deal with the problem in a different way. However, it should be noted at the outset that there are few artists who are willing to make invisible settings for their ornaments, since this is the sign of their own personal touch. Dali is perhaps the only one to design jewelry entirely of pearls and gems, and in order to avoid any confusion with so-called traditional jewlry, the states unequivocally that his ornaments are not made to be worn.

Especially since the nineteenth century, precious stones have come to be regarded as a symbol of wealth and social success—another good reason for avoiding them, in the opinion of various artists who sometimes amuse themselves with expensive sacrileges. Man Ray, in a ring, encircled a diamond so closely in gold that it was almost invisible. Dubuffet's rings scarcely show off the stones any better. Indeed, some artists seem to dislike not only contemporary jewelry, the poverty of imagination of which they deplore, but even the material of which it is made, in that it limits their scope and the expression of their personalities.

It is precisely this latent conflict that fires certain painters and sculptors, and they are given a place here because every work of art, no matter how decried, influences its age to some degree. Their jewels are not likable, but it is impossible to ignore them or their influence.

"A Hundred Ornaments by Braque set all Paris Running" is the title chosen by a critic for an article published in 1963 (Claude Salvy, "Cent bijoux de Braque font courir tout Paris," *Journal suisse des horlogers,* July 1963). This is no exaggeration. The first exhibition of Braque's jewelry was an important event, and no one wanted to miss it. Everyone flocked to it with even more enthusiasm, perhaps, than if it had been a show of paintings. The painter, his style and his favorite motifs were familiar, and everyone was curious to see how the artist would adapt them to ornaments and how he would prosper in this new medium.

The story of Braque's jewelry is well known, but we will review it briefly. The idea is said to have come to him by chance. Thinking that his "Greek Head" could be the motif for a cameo, Braque one day stuck a small photograph of it to a piece of pasteboard which he wrapped around his finger. Please with the result of this try-out, he decided to make a ring for his wife. To carry out this scheme he needed the help of a collaborator who was thoroughly familiar with the material and technique. He turned to a lapidary named Heger de Löwenfeld who set to work to transcribe the painter's design as faithfully as possible. This was not achieved without difficulty because, as Claude Salvy says, "The artist refused to allow for the limitations of the equipment, blowpipe or wheel. The gold was not matt enough and the lines were not what he had in mind. Some pieces were achieved with great labor only to be rejected as soon as they were finished. However, a hundred jewels were exhibited in 1963, i.e., two years after the first experiments."

They draw on the artist's favorite motifs of profiles, birds and fish. Each piece has a title, usually the name of a god or hero of ancient mythology, and consequently a symbolic meaning. Hemera brings the daylight to

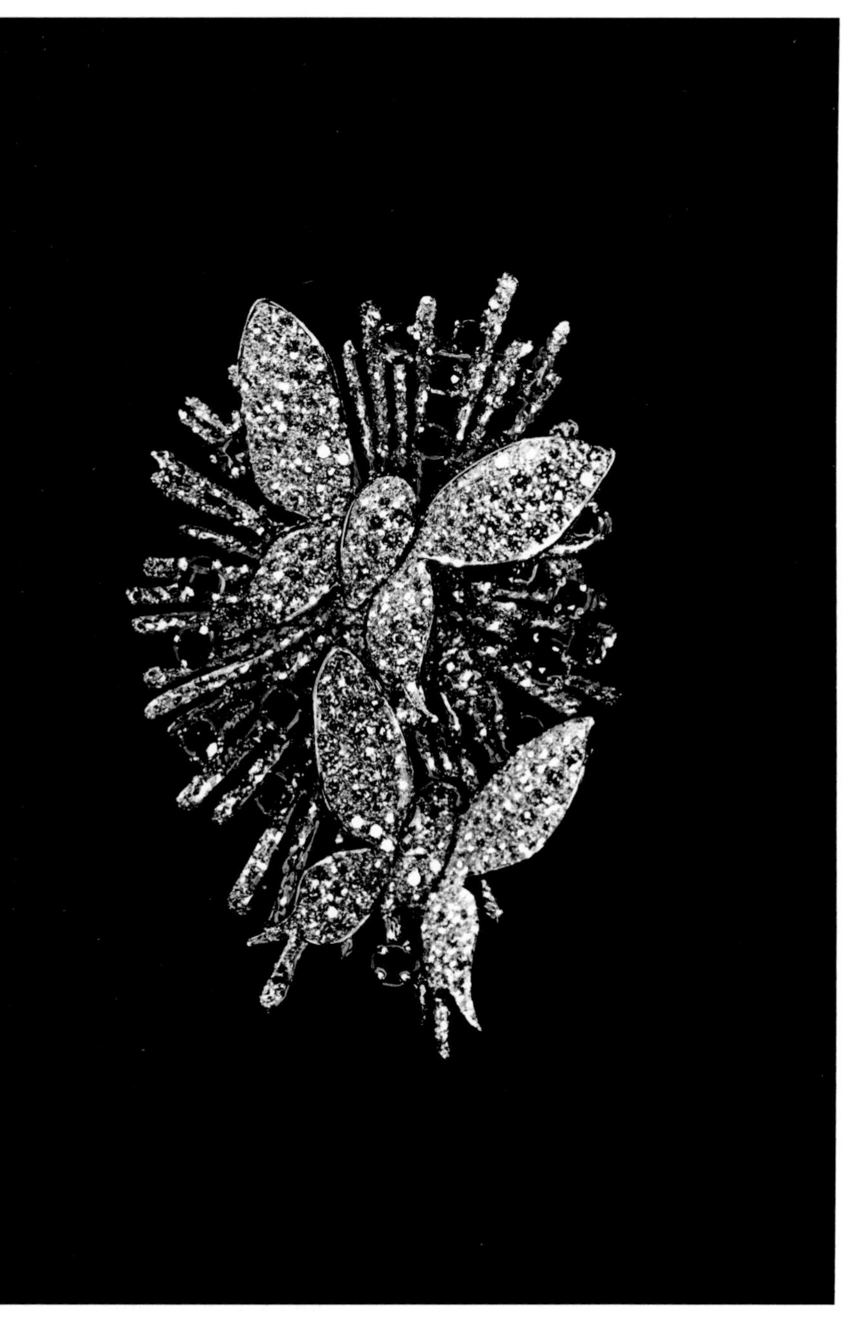

Braque: "Triptolemus." Clip: gold, brilliants and rubies. Mme. Heger de Löwenfeld's Collection, Paris.

Braque: "The Pleiades." Clip: gold and brilliants. Mme. Heger de Löwenfeld's Collection, Paris.

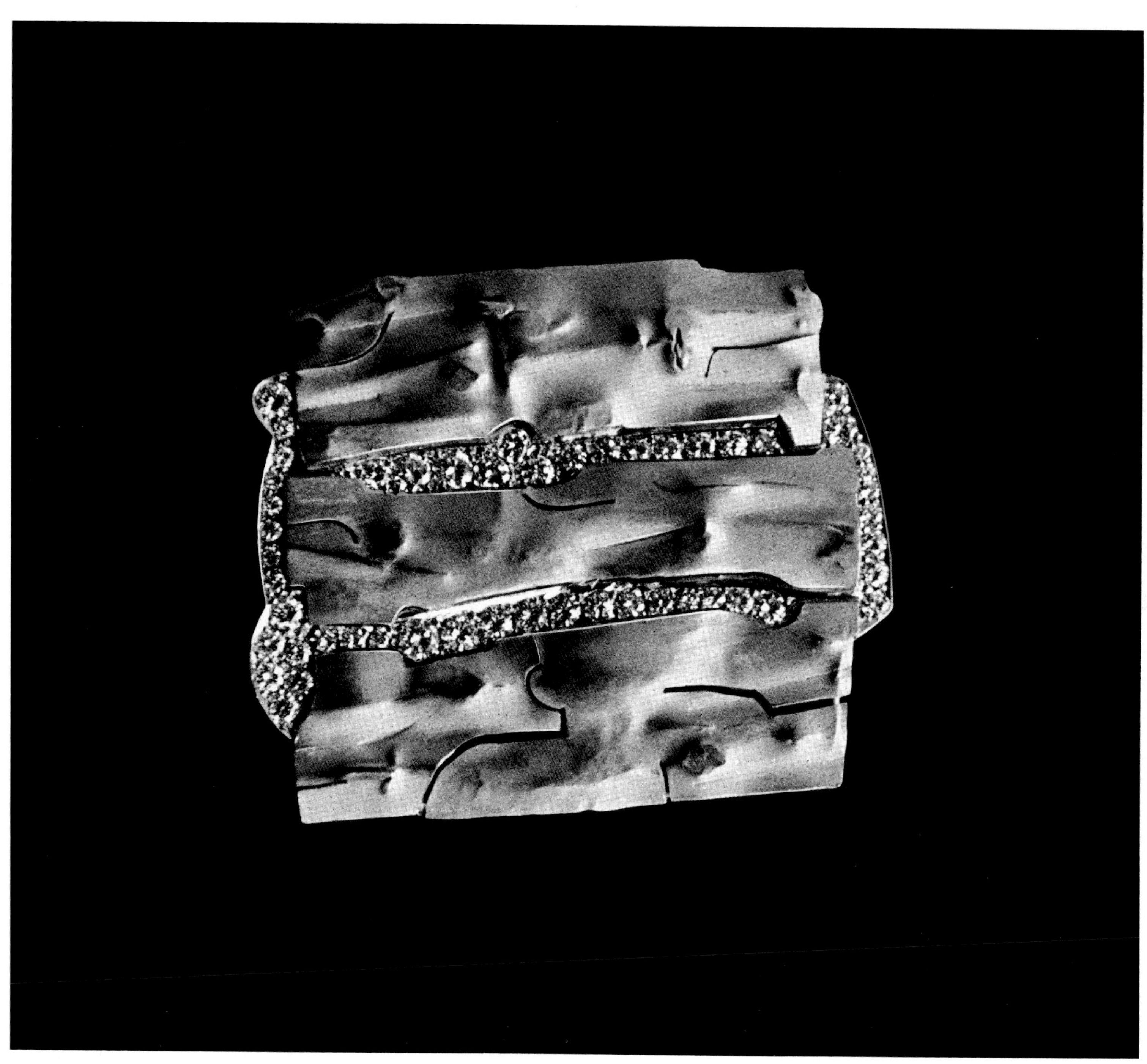

Consagra: brooch. Gold and brilliants. G. Masenza and Co., Rome.

Braque: "Zephir." Ring: platinum and diamonds. Galerie Stadler, Paris.

mankind; the jewel of this name is a bird entirely carried out in brilliants on a gold cloud bearing a clear red opal. A gold Hera bathes in waves represented by a sapphire background. That is to say, these jewels are already more than ornaments and are closely allied to painting in spirit. They are also related to painting by the handling of the raw materials and the composition. There are usually two superimposed contrasting planes, one acting as a background and the other consisting of the subject. Stones and gold are therefore treated as colors and values, but are still subservient to the design and do not determine it. Braque's jewels, which are very beautiful, were conceived in terms of painting, as shapes, planes and colors, rather than in terms of pure jewelry. This does not detract from their charm and originality, but it leads some critics to think that the master's talent is more admirable than the object itself. It was reported that one jeweler said, "It's Braque who is the gem."

This critique could equally well be applied to the jewels of Salvador Dali, since they are stamped, like all his work, with his own myths and motifs. They are unquestionably very beautiful pieces of jewelry, and their execution by Alemany & Co. is a veritable technical *tour de force,* but they are first and foremost works by Dali, a painter, translating his fantastic world of bleeding hearts, time-keeping eyes and melting watches into gems and pearls. He himself explains what he is trying to achieve: "My jewels are a protest against the emphasis upon the cost of the materials of jewelry. My object is to show the jeweler's art in true perspective—where the design and craftsmanship are to be valued above the material worth of the gems, as they were in Renaissance times." (*Salvador Dali: A Study of his Art-in-Jewels,* London and New York, 1959.)

The problem is stated here very neatly, and sheds further light on the radical difference between the artists' and the jewelers' points of view. Dali's position opposes the stand taken by Régine Gabbey (*Réalités,* December 1969), according to whom the jewel "should include more stones than workmanship, because workmanship is out of date." It is true that this refers to the selling of jewelry, but Dali

Dali: "The Pomegranate Heart." Gold, diamonds and cabochon rubies. Owen Cheatham Foundation, New York.

Dali: "The Bleeding World", gold, rubies, pearls and diamonds. Owen Cheatham Foundation, New York

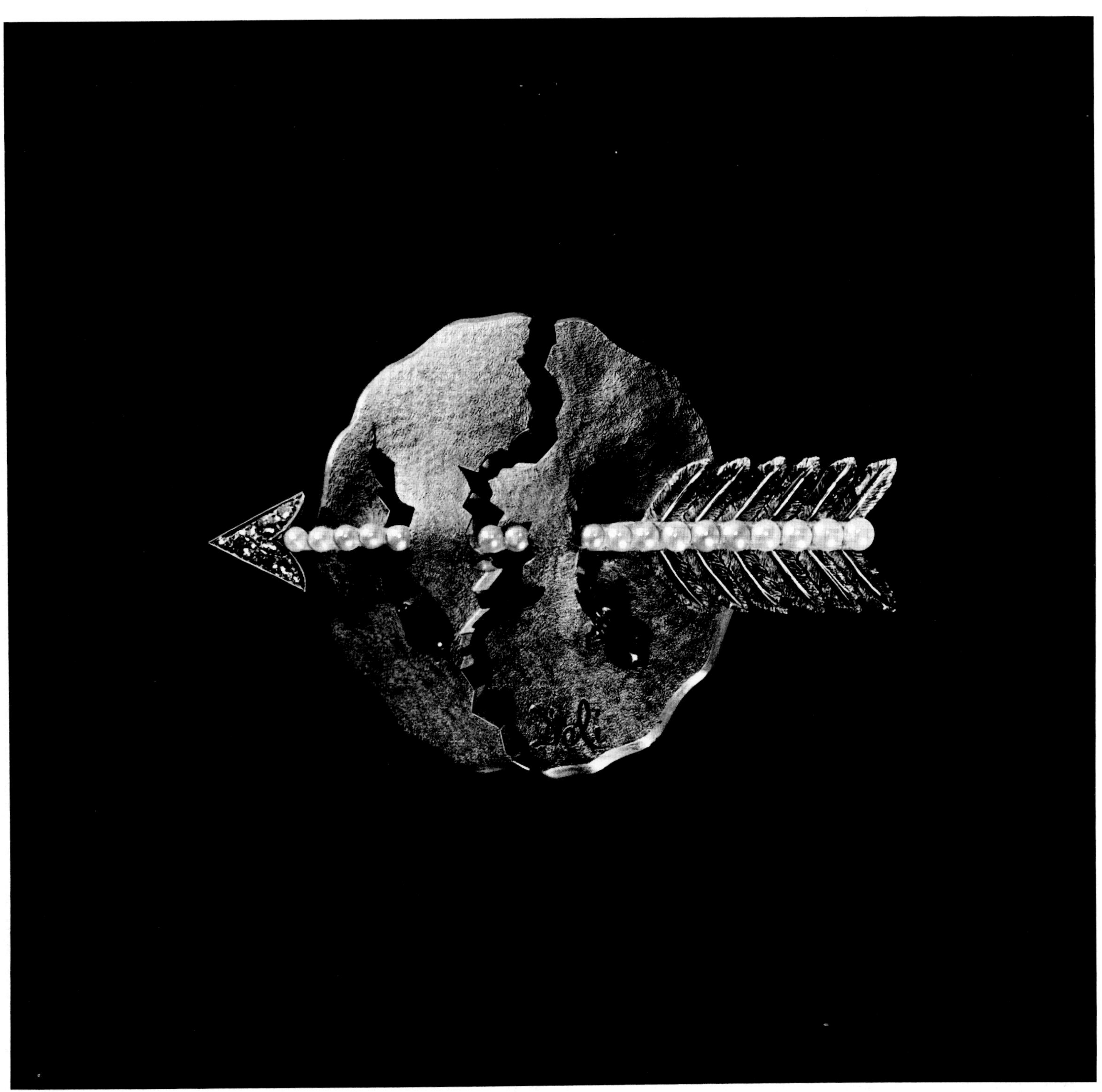

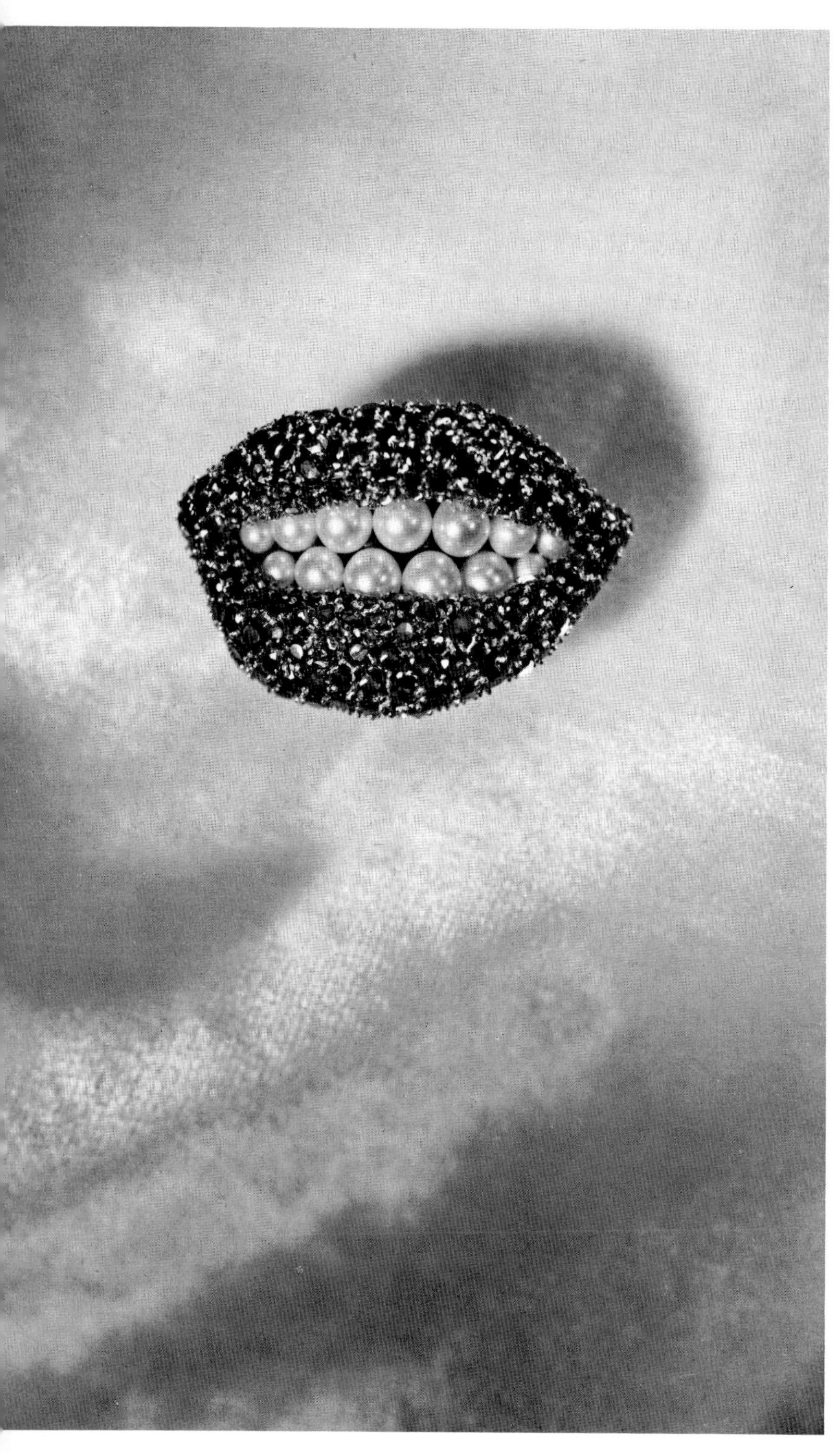

takes his stand against precisely this theory of jewelry. He shows the same concern as the Art Nouveau artists to make the jewel primarily a work of art, the raw material of which, whether valuable or not, should be subservient. Guimard, the well known designer of the Paris Métro entrances, tried experiments with bronze rings with artificial stones. Dali works differently. He uses gold, platinum, diamonds, rubies, sapphires and pearls to translate his images and phantoms. The bleeding world is a mass of hammered and cracked gold with splits here and there from which drops of rubies pour. The pearl-and-diamond arrow transfixing it also holds it together. According to the artist, it symbolizes "the Love of Christ and the hope of peace" in a "world divided by war and chaos." The ambiguity of life is represented by a gold heart split like a ripe pomegranate revealing its shimmering diamond flesh and ruby seeds. "The slightly acid taste of the fruit is agreeable—as acidity stimulates human accomplishment." Ruby lips half-open over pearl teeth and the Eye of Time, an enamel watch framed in diamond eyelids, are among Dali's most Surrealist jewels. The eye motif which sees the present and the future is familiar. The living, natural mouth without any face exerts a peculiar fascination over the spectator. This ornament would be difficult to wear even if it had been meant to be worn. But as we have seen, Dali is not interested in practical considerations. On the contrary, he designed his jewels to scratch and cut anyone who tries to wear them. Such designs are works of art, but they are also unquestionably related to jewelry.

There is little common ground between the works of Braque and those of Dali. Their jewels, however, share a recognizable principle which arises from the medium of expression. These are jewels by painters working with a palette of precious stones. They are often criticized as

Dali: "Ruby Lips." Gold, rubies and pearls. Owen Cheatham Foundation, New York.

Dali: "The Eye of Time." Platinum, round and baguette diamonds, cabochon ruby, blue enamel. Owen Cheatham Foundation, New York.

Dalí

Dali: "Explosion." Lapis lazuli, diamonds and fluorite rubies. Owen Cheatham Foundation, New York.

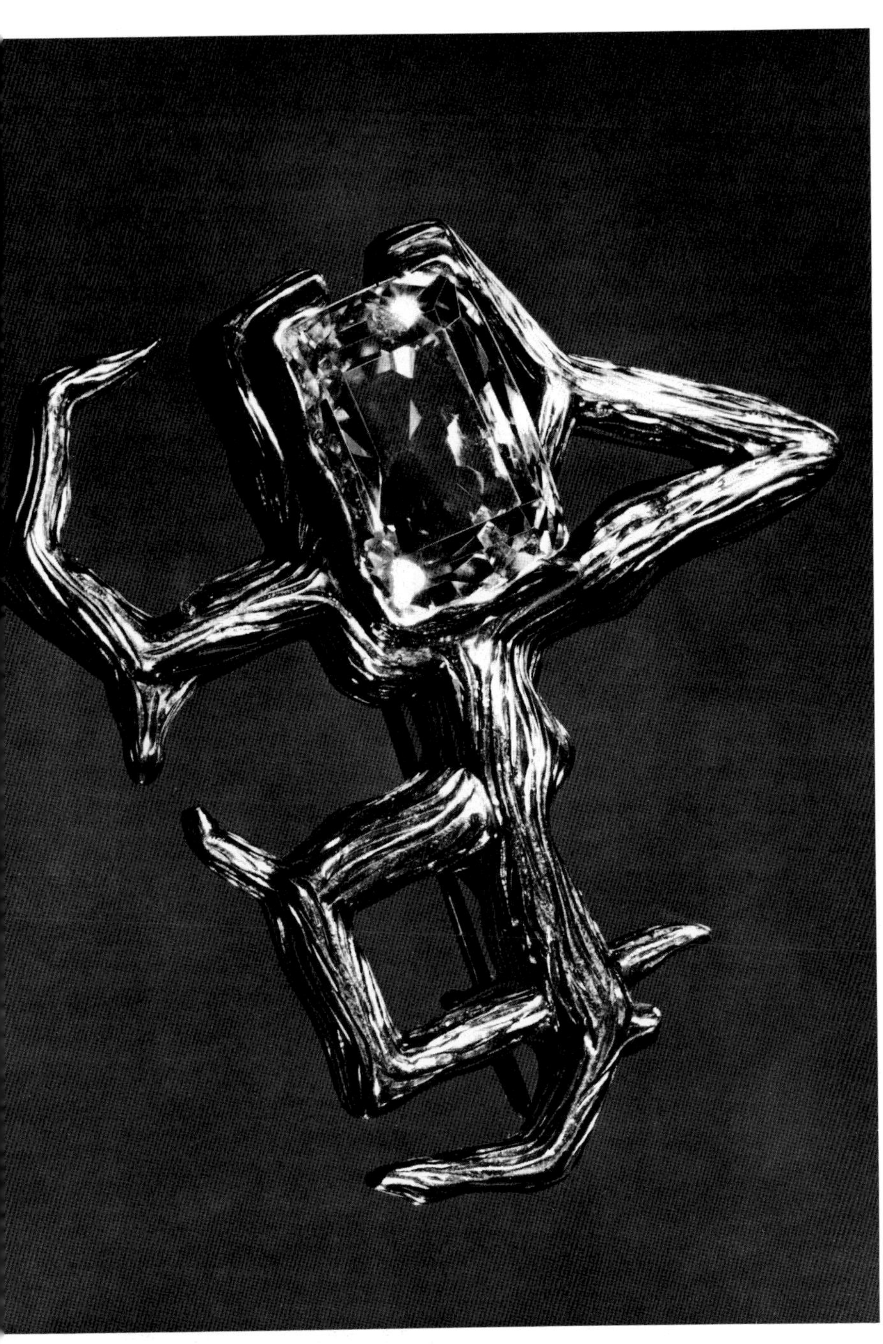

Herbert Jochems: "Femme fatale." Gold and yellow sapphires. Herbert Jochems Collection, The Hague.

being too linear, ignoring the third dimension and the necessity for relief—a criticism that has more justice in the case of some of Braque's work than Dali's, which is sometimes almost sculptural. Painters' jewels certainly tend to be marked by emphasis on graphic qualities and the interplay of lines rather than volumes, but this is not necessarily always true. Abstract painters seem to be particularly interested in exploring space and frequently attempt this on their canvases. It is sometimes difficult to determine what is painting and what is relief. Canvases with holes, impasto and superstructures as well as deliberately contrived optical effects are also experiments in expessing the third dimension in a concrete, factual manner.

This is why a painter like Herbert Jochems uses lines which spread in all directions until some of his jewels look like marine life, plant or animal, surrounded by moving tentacles. The repertoire of forms is the same as on canvas, but they acquire a different significance for the artist on being translated into precious materials. "Our pursuit of eternal beauty," he says, "impelled us to discover the jewel." The meaning of his work becomes even clearer when he discusses his materials. "Precious jewels, mined from the earth and sought at its very heart. To contemplate their secrets, to caress them and enjoy them to the point of intoxication, and then set them in the joy of a creation from the soul" (quoted in *Style* 4, 1963; article by Georges Peillex). For him, therefore, precious and semi-precious stones are more than touches of color at the service of the design. The material is regarded as having an intrinsic value, but its setting is determined by the will and choice of the artists, and this is where the human element comes in, and becomes predominant once more. We have strayed rather a long way from the purely painterly conception of jewelry, but without losing sight of the principle which the artists emphasize most strongly: the necessity for stamping the jewel with the personal touch. This sort of signature is found in the setting, the man-made accompaniment to the natural treasure man has in no way helped to make.

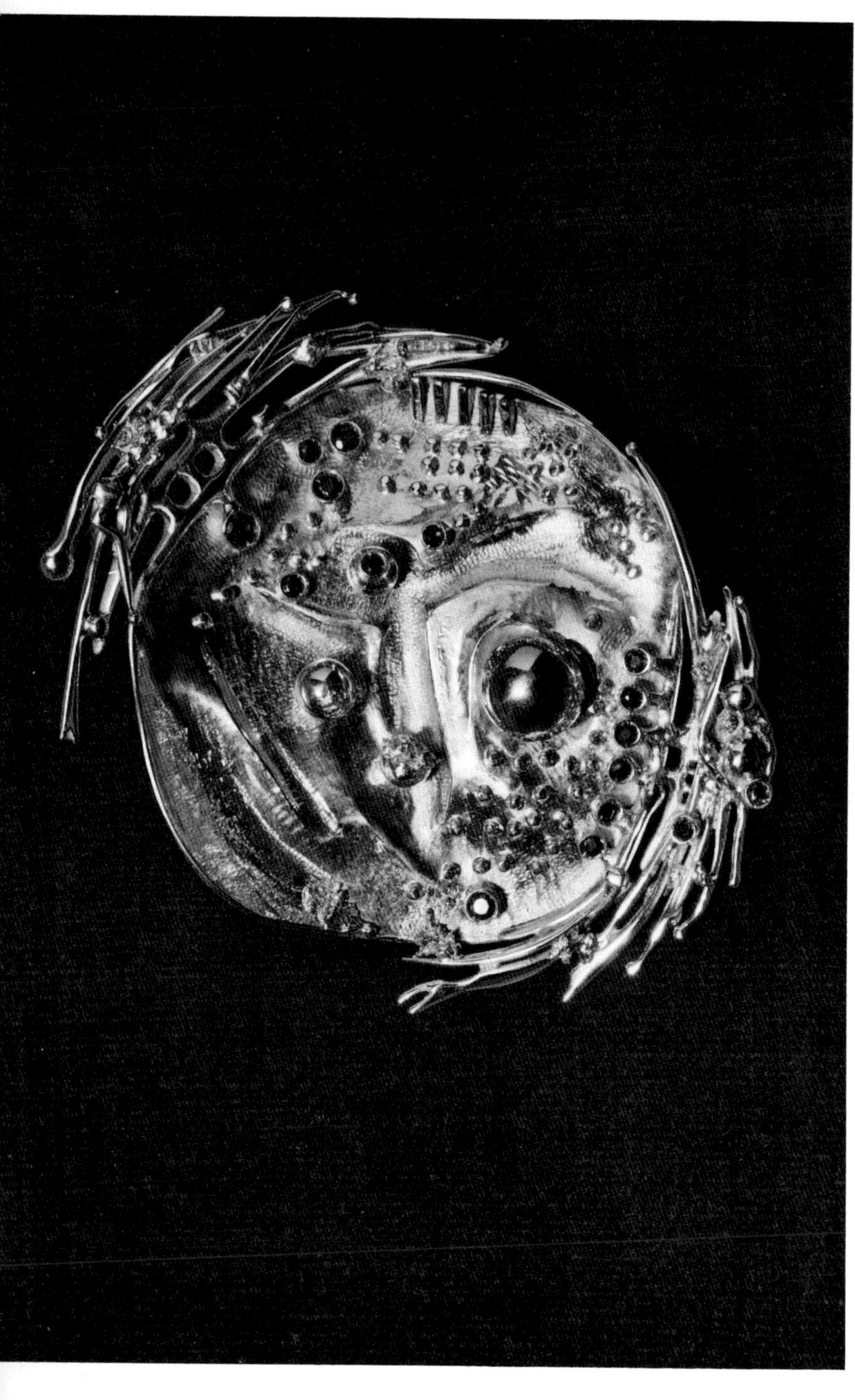

The same principle is expressed by the sculptor and architect Filhos who has been making jewelry for some years and who took part in the 1962 exhibition "Ten Centuries of French Jewelry" at the Louvre. For him, precious stones, however beautiful, have something inhuman about them. They need to be surrounded, framed, extended and brought to life in a world of signs and volumes designed and fashioned by the artist. Only under these conditions can they be integrated into a work of art. Filhos, like all the artists discussed here, stresses the value of the artist's and craftsman's contribution, the creative work surrounding a given element, the stone, even the cut of which allows little variation. For him, an ornament is not just an object made of precious materials; it is also the result of a labor of invention which is the exclusive mark of the artist. He would agree with Dali's statement quoted above, stressing the value of the craftsmanship after the example of Renaissance jewels.

Filhos, too, evokes this period by requiring the jewel not only to be a work of art, but to convey one or more symbolic messages. No anecdotes or paltry figures, and no superfluous forms. Filhos reintroduces the human figure into his jewels and chooses the symbolism which he considers best suited to contemporary feminine ornament: eroticism. Closely allied to the emancipation of women in the twentieth century, eroticism is also a permanent element in human history. Filhos' ambition is to make jewels for our times while keeping in tune with past traditions. He also assumes that the jewel is made for a specific person, and that the artist must know not only her tastes but her innermost motivations.

The great masters of the Renaissance such as Hornick and Cellini knew who their jewels were meant for, and contemporary artists must similarly create an ornament specifically for the woman who is to wear it. He describes

Gio Pomodoro: round brooch. Gold and rubies. Marlborough Gallery, London.

Arnaldo Pomodoro: necklace and pendant. Red and white gold, rubies and brilliants. Marlborough Gallery, London.

Arnaldo Pomodoro: necklace.
Red and white gold and brilliants and rubies.
Marlborough Gallery, London.

Arnaldo Pomodoro: necklace.
Red gold and brilliants, 1966. 
Marlborough Gallery, London.

his own methods—the picture he forms for himself of the woman for whom he is working and the feelings she inspires in him. The ornament then becomes a jewel in that its value is not just that of gems and metal. Filhos makes his jewelry of gold, which is more malleable, velvety and warm than platinum. He loves to work and fashion it, drawing it out into thin strands which become outlines, labyrinths in which the eye is lost only to discover the true subject all of a sudden in the subtle interplay of its windings. This golden embroidery shines out round the stone, strays from it, comes back to it and creates a glowing framework around it. Sculptors' jewels are conceived as masses more than those of most painters. Filhos' jewels do not deviate from this rule, and our eye is even more aware of it in that the very open treatment of the motif emphasizes the space it occupies.

Several exhibitions from 1962 on have made the name of Filhos famous. Charles de Temple, too, became known in London about this time, after a wide variety of experiments. Devoted to craftsmanship, fine materials and all branches of creative work, Charles de Temple does not receive you in his Bond Street establishment as a traditional jeweler. His welcome is courteous and warm, but he observes his client like a portrait painter. The basic question, never openly asked, is "Who are you?" His designs and shapes are devised in accordance with the answer he deduces. He believes that jewel should not just reflect the personality, but should emphasize the characteristics, even at the expense of shocking the client. He feels that it must attract and hold the glance of the spectator, and never leave him indifferent. Charles de Temple tries to infect his clients with his own love of craftsmanship. His jewels can be taken to pieces, separated and reformed. He sometimes even changes the color; he has been known to remove a cluster of sapphires and replace them with rubies and brilliants. His gems are generally set in platinum for reasons of strength, but the ornament

Herbert Jochems: "Oriental Mystery." Gold, brilliants and star sapphire. Herbert Jochems Collection, The Hague.

Jean Filhos: "Through the Looking-glass." Pendant in gold and brilliants. Galerie F.& F. Gennari, Paris.

prominently features gold treated with the "caviar" or "stalactite" finish, hammered and worked to a rough, uneven but nevertheless very light look. Semi-precious stones left in their natural state are inlaid with tiny brilliants that seem to start out spontaneously from every irregularity in the surface. Charles de Temple bejewels his customers with an immense variety of discreet or fantastic forms that always remain real jewelry. He is, in fact, one the rare artists to devote a lot of his time to jewelry and to work in collaboration with a shop and a permanent clientele. He is also a decorator, painter and sculptor. His taste for everything to do with handworking and craftsmanship enabled him to learn the technique of jewelry and to discover its secrets very rapidly. He draws on every age and culture to create jewels that are often both strange and fascinating.

Arnaldo and Gio Pomodoro's jewels are also strikingly strange. They are reminiscent of Arnaldo's powerful sculptures in which blocks split open to reveal an inside that is twisted as though it were still in a state of fusion, or of Gio's more polished but still crumpled and cracked pieces. Strongly sculptural qualities and the dynamic forms and volumes which characterize each of them in his own way are to be found in their jewelry.

Arnaldo's necklaces and pendants jeweled with brilliants and rubies have a pared-down, almost shredded look which gives them a deliberately primitive feeling. White and red gold is treated in stems, curved lines, striped or smooth links, and neat or roughly defined geometric forms. An important role is played by the stones, which are nearly as fundamental a part of the jewel as the metal, and not accompanied, framed or set in it. Rubies and diamonds give an illusion of enjoying the same independence as gold. Arnaldo Pomodoro bends them to his will like commonplace materials—or that is the effect he produces. This is a completely new form of association, and very different from anything we have encountered so far. It is difficult to speak of the setting of some of his jewels, since the stone is separated as far as possible from the gold. By his use of spaces and masses, the artist succeeds in giving the contrasting shapes and volumes a lightness which counterbalances the rude effect of the object. The more uncluttered, less lyrical pieces use the same processes but with regular shapes.

Gio's jewels are less open and more compact. Gems are set in the mass of metal and though these ornaments, too, can be described as primitive, they are more restrained and simpler. Emeralds and rubies are relegated to a subsidiary position, to enhance the effects of color and light. They are fixed in deliberately visible settings which are part of the composition. We are therefore a far cry from jewelry as it is usually defined, but this aspect of contemporary jewelry cannot be overlooked.

Many other artists have translated the signs and shapes they fashion in their pictures and sculptures into the raw materials of jewelry. A brooch by Capogrossi features this same interplay of space and volume to be found in his reliefs. Afro and Mirko fashion fantastic half-vegetable, half-animal creatures in gold and gems and, like Franchina and Manucci, have a liking for spontaneous shapes, natural-looking materials and rough, almost crude ornaments that force us to question once more the achievements we too often take for granted.

Charles de Temple: "The Burning Bush." Earrings in gold, "stalactites" and brilliants.
Parure: sapphires or rubies, brilliants and gold.
Charles de Temple, London.

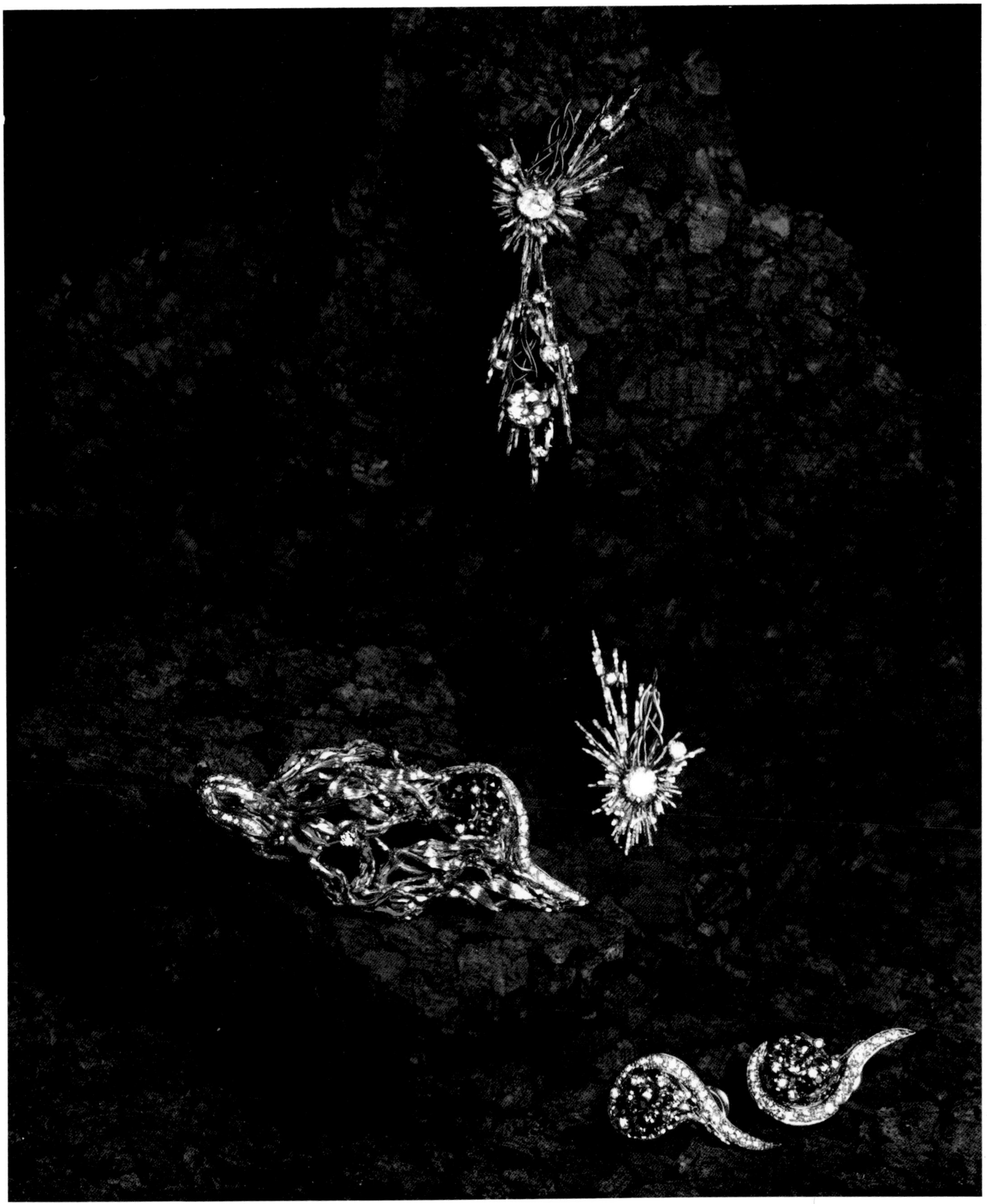

Gio Pomodoro: brooch. Red and white gold and emeralds. Marlborough Gallery, London.

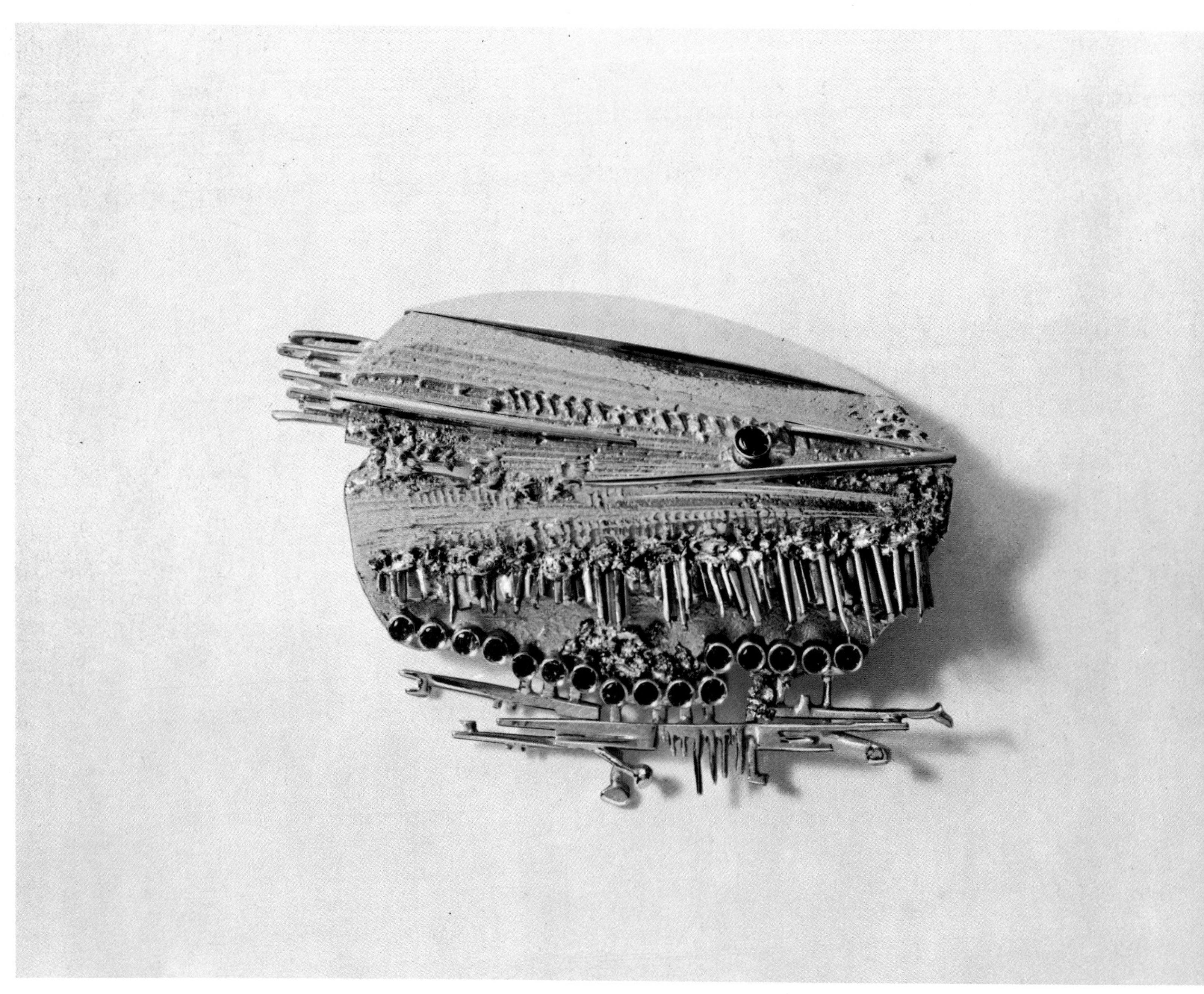

Charles de Temple: Pendant: gold, agate, rubies and diamonds. Ring: sapphires and meteorite. Ring: brilliant. Ring: amethyst and "caviar" gold. Ring: emerald and baguette brilliants. Ring: diamonds and "icicle" gold. Charles de Temple, London.

Franchina: earrings. Gold and rubies. Galerie Masenza, Rome.

The artist reflects his own time and in this respect he is in advance of it. However rare and surprising they may be, artists' jewels suggest a possible direction for the development of jewelry which may perhaps, in a tempered, softened form better adapted to the function of the ornament, be recognizable later. Painters' and sculptors' volumes, signs and symbols influence and alter our tastes even when we are not aware of it. The fact that we do not always accept their translation into jewelry or that we are rather slow to assimlate them does not prevent

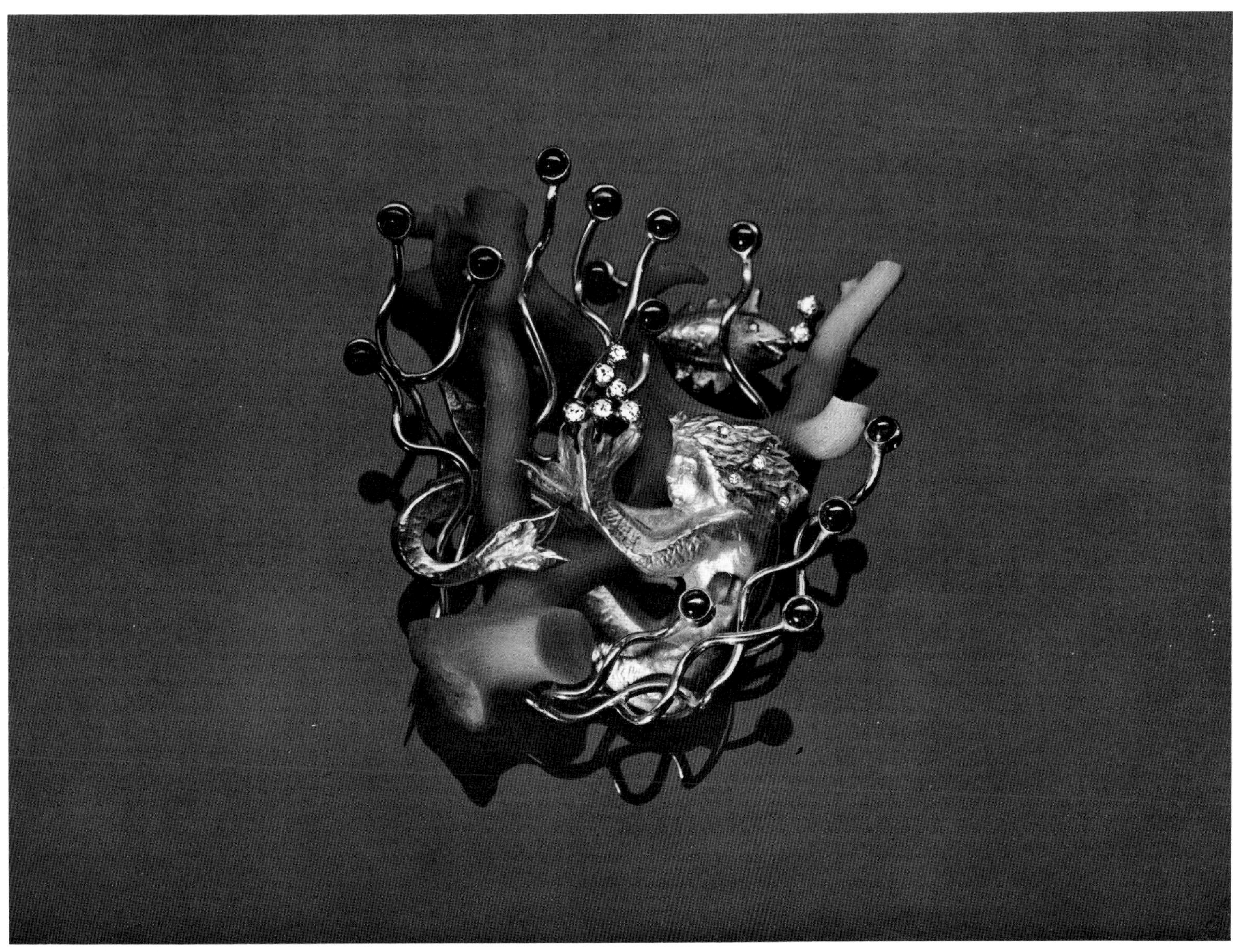

Mirko: brooch. Coral, gold, sapphires and brilliants. Galerie Masenza, Rome.

them from making their secret way into our subconscious and shaping it. This is why these works deserve to be mentioned here. They bear witness in their own way to the fact that jewelry is a living art which unceasingly challenges its own findings.

We may therefore conclude this brief review of five centuries of jewelry on an optimistic note. Throughout it we have noticed the vitality which is indispensable to the development of any art, and the jewelers' interest in adapting themselves to modern times and assimilating all the

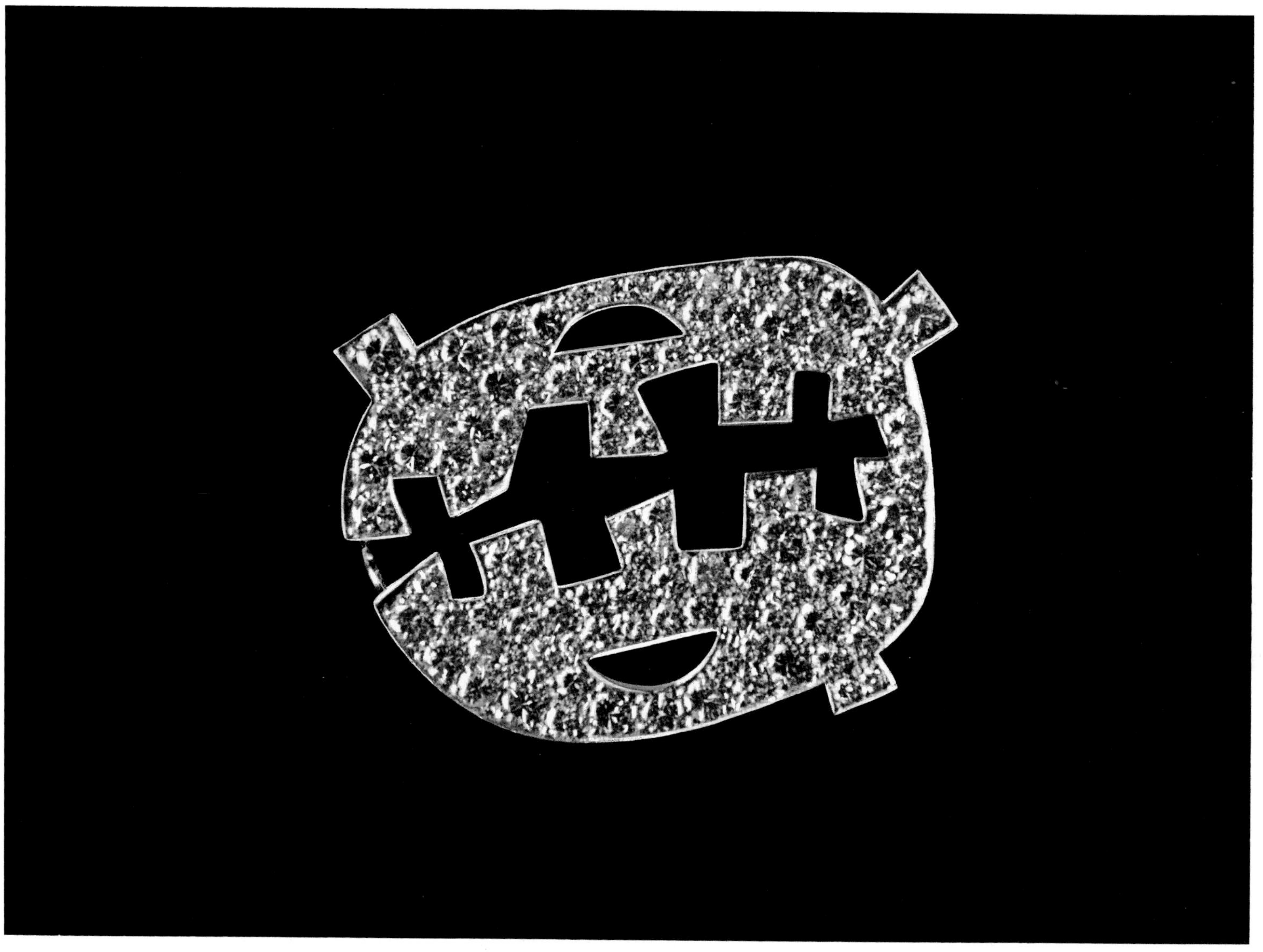

Capogrossi: brooch. Platinum and brilliants. Galerie Masenza, Rome.

most recent trends while preserving the precious traditions of quality, technical excellence and elegance. Jewelry is alive and growing, each country finding its own style and rhythm while accepting a wide variety of influences. In the twentieth century, it is harder than ever to determine the provenance of a jewel at a glance. Perhaps the faintly oriental forms and taste for rich colors of Bulgari's jewels, or the sober linear ornaments of Jensen or Michelsen are recognizable; but we can no longer say that English jewelry is massive and heavy, or that some countries con-

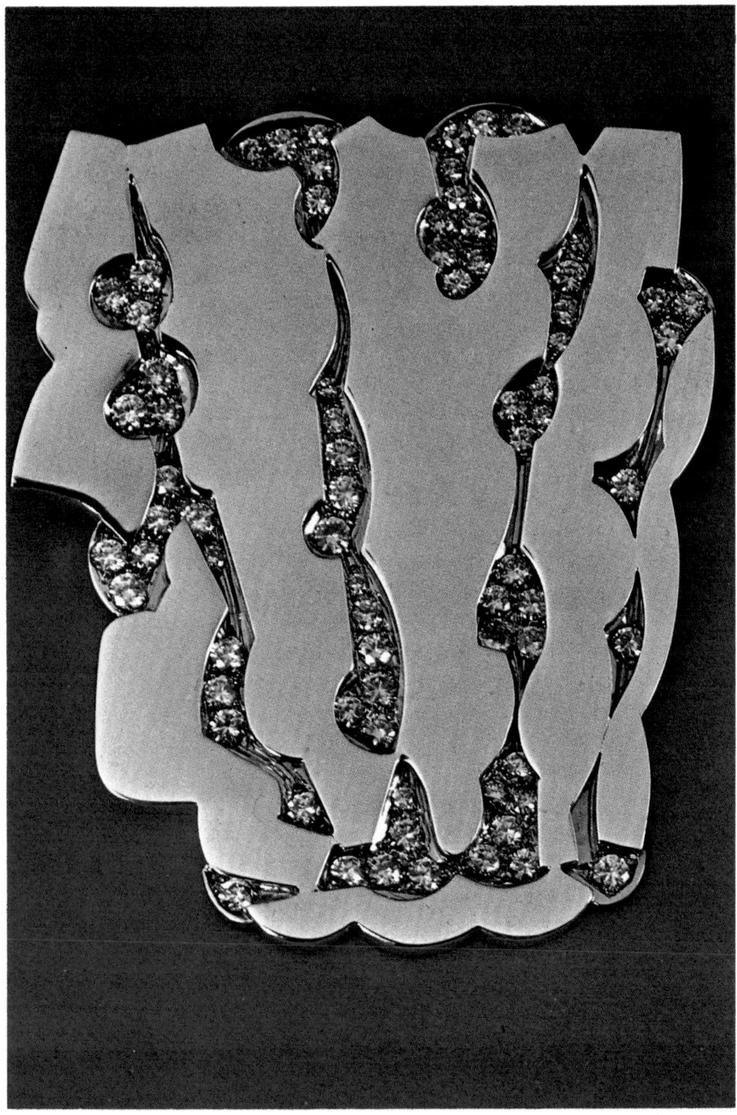

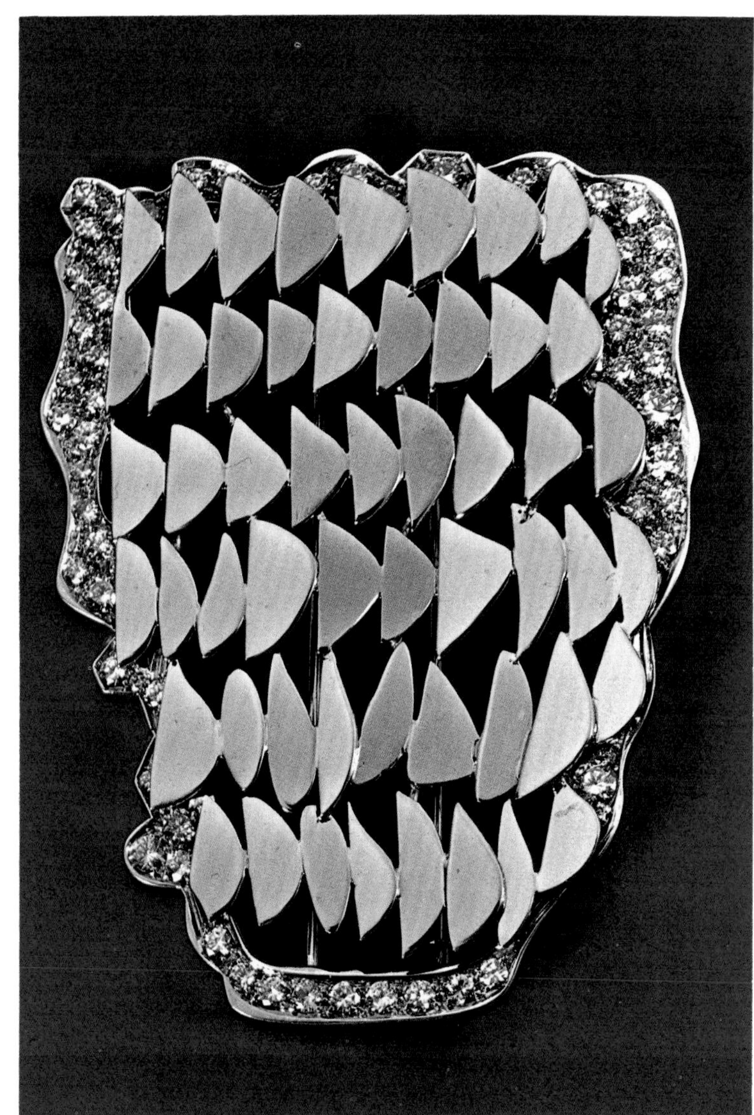

Consagra: two brooches. Gold and brilliants. Fumanti, Rome.

fine themselves to plagiarizing the creations of others. The twentieth century style of jewelry is international, like that of the other arts, but this does not prevent it from assuming a wide variety of forms all over the world.

Jewelers in most capitals and major cities have opened branches alongside their foreign colleagues or compatriots. However, they do not try to put each other out of business, and one is less inclined to speak of competition than emulation. It is pre-eminently a sign of soundness that the great houses have persisted for hundreds of years, through

Afro: brooch. Gold, brilliants, emerald and ruby leaves. Galerie Masenza, Rome.

so many wars and economic, social and artistic disturbances, and that there is still room for new firms. The fact that these same houses are ready to take risks, engage young designers and introduce innovations in jewelry allows us to hope for an even more brilliant future for the art.

The variety of styles is rather disconcerting. We have asked all the jewelers we have met, "Are there jewels for the young and others for the not-so-young? Are there certain styles specifically designed for a particular clientele?"

The answer is always the same. It is impossible to generalize, or to define types and categories. The way we adorn ourselves reflects the way we think. Jewelry is still a sign.

Mannucci: brooch. Gold and emeralds. Galerie Masenza, Rome.

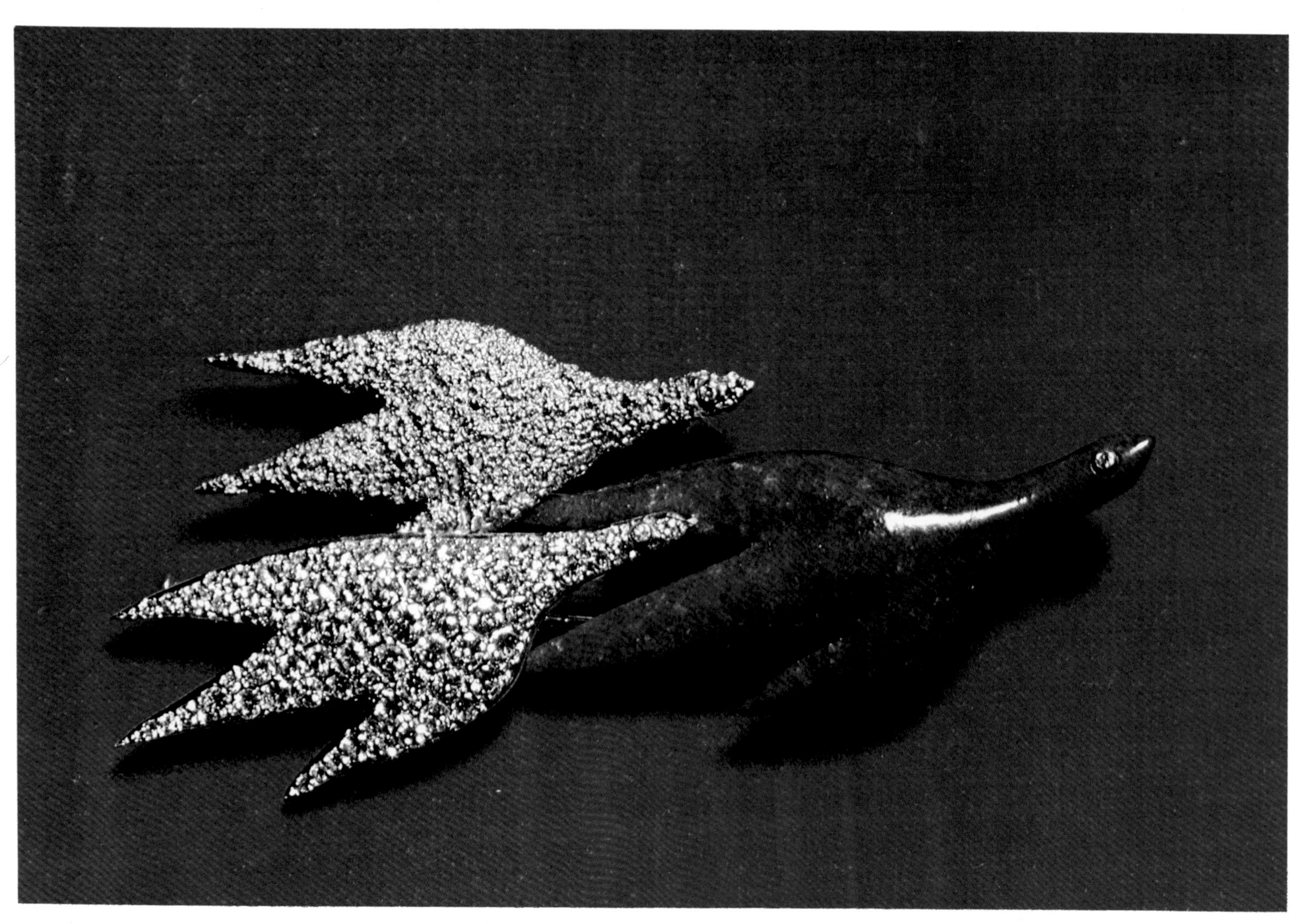

Braque: "Two Sons of Eos." Clip: diamonds, gold and lapis lazuli. Galerie Stadler, Paris.

BIBLIOGRAPHY

Alazard, Jean: *La Venise de la Renaissance,* Paris, 1956. *Les Années "25":* Musée des Arts Décoratifs, Paris. Exhibition catalogue, March-May 1966, Paris, 1966.

Aslin, E: *The Aesthetic Movement,* London, 1969.

Bailly, Auguste: *La Florence des Médicis,* Paris, 1956.

Bainbridge, H.C.: *The Life and Work of Carl Fabergé,* London, 1950.

Bapst, Germain: *Histoire des joyaux de la couronne de France,* Paris, 1889.

Berliner, Rudolf: *Italian Drawings for Jewelry, 1700-1875,* Cooper Union Museum for the Arts of Decoration. Exhibition catalogue, September-October 1940, New York, 1940.

Le Bijou 1900, Hotel Solvay, Brussels. Exhibition catalogue, May 1965, Brussels, 1965.

Bloche, A.: *La vente des diamants de la couronne,* Paris, 1886.

Le Blon, Michel: *Recueil d'ornements,* The Hague, 1900.

De Boot, Anselmus Boetius: *Le Parfait Joaillier,* Lyon, 1644.

Boue, Placide: *Traité d'orfèvrerie, bijouterie et joaillerie,* Paris, 1832.

Bradford, Ernle: *Four Centuries of European Jewelry,* London, 1953.

Le Brun, Corneille: *Voyages de Corneille Le Brun par la Moscovie, en Perse et aux Indes Orientales,* Amsterdam, 1718.

Bulgari, Costantino: *Argentieri, gemmari e orafi d'Italia,* Rome, 1958-9.

Clifford Smith, H.: *Jewelry,* London, 1908.

Clouzot, Henri: *Les arts précieux à l'Exposition Coloniale,* Paris, 1931.

Dali, Salvador: *A Study of His Art-in-Jewels,* London and New York, 1959.

Dalton, O.M.: *Catalogue of the Post-Classical Gems in the British Museum,* London, 1915.

Davillier, C.: *Recherches sur l'orfèvrerie en Espagne, au Moyen Age et à la Renaissance,* Paris, 1879.

Le Décor de la Vie sous la IIIème République, de 1870 à 1900: Louvre, Pavillon de Marsan, Paris, April-July 1933, Paris, 1933.

Diamants, perles et pierreries provenant de la collection dite des joyaux de la couronne, Paris, 1887.

Dix siècles de joaillerie francaise: Musée du Louvre, Paris. Exhibition catalogue, Paris, 1962.

Duflos, Augustin: *Recueil de dessins de joaillerie, dessiné par Augustin Duflos, joaillier du Roy d'Espagne,* Paris, 1767.

Duncan, David D.: *The Kremlin,* London, 1960.

Europa 1900: Musée des Beaux-Arts, Ostend. Exhibition catalogue, June-September 1967, Brussels, 1967.

Evans, Joan: *A History of Jewelry, 1100-1870,* London, 1953. *English Jewelry from the Fifth Century A.D. to 1800.*

Fairholt, F.W.: *Costume in England,* London, 1885.

Flower, Margaret: *Victorian Jewelry,* London, 1951.

Fontenay, Eugène: *Les Bijoux anciens et modernes,* Paris, 1881. *Diamants et pierres précieuses,* Paris, 1881.

Fontenelle, Julia de, and Malepeyre, F.: *Nouveau manuel complet du bijoutier-joaillier,* Paris, 1927.

Fouquet, G.: *La bijouterie, la joaillerie au XXe siècle.* Paris, 1934.

Frégnac, Claude: *Les bijoux de la Renaissance à la Belle Epoque,* Paris, 1967.

Gibbs-Smith, Charles H.: *The Great Exhibition of 1851,* London, 1950. *The Fashionable Lady in the 19th Century,* Victoria & Albert Museum, London, 1960, Exhibition Catalogue, 1960.

La Gioielleria, l'oreficeria e l'argenteria in Italia. Giorgio Kaisserlian's Introduction, Rome, 1964.

Gregorietti, Guido: *Jewelry through the Ages* (translation from the Italian by Helen Lawrence). New York, 1969.

Guide-album de l'Exposition internationale des arts décoratifs et industriels modernes, Paris, 1925.

Guilmard, Désiré: *Les maîtres ornemanistes, dessinateurs, peintres, architectes, sculpteurs et graveurs, écoles française, italienne, allemande et des Pays-Bas,* Paris, 1880-81.

Hackenbroh, Yvonne: *Erasmus Hornick as a Jeweler,* 1967.

Hughes, Graham: *Modern Jewelry,* London, 1964.

Janneau, Guillaume and Benoist, Luc: L'exposition internationale des arts décoratifs et industriels modernes, Paris, 1925.

Lafuë, Pierre: *La vie quotidienne des cours allemandes au XVIIIème siècle,* Paris, 1963.

Lavater-Sloman, Mary: *Cathérine II et son temps,* Paris, 1952.

Lucas-Dubreton, Jean: *Everyday Life in Florence in the Time of the Medici,* London, 1960.

Luthmer, F.: *Joaillerie de la Renaissance,* Paris, no date.

Margeret, Capitaine: *Estat de l'Empire de Russie et Grand Duché de Moscovie,* 1669.

Maria: *Premier livre de desseins de joaillerie et bijouterie, inventés par Maria et gravés par Babel,* Paris, no date.

Menzhausen, Joachim: *La Voûte Verte,* Leipzig, 1968.

"Modern Design in Jewelry and Fans," *The Studio,* 1902.

Molinier, Emile: *Chefs-d'oeuvre d'orfèvrerie,* Paris, 1884-88.

Mondon: *Premier livre de pierreries pour la parure des dames,* Paris, no date.

Nineteenth Century Jewelry from the First Empire to the First World War, Cooper Union Museum for the Arts of Decoration, New York. Exhibition catalogue, April-June, 1955, New York, 1955.

Official Catalogue of the Great Exhibition of the Works of Industry of All Nations (corrected edition), London, 1851.

Pierres précieuses, gemmes et pierres dures. Documentaires en couleurs, Paris, 1968.

Une Pléiade de Maîtres-joailliers, Paris, 1930.

Pouget: *Traité des pierres précieuses et de la manière de les employer en parure,* Paris, 1762.

Read, C.H.: *Catalogue of the Waddesdon Bequest,* London, 1927.

Rossi, F.: *Italian Jeweled Arts,* London, 1957.

Schick, Leon: *Un grand homme d'affaires au début du XVIème siècle: Jacob Fugger,* Paris, 1957.

Snowman, A.K.: *The Art of Carl Fabergé.* London, 1965.

Tillander, H.: *Six centuries of diamond design.* London, 1965.

Twining, Lord E.: *A History of the Crown Jewels of Europe,* London, 1960.

Van der Cruycen, L.: *Nouveau livre de desseins concernant la joaillerie.*

Vever, Henri: *La bijouterie française au XIXème siècle.* Paris, 1908.

Wagner de Kertesz: *Historia Universal de las joyas,* Buenos Aires, 1947.

Weltmann, A.: *Le Trésor de Moscou,* Moscow, 1861.

Wilson, Mab: *Pierres précieuses,* Paris, 1968.

Wolfers, Marcel: *Philippe Wolfers, précurseur de l'Art Nouveau,* Brussels, 1965.

PHOTOGRAPHIC CREDITS

Gilbert Albert, Geneva: 287, 288, 289, 290, and 292
Klaus Bohnenberger, Schwäbisch Gmünd: 291 and 293
Boucheron, Paris: 34, 248, 249, 246, 247, 250, 258, 259, and 272
British Museum, London: 41, 48, 52, 55 (photo C. Ridley), 72, 97, and 105 (2 photos C. Ridley)
Bureau of Soviet Information, Paris: 125
Cartier, Paris: 251, 262, 264, and 266
Château de Nymphenburg, Munich: 57, 61, 78, 83, 143 and 163
Château de Rosenborg, Copenhagen: 44, 126, 127, and 128
Chaumet, Paris: 35, 231, 232, 235, 236, 237, 239, 242, 263, 267, and 271
Owen Cheatham Foundation, New York: 302, 303, 304, 305, and 306
Christie's London: 123, 125, 179, and 181
The Cooper Union Museum for the Arts of Decoration, New York: 116, 136, 137, 151, 153, 189 and 196 (photo Bernhardt)
De Beers, London: 14, 15, 18, 19, 20, 21, 22, 23, 27, 110, 280, 285 and 286
Forney Library, Paris: 187, 193, and 208 (photos M. Nahmias)
Fumanti, Rome: 321
Isabella Stewart Gardner Museum, Boston: 50 and 51
Garrard, London: 139 (photo C. Ridley), 165, 223, 270 (2 photos C. Ridley) and 278
Gennari Gallery, Paris: 313
Gübelin, Lucerne: 261, 268, 269 and 270
Jensen, Copenhagen: 213, 218, 284 and 286
Herbert Jochems, La Haye: 307 and 312
Kern, Düsseldorf: 281, 282 and 283
Kunstindustrimuseet, Copenhagen: 65, 112 and 119 (photos O. Woldbye)
Louvre Museum, Paris: 59, 67,, 69 (photos Giraudon), 173 and 183 (National Museum photos)
Mme Heger de Löwenfeld, Paris: 297 and 299
Marlborough Gallery, Rome: 316, 308, 309, 310 and 311
Masenza Gallery, Rome: 302, 320, 322 (photo O. Savio), 320 (photo De Antonis), 322 and 323 (photos O. Savio)
Mauboussin, Paris: 147 (photo M. Nahmias) 233, 234, 250, and 251
The Metropolitan Museum of Art, New York: 54, 68, 203, and 206
Museum of Decorative Arts, Paris: 144, 159, 161, 201, 203, 207, 225 and 227
Museum of Fine Arts, Dijon: 62, 63 (photo Giraudon)
National Library, Cabinet des Estampes, Paris: 9, 29, 42, 48, 64, 66, 68, 69, 77, 79, 80, 85, 86, 87, 95, 103, 106, 107, 108, 111, 113, 140, 141 and 142
National Portrait Gallery, London: 42, 43, 45, 53, 94 and 101
Prince Napoleon, Paris: 148 (photo Giraudon)
Picardy Museum, Amiens: 155
Poldi-Pezzoli Museum, Milan: 56, 78, 92, 100, 105, 109, and 121
Stadler Gallery, Paris: 301 and 324
Charles de Temple, London: 315 and 317 (photos C. Ridley)
Tiffany, New York: 274, 275, 276, 277 and 278
Van Cleef and Arpels, Paris: 31, 33, 147, 252, 253, 254, 255, 256, 257 and 273
Victoria & Albert Museum, London: 39, 47, 49, 56, 64, 73, 81, 82, 84, 85, 88 (photo C. Ridley), 89, 90, 96, 98, 99, 102, 104 (2 photos C. Ridley), 114, 115, 117 (2 photos C. Ridley), 118, 119, 120 (2 photos C. Ridley), 124 (photo c. Ridley), 129, 134, 135 (photo C. Ridley), 138, 157 (photo C. Ridley), 167, 169 (photo C. Ridley), 170, 171, 175, 177, 178 (photo C. Ridley), 185, 191, 194, 195, 205, 206, 209 (photo C. Ridley)
Wartski, London: 168, 180 and 196
Harry Winston, New York: 26, 149, 240, 241 (2 photos Toscas), 243, 244, 245 (photo Toscas)
Wolfers, Brussels: 199, 210, 211, 212, 214, 215, 216, 218, 219, 229, 230 (2 photos M. Nahmias), 236, 238, 260, 261, 264 and 265
Designs on pages 11 and 21 are by Michel Labarthe.